PHILADELPHIA

ORIGINALS

Joseph Glantz

Schiffer Publishing Ltd

4880 Lower Valley Road · Atglen, PA · 19310

Title Page:
Philadelphia skyline with Cira Center by Charles Cushing.
Courtesy of Charles Cushing.

"What a warm-hearted and wonderful book this is. Its embrace of all things Philadelphia, past and present, showcases a great and vibrant American City. Joe Glantz has written a remarkable compendium about a remarkable city. The pages are studded with gems of accomplishment in culture and industry that make our city sparkle. To borrow a great Philadelphia phrase, the book offers readers 'acres of diamonds'."

Joseph Torsella, President & CEO,
National Constitution Center

"Mr. Glantz has undertaken the daunting, yet noble task of telling the story of Philadelphia by tying business, art, and culture to the people, places, and things of Philadelphia's past and present. The premise of *Philadelphia Originals* is that Philadelphia has a style unto itself that was birthed from two of its founding fathers and well-known citizens, William Penn and Benjamin Franklin. Focusing on the style and tradition of all things 'Philadelphia', Mr. Glantz has pioneered a fresh approach that can be adapted by other historians who wish to tell the story of their city."

Kim Sajet, President & CEO,
Historical Society of Pennsylvania

"Philadelphia Originals is an important book that all Philadelphians need to read. Through a series of historical vignettes and corresponding images, Mr. Glantz has captured the distinctive character of the city's 'civic culture' that has emerged over the past three centuries. As the former Executive Director of the city's history museum—the Atwater Kent Museum—I highly recommend *Philadelphia Originals*."

John V. Alviti, Senior Curator of Collections,
Franklin Institute Science Museum

"*Philadelphia Originals* is a delightful blend of profiles and history, of culture and business. It will be of interest not only to tourists, but also to people who live or work in Greater Philadelphia. The unique approach of organizing the book by profession will make it easy and enjoyable to read."

Meryl Levitz, President and CEO,
Greater Philadelphia Tourism
Marketing Corporation

Schiffer Books are available at special discounts for bulk purchases for sales promotions or premiums. Special editions, including personalized covers, corporate imprints, and excerpts can be created in large quantities for special needs. For more information contact the publisher:

Published by Schiffer Publishing Ltd.
4880 Lower Valley Road
Atglen, PA 19310
Phone: (610) 593-1777; Fax: (610) 593-2002
E-mail: Info@schifferbooks.com

For the largest selection of fine reference books on this and related subjects, please visit our web site at **www.schifferbooks.com**
We are always looking for people to write books on new and related subjects. If you have an idea for a book please contact us at the above address.

This book may be purchased from the publisher.
Include $5.00 for shipping.
Please try your bookstore first.
You may write for a free catalog.

In Europe, Schiffer books are distributed by
Bushwood Books
6 Marksbury Ave.
Kew Gardens
Surrey TW9 4JF England
Phone: 44 (0) 20 8392 8585; Fax: 44 (0) 20 8392 9876
E-mail: info@bushwoodbooks.co.uk
Website: www.bushwoodbooks.co.uk

Copyright © 2009 by Joseph Glantz
Library of Congress Control Number: 2009929646

Designed by RoS
Type set in Bernhard Modern BT/Aldine 721 BT

ISBN: 978-0-7643-3338-5
Printed in China

Art Museum and Waterworks by Charles Cushing. Courtesy of Charles Cushing.

CONTENTS

PROLOGUE

Philadelphia compared to other cities:

Philadelphia has been financially compared to London, culturally compared to Athens, and esthetically compared to Paris. Yet it is the truest of American cities – where our democracy was founded, whose physical design was copied westward, where diversity flourishes and neighborhoods coexist. New York may be the biggest. Boston may claim to be the best. California's cities may have the latest fads. In Texas even the small cities boast largesse. But only Philadelphia can define all its professions, its persona, its history, and its future by one unique label

"Philadelphia Style"

Philadelphia's Most Notable Professions

The Philadelphia Lawyer – Andrew Hamilton, William Penn's lawyer, defended the press in New York against a charge of libel. Because of his brilliant tactics and speeches, Philadelphia lawyers have been noted, ever since, for their ability to defend and pursue any good cause.

The Philadelphia Merchant – John Wanamaker emphasized advertising and honesty in dealing. Philadelphia businesses are known for their innovation, their attention to detail, and their integrity in dealing with the consumer.

The Experimental Philadelphian – Benjamin Franklin's experiments and self-starter qualities have enabled Philadelphia to be a leader in creativity whether it be the wide variety of communication inventions which have captivated the world, the Philadelphia Flower Show, the Franklin Award honorees or just the beautiful greenery which is a signature of Penn's 'Greene' Country Towne.

Philadelphia Art – Thomas Eakin's practical realism combined with the teachings of the Pennsylvania Academy of Fine Arts helped create a wide variety of recognizable artistic movements from the Ashcan movement to Pennsylvania Impressionism. From portraits and illustrations to photography and murals, from the Barnes and the Pennsylvania Academy of the Fine Arts to the Philadelphia Museum of Art – Philadelphia art is a world treasure.

Philadelphia Movies – Eadweard Muybridge helped invent film at Penn's Veterinary School. Siegmund Lubin was the first movie mogul. Numerous movies like *The Young Philadelphians*, *The Philadelphia Story*, *Trading Places*, and *Philadelphia* could only have been made right here in Philadelphia. The actress who put Philadelphia on the Hollywood map was Grace Kelly who combined, as do many Philadelphia performers, talents from other disciplines and a touch of class.

The Philadelphia Sound – Leopold Stokowski's lush string sounds led to a century of great symphonies. A variety of other fabulous Philadelphia sounds from gospel to rock, opera, folk, hip-hop, jazz, and the soulful Gamble and Huff's "Sound of Philadelphia" can share the same moniker.

Philadelphia Sports – Win a couple, lose a bunch. Never do anything easily. Philadelphia sports has the best of all possible worlds, the union of five diverse teams in the Big Five, and the worst of all possible worlds – they're infected by the bizarre. Philadelphia has the best announcers and sportswriters. The city helped start the NBA and the NFL, sports talk radio, and many of the national sports awards.

The Philadelphia Food Renaissance – Until Steve Poses arrived, Philadelphia food was finger food, seafood, great drink, and the best desserts. With the arrival of Poses the Philadelphia food restaurant now means Philadelphians have Georges Perrier's five star restaurant, numerous four and three star locations, and recipes for every taste.

Philadelphia Humor – Clean humor, wonderful essays and stories. Great cartoons. Benjamin Franklin helped set the stage that Bill Cosby perfected. Philadelphia cartoonists are some of the best. Many comedians have gone on to great movie careers. Other locals like Upper Darby's Tina Fey are wonderful producers and writers.

*Penn and Franklin
by Perry Milou.
Courtesy of Perry
Milou*

INTRODUCTION

NOTES FROM THE AUTHOR
CRITERIA

Philadelphia Originals is an impressionist look at the city. Its purpose is to show the unique styles and traditions of Philadelphia through its most notable professions.

There was no precise formula for the book other than noting, as John Alviti, the Senior Curator of Collections for the Franklin Institute Science Museum, did that "*Philadelphia Originals* is the product of a number of years of extensive research in the archives, galleries, libraries, and museums of metropolitan Philadelphia. Drawing upon their respective collections – there are about 250 images – Mr. Glantz has matched their visual power with an engaging narrative that explains why Philadelphia became American's first great city."

Each chapter, except Food, was reviewed by at least one expert in the respective profession, though the final decisions of which people, events, and places to include were exclusively those of the author. Priority was given to a specific style. After that, selections were made to give each chapter an appropriate balance – except that where the profession had articulated its own preferences, such as the Philadelphia Bar Association – the author respected those preferences.

FACT CHECKING

To the extent possible, a request was asked of the subject matter – usually when permission was asked of a corresponding image – to verify the facts. The author did the remaining fact checking. If there are any errors or omissions, please notify the author directly at philadelphia_originals@yahoo.com

HOW THE BOOK IS ORGANIZED

Law, Business, and Science

The business and science chapters are interrelated and many of the topics in science – television, computers, cable, etc. – could be discussed in the business section. What the reader should know is that Philadelphia can easily be thought of as the "Media Innovator to the World." Newspapers, magazines, radio, television, computer, cable – all were either invented or had major innovations in Philadelphia. Another moniker is "Workshop to the World." Philadelphia has long been known for its industry – car parts, plane parts, railroad engines, and textiles to name a few.

After the American Revolution, Philadelphia was also known as the Cradle of Finance. The First Bank of the United States was here and Philadelphia, then, was the wealthiest city in the newly formed United States. In order for these businesses and inventions to prosper, lawyers were needed to set the rules. The legal chapter profiles the leading lawyers, the most memorable cases, how lawyers are portrayed in the media, and some of the places where lawyers practice.

Cultural Activities – Art, Music, and Film

The arts chapter is mostly historical, beginning with early painters and moving to current artists. It includes the various art movements that began in Philadelphia, the places where the art is housed, and ends with a showing of some of the best art of Philadelphia scenes. Music begins with the classical sound, though it could easily begin with rock and roll or the "Sound of Philadelphia" invented by Kenny Gamble and Leon Huff. The various styles of music are reviewed along with the venues where the music is played. The music chapter ends with some of the best-known songs about Philadelphia. Film begins with the performers and directors before moving on to the innovators and movies about Philadelphia.

Leisure Activities – Sports, Food, and Humor

The sports chapter begins with Connie Mack, who was a mainstay of Philadelphia baseball for about fifty years and focuses on the ups and downs of the local teams and some of the more notable players. The food section begins with the ingredients, moves through finger foods, goes on to entrees, and ends with a classic Philadelphia dessert. Humor takes a look at the comedians, cartoonists, and essayists who have made the city famous.

The Book's Preface

The preface argues that most of these 'Philadelphia' styles can be traced back to the way William Penn designed the city and Benjamin Franklin developed it. At its core Penn's respect for diversity helped create a cauldron where different communities could create their own cultures. Franklin wanted these cultures to mix by encouraging voluntary associations where people from different communities could come together and share and test their cultures.

This mix of different communities coming together for practical and charitable purposes helps define Philadelphia in ways that no other American city can.

DEDICATION and ACKNOWLDEGMENTS

NAME	PROFESSIONAL RELATIONSHIP
John Alviti	*Senior Curator. Franklin Institute*
Michael Barkann	*Host. ComcastSportsNet*
Peter Binzen	*Columnist. Philadelphia Inquirer*
Ray Didinger	*Author. NFL Films and ComcastSportsnet*
Joseph Gerber, Esquire	*Managing Partner. Cozen and O'Connor*
Bo Hammer	*Vice President. Franklin Institute*
Stephen Harmelin, Esquire	*Managing Partner. Dilworth Paxson*
Erika Jaeger-Smith	*Assistant Curator. James Michener Museum*
Bill Lyon	*Sports Columnist. Philadelphia Inquirer*
Kate Maxwell	*Former Managing Editor. Philadelphia Lawyer*
David Moltke-Hansen	*President and CEO. Historical Society of Pennsylvania*
Sharon Pinkenson	*Executive Director, Greater Philadelphia Film Office*
Carrie Rickey	*Film Critic. Philadelphia Inquirer*
Paul Savedow	*Chair, Music Department. Philadelphia Free Library*
Jerome Shestack, Esquire	*Former President. American Bar Association*
Katharine Steele Renninger	*Artist. Former Director for the James Michener Museum*
Gerard St. John	*Partner. Schnader Harrison LLP*
Gerald Wilkneson	*President, Broadcast Pioneers*
Signe Wilkinson	*Pulitzer Prize Winning Cartoonist. Philadelphia Daily News*
	Abington Free Library
	Margaret Grundy Library
	Levittown Free Library
	Pendel Free Library

ARTIST	WEBSITE
Bruce Johnson	*www.bjohnson ltd.com*
Charles Cushing	*www.charlescushing.com*
Dick Perez	*www.dickperez.com*
Elaine Lisle	*www.elainelise.com*
Gross McCleaf Gallery	*www.grossmccleaf.com*
Howard N. Watson	*www.howardwat.com*
James Kelly	*www.flickr.com*
Larry Berman	*www.larryberman.com*
Perry Milou	*www.perrymilou.com*
Rob Lawlor	*www.lawlorgallery.com*
Ruth Savitz	*www.photosofphiladelphia.com*
Stan Kotzen	*www.stankotzen.com*
The Rosenfeld Gallery	*www.therosenfeldgallery.com*
Tim Ogline	*www.timogline.com*
Tom Stiglich	*ww.tomstiglich.com*
Valerie Craig	*www.valeriecraig.com*
Wally Neibart	*www.wallyneibart.net*
Woodmere Art Gallery	*www.woodmereartmuseum.org*

Gross McCleaf Gallery Artists
www.grossmccleaf.com
Thomas F. Dougherty, Eileen Goodman,
Bertha Leonard, Max Mason, Celia B. Reisman,
Frank Trefny

Special thanks to the following people whose help was invaluable:

My Parents – Anne and Samuel Glantz, who gave me the well rounded background and the love of so many things to make this book possible. My mother always quoted Robert Louis Stevenson who said, "The World is so full of a number of things, I'm sure we should all be as happy as kings." My father always said, "Life is about having the questions, not the answers."

John McPhee's *Levels of the Game*, which showed how the style of play of two tennis players, Arthur Ashe and Clark Graebner, was a mirror of their backgrounds.

E. Digby Baltzell's *Puritan Boston Quaker Philadelphia*, which compared the styles and backgrounds of Boston and Philadelphia.

Thanks to the following artists who gave me permission:

Websites and studios of local Philadelphia Artists and Galleries who have artwork in this book

Flies Crawling on the Skeleton (1895) by Daniel Beard. Original Image from Philadelphia Press – Public Domain

WEBSITES of PLACES to VISIT
(A selection)

For more places try typing in the name of the place into your web-browser

LOCATION	Website
Avenue of the Arts	www.avenueofthearts.org
Chanticleer	www.chanticleergarden.org
City of Philadelphia Mural Arts Program	www.muralarts.org
Drexel University	www.drexel.edu
Elfreths Alley	www.elfrethsalley.org
Fairmount Park	www.fairmountpark.org
Franklin Institute	www2.fi.edu
Free Library of Philadelphia	www.library.phila.gov
Greater Philadelphia Film Office	www.film.org
Independence Hall	www.ushistory.org
Kimmel Center	www.kimmelcenter.org
LaSalle University	www.lasalle.edu
Lights of Liberty	www.lightsofliberty.org
Longwood Gardens	www.longwoodgardens.org
Mann Music Center	www.manncenter.org
Michener Museum	www.michenermuseum.org
Moore College of Art	www.moore.edu
Morris Arboretum	www.upenn.edu/arboretum
Mutter Museum	www.collphyphil.org/mutter.asp
National Constitution Center	constitutioncenter.org
Pennsylvania Academy of Fine Arts	www.pafa.org
Philadelphia Museum of Art	www.philamuseum.org
Rittenhouse Square	www.rittenhouserow.org
Rodin Museum	www.rodinmueum.org
South Street	www.southstreet.org
St Joseph's University	www.sju.edu
Temple University	www.temple.edu
Union League	www.unionleague.org
University of Pennsylvania	www.upenn.edu
Villanova University	www.villanova.edu
Wistar Institute	www.wistar.org

SPONSORS

An extra special thanks to the Thomas Skelton Harrison Foundation for providing the initial seed money to help get the book started.

Disclaimer: The Thomas Skelton Harrison Foundation exercised no control over the content of the book.

None of the people, organizations, grant–givers or sponsors, nor their employers, listed exercised any editorial control over the contents of this book.

The professions, people, venues, and events are only a starting point – not an exhaustive list. Professions like Philadelphia literature and politics are also worthy of study. The book is meant to give the visitor and student of Philadelphia a taste, a menu, of what makes Philadelphia such a remarkable city. I have tried to have an expert review each section but the details in the book are mine. If there are any errors or omissions please let me know and I will review them for any subsequent editions.

Washington Square Afternoon, 11" x 14", oil on board, by Elaine Moynihan Lisle. Courtesy of Elaine Moynihan Lisle

*Cypress at 19th, Oil on Board, 16" x 12", ©
2007 (available) by Elaine Moynihan Lisle.
Courtesy of Elaine Moynihan Lisle*

PHILADELPHIA'S DESIGN

Penn's First Sight of the Shores of Pennsylvania as He Ascends the River "From Whence the Air Smelt as Sweet as a New-Blown Garden," 1902-1906, Oil on canvas by Violet Oakley. Courtesy of Pennsylvania Capitol Preservation Committee and Brian Hunt

Picture – William Penn

"Franklin represented the city's mind. Penn, its heart. Penn was the idealist. Franklin, the pragmatist. Penn believed in the individual conscience as the 'Inner Light', while Franklin believed in voluntary associations to set the standard for behavior."

John Lukacs, Author Patricians and Philistines

NINGS

PHILADELPHIA'S DESIGN

NOTABLE STYLES
Planned Designs
Religious Tolerance
Neighborhoods
Voluntary Associations
Pragmatism
Charity

CONTENTS

GINNINGS

PHILADELPHIA'S DESIGN

Definitions of a city are many. A city can refer to a civilization like the Egyptians or the Israelites. A city can be a city-state like ancient Athens, Sparta or Rome. A city can be a theology like St. Augustine's City of God.

A literary characterization, by Philadelphia author Buzz Bissinger, says cities are wonderful because they are where "the spontaneity, the togetherness of community, the creativity, the endless characters populating the streets, the chaos" happen.[1]

American cities evolved out of the desire for freedom from religious persecution in Europe. In the 1600, 1700s, and early 1800s, the cities of the colonies were also defined by their means of access.

Philadelphia's definition was, is, and always will be defined by William Penn and Benjamin Franklin.

Penn liked Philadelphia because it was a seaport city. In Philadelphia, the Delaware River and the Atlantic Ocean allowed for easy access. The valleys of the Schuylkill allowed for agriculture, mining, and industry. Philadelphia was the place where Penn could test his theories of grand-design: his planned layout of the city which many other American cities copied in some form and his "Holy Experiment," which uniquely, among early American cities, allowed for religious toleration.

Franklin liked Philadelphia because it gave him and everybody else a chance to set their own imprints on the city. It was a city where a self-starter could thrive. It was a city that encouraged voluntary associations because there was no central ideology. Penn had set up the city so that no one point of view was supposed to dominate. This concept encouraged the free exchange necessary for people to feel free to associate with others of different backgrounds or different views.[2]

The noted historian John Lukacs wrote of Philadelphia and these two men.

"Its character was shaped partly by William Penn, partly by Benjamin Franklin. One was the contemplative humanitarian; the other the utilitarian eager beaver.

Penn was the essential English (or rather, Anglo-Celtic) case of the Rich Young Man turned Humanist; Franklin was the more Germanic (and essentially Bostonian) ideal of the Poor Apprentice who became a Famous Scientist.

Penn was the founder; Franklin, after all, a newcomer from Boston; but newcomers in Philadelphia do not have a hard row to hoe.

It is easy to fancy Franklin addressing the assembled ironmongers in the elephantine vault of the Masonic Temple in 1875, inaugurating the first nickelodeon movie in 1900, judging the Miss America contest in Atlantic City in 1925; or introducing someone like Buckminster Fuller at the American Philosophical Society in 1975.

It is difficult to imagine Penn doing anything of the sort. The shy, the gentle, the introverted, the myrtle-and-brick Philadelphia, where houses were named "Strawberry Mansion" and "Solitude" was that of William Penn.

Franklin's world included the first utilitarian prison, the first national advertising agency (N.W. Ayer, in 1901), and the Curtis Publishing Company.

Franklin represented the city's mind. Penn, its heart. Penn was the idealist. Franklin, the pragmatist. Penn believed in the individual conscience as the 'Inner Light', while Franklin believed in voluntary associations to set the standard for behavior."[3, 4]

These two men set the tone for the city's character into the twenty-first century.

Each profession covered in this book owes something to Penn's desire for independent communities tempered by Franklin's view that the members of these communities should work with each other. Each of the professions reviewed can be seen to have a mix of the ingredients/influences established by Penn and Franklin: Penn's Quaker ideals and his utopian desires, Franklin's charity, pragmatism, and self-starter qualities.

WILLIAM PENN'S INFLUENCES

RELIGIOUS DIVERSITY

Religious persecution in England

William Penn was born on October 14, 1644, in London.[5] His father was Sir Admiral William Penn who sent his son to Oxford and to France for his education. Penn also studied law in London but he was dismissed from Oxford in his second year for "nonconformity" and only briefly studied law. His legal education proved useful in his own writings, his own trials, and mostly in the laws that he would create for his new colony.

In 1647, George Fox founded the Quaker religion. Penn became one of Fox's disciples while in Ireland, in 1667, where Penn was sent to manage some of his father's properties.[6]

The Quakers believe that members should be able to pray directly to God without intermediaries like ministers and bishops. Their "Inner Light" guides them to the proper understandings. The Quakers gather at Meetinghouses where they pray and speak only when moved. They believe they have a friendship with God and call themselves "Friends." Their enemies, believing that the method of praying only when moved resembled "quaking" called them Quakers. Quakers do not have an organized clergy. They read the Bible for the stories it tells rather than for literal meaning.

Because they failed to respect the authority of the King of England and because they refused to take an oath of loyalty to the king (Quakers don't swear oaths), they became a target for their heretical beliefs.[7, 8, 9] It was while in prison for some of these trials that William Penn set forth, in writing, his core beliefs, many of which were to find their way to Philadelphia.

Trial 1

In September 1667, Penn and his congregation were jailed for practicing their faith. Penn wrote to the Earl of Orrery, the lord-president of Munster. On reading Penn's letter an order was issued for his immediate discharge. His father became outraged and threatened to disinherit him. Luckily for Philadelphians his father didn't. Penn's father reconciled with his son and his son's Quaker beliefs before Penn's father died in 1670.[10]

Trial 2

Subsequent writings earned Penn a stint in the Tower of London for eight months. In jail he wrote a number of pamphlets in support of his faith. The best known was No Cross, No Crown, a historical case for religious toleration, which Penn wrote in 1669. Through his influence with the Duke of York, Penn was subsequently released.[11]

Trial 3 – Right to Trial by Jury Established

Penn was arrested a third time by the Lord Mayor of London, in 1670, for preaching in the streets after authorities had padlocked his Meetinghouse. It was in this trial that the right of juries to decide verdicts was established.

The jury acquitted Penn and the other defendants but the Lord Mayor rejected the verdict and had Penn imprisoned. "The Lord Mayor of London gave the jury members fines and ordered them held in Newgate prison. Still, the jury affirmed their verdict.

After two months, the Court of Common Pleas reversed the verdict and freed the jury and Penn and his co-defendants. The jury then sued the Lord Mayor of London for false arrest. The Lord Chief Justice of England, together with his eleven associates, ruled unanimously that juries must not be imprisoned for doing their duty."[12, 13]

Sir John Vaugh, the Lord Chief Justice, wrote a judge "may try to open the eyes of the jurors, but not to lead them by the nose."

Trial 4

A fourth arrest resulted in an acquittal of the main charges but imprisonment for refusing to take an oath of allegiance.[14]

THE HOLY EXPERIMENT

Creation of Philadelphia

While traveling in Germany and Holland, William Penn began to think of creating his own colony for religious freedom. Holland, especially, influenced Penn because its freedoms encouraged many Jews and Protestants to move there.[15]

Penn sought an area away from New England where many Quakers were treated unfavorably by the New England Puritans.[16] Penn, convinced that the Quakers could not practice freely in England, asked King Charles II for a charter for an American Colony, on March 4, 1681. Penn wrote of Pennsylvania – "There may be room there, though not here [England] for such a holy experiment."

In return for canceling the 16,000 pound debt owed to Penn's father, the Admiral, Charles II granted to William Penn land close to the present boundaries of the state of Pennsylvania. The King proposed the name "Pennsylvania" which meant "Forests of Penn"—honoring Penn's late father, the Admiral.

Penn became proprietor, owing to the King two beaver skins and a fifth of any gold and silver mined within the territory.[17]

Penn arrived on November 8, 1682, where he founded "Philadelphia." He chose the name, which means "City of Brotherly Love" in Greek.

Rights in the New City

Penn's First Frame of Government provided for secure private property, virtually unlimited free enterprise, a free press, trial by jury, and religious toleration. It was the first Constitution to provide for peaceful change through amendments with the approval of the governor and eighty-five percent of the elected officials. The Constitution was amended several times, often because of complaints that Penn's power, though exercised with restraint, was still too much for the legislature. Adopted on October 28, 1701, Penn's Constitution lasted until 1776, where it became a model for Pennsylvania's own Constitution.

Penn limited the death penalty to murder and treason, unlike England which had about 200 offenses that could result in the death penalty.

Religious Freedom

Penn's Constitution was the first in modern history to offer equal rights to people of different races and religions.

The French philosopher Voltaire, a champion of religious toleration, lauded Penn: "William Penn might, with reason, boast of having brought down upon earth the Golden Age, which in all probability, never had any real existence but in his dominions."[18, 19]

In other words, only in Philadelphia, Pennsylvania, was one truly free to practice one's religious beliefs. This was unlike England or Puritan New England, which made political dissent a crime. New England whipped, tarred, and hanged Quakers. [20]

Peace with the Indians

Penn achieved peaceful relations with a number of local Indian tribes including the Susquehannocks, Shawnees, and Lenni-Lenape. The Indians respected Penn because he visited them without guards or personal weapons and because Penn took the time to learn their dialects so he could conduct negotiations without interpreters. Penn acquired Indian lands through peaceful, voluntary exchange. Reportedly, Penn concluded a "Great Treaty" with the Indians at Shackamaxon, near what is now the Kensington district of Philadelphia.[21] Benjamin West and later Edward Hicks [see the art section] immortalized an imaginative view of the treaty in their art.

Voltaire noted this treaty as well. He praised Penn's treaty with the Indians as "the only treaty between those people [Indians and Christians] that was not ratified by an oath, and that was never infringed."

While Penn encouraged women to get an education and speak, Penn did not require equal rights for women. "He had slaves and never believed that the Indians would be acceptable citizens."[22]

NEIGHBORHOODS

"Penn's policy of religious toleration and peace—no military conscription—attracted all kinds of European immigrants. English, Irish, Germans, Catholics, Jews, and an assortment of Protestant sects including Dunkers, Huguenots, Lutherans, Mennonites, Moravians, Pietists, and Schwenkfelders. Liberty brought so many immigrants that by the American Revolution Pennsylvania had grown to some 300,000 people and had became one of the largest colonies.

Pennsylvania was America's first great melting pot."[23]

In the nineteenth and twentieth centuries, neighborhoods took more of an ethnic flavor. Many of these neighborhoods couldn't have been more opposite. In 1900 few New Yorkers and few Bostonians had failed to visit Times Square and Boston Common, yet many Philadelphians had never been in Rittenhouse Square.

"When an Irish Catholic boy from Manyunk married a Polish Catholic girl from Port Richmond, his people would speak of a Mixed Marriage. The lack of interest of most people in those outside their circle was as genuine as it was self-willed. It was not the result of ethnic fears or hatred. It was, rather, the result of indifference. They did not know because they did not wish to know."[24]

1900 Waverly by Ruth Savitz. Courtesy of Ruth Savitz

CITY DESIGN

Penn's Green Country Towne

While other cities evolved haphazardly, Penn designed as much of Philadelphia as he could. The designs of the city were geographical and philosophical. Penn laid out and sold plots of land he had mapped from the Delaware River to the Schuylkill River.

Penn wanted to get along with the Indians so there were no provisions for city walls or a garrison of soldiers. He didn't want factional politics, so there was no provision for traditional municipal institutions.

He wanted a city that wouldn't burn (as London had in 1666), so much of the city was built with bricks.[25]

Penn's hope was that various trades-people, many of whom were in the building or merchant industries, would live in homes according to their profession.[26]

Penn negotiated a peace treaty with the Lenni Lenape Indians (The Delawarians) at what is now Kensington [The aforesaid "Great Treaty"]. He bought out the tribes' rights to what are now Chester, Bucks, and Philadelphia (which then contained much of Montgomery) counties.[27] Soon after his charter was granted, Penn began to sell plots and establish the city, which was incorporated in 1701.

Most early settlers lived near the Delaware River. Those who ventured beyond to Chester and Bucks County were farmers. Most early Philadelphians worked hard. Public displays, where public disorder could occur, were frowned upon. There was little early theater or public card playing in Philadelphia.[28]

The arts were most notable in the architecture of the buildings and the furniture.

Design Details

"Penn's conceptions of Philadelphia is one of the earliest attempts at utopian city planning. His design represented the most extensively 'pre-planned' American city at that time.

His early plans grew from his love of the country estate, as opposed to the metropolis. His original vision of a 'Greene Country Towne' sought to replicate this model of life in the New World.

The first plan called for individual houses to be separated from their neighbors by sizable areas of green, thus replicating the gentleman's farm that he so loved."[29]

Philadelphia was chosen by Penn because it was a place where trade could flourish. It was accessible to the Atlantic Ocean and thus to Europe and other eastern seaports. The city of Philadelphia was the commercial center of this "Towne." Eighty acre "gentleman's estates" were to surround it.

William Penn's City described:

Elizabeth Pennell, in *Our Philadelphia*, wrote that New York and Boston boast of the disorderly picturesqueness of streets that follow the old cow tracks. Penn, however, understood the value of order in architecture as in conduct. Along with her husband, Joseph Pennell, Elizabeth emphasized the beauty of Philadelphia's [and the suburb's] streets.

"Philadelphia's despised regularity gives it the repose, the serenity, which is an essential of great art. Few towns, if any, have more lovelier suburbs than Philadelphia. Their loveliness is another part of our inheritance from William Penn who set no limits to his dream of a green country town, and from the old Friends who, in deference to his desire, lined not only their streets but their roads with trees."

"Main street in Germantown, with its peaceful old grey stone houses and great overshadowing trees, has no rival at home or abroad, and I have seen as commonplace a street as Walnut in West Philadelphia, its houses screened behind the two lines of trees, become in the golden light of a summer afternoon as stately as any at Versailles or St. Germain." As for Philadelphia, she wrote, "Can the spring be fairer than in and around Philadelphia when wisteria blossoms on every wall and the coating is white with dogwood?"[30]

John Adams, in his letters, remarked about the road to Kensington and beyond that the road was "Straight as the streets of Philadelphia …beautiful rows of trees: buttonwoods, oaks, walnuts, cherries and willows" lined both sides of the street.[31]

Penn's Philadelphia thoroughfares were named after trees. Pine. Walnut, Spruce, Chestnut, Sasafras (now Race), Mulberry (now Arch) and Cedar (now Spruce).[32]

Homes

The availability of lots was advertised in Thomas Holme's *Portraiture of the City of Philadelphia*, published in 1683.

Penn designed the city with Broad and High [now Market] as the main streets which cross each other at "centre square," now the home of City Hall, thus dividing the city into quadrants.

Ideally, Penn would have liked each mansion, bounded with fields and gardens, to be 800 feet from each neighbor. Penn reduced the geographical limit but kept the general concept as well as the idea of a "greenbelt" around the city to allow for expansion and to provide for additional needs. The idea was the forerunner to the suburbs. The avenues were 100 feet wide (more than any street in London). The grid design was revolutionary in its day. Penn's hope, in part, was that the "green" of the town would aid against diseases like London's bubonic plague and also aid against fire.

The main square, Centre Square, was to be surrounded by the city's main public buildings; the meeting house, state house, and school. The other four squares of Penn's "Green Country Town" were:

Northeast
[Now] Ben Franklin Bridge
Southwest
Rittenhouse Square
Southeast
Washington Square
Northwest
[Now] Logan Circle[33]

Rittenhouse Square, shown, is the most used and maybe the nicest of the parks that Penn envisioned. It is surrounded by a number of Philadelphia cultural institutions, including the Philadelphia Art Alliance, The Curtis Institute of Music, The Philadelphia Ethical Society, Holy Trinity Church, the homes (at least before he died) of Henry McIlhenny, a noted art collector and chair of the Philadelphia Art Museum, and the Rittenhouse Club, one of the old-boys club, until women were finally admitted.[34]

Rittenhouse Square by Perry Milou. Courtesy of Perry Milou

The park draws a wide variety of people and is named after the scientist David Rittenhouse.

During the second half of the nineteenth century, E. Digby Baltzell wrote in his book, *Philadelphia Gentlemen: The Making of a National Upper Class*:

"Rittenhouse Square was surrounded by the mansions of Philadelphia's Victorian aristocracy. At no other time in the city's history, before, or since, have so many wealthy and fashionable families lived so near one another."

Drexels, Wanamakers, Lippincotts, Ingersolls, Peppers, Cassatts, Wyeths, Van Rensselaers, Biddles, Brown, Bullits (William C. Bullitt's *It's Not Done* was written about the Square) have lived on the Square.

In the twentieth century some of the mansions around the square were replaced by apartment buildings and the square was redesigned by Paul Cret, who was also instrumental in the design of the Benjamin Franklin Parkway. Today Rittenhouse Square still attracts a wide variety of guests.[35]

SUBSEQUENT PHILADELPHIA GRAND DESIGNS

Benjamin Franklin Parkway

The Benjamin Franklin Parkway is another planned enterprise whose purpose, like Penn's grand layout of the city, was to create an avenue that would connect the city to the western suburbs of Fairmount Park and would serve as a street that people could easily travel.

The Parkway gives Philadelphia another identity. It is to Philadelphia what the Champs-Elysées, is to Paris. In addition to the buildings, a number of fountains, statues, and memorials give the Parkway a special feel. Monuments all lend a tone that gives the Parkway its own special atmosphere.

Creation of the Parkway

The original idea for the Parkway came from C. K. Landis of Sea Isle City. The dimensions of the Parkway were intended to be one mile long and one hundred and fifty feet wide.

"Landis chose this land because he felt that a convenient approach to Fairmount Park was a necessity. He thought that by placing a view of the park at one end, and a view of the Public Buildings at the other, he would have 'Something worthy of the magnificent City of Philadelphia'."[36] William J. McAuley gave another proposal with the design of a Boulevard straight from the Plaza at Northern City Hall to the foot of Fairmount Park. The "City Beautiful" movement finally approved the project and ground was finally struck in 1907.

Skyline, oil on canvas, 36 x 48 inches, by Thomas F. Dougherty. Courtesy of Gross McCleaf Gallery

More City Planning

Within the city, the Redevelopment Authority, established in 1945, helped.

"In the creation of low-income and middle-income housing, the rehabilitation of certain old row houses, the development of new industrial cites, the conversion of blighted areas into improved and enlarged campuses for several of the city's universities [including Penn and Temple], the provision of new parks and playgrounds and projects for automobile parking and street widening." "About the same time private enterprise helped rebuild downtown Philadelphia "into a planned commercial area – Penn Center."[37]

Later, the Philadelphia's PSFS building was a pioneer in skyscraper construction.

Lately, like most cities, Philadelphia, has struggled to keep its population from moving to the suburbs, but mayors like Ed Rendell, who helped open up Center City at night, and John Street, who has seen the construction of a new arts center, have kept the dream of William Penn alive. Mayor Michael Nutter has the same aim.

The vertical limit of the City, limited to be the brim of Penn's hat atop City Hall, was broken when Willard Rouse developed his two twin Liberty towers in the 1980s over the protests of Edmund Bacon, a noted city planner and father of actor Kevin Bacon.[38]

The tallest Philadelphia building, as of 2008, is the Comcast Center.

The Avenue of the Arts

Just as the planned design of the Parkway led to an architectural identity for the city and the Redevelopment Authority led to a new residential and commercial identity for the city, the Avenue of The Arts has given a cultural focus to the city.

The Avenue of the Arts, Inc., an independent non-profit organization, was created in 1993 to coordinate and support cultural and related development along North and South Broad Street in Philadelphia.

This isn't to say that there aren't many other cultural arts centers, like the Walnut Street Theater [the nation's oldest continually functioning theater] but Broad Street, the Avenue of the Arts, is now the focus for many arts projects.

The most recent addition to the Avenue of the Arts (as of this writing) is the Kimmel Center for the Performing Arts, which is the

Wilma Theater, 20" x 30", by Charles Cushing. Courtesy of Charles Cushing

Italian Fountain, Art Museum, by Charles Cushing. Courtesy of Charles Cushing

home for the Philadelphia Orchestra and numerous performing groups.

The old Academy of Music, built in the 1850s, is home to the Pennsylvania Ballet and the Philadelphia Opera Company, and a number of other arts companies.

Other Arts buildings on Broad Street include The University of the Arts, The Wilma, Merriam, and Freedom Theaters, The Pennsylvania Academy of the Fines Arts, The Liacouras Center at Temple, and the Black Family Reunion Cultural Center.

Artists of Pennsylvania Ballet in Christopher Wheeldon's Swan Lake by Photo: Paul Kolnik. Courtesy of The Pennsylvania Ballet

Pennsylvania Ballet

Text reprinted with permission of Pennsylvania Ballet (source: email communication).

Since its inception in 1963, Pennsylvania Ballet has been at the forefront of dance in America and is widely regarded as one of the premier ballet companies in the nation. The School and Company were established by Barbara Weisberger, a Balanchine protégée, through a Ford Foundation initiative to develop regional professional dance companies.

During its first decade, the Company forged the unique identity for which it is still known today: a diverse classical repertoire with a Balanchine backbone performed by versatile dancers whose energy and exuberance are the Company's enduring signature

Drawing its audiences from throughout the tri-state region,

Pennsylvania Ballet presents a season of six productions in Philadelphia, including a new production of the holiday spectacular, *George Balanchine's The Nutcracker*, balancing classic ballets with new works that challenge the dancers and attract a diverse audience. The Company also tours throughout the Commonwealth of Pennsylvania, as well as in other locations in the Northeastern U.S.

Over the past several years, Pennsylvania Ballet has enhanced its artistic integrity while continually increasing its reach and strengthening its foundation through creative programming; initiatives such as the Family Matinee Series and Prologue Lecture Series; and educational outreach programs such as Accent on Dance

Artists of Pennsylvania Ballet in George Balanchine's The Nutcracker, Choreography by George Balanchine, © The George Balanchine Trust. Courtesy of The Pennsylvania Ballet

BENJAMIN FRANKLIN'S
INFLUENCES

Self-Starter

Benjamin Franklin had a curiosity about how things (human as well as mechanical) worked. He had an ability to read, to study, to experiment, and to keep trying until he saw the necessary connections to make an idea work. He was also willing to take the necessary risks. He was lucky he wasn't electrocuted in his famous kite experiment, which legend has it took place around 10th and Market Streets (the country at the time).

Due to Franklin's example, Philadelphia is best known by the following comparison. Boston is best. New York is biggest. Philadelphia is first.

The core communication equipment was invented in and around Philadelphia – television, the first general purpose computer, the first advertising company, cable, and, of course, the first "readable" newspaper – Franklin's *Pennsylvania Gazette*. Even film got started at Penn's Veterinary School with experiments on capturing the motion of animals.

[For a list of many other Philadelphia firsts, please see the beginning of the science section].

Pragmatism

Fads are temporary. A constant theme with Franklin was that his experiments, his businesses, should have some useful value. But Franklin's pragmatism went much further. It applied to the way he conducted himself and the image that he portrayed. Franklin would always make a point of hustling, working physically hard, and scurrying to the printing press office because it gave customers the perception that he was up to something or that he would apply the same hustle to their concerns. Practically, Franklin would often let others take credit, at least partial credit, for his ideas, for he knew that the salesmanship of others would help launch his projects.

In order to write for his brother's newspaper, *The Courant*, in Boston, Franklin created fictional characters like Silence DoGood. These assumed identities allowed Franklin to reach a wider audience, allowed him to look at issues from different viewpoints, and, at the core, allowed him to express his own views. When he understood that he could never run the paper while his brother was in charge, Franklin understood another principal of innovation. If the rules are constricting you – leave. That's what he did by fleeing to Philadelphia.

In his biography Franklin identified thirteen attributes for the successful man. Practicality is at the core of many of these.

1. Temperance. Eat not to dullness; drink not to elevation.
2. Silence. Speak not but what may benefit others or yourself. Avoid trifling conversation.
3. Order. Let all your things have their places; let each part of your business have its time.
4. Resolution. Resolve to perform what you ought; perform without fail what you resolve.
5. Frugality. Make no expense but to do good to others or yourself. Waste Nothing.
6. Industry. Lose no time; be always employed in something useful; cut off all unnecessary activities.
7. Sincerity. Use no hurtful deceit; think innocently and justly; and, if you speak, speak accordingly.
8. Justice. Wrong none by doing injuries or omitting the benefits that are your duty.
9. Moderation. Avoid Extremes; Forbear resenting injuries, so much as you think they deserve.
10. Cleanliness. Tolerate no uncleanliness in body, shelter, or habitation.
11. Tranquility. Be not disturbed at trifles or at accidents common or unavoidable.
12. Chastity.
13. Humility. Imitate Jesus and Socrates.[39]

Among his many sayings was that "When a man's life was over, it should be said that he lived usefully, not that he died rich."

Franklin knew that to reach his readers he had to make the news accessible. Accessibility meant making it fun and making it personal. In this vein Franklin employed numerous devices, mostly in his Poor Richard's Almanac (which literally means All Man's Knack) but also in his *Pennsylvania Gazette*. He used his famous Poor Richard's sayings, numerous anecdotes, creative stories, humor and even poems to engage the reader.

A second practical side to Franklin's printing business was that he franchised his writings across the seaboard, mainly through relatives.[40] Spreading his writings out helped Franklin amass a fortune so that he could focus on innovation – his scientific projects. The post office was created by Franklin mainly to assist in the mailings of his writings. It should be noted that the "Almanac" was not Franklin's invention. Franklin would often use the inventions of others to his advantage by recreating them in a more usable format.

Franklin's scientific achievements were mostly the result of his aforesaid self-starter qualities and his pragmatism. The lightning rod was a practical solution to fire. That's one reason it was so successful. People needed it. But Franklin also made sure that the lightning rod was free (in the sense that he didn't charge a fee for its usage and he wanted the world to know how it worked). This free usage had, again, a practical side. It enhanced his reputation throughout the world.

A review of all the professions in this book shows this practical side. Philadelphia businesses took advantage of their location to be a leader in shipping, finance, and textiles until the world expanded. Lawyers look to serve their clients – not to be on the United States Supreme Court. Philadelphia artists serve their clients by giving them art they can show and use. Philadelphia comedians tell stories to make their points. The city has some of the finest medical facilities in the country and several that are also teaching hospitals. There's nothing more practical than good health. The University's Wharton School is one of the few undergraduate business schools in the country.

Voluntary Associations

Practically, Franklin knew that he could only do so much by himself. Franklin, with the aid of some members of the Samuel Keimer press, began a "voluntary association" called the Junto. It was devoted to helping businessmen improve their ventures and their daily life.

"The club, the Junto, met Friday nights, first in a tavern and later in a house, to discuss moral, political, and scientific topics of the day. To guide and focus discussions, Franklin formulated a series of questions that included asking for reasons why local businesses were succeeding or failing, whether a citizen had done something praiseworthy and, if so, how might this be emulated. Common readings in literature were regularly assigned and used to debate topics related to morals, philosophy, and civic life. Members were required to write essays that would be critiqued by the group in the form of suggestions, hypotheses, and polite questions. Franklin required that any member who became harsh and assertive in his comments would receive a small but embarrassing fine. While being more of a skeptic than a rebel and refraining from disagreement just for the sake of argument, this fine was meant to keep him in line as well. He was one of the youngest members of the club, had no wealth or position to speak of, and yet, his leadership skills shone through in his intelligence and moral force."

Some of the questions to be answered in each meeting (*Junto* is Latin for meeting) included the following:

• Hath any citizen in your knowledge failed in his business lately, and what have you heard of the cause?

• Have you heard of any citizen's thriving well, and by what means?

• Do you know of any fellow citizen, who has lately done a worthy action, deserving praise and imitation? Or who has committed an error proper for us to be warned against and avoid?

• What unhappy effects of intemperance have you lately observed or heard? Of imprudence? Of passion? Or of any vice or folly?

• What happy effects of temperance? Of prudence? Of moderation? Or of any other virtue?

• Have you or any of your acquaintances been lately sick or wounded? If so, what remedies were used, and what were their effects?

• Whom do you know that are shortly going voyages or journeys, if one should have occasion to send by them?

The Junto was only one example of showing that citizens functioned best when they voluntarily (as opposed to any governmental mandate or religious or moral dictate) came together to work in common purposes.

Other "voluntary associations" included a subscription library where members of the association agreed to contribute a small sum to buy a start-up set of books for a public library – the Library Company of Philadelphia. He and the Junto also helped start the American Philosophical Society for discussion of science, the first volunteer Fire Company and the first public hospital and police departments.

These voluntary associations have been a foundation of public life in Philadelphia and touch every profession covered in this book.

Some of the numerous voluntary associations include: [Voluntary is used in the sense that individuals or groups have come together for a common good. In some of these associations there may be dues]

The Greater Philadelphia Cultural Alliance
The Greater Philadelphia Film Society
The Philadelphia Big Five
The Philadelphia Art Alliance
The Philadelphia Bar Association
The Philadelphia Cartoon Society
The Philadelphia Chamber of Commerce
The Philadelphia Free Library

Versatility

Franklin's versatility (printing, science, humor, business associations) gave him a remarkable scope. He understood, perhaps better than anybody since his time, how things connected. How he could apply one set of skills to other areas. His curiosity gave him range, a range that he would most notably employ in his political dealings in France and the United States.

A study of his participation in these ventures would take volumes. A wonderful recent example is Stacy Schiff's *A Great Improvisation: Franklin, France, and the Birth of America*, which marvels at how Franklin's negotiations with France took place while Franklin was in his 70s and how Franklin literally invented American foreign policy in a climate of spies, double agents, backroom deals, and anger in the colonies over reliance on a foreign power.[41]

It was through Franklin's remarkable versatility that he was able to secure from the French (who a short time before had been the enemy of the colonies in the French and Indian War) the financing and weapons and military assistance to win the Revolutionary War and to create the preeminent voluntary association – the United States of America. Franklin was the only American to sign all four of the principal founding documents:

• *The Declaration of Independence* (1776)
• *The Treaty of Alliance, Amity, and Commerce with France* (1778)
• *The Treaty of Paris*, establishing an end to the Revolutionary War (1782)
• *The United States Constitution* (1787).

Several anecdotes show the creativity of Franklin's diplomatic mind.

While serving as an American representative in France during the American Revolution, Franklin was told that General Howe, the British commanding officer, had captured Philadelphia. However, Franklin, aware that maintaining control of the city would be a great burden, replied, "I beg your pardon, Sir, Philadelphia has taken Howe."

In France, Franklin wore a coonskin cap. Franklin, who helped launch the University of Pennsylvania, was no dummy. But it played into his negotiations for the French to think that he was just an American country bumpkin.

Philadelphia's Versatility

Philadelphia has shown Franklin's versatility by being able to adapt to the times as an examination of the City through the centuries shows:

Revolutionary City

It was not merely the geography of being near the middle of the Eastern colonies that made Philadelphia the home for Revolution and Democracy. It was Penn's willingness to experiment, combined with Franklin's love of voluntary associations, that forged the greatest Democratic Experiment – an experiment that recognized while the states should be free to conduct their own social experiments they could only, practically, do so if they voluntarily came together to form a Union to protect and enhance those social experiments.

Athens Age

In the last decade of the 1790s Philadelphia had its most successful age, its "Athens" age. In this decade Philadelphia was the political, economic, and cultural leader of American. It also had the largest population [soon to be supplanted by New York] as well as the largest city. It was home to the Congress and the United States Supreme Court. The first Bank of the United States was centered there. It was during this period when many notable Philadelphians like Benjamin Rush lived and many organizations like the Philadelphia Academy of Fine Arts were formed.

Biddle Age

The period from 1825-1841 is known as the Biddle Age, named for the wealthy Nicholas Biddle who ran the country's Second National Bank. The period was another prosperous age for Philadelphia.

When New York built the Erie Canal, which allowed for New York City to have easy access to the riches of the hinterland, Pennsylvania tried to counter this commercial shift by building a "Pennsylvania System" west to Pittsburgh. In 1834 one could travel from Philadelphia to Pittsburgh over a 394-mile route combining railroads and canals.[42, 43]

Workshop to the World

While the national focus would shift from Philadelphia to New York and Washington, Philadelphia began to focus its creative energies in other areas. It became a leader in textiles and in 1876 was host to the country's Centennial exhibitions, which emphasized new technology and new industries. It would later create car parts, helicopters, railroad engines, and a variety of manufactured items for national and international use while still being a major provider of ships. The United States Steel Corporation provided jobs to laborers for decades.

Consolidation

In the second half of the nineteenth century and the beginning of the twentieth, Philadelphia was noted for its spread beyond the city limits and by the entry of many new immigrants who forged their own ethnic neighborhoods. In South Philadelphia the dividing lines between the Irish, Jewish, Italian, and African-American communities were often just a matter of several city blocks.

Reform

In the 1950s Philadelphia joined Roosevelt's New Deal with the elections of Joseph Clark and Richardson Dilworth. These two mayors instituted many city reforms and changes including the home rule and the aforesaid redevelopment of Center City and Society Hill.

A New Renaissance

In the latter part of the twentieth century and the early part of the twenty-first, Philadelphia is again becoming a cultural leader. Philadelphia is home to a new Convention Center, the National Constitution Center, and the Kimmel Center for the Performing Arts. Two new stadiums were constructed: Lincoln Financial Field (for the Eagles football team) and Citizens Bank Park (for the Phillies baseball team).

The Barnes Foundation is getting ready to line the Benjamin Franklin Parkway making the Parkway an "Artistic" Mile. The restaurants are home to some of the most creative ideas in the county.

The Greater Philadelphia Film Office has helped make Philadelphia an exciting and practical alternative to Hollywood.

Philadelphia's Fringe Festival encourages experimentation in the arts.

Charity

Franklin also thought that one of the goals of these associations was to do some public good. The goal of these associations was not, in Franklin's world, to be exclusive, to make its members rich or famous. Franklin put it thus, "Nor is a duty beneficial because it is commanded, but it is commanded, because it is beneficial."

Before he died, Franklin freed his slaves and thus his conscience. In his will Franklin left money to be used for tradesmen to start their own businesses.

Charity has been essential to Philadelphia's life. The Franklin Institute was founded with money from Franklin's will. The Kimmel Center was founded with the money of Sidney Kimmel and thousands of others, including donators of $100 whose names appear on glass inside the center. Philadelphians have contributed to this tradition throughout the decades, from small donations to the very large.

*the*PHILADELPHIALAWYER

*Andrew Hamilton. Courtesy of
Historical Society of Pennsylvania*

**Picture – Andrew Hamilton, the
Original Philadelphia Lawyer**

*"I think Philadelphia Lawyers
tend to be competitive and combative,
very much like the spirit of the town.
There's a feistiness here. It's a town that
tends to get its juices flowing. We're not
New York and we're not Washington,
so I think we're forced to fight a little
harder to get what we want. And we
get it more often than not."*[1]

Quote by Ed Rendell,
Former mayor of Philadelphia
who became a governor of
Pennsylvania

A LAWYER

THE PHILADELPHIA LAWYER

NOTABLE STYLES
Sharp and Aggressive Fighters
Tenacity
Able To Handle All Aspects of Law
Favor Freedom of Expression

CONTENTS

EPHIA LAWYER

A PHILADELPHIA LAWYER

Philadelphia Lawyer: A song, Woody Guthrie's "Philadelphia Lawyer" is named after this profession. An autobiography, George Wharton Pepper's *Philadelphia Lawyer*, is named after it. A movie, Paul Newman's *The Young Philadelphians*, is about lawyers in the title city.

No other city's lawyers are as identifiable by their geography. Philadelphia lawyers are known for their tactics and abilities to plead cases. They're known for their abilities to switch from handling corporate acquisitions and utility law to handling the cases of individuals – criminal defense, personal injury, and more.

They're primarily local lawyers (representing local clients), though they've been known to argue cases nationally and internationally. Although very few have gone on to the Supreme Court, many have argued before it and several turned down nominations. It was a Philadelphia lawyer who argued a New York case that gave rise to the very phrase – "Philadelphia Lawyer."

They are not afraid to take on unpopular causes or make unpopular decisions and they have set or been involved in many firsts, such as the first law school and the first law library. According to Gerard J. St. John (retired partner at Schnader Harrison) The Philadelphia Bar Association is the oldest bar Association in the country, "In the pre-American Revolution era, Philadelphia lawyers litigated disputes over insurance claims for oceangoing cargo. After the war, they sat as members on boards that managed the nation's financial system. In the mid-19th century, they represented the interests of railroads and industrial companies. After World War I, they moved into global politics and, in the 1960s, into civil rights causes. In the 1990s, Philadelphia lawyers had pushed into other areas – personal-injury, product liability, and class-action lawsuits."[2]

Dan Rottenberg, a Philadelphia author and editor, wrote for *The Philadelphia Lawyer*: "It has taken a peculiarly Philadelphian kind of lawyer – marinated in this city's uniquely egalitarian culture – to promote and nurture democracy's ideology over two centuries."[3]

Early in Philadelphia history and up to the 1900s, law was largely a family tradition. The leaders of the Bar Association were also leaders of Philadelphia society. Tocqueville wrote, "If you ask me where I should put aristocracy in America, I should not hesitate to answer that it is not among the rich, who have no common bond uniting them. It is at the bar or on the bench that the American aristocracy may be found."

According to John Lukacs, a noted Philadelphia historian, the notion of a legal aristocracy serving as "[a] counterweight to unbridled democracy, may have crystallized in [Tocqueville's] mind during a sixteen day visit to Philadelphia in 1831."

Lukacs argues in *Philadelphia – Patricians and Philistines 1900-1950* that the reputation of the "Philadelphia lawyer" changed in the 1900s as the leaders of the bar were less associated with families and became more interested in finding new causes of action than protecting the status quo.[4] The Philadelphia Bar would probably argue that opening up the practice of law to the non-elite helped make for better lawyers and for better law.

In the twenty-first century some of the city's biggest law firms approach or exceed 500 and even 1,000 lawyers. Many of the big firms now have international offices.

At its best, law defines the boundaries of proper behavior. Since Philadelphia is made up of a variety of neighborhoods (be they geographical or ethnic or religious or cultural), Philadelphia law, at its best, has sought to define the boundaries of these neighborhoods. Are there boundaries? Are there limits on access? To what extent does inclusion mean the end of the neighborhood? Who decides when inclusion is good or bad? Examples abound. Can a municipal agency exclude blacks from an education at a school run by that agency under the terms of a private will? How much can the religious dictate norms of behavior to the non-religious and vice-versa? Can women be precluded from attending the best public school in the city? Do only the rich own the right to travel down Broad Street? How far can the majority dictate what the minority says and how it says it? Can the rights of heirs trump the rights of the city?

Winning also means persistence. In the Girard College and Central High School cases, appeals in an initial case were exhausted. It was through the need to bring a second case that the case was ultimately won.

When you're in trouble–get a "Philadelphia lawyer."

THE OLD GUARD

Andrew Hamilton (1676-1741)
Freedom of the Press and the Right to a Jury Trial

It was the John Peter Zenger case, in 1735, which first gave rise to the phrase "Philadelphia Lawyer."

In 1735, Governor William Cosby of New York, who was known for his corrupt ways, fired Lewis Morris, a Chief Justice of the New York Supreme Court, because of a dispute. Morris and some others started a newspaper, the *New York Weekly Journal*. They got John Peter Zenger to print the paper cheaply.

The newspaper championed a number of causes we take for granted now, including the right to trial by jury, the right to print the truth, and the right of citizens to object to a tyrant like William Cosby. Because the articles were not signed (no byline), Cosby had the publisher, Zenger, arrested for seditious libel. When Morris and his friends, James Alexander and William Smith, said they would defend Zenger, Cosby (through Chief Justice James Delancey, a handpicked choice of Cosby's) had them disbarred.

On the day of the trial, Andrew Hamilton, from Philadelphia, announced his representation of Zenger. Zenger had retained Hamilton because of his brilliance and because Cosby couldn't (even through Justice Delancey) disbar a Pennsylvania lawyer (only New York lawyers).[5]

The Trial Judge, Justice DeLancey, announced that the jury would decide whether Zenger had published the items, but the justices would decide the issue of libel. Hamilton admitted that the items in dispute had been published by Zenger. He argued that truth was a defense and that the libel law of England (where truth was not a defense) should not apply to New York.

Hamilton told the jury they [and not the trial judge] could and should decide libel, too. Essentially Hamilton was arguing for jury nullification.

"I know, may it please Your Honor, the jury may do so [return a finding of libel]. But I do likewise know that they may do otherwise. I know that they have the right beyond all dispute to determine both the law and the fact; and where they do not doubt of the law, they ought to do so. Leaving it to judgment of the court whether the words are libelous or not in effect renders juries useless (to say no worse) in many cases. But this I shall have occasion to speak to by and by."[6] Hamilton told the jury that, "… the judge, how great so ever he be, has no right to fine, imprison, or punish a jury, for not finding a verdict according to the direction of the court." The jury should use their own eyes, ears, and consciences.[7]

The Chief Justice was in no position, in 1735, in a hostile courtroom, to control the jury. Hamilton defended Zenger and the right to a free press and won. The right to freedom of speech and expression survived, though it would be sixty-three years before truth was accepted as a defense in libel cases.[8, 9]

Gouvernor Morris would write of the Zenger case: "The trial of Zenger in 1735 was the germ of American freedom, the morning star of that liberty which subsequently revolutionized America."[10]

After the victory, Andrew Hamilton, the lawyer who won in New York, was given the moniker – "Philadelphia Lawyer" – and it has stuck through the ages. Hamilton was sixty years old at the time of the Zenger trial.

Hamilton came to Philadelphia to help William Penn in a number of lawsuits. He was a Prothonotary of the Supreme Court and Speaker of the Pennsylvania Assembly. "In 1732, he designed and supervised the construction of Philadelphia's Independence Hall."[11] His plan called for the new Hall to be outside the central part of the city, which back then was Second and Market (High) Streets. Hamilton's design called for the Georgian style (named after Britain's King George) building to be built at 6th and Chestnut Streets.[12]

Other Eighteenth Century Attorneys[13]
Profiles excerpted from the Legends of the Bar Issue of the Philadelphia Lawyer Magazine (Winter, 2002).

Benjamin Chew (1722–1810)
John Dickinson (1732–1808)
James Wilson (1742–1798)
Jared Ingersoll (1749–1822)
William Lewis (1750–1819
George M. Dallas (1792–1864)
William Morris Meredith (1799–1873)

The early practice of law was an apprenticeship system where aspiring lawyers studied with practicing lawyers, primarily in the areas of "equity, property, and wrongs."[14]

Horace Binney (1780-1875)[15]

Horace Binney studied law in the Philadelphia office of Jared Ingersoll (1749-1822). He was a member of the Pennsylvania legislature (1806-07) and a Whig member of the National House of Representatives (1833-35), where he defended the United States Bank and opposed the policy of President Andrew Jackson.

As a prominent Philadelphia lawyer for over half a century, he was known for his expertise in banking and insurance law. His most famous case, in which he successfully opposed Daniel Webster, was Vidal v. Girard's Executors, 43 U.S. 127, 2 How. 127, 11 L. Ed. 205 (1844), a case that influenced the law of charities. [For more on this case read about Stephen Girard's will]. In 1844 he showed leadership in helping to restore order during the anti-Catholic riots in Philadelphia.

EARLY LAWSUITS

William Penn – Mason-Dixon Line

One early lawsuit brought by William Penn against Lord Baltimore involved the marking of the boundary line(s) between Pennsylvania and Maryland. The case was settled when the two agreed to a formal survey, which was completed by Charles Mason and Jeremiah Dixon. It became known as the Mason-Dixon line (along with the Delaware border) and during the Civil War it was a border between the free North and the slavery South.

St. Mark's Bells

St. Mark's, on Locust Street near Rittenhouse Square, was an Episcopalian Church and one of Philadelphia's most fashionable churches. It was completed in 1851 except for the bells in the belfry. The bells were installed in the 1870s and began to ring on Sundays. A number of old Philadelphia residents who lived nearby were not pleased with the noise and brought suit against the Rector and the Church. These old residents hired William Henry Rawle. The Church retained George Washington Biddle. Rawle and Biddle had a field day with their arguments.

Rawle quoted Shakespeare, "Me thought I heard a voice cry. 'Sleep no more, Macbeth doth murder sleep'. He implied that the Reverend Dr Hoffman was the Macbeth of Locust Street. He refused to contrast his clients, 'The affidavits of Harrison and Cadwalader and Norris' with those of the churchgoers 'Michael Fitzgerald, Catherine Harkins, Adeline Blizzard, and Patrick Mahony, many of whom cannot even read and write'."

Biddle defended the lower class. "Blizzard perhaps is not a highly aristocratic name but such people [who, after all, have to stay in town all year] have their right and should not have their little pleasures disturbed."

Biddle argued that the rich plaintiffs could move West. The Court granted the injunction to quiet the playing of the bells and years later the rich plaintiffs would indeed move West to the Main Line.[16]

Smithsonian Institute and Philadelphia Public Library

In 1836 President Andrew Jackson sent Philadelphia lawyer Richard Rush to England to pursue from a British court the legacy of James Smithson to the United States. Rush was successful in gaining the full amount of the legacy ($515,169). This money was used to create the Smithsonian Institution. Rush bequeathed his estate to the Philadelphia Public Library. **Rush** (1780–1859) served as U.S. attorney general, secretary of state, and was a U.S. minister to England until 1825, when President John Quincy Adams appointed him secretary of the Treasury. As minister to Great Britain in 1818, Rush negotiated the agreement that fixed the 49th parallel as the boundary between Canada and the United States from Minnesota west.

EARLY TWENTIETH CENTURY LAWYERS[17]

Profiles excerpted from the Legends of the Bar Issue of the Philadelphia Lawyer Magazine (Winter, 2002).

George Washington Biddle (1818–1897)
Francis Rawle (1846–1930)
John Christian Bullitt (1827–1902)
George Harding (1827–1902)
Samuel Dickson (1837–1915)
Christopher Stuart "Chippy" Patterson Jr. (1875–1933)
Eugene V. Alessandroni (1887–1966)
Francis Biddle (1886–1968), 1938 to 1940
Walter B. Gibbons (1894–1972)
Stevens Heckscher (1875-1931)
William Draper Lewis (1867–1949)
Herbert E. Millen (1890–1957)
J. Austin Norris (1893–1976)

John Graver Johnson (1841-1917)

For most of Philadelphia's history, up until the early 1900s, most lawyers were also solo practitioners. The most famous was John G. Johnson, who represented many railroads in antitrust cases and was a noted contributor to the Philadelphia Museum of Art.

Johnson was a graduate of Philadelphia's Central High School, two years before the artist Thomas Eakins. Johnson was not from an aristocratic background.

In the 1800s Philadelphia, like the nation, joined the industrial revolution. Many new businesses were being formed and lawyers were crucial partners in deciding how these businesses should be formed, under what terms they could compete, and how workers and users of these new products should be protected. If Johnson was to have an epitaph it might have been "What J.P. Morgan was to finance, John G. Johnson was to corporation law."[18] During Johnson's legal practice he was known for giving what the financial community considered "judicial decisions." If Johnson gave an opinion on the legality of some business move, it was considered golden.

Nationally, Johnson "represented the tobacco industry, Northern Pacific Railroad, U.S. Steel and Standard Oil Company. ... Locally, Johnson represented Peter A. B. Widener and George Elkins in obtaining the right to operate electric trolleys in Philadelphia."[19]

Johnson represented clients for the challenge of the case as opposed to a belief in any cause which might lead an attorney to represent only a certain class of clients.[20] Once, legend has it, a Supreme Court Justice said, "Weren't you here earlier representing the opposite point of view?" Johnson, memorably replied, "I hope, your Honor, I don't lose them both."

Johnson appeared before the United States Supreme Court 168 times – more than any other attorney of his generation. He, like Horace Binney and John Sergeant, declined requests by Presidents Garfield and Cleveland to be a Supreme Court Judge.[21]

JOHN GROVER JOHNSON,
Attorney-at-Law.

John Graver Johnson. Original from Philadelphians in Cartoons – Public Domain

Owen Josephus Roberts (1875–1955)

Owen Josephus Roberts was an associate justice of the U.S. Supreme Court from 1930 to 1945.

Roberts first gained nationwide attention in 1924 when President Calvin Coolidge appointed him special counsel to investigate and prosecute criminal activity associated with the government's lease to private interests of oil reserves valued at more than $100 million. The highly publicized "Teapot Dome" investigation lasted six years and was an acknowledged success.

Roberts also led the fact-finding commission that investigated Pearl Harbor.

After retiring from the Supreme Court, Roberts was appointed dean of the University of Pennsylvania Law School. He was one of the founders of Montgomery, McCracken, Walker & Rhoads.

George Wharton Peppr (1867-1961)

George Wharton Pepper was first in many ways. He was the first in a family of doctors to go to law school, the University of Pennsylvania Law School. There he finished first in his class. He taught law at Penn while practicing. He went on to be appointed Senator. He was also the first to start one of the new large firms, Pepper Hamilton LLP, that would become the standard in the twentieth century. Senator Pepper represented a full range of clients and was on the Board of Trustees of virtually every major organization in Philadelphia.

BIG FIRMS, OLD NAMES

The firm of **Ballard Spahr Andrews & Ingersoll LLP** can trace its roots to Jared Ingersoll. R. Sturgess Ingersoll, who became president of the Philadelphia Art Museum in the mid-1900s.[22] Ballard was also an old family name. Henry S. Drinker of **Drinker Biddle & Reath** was the brother of the famous writer Catherine Drinker Bowen. **Rawle & Henderson LLP** practiced law from 1725 to 1930. Other famous families of lawyers included the Biddles, the Cadwaladers, and the Chews.

Profiles excerpted from the Legends of the Bar Issue of the Philadelphia Lawyer Magazine (Winter, 2002).

Clark, Ladner, Fortenbaugh & Young. Grover Ladner (1885-1954) was a Pennsylvania Supreme Court justice and founder of Clark, Ladner, Fortenbaugh & Young. While in practice, he was considered an expert on conveyancing. A great conservationist, he was instrumental in the passage of the Pure Streams Act and fought to improve the quality of Philadelphia's water.

Blank Rome LLP. Edwin P. Rome (1916-1987) holds the reputation as one of the most tenacious, yet also compassionate and respected, lawyers in Philadelphia history. He joined the firm of Blank & Rudenko in 1954 and was one of the named partners in Blank Rome Comisky & McCauley. He is best known for his court-appointed and pro bono criminal defense work.

Dechert Price Rhoads (now Dechert LLP) was founded by Robert Dechert (1895-1975), who distinguished himself by mentoring young lawyers in the firm he managed with Curtis Bok and Owen Rhoads. President Dwight D. Eisenhower named him general counsel of the Department of Defense in 1957. The taxation course he taught at the University of Pennsylvania Law School is believed to have been the first in a major law school.

Fox Rothschild LLP. Charles Edwin Fox (1883-1937) was co-founder of Fox & Rothschild, which later became Fox, Rothschild, O'Brien & Frankel. Although he never attended college, he graduated from the University of Pennsylvania Law School. He served as Philadelphia district attorney, first president of the Big Brother and Big Sister Foundation and chairman of the board of the Crime Prevention Association of Philadelphia.

Montgomery, McCracken, Walker & Rhoads LLP. Robert T. McCracken (1883-1960) played an influential role in the fields of law, municipal reform, higher education, religion, and business. He was a leading member of the commission that drafted Philadelphia's Home Rule Charter; a trustee of the University of Pennsylvania, serving as chairman of the board from 1948 to 1956; chancellor of the Pennsylvania Diocese of the Episcopal Church; and a director of the Pennsylvania Railroad.

Morgan, Lewis and Bockius LLP. Founded in Philadelphia on March 10, 1873, by Charles Eldridge Morgan, Jr. and Francis Draper Lewis, the firm began as a two-man operation. In 1883, Morgan & Lewis hired Morris Rex Bockius, who dominated the firm from the turn of the century until his death in 1939. As of this writing, the firm is the largest in the city and one of the largest in the world.[23]

Rawle and Henderson LLP (according to their website) was founded in 1783.

Saul Ewing LLP. Walter Biddle Saul (1881-1966) was a trial lawyer in the field of construction and engineering liability. He helped found Saul, Ewing, Remick & Saul in 1921. Saul was on the Board of Education for twenty-five years and was so invaluable to public education that a high school was named after him while he was still alive.

Schnader Harrison Segal & Lewis LLP. William A. Schnader (1886-1968) was responsible for drafting a comprehensive codification of Pennsylvania's administrative, banking, corporation, fiscal, and insurance laws during his four years as attorney general (1931-1934) and another eight years as a deputy in that office (1922-1930). He was also responsible for the successful defense of those laws in court. In 1940, during an argument in the Pennsylvania Supreme Court, Schnader suffered a massive stroke. His right arm was permanently paralyzed. He required the frequent use of a wheelchair. Undaunted, Schnader turned his talents to the improvement of the law. He forged an alliance of the National Conference of Commissioners on Uniform State Laws and the American Law Institute to promulgate a Uniform Commercial Code that was eventually adopted by all fifty states. Schnader's leadership role in that effort earned him the title of "The Father of the Uniform Commercial Code." In 1949, Schnader was appointed chairman of the committee that drafted Philadelphia's Home Rule Charter; and in 1968 he was a leading force in the revision of the Pennsylvania Constitution.

White and Williams LLP. Thomas Raeburn White Sr. (1875-1959) was a prominent corporate lawyer. In 1924, he formed the partnership of White, Parry, and Maris, the beginnings of what is now White and Williams. He fought political corruption as counsel to the Committee of Seventy and as a city solicitor, ultimately directing the arrest of more than 200 people for various political crimes.

Wolf Block LLP (formerly Wolf, Block, Schorr and Solis-Cohen). Horace Stern (1878-1969), son of immigrants, became a brilliant and esteemed chief justice of the Pennsylvania Supreme Court. His legal opinions were marked by clarity of thought and intellectual integrity. Stern was the first Jew to sit on the Pennsylvania Supreme Court and the first Jewish trustee of the University of Pennsylvania. As a young law professor at the University of Pennsylvania Law School, Stern teamed up with student Morris Wolf to form the law firm Stern and Wolf, the predecessor of Wolf, Block, Schorr and Solis-Cohen. Stern was also very active in the community, having served as president of the Federation of Jewish Charities and having been a founder of the American Jewish Committee.

VENUES

City Hall[24]

City Hall is the home for the Mayor's office, many of the judicial courts, and many Philadelphia government offices like the Recorder of Deeds. Next to the U.S. Capitol, it is the nation's largest city building and one of the grandest. It is the country's largest masonry building. The exterior materials include limestone, granite, and marble.

It was designed (the winner of a contest) by John McArthur Jr., a student of Thomas U. Walter, one of the city's most renowned architects. McArthur originally chose Independence Square but voters approved its present location in Center Square.

Before building began, in 1871, Center Square was used for hangings and for the City's Waterworks. City Hall is over 500 feet high. The architecture is "French Second-Empire." City Hall took thirty years to complete as "designers struggled to keep abreast of major technological advances like electricity and elevators." It wasn't finished until 1901. It has close to 700 rooms, more than any municipal building in America. (www.whyy.org)

It is topped by the statue of William Penn, which was designed by Alexander Calder. [For more on Calder see the art section]. For much of its history, pursuant to a gentleman's agreement, it was the tallest building in the City. It lost that distinction in 1987, when it was replaced by Willard Rouse's One Liberty Place.

Penn Overlooking his Splendor (or Lack Thereof). Courtesy of John Gledhill

The South Portal. The Judicial Wing.

City Hall is composed of four wings. "The South Portal, known as the Judicial Entrance, was designed for the courts." The classic allegory that Justice should be blind appears throughout City Hall. The only lawyer in the City Hall sculpture is Horace Binney. (www.ajaxelectric.com)

State Supreme Court – Room 454

City Hall's first permanent resident was the Pennsylvania Supreme Court. The grandest room is Courtroom 454. Like many of the courtrooms, Courtroom 454 is decorated on the walls, ceiling, and "fluted pilasters" in a variety of rich oils. Courtroom 454 was designed by the German painter George Herzog. Unfortunately, much of his work has been painted over. (www.ajaxelectric.com)

Law Library – Room 600

The first Law Library Association began in Philadelphia in 1802. It moved to City Hall in 1898. When designed, the quarters for the Law Library Association were described as the most elegant in America, with amazing frescoes and incandescent lights. The most precious books were stored in the balcony, which was accessible only through a spiral staircase. A popular feature of libraries of its day, the balcony has a glass floor, which may still be seen today.

By 2003, many of the trials had moved to more functional locales. (www.ajaxelectric.com)

Liberty Bell

LOCATION: *Market Street between 5th and 6th Streets, in Philadelphia, Pennsylvania.*
The primary information sources are "The Liberty Bell: A Special History Study," by John Paige and "The Story of the Liberty Bell," by David Kimble.

Reflections on Market Street, oil on wood, 48 x 38 inches, © 2001 by Chris Zmijewski. Courtesy of Gross McCleaf Gallery

Nearly Noon, oil on wood, 48 x 48 inches, Chris Zmijewski © 1998, by Chris Zmijewski. Courtesy of Gross McCleaf Gallery

Philadelphia Tulips by Rob Lawlor. Courtesy of Rob Lawlor

City Hall Tunnel by Rob Lawlor. Courtesy of Rob Lawlor

Logan Circle Wedding by Rob Lawlor. Courtesy of Rob Lawlor

*Liberty Bell.
Courtesy of Mike
Fitzpatrick*

Some highlights from the Liberty Bell's website [with permission of Independence Hall Association] show the following history:

1701 Charter of Privileges. William Penn issued the Charter of Privileges, which transferred legislative power from William Penn and the Proprietorship to the Assembly. Many historians believe this event was celebrated 50 years later by purchasing the original Liberty Bell.

1732 The State House (Independence Hall) was finished. Considered colonial America's grandest public building it later became home to the Liberty Bell.

1749 An addition to the State House was ordered to house a bell.

1751 The Pennsylvania Assembly issued an order for the bell.

1752 Bell arrived sometime before September 1. The journey took 11 weeks in rough seas.

1753 Several days after arriving, the bell was set up in Independence Square to be tested and promptly cracked. Norris described the event in a letter to agent Charles: Second-generation Bell completed. Cast from the metal of the original bell, an extra 1.5 oz. of copper was added for each pound of the bell. After the twenty-day effort to raise the bell to belfry was complete on April 17, 1753, a big feast was served to the workmen in celebration. However, most agreed its tone was less than pleasing. Isaac Norris noted that "they were so teized (teased) by the witicisms of the Town that they...will be very soon ready to make a second essay." It's believed that excessive copper ruined the bell's tone.

1753 Third-generation Bell completed. The second-generation Bell was melted down and recast into a new bell – supposedly some silver was added to improve the sound. It was this third-generation Bell that became the celebrated Liberty Bell that today hangs in Philadelphia's Liberty Bell Pavilion. The New York Mercury reported on June 11, 1753, "Last Week was raised and fix'd in the Statehouse Steeple, the new great Bell, cast here by Pass and Stow, weighing 2080 lbs." Master-builder Edmund Woolley built the steeple in March of 1753. He was a member of Philadelphia's Carpenters' Company and overseer of the original State House construction. Pass and Stow charged slightly over 36 Pounds for the repair. According to their bill, the Bell weighed 2,081 pounds. ...

July 4, 1776 Bell did not ring. Contrary to popular belief, the Liberty Bell did not ring on July 4, 1776 for the Declaration of Independence.

July 8, 1776 The Bell tolled at the first public reading of the Declaration of Independence to the accompaniment of many other bells throughout the city. Some historians note that the steeple was in bad condition and that perhaps the Liberty Bell did not toll this day. Lacking any record of a replacement bell or measures taken to find an alternate way to ring major events, it's fairly certain that the Liberty Bell rang.

Feb. 12,1846 Fix the Bell for Washington's birthday. Fix it? When did it break? There is no unanimous agreement when the first crack appeared. On this day the Common Council and Select Council requested that the "Independence Bell" be repaired for ringing on George Washington's birthday – February 22. The work was performed by bell hanger Henry Stone of 79 South Fifth Street. William Eckel, Superintendent of the State House, supervised the operation and had at least one small bell made from its filings. Most significantly, this operation resulted in the bell's trademark feature – the visible "crack" that we see today.

Feb. 22, 1846 It rang its "last clear note" while tolling for Washington's birthday Monday February 22, 1846. The Philadelphia Public Ledger February 26, 1846 reported,

"... It gave out clear notes and loud, and appeared to be in excellent condition until noon, when it received a sort of compound fracture in a zig-zag direction through one of its sides which put it completely out of tune and left it a mere wreck of what it was."

1852 Move to Independence Hall – its home for the next 114 years. The Bell was brought down from the steeple and placed in "Declaration Chamber" of Independence Hall.

1876 Centennial Exposition. Displayed at the Centennial Exposition in Philadelphia

1976 Moved to Liberty Pavilion. Celebrating America's Bicentennial, the Liberty Bell was moved from Independence Hall to a specially built pavilion across the street on Independence Mall. The Pavilion allowed visitors to view the Bell at any time of day. It was designed by Mitchell/Giurgola and Associates.[25]

2003 The new Liberty Bell Center, costing $12.6 million, opened to the public.

Independence Hall by Valerie Craig. Courtesy of Valerie Craig

Independence Hall

Independence Hall is the site of the preparation and signing of the Declaration of Independence and the United States Constitution. It was first known as the Pennsylvania State House. It was built between 1732 and 1753. The second floor was once home to Charles Willson Peale's museum of natural history. George Washington, knowing that his opinion would carry undue weight, contributed little to the debate over the Constitution. Even though the days were very hot in the summer of 1787, windows were kept closed so others could not overhear their discussions.

PHILADELPHIA'S INFLUENCES
on the
NATIONAL CONSTITUTION

The United States Constitution, in addition to being drafted in Philadelphia, was also influenced by the Pennsylvania Constitution framed by Philadelphian William Penn. Additionally, the right to trial by jury in the United States Constitution can be traced back to William Penn's insistence on a trial by a jury of his peers (see the Preface).

The following statement, from William Penn's Declaration of Rights, inspired Jefferson's language in the Declaration of Independence:

"All peace is inherent in the people, and all free governments are founded on their authority and instituted for their peace, safety, and happiness. For the advancement of these ends they have at all times, an inalienable and indefeasible right to alter, reform or abolish their government in such a manner as they may think proper. – William Penn, "Declarations of Rights."

"Government seems to me a part of religion itself, a thing sacred in its institution and ends. ... And government is free to the people under it, whatever be the frame, where the laws rule and the people are a party to those laws; and more than this is tyranny, oligarchy, or confusion. ... As governments are made and moved by men, so by them they are ruined too. Wherefore governments rather depend upon men than men upon governments. Let men be good, and the government cannot be bad. If it be ill, they will cure it. But if men be bad, let the government be ever so good, they will endeavor to warp and spoil it to their turn."

— William Penn, "First Frame of
Government", 1682[26]

Violet Oakley (1874-1961) was a disciple of Howard Pyle. She received a Doctorate of laws from Drexel Institute. She was also a faculty member of the Pennsylvania Academy of Fine Arts.

She painted forty-three murals for the Pennsylvania State Capitol. The murals focus on William Penn and the founding of Pennsylvania. Other legal murals include:

Keynote, Divine Law...Love and Wisdom;
The Golden Age, Law of Nature;
Themis – Greek Idea of Revealed Law;
The Decalogue...Hebrew Idea of Revealed Law;
The Beatitudes...Christian Idea of Revealed Law;
Code of Justinian...Law of Reason;
The Spirit of William Gladston...Common Law;
Supreme Court of the State...Law of Nations;
Supreme Court of the Nation...Law of Nations;
Supreme Court of the World...International Law;
Christ and Disarmament...International Law

National Constitution Center

Text courtesy of the National Constitution Center (source: email communication)

The United States Constitution, the document the United States Supreme Court uses for its final authority, was written in Philadelphia in 1787.

The National Constitution Center, located at 525 Arch St. on Philadelphia's Independence Mall, is an independent, nonpartisan, nonprofit organization dedicated to increasing public understanding of the U.S. Constitution and the ideas and values it represents. The Center serves as a museum, an education center, and a forum for debate on constitutional issues. The museum dramatically tells the story of the Constitution from Revolutionary times to the present through more than 100 interactive, multimedia exhibits, film, photographs, text, sculpture, and artifacts, and features a powerful, award-winning theatrical performance, "Freedom Rising." The Center also houses the Annenberg Center for Education and Outreach, which serves as the hub for national constitutional education. Also, as a nonpartisan forum for constitutional discourse, the Center presents – without endorsement – programs that contain diverse viewpoints on a broad range of issues. For more information, call 215.409.6700 or visit www.constitutioncenter.org

A pivotal moment of the 2008 presidential campaign took place at the National Constitution Center, providing another original document for the Center's permanent collection. Barack Obama's Race Speech at the Constitution Center took place on March 18, 2008. Following the historic speech, a Constitution Center staff member had the presence of mind to save the original copy of the speech, which was left behind

William Penn as Law-Giver, Mural, Supreme Court room, State Capitol, Harrisburg, Pennsylvania, by Violet Oakley. Courtesy of Pennsylvania Capitol Preservation Committee and Brian Hunt

Signers Hall. Courtesy of National Constitution Center

at the podium. When Senator Obama returned to the Center for the Democratic Presidential Primary Debate in April, he signed the document.

Philadelphia also was the site of a curious sting operation, months before the Constitution Center was to open. Someone in possession of one of the fourteen originals of the Bill of Rights tried to sell that original, North Carolina's, to the Center through the Center's attorney, Stephen Harmelin. A Union soldier in the Civil War had taken the original and there had been several attempts to sell it earlier. At Harmelin's Dilworth Paxson office, the FBI and Harmelin, posing as a buyer, nabbed the seller who was looking for a four million dollar payout. The FBI took temporary custody of the Bill of Rights subject to court hearings to determine the proper disposition.

The American Experience. Courtesy of National Constitution Center

LAWYERS PORTRAYED

The Movies
Paul Newman in *The Young Philadelphians*

Paul Newman starred in the movie called *The Young Philadelphians*. Though he seeks to become a prestigious lawyer and rise up the firm ladder of his father, like many "Philadelphia Lawyers" he has an independent streak.

When his friend (played by Robert Vaughn) is tried for murder, the firm and the rest of his high society want him to resolve it quickly but the Newman character knows an injustice when he sees it.

He switches gears and tries a criminal defense case, though he's never tried one before. With guile and skill he shows that his client is not only innocent but has been taken advantage by the high society people who wanted a quick deal.

The legal advisor to the film was Jerome Shestack of Wolf Block Schorr and Solis-Cohen LLP. Shestack noted: "I made up a fictional name of a Philadelphia law firm for the movie. Unbeknownst to me, the director put my name on the office billboard shown in the movie. Then when Paul Newman captured a wealthy widow for a client he showed Newman's name moving up the billboard ahead of mine. I told Newman he was a better actor than I, but I took exception to his legal prowess exceeding mine. He said he was in enough lawsuits to quality for the bar. When the movie came out the Police Commissioner called me and said I thought lawyers couldn't advertise (in those days we couldn't). I said, I thought Police Commissioners couldn't censor. So it was a standoff."[27]

The movie was based on the novel *The Philadelphians* by James Gunn. The film helped solidify the aristocratic notion that Philadelphia lawyers advance through having the right connections.

Philadelphia – The Movie

In this movie, Andrew Beckett, played by Tom Hanks, works for a prestigious Philadelphia large law firm until one of the firm's partners suspects the Beckett character of having AIDS.

Beckett enlists a solo practitioner, played by Denzel Washington, when he is fired. The lawsuit revolves around a new legal trend – employment litigation suits.

Beckett contends he was fired because of his disease, while the firm claims that the Beckett was fired for cause. The legal verdict in the case goes in favor of Beckett, though AIDS determines his ultimate fate. [For more on the film see the movie section]

Music
Woody Guthrie's Song – "Philadelphia Lawyer"

Woody Guthrie wrote a song on his famous *This Land is Your Land* album about a Philadelphia lawyer who tries to get a divorce for his client. When the lawyer sleeps with the client, the client's husband takes a fatal revenge with the result that there's one less "Philadelphia Lawyer." The references to Philadelphia lawyers are not meant to be kind. Philadelphia lawyers know "it's just a song."

LEGAL WRITING

History

A celebrated writer of legal history was **Catherine Drinker Bowen**, a graduate of the University of Pennsylvania Law School. Ms. Bowen's biographies included profiles of Justice Oliver Wendell Holmes and Edward Coke. She also wrote *Miracle at Philadelphia* the story of the Constitutional Convention and *The Most Dangerous Man in America: Scenes from the Life of Benjamin Franklin*, among other history books.

Profile excerpted from the Legends of the Bar issue of the Philadelphia Lawyer Magazine, (Winter 2002)

Peter S. DuPonceau who, as a teenager, left an abbey in France and, using his facility with languages, accompanied Baron Steuben to America. DuPonceau's linguistic ability led to his employment in a Philadelphia law office, and he was admitted to practice in 1785. He was also author or translator of a number of legal or historical treatises, but his fame rests chiefly upon his studies of the Native American languages.

The Throwaway Children by Lisa Richette

Lisa Aversa Richette, a Common Pleas Judge and former assistant district attorney, wrote *The Throwaway Children*, which reviews and criticizes the juvenile court system.

In her conversations with Studs Terkel, Judge Richette notes for years that the decisions of judges in juvenile courts could not be appealed. She reviews the relationships between adults and children and what makes them fail; how the white suburban parents are much less willing to acknowledge their childrens' problems or react more severely to the acknowledgement than blacks; how children who are too good can have problems; and how juvenile prisons are often just warehouses.[28] One of her comments in the interview is that "A District Attorney should be the conscience of the community, not a megaphone."

Owen Wister (1860-1938)

According to Gerard J. St. John, writer Owen Wister began his career as a Philadelphia lawyer. He grew up in Germantown, was a graduate of Harvard Law School, and was friends with Oliver Wendell Holmes and Theodore Roosevelt. He apprenticed in Philadelphia with Francis Rawle.

Wister left for greener pastures, where he wrote Western short stories for Harper's. In 1902 Wister wrote his classic, the first "Cowboy" novel – *The Virginian*, where disputes were settled not by a Philadelphia judge but by a couple of fellows named Smith and Wesson.[29]

The Novelists

Several Philadelphia lawyers have written novels or mysteries where the main characters and main scenes involve the Philadelphia legal profession and Philadelphia.

Arthur R. G. Solmssen wrote *The Comfort Letter, Rittenhouse Square, Takeover Time, Alexander's Feast*, and several non-legal novels.

Catherine Drinker Bowen by R. Cooke. Courtesy of University of Pennsylvania Law School

The Comfort Letter is about a securities transaction and the issues (ethical, legal, and emotional) that bear on a "closing." The book has been the subject of Law Review articles on the ethics of closings but is readable by non-lawyers as well.

William Lashner writes mysteries where a Philadelphia male lawyer, Victor Carl, is the star. The mysteries are *A Killer's Kiss, Bitter Truth, Falls the Shadow, Fatal Flaw, Hostile Witness, Marked Man*, and *Past Due and Verita*s. His newest offering is *Blood and Bone*.

Lisa Scottoline is a University of Pennsylvania Law graduate who worked for a major Center City law firm and who, now, lectures at the University of Pennsylvania Law School and writes for the *Philadelphia Inquirer*. Lisa's writings are known for her quick wit, absorbing storytelling, getting the law right, and references to the city. Her most recent book, as of this writing, is *Look Again*. Other writings include:

Courting Trouble, Daddy's Girl, Dead Ringer, Devil's Corner, Dirty Blonde, Everywhere That Mary Went, Final Appeal, Killer Smile, Lady Killer, Legal Tender, Mistaken Identity, Moment of Truth, Rough Justice, Running from the Law, The Vendetta Defense

Law Reviews

Each of the law schools in the city has several Law Reviews that are now run by students at the respective law schools.

Villanova has an Environmental Law Journal and Sports and Entertainment Law Journal. Temple has a Political and Civil Rights Law Review and an International and Comparative Law Journal.

Penn's Law Review originated in 1852 as the American Law Register. Originally run by lawyers for lawyers, Penn's Law Review produced its first student run review in 1896.[30] In addition to the standard Law Review, the University of Pennsylvania has a Journal of Constitutional Law, The University of Pennsylvania Journal of Labor and Employment Law and The University of Pennsylvania Journal of International Economic Law.

All reviews attempt to analyze in a scholarly manner legal issues of the day. Additionally, special articles are meant for the interest of the local bar associations. Topics range from the finer points of Antitrust Law to the Common Law origins of the Infield Fly Rule. Most articles are for the serious-minded scholar.

One sample article from a recent University of Pennsylvania Law Review sought to examine the issues in a new publication, the *Metro*, which is a combined newspaper of SEPTA, the local transit agency and Transit Publications Inc. The author, Michael A. Mugman, cleverly titled the review "Broadsheet Bullies" [a reference to the Flyers hockey team's reputation for toughness – the Broad Street Bullies].[31] The *Metro*, which was free, was available, at the time of the article, at various train and bus platforms in the city, while those of the *Inquirer*, *New York Times*, and *USA Today* were not. The latter papers sued but an out of court settlement was reached.

Mugman's article, typical of many law review articles, tried to identify the key legal issues and how similar cases might be decided.

Bar Association Magazines
The Shingle and The Philadelphia Lawyer

The Shingle (founded by Leon J. Obermayer in 1938) was the early official publication of the Philadelphia Bar Association. Its name was changed in 1992 to *The Philadelphia Lawyer*. Some noted writers included Magistrate Judge Jake Hart, Harry Lore, and Judge Curtis Bok.[32] Judge Bok served on the Philadelphia Court of Common Pleas for twenty years and then served on the Pennsylvania Supreme Court during the last four years of his life. In one noted case on the Common Pleas bench, Bok ruled that a Philadelphia bookseller had not violated obscenity laws by selling works by authors like William Faulkner.

The best legal fiction writing, like Melville's *Bartleby the Scrivener*, tries to examine the boundaries of proper and improper civil conduct and how to determine those boundaries.

Judge Curtis Bok for several years penned a fictional column about a local judge named Ulen. Bok, in reply to a poll about his stories, wrote that: "There is drama in the courts, and hurt, and merriment. If life can raise an ache in the heart, one must serve these things in the spirit of him who bears the patent."

LAW and RACE

Progress in Philadelphia, for African-Americans, until the late 1950s was painfully slow.

Profiles excerpted from the Legends of the Bar Issue of the Philadelphia Lawyer Magazine (Winter, 2002).

Sadie Tanner Mosell Alexander (1898–1989) blazed trails. She was the first African-American woman to earn a Ph.D. (in 1921, one of three awarded to African-American women that year, and the first in economics); to attend or graduate from the University of Pennsylvania Law School or to be an editor of its Law Review; to be admitted to the Pennsylvania bar (in 1927); and to serve as a lawyer in the Philadelphia City Solicitor's Office. She drafted the section of the Philadelphia Home Rule Charter that created the Commission on Human Relations, and served on it for many years. President Harry S. Truman appointed her to the President's Committee on Civil Rights, President John F. Kennedy appointed her to the Lawyers' Committee on Civil Rights Under Law, and President Jimmy Carter appointed her chair of the White House Conference on Aging. Her father, Aaron Albert Mossell, was the first African-American to graduate from the University of Pennsylvania Law School.[33]

Raymond Pace Alexander (1898-1974) was the first African-American judge of the Philadelphia Court of Common Pleas, appointed in 1959. He was largely responsible for the end of de jure segregation in Pennsylvania public schools, and urged General George C. Marshall to end segregation in the armed forces. A president of the National Bar Association and a co-founder of the *National Bar Journal*, he also served on Philadelphia City Council from 1956 until his appointment to the bench. Mr. Alexander noted that until the 1950s it was almost impossible for blacks to get downtown office space. For black lawyers before the 1950s the practice of law included "ill will, insults, ostracism, and rejection."

Two Philadelphia organizations, the John M. L. Ganston Law Club and the Barristers' Club, were formed to aid black lawyers.

OTHER PIONEERS

Hiliary H. Holloway (1928-2000) excelled as a public sector attorney and large-firm partner while retaining the core values that made him an example to the young, starting in his own household. He was the first African-American officer at the Federal Reserve Bank of Philadelphia, where he advanced to first vice president and general counsel. The positions, while challenging, allowed him a schedule that permitted him to be a real father. After retiring from the Federal Reserve, he became the first African-American partner at the Marshall Dennehey firm. He frequently summarized his life view with: "It's not the I.Q., it's the I will."

Robert Nelson Cornelius Nix Sr. (1905–1987) was a Philadelphia lawyer and a member of the U.S. Congress from 1958 to 1979. He was one of the first African-American lawyers to become a major political leader in Philadelphia and the first black representative from Pennsylvania. Congressman Nix's son later served as chief justice of the Pennsylvania Supreme Court.

Cecil B. Moore (1915-1979) was mostly known as a political activist. He was the local chair of Philadelphia's NAACP and was instrumental in the picketing of Stephen Girard College. Moore, a WWII marine, went to law school on the GI Bill. Moore represented

Sadie Alexander by Alonzo Adams. Courtesy of University of Pennsylvania Law School

STEPHEN GIRARD'S WILL
Stephen Girard's Will – Enjoining of religious teaching

Two Philadelphia attorneys, John Sergeant and Horace Binney, were involved in the various suits involving Stephen Girard's Will. Girard College wanted practical study and provided in his will that "I do not forbid, but I do not recommend, the Greek and Latin languages." This was the path that Benjamin Franklin recommended and was a common theme – the resistance of some Philadelphians to "belles-lettres."[35]

It was the following provision that caused a lawsuit:

I enjoin and require that no ecclesiastic, missionary or minister of any sect whatsoever shall ever hold or exercise any station or duty whatever in the said college: nor shall any such person ever be admitted for any purpose or as a visitor with the premises… In making this restriction I do no mean to cast any reflection upon any sect or person whatsoever: but as there is such a multitude of sects and such a diversity of opinion amongst them I desire to keep the tender minds of the orphans…free from the excitements which clashing doctrines…are so apt to produce.

However, "all the teacher in the college shall take pains to instill…the purest principles of morality…" so that when the students grow up, they can adopt "such religious tenets as their matured reason may enable them to prefer.

The relations of Girard sued to break the will, claiming that the anti-religion clause made the will invalid. Most early colleges in the North had a religious foundation (as opposed to Jefferson's University of Virginia, for example, which was secular). The case reached the Supreme Court where the final arguments took place, in 1844, before Justice Story and his associates. Horace Binney and John Sergeant argued for the city. The Girard heirs were represented by none other than Daniel Webster, hired for the huge sum of fifty thousand dollars. Webster's oration went on for three days and argued that:

To argue upon the merits of such a will is an insult to the understanding of every man…it opposes all that is in heaven and all on earth that is worth being on earth.

The audience broke into frenzied applause after Webster's argument. The Supreme Court, which rule for the College and City of Philadelphia, was not so impressed.

After the case Webster told Binney "Mr. Binney, you buried my argument in granite" – a reference to how solid Binney's argument was.[36]

President Tyler offered a seat on the Supreme Court to Sergeant after the case. Sergeant refused but suggested Binney with the proviso that Binney shouldn't know Sergeant suggested Binney. An equivalent offer to Binney was met with the same equivalent reply – Choose Sergeant but don't let him know it was Binney. Neither accepted. Better to practice law locally than make national decisions."[37]

Horace Binney's sculpture is one of only three real people on the exterior of City Hall. (The other two are Penn and Franklin.)[38] According to The Philadelphia Lawyer's Legends of the Bar issue, Mr. Binney (1780-1875) was a charter member of the Philadelphia Bar Association and represented the First and Second Banks of the

mostly poor blacks. He saw the court system and the district attorneys office as being prejudiced in favor of whites.

The manipulation of the docket (Moore was often in another courtroom or out picketing) led to the creation of an administrative rule – 301, limiting the number of cases an attorney could have in court at one time. It was a specific attempt to regulate Moore's cases. Moore argued that this "Cecil B. Moore Rule" was unconstitutional because clients had the right to choose their own lawyer and in the 1960s Moore was the lawyer of choice for most poor blacks. Then District Attorney Arlen Specter (who would become a Pennsylvania Senator) said Moore won cases because the evidence became stale because of so many continuances – Moore argued that most of the charges brought against his clients shouldn't have been brought in the first place. On March 29, 1973, the Pennsylvania Supreme Court held that the "Cecil B. Moore" – Rule 301 was unconstitutional.

Moore would go on to run for Mayor. Though he lost, he set the stage for other successful black mayoral candidates, Wilson Goode and John Street. Moore did become a city councilman near the end of his life in 1975. Moore was a graduate of Temple Law School.[34]

Girard College Portrait Views of Philadelphia and its Vicinity by John Caspar Wild. Courtesy of Bryn Mawr University

United States. He came out of retirement to argue the Girard case. Binney was the official reporter for the Pennsylvania Supreme Court from 1807 to 1814 and Chancellor of the Philadelphia Bar Association from 1852 to 1854. Binney also wrote historical sketches of some of the Philadelphia lawyers and judges of his day.

John Sergeant was a Whig candidate for Vice President in 1832, served in Congress for six years and was Chancellor of the Law Association for eight years.

Rights of Nonwhites to Attend Girard College

This case involved the probate of the will of Stephen Girard, a native of France. He arrived in America before the Declaration of Independence was written and settled in the city of Philadelphia, where he lived until his death in 1831. He bequeathed his entire estate and personal property, valued at over $7 million, to the city of Philadelphia. The provisions of his will required the city to construct both an orphanage and a college according to his specific stipulations. Two million was set aside for this purpose. The will was drafted by Girard with help from William J. Duane, a Franklin-in-law.[39, 40]

There was an architectural competition to determine who would design the college according to the many detailed specifications in the will. The contest was sponsored and judged by Nicholas Biddle. The winner was Thomas Walter, who remodeled the United States Capitol in Washington.[41]

The litigation over the second series of suits involving Girard College centered around the provisions in Mr. Girard's will that provided an education for poor white orphans. In the 1950s and 1960s, a number of poor black orphans sought admission. The litigation that followed could fill several mainframes. There were thirteen rulings (including two no decisions by the U.S. Supreme Court) before a final decision was reached requiring the College to admit non-white students.

The Parties

The principal parties in the various suits were the Estate of Stephen Girard, the individual students seeking admission, the Trustees of the College, the City of Philadelphia and the Commonwealth of Pennsylvania.

The Courts involved were the Philadelphia Orphans Court, which handles the wills and trusts of Philadelphia citizens, the Pennsylvania Superior and Supreme Court, The Eastern District Court (Federal Court), the United States Court of Appeals (3rd circuit), and the United States Supreme Court.

The legal issues involved the following (in non-legal terms):

The doctrine that the desires of a testator (the writer of a will) should have his desires enforced.

The Equal Protection Clause of the Fourteenth Amendment to the United States Constitution requires the Federal Government and the various states to treat different classes of citizens equally unless there is at least a rational reason not to.

Various state laws including the Pennsylvania Public Accommodation Act of May 19, 1887, and subsequent amendments.

The doctrine of "res judicata" which holds that parties and issues who have already had their day in court should not have repeated chances.

The doctrine of "State Action" which says that the conduct of any state, such as Pennsylvania, may give rise to the state being required to comply with the United States Constitution's provisions; for this discussion – item 2, the Equal Protection Clause. Justice Frankfurter described it as follows: "somewhere, somehow, to some extent, there be an infusion of conduct by officials, panoplied with State power, into any scheme" to deny protected rights.[42] In other words the action should appear to be state sanctioned, i.e., public over private. The courts continually wrestle with the precise definition.

The Cases

The legal summaries of the various cases involving the non-white access issue of Girard College span can be reduced to the following:

Case 1

A. The Orphans Court of Philadelphia decided that the non-white provision of Girard's will was a rational reason (the desire to see that the terms of wills are respected) for precluding non-whites. This view was upheld by the Pennsylvania Superior and Supreme Courts.

B. The United States Supreme Court reversed this decision, saying that the Equal Protection Clause applied to the Trustees of the College, since the Trustees were representatives of the City of Philadelphia.

C. The case was sent back to the Orphans Court of Philadelphia. The City in the meantime had appointed "private" trustees. The Orphans Court said this act was allowed. Private is private. The Pennsylvania Superior and Supreme Courts agreed. The United States Supreme Court was not willing to say otherwise. This ended the first case after eight separate court orders.[43]

Legal challenges to Girard's whites only policy were dormant until 1965, when Cecil B. Moore, then president of the Philadelphia NAACP, picketed the school. Gov. William Scranton named two lawyers to try to persuade Girard officials to drop the racial barriers: Charles J. Biddle and William T. Coleman, Jr. Raymond Pace Alexander was also counsel in the first set of cases for the individuals.

Case 2

A. A second suit was brought in 1966 by seven individual orphans through their legal guardians, the city of Philadelphia and the Commonwealth of Pennsylvania. Judge Joseph Lord III held that the individual orphans had a viable claim – that the decision to exclude non-whites violated the provisions of the Accommodation Act, which made it a misdemeanor to racially discriminate. He held that Girard College was a "public accommodation" and moreover an "educational institution" under the supervision of the Commonwealth of Pennsylvania. He further held that Girard College was not "distinctively private" [as might be a gathering of friends at a pool party] and did not qualify for exemption from the Act. He heard the claim and determined that it was with merit as to the individuals.

Judge Lord left open the Equal Protection argument and a doctrine called "cy pres," which allows for a will to be changed if the underlying conditions surrounding the will have drastically changed.

B. On appeal the Third Circuit of Appeals applied the doctrine of "res judicata" saying that the matter had been decided in [Case 1]. It reversed this part of Judge Lord's decision but said the items that Judge Lord had left open could proceed.

C. Judge Lord decided that the exclusionary policy was a violation of the Equal Protection clause based on an intervening Supreme Court Case, which held that a similar substitution of private trustees was still "state action" in a Macon, Georgia, case involving the creation of a park. Judge Lord found similar "state action" in the Girard case based, among other facts, on a variety of public acts by Girard to get applicants to apply to the school.

This decision was appealed to the Third Circuit, which affirmed Judge Lord's opinion. The United States Supreme Court declined to hear the case. So five more rulings added to the previous eight were needed to win the ultimate issue.[44]

As in most cases the backdrop was the climate of the times. In the 1950s it was common practice, albeit unacceptable, for blacks to be treated differently. Through the Civil Rights movement changes in views about the rights of blacks and other minorities were a principal reason for the changes in the way the Courts handled Civil Rights issues like the ones handled by the attorneys here.

Non-whites now make up a substantial percentage of Girard College students, as do females who were admitted in the 1980s.

WOMEN AND THE
PHILADELPHIA BAR

It wasn't until the 1970s that women started to become members of the Bar Association on a regular basis. One of the early lawyers and later the first woman partner in a major firm, the first woman elected to the Board of Governors of the Philadelphia Bar Association, and the first woman to sit on the U.S. District Court for the Eastern District of Pennsylvania, is the Honorable Norma L. Shapiro. In an interview with Elizabeth Vrato, Judge Shaprio advised women attorneys: "I recommend not only networking but actually forming a network of mentors," and "conversation is not successful because of what you're saying – it is successful based upon what the other person is hearing." One of her most controversial decisions was the one that placed a lid on the number of prisoners the city could keep in jail. The city ultimately had to release a number of prisoners because of poor prison conditions. [45]

Notable Female Attorneys
Profiles excerpted from the Legends of the Bar Issue of the Philadelphia Lawyer Magazine (Winter, 2002).

Lynne M. Abraham was the first woman district attorney of Philadelphia. Her many triumphs include the return from exile in France of Ira Einhorn for the murder of Holly Maddux.

Helen Chait (1914-1992) became the first woman lawyer to hold a leadership position in the City Law Department. She was appointed chief counselor of the Department in 1957, the third-highest position. She served as chair of the Philadelphia Tax Revenue Board from 1960 to 1966.

Caroline Burnham Kilgore (1838-1909) was a trailblazer, the first woman to be admitted to the bar in the Commonwealth of Pennsylvania. Hers is a story of persistence in the face of adversity. She struggled for sixteen years, from 1870 to 1886, against cultural and statutory obstacles, knowing full well that even if she succeeded, she would not be afforded the opportunity to achieve a status comparable to that of the significant lawyers of her time. Nonetheless, Kilgore persevered, reading the law in the office of her husband-to-be, applying to attend lectures given by prominent Philadelphia judges at the University of Pennsylvania, reapplying when her requests were refused, applying for admission to the bar, lobbying the legislature to change the applicable statutory law, and finally gaining admission to the courts of Philadelphia and Pennsylvania after the law was amended. Kilgore joined her husband in the practice of law, and continued the practice after his death. She persevered in her quest for admission to the bar not for herself, but for the benefit of generations of women lawyers who would follow. In so doing, Kilgore achieved a status in the bar above and beyond most of her contemporaries.

Frederica Massiah-Jackson was the first African-American woman to serve as President Judge of the Philadelphia Court of Common Pleas.[46]

Leslie Anne Miller was the first woman president of the Pennsylvania Bar Association.

Audrey C. Talley was the first African-American woman Chancellor of the Philadelphia Bar Association.

Notable Cases
Vorchheimer vs. Central High School. Rights of women to attend an all-boys school.

This case was a challenge by several female students at neighboring Girl's High to be admitted to Central High School's all-boy's school.

A large amount of evidence was entered to show that Central received more funding, had better teachers, larger endowments, and was a better school. Additionally, it was argued that single-sex schools that exclude women were not equal schools. The premise of this argument was that even if Girl's High was equivalent to Central in the empirical standards, Girl's High and single-sex schools did not have the better reputation, which made it tougher for the female applicants to advance to college and their careers. Another argument was that the single-sex schools, at the top academic level, continued the stereotype that women could be teachers and secretaries but couldn't be professionals.

While the female students won in the lower court, the case was reversed on appeal before the Third Circuit Court of Appeals, where the Third Circuit Court applied a minimal standard for equal protection cases involving women. The Equal protection clause, under the Fourteenth Amendment to the United States Constitution, required that in certain cases, those where a "fundamental right" was at issue or a "protected class" like race was at issue, that the Court apply a "strict" standard – a standard that said if the government acts it must not only have a rational basis but that a "strict standard" should be applied to see if the Equal Protection clause wasn't violated.

The plaintiff women litigants sought to have this "strict standard" or some intermediate standard applied but the Third Circuit Court of Appeals held that the Board of Education only needed to provide a rational explanation for single-sex schools. The case went to the United States Supreme Court where a 4-4 decision affirmed the Third Circuit.[47]

In a second suit by three new Girl's High students, through their parents, Central High was forced to allow female students. An appeal was taken by other students of Girl's High who wanted separate schools. Their appeal was denied.[48]

The standard for reviewing discrimination cases involving women has been modified to be more than a "rational basis" and less than a "strict standard."

The presiding Judge William M. Marutani (who is also a Philadelphia Legend of the Bar) was a victim of discrimination himself. Marutani was interned along with many other Japanese during World War II. He enlisted and served in World War II, helping the United States in the Pacific. Judge Marutani was involved in anti-discrimination matters throughout his life; he represented and helped support the Japanese American Citizens League. He was appointed to the bench in 1975, the first Asian American so appointed outside the West Coast. Elected in 1977, he served as judge for ten years.[49]

In recent Philadelphia history, the doors to clubs, the head of the district Attorney's and Public Defender's Office, have been open to women.

OTHER LEGENDS

OTHER LEGENDS
Profiles excerpted from the Legends of the Bar Issue of the Philadelphia Lawyer Magazine (Winter, 2002).

Abraham D. Caesar (1901-1995) was founder of Caesar, Rivise, Bernstein, Cohen & Pokotilow. He co-authored with his partner, Charles W. Rivise, Interference Law and Practice, which has been cited and relied on by the courts and the U.S. Patent and Trademark Office in hundreds of reported opinions. He is founder of the South Philadelphia High School Alumni Association Scholarship Fund.

Carl W. Funk (1900-1981) was a nationally recognized authority on banking law. A member of Drinker Biddle & Reath, he served as legal counsel to the banking industry, including the Philadelphia Clearing House. A captain in the U.S. Naval Reserve, he became an expert on priorities and allocations and wrote Navy manuals on termination of contracts.

Earl G. Harrison (1899-1955), serving under Presidents Franklin D. Roosevelt and Harry S. Truman, presided over alien registration work on the plight of refugees in the aftermath of World War II. Harrison returned from government service to become dean of the University of Pennsylvania Law School and vice president of the university. When he resigned from the university, he returned to private practice. He remained a public servant throughout his life.

Harold E. Kohn (1914-1999) achieved his national reputation in the early 1960s by winning a $29 million judgment against the giants of the electrical equipment industry for conspiring to fix prices. Following that triumph, he achieved great success in antitrust litigation involving numerous other industries. He was also instrumental in creating the procedural means for courts to deal with matters of such vast magnitude: the class action rules and the Panel on Multidistrict Litigation. Not a lawyer of one dimension, Kohn was also recognized for his devotion to civil liberties. He represented Ralph Ginzburg in appeals of a 1963 conviction for mailing obscene literature, argued the Two Guys store chain's challenge to the constitutionality of Sunday-closing laws, and handled a Vietnam War-era challenge to the draft as unconstitutional sex discrimination.

NOTABLE JUDGES

Only Philadelphians Owen J. Roberts and James Wilson became United States Supreme Court judges. Many Philadelphians have gone on to serve on federal benches and state benches. Philadelphia's lawyers attracted praise from *The Wall Street Journal* when, in 1991, forty judges volunteered their time to help ease the backlog of civil jury cases that had lingered between five and six years before trial.[50]

Phyllis W. Beck: After starting law school as a mother of four at age thirty-two, Phyllis Beck finished at the top of her Temple night-school class; spent eight years in private practice; taught at Temple; served five years as Penn Law School vice dean; and, in 1981, became the first woman ever appointed to the post of Pennsylvania Superior Court judge.[51] She has since left the bench and is now general counsel to the Barnes Foundation.
Profiles excerpted from the Legends of the Bar Issue of the Philadelphia Lawyer Magazine (Winter, 2002).

Raymond J. Broderick (1914-2000) was a U.S. District Court judge for the Eastern District of Pennsylvania. He served on the federal bench for twenty-nine years. His groundbreaking rulings in Halderman v. Pennhurst State School and Hospital went to the U.S. Supreme Court and are credited with ushering in a new era of legal rights for the mentally disabled.

M. Patricia Carroll (1937-2000) took an active role in aiding lawyers who suffered from addictive diseases. She was the founding director of Lawyers Concerned for Lawyers of Pennsylvania. A civil litigation attorney, she practiced law with her husband, John Rogers Carroll, for twenty years.

Lois G. Forer (1914-1994) was an advocate for the powerless. In practice, she was co-founder and first director of the Juvenile Law Center, established in 1966. Some years earlier, while a deputy attorney general of Pennsylvania, she handled the case that compelled the Barnes Foundation to open to the public. She voiced outrage at how the legal system handled those unable to manipulate it to their advantage.

Clifford Scott Green (1923-2007) was a senior judge on the U.S. District Court of the Eastern District of Pennsylvania. Before that he graduated from Temple Law School, Green worked in private practice and was a Common Pleas judge.

William Henry Hastie (1904-1976) earned an LLB and a Doctor of Juridical Science from Harvard. FDR appointed him judge of the Federal District Court in the Virgin Islands, becoming the nation's first African-American federal magistrate. Although the Virgin Islands were ninety percent black, no person of African descent before Hastie had been appointed to a federal judgeship. Judge Hastie served on the bench for two years before resigning his judgeship to return to Howard University's School of Law as dean and professor of law. From 1941 to 1943, Hastie served as civilian aide to Secretary of War Henry L. Stimson. On January 15, 1943, he resigned his position as Secretary of War Stimson's civilian aide to protest the government's racial policies of segregation and discrimination in America's armed forces. On May 7, 1946, Hastie was inaugurated as the first African-American governor of the Virgin Islands. On October 15, 1949, he was nominated judge of the Third United States Circuit Court of Appeals, based in Philadelphia, by President Harry S. Truman. At the time, it was the highest judicial position attained by an African-American. He served on the appellate court bench for twenty-one years. In 1968, he became chief judge of his circuit.[52]

Leon Higginbotham Jr. (1928-1998) was a towering man with a voice like thunder. He articulated the legal experience of black America with scholarship and understanding. He was a successful lawyer, a partner in Philadelphia's premier black law firm during an era when black lawyers were subjected to many inequities. From 1964 to 1977, Higginbotham was a highly respected federal trial judge, and then served sixteen years on the Third Circuit Court of Appeals, holding the position of chief judge before his retirement in 1993. From 1965 to 1966, he was vice-chairman of the National Commission on the Cause and Prevention of Violence. Higginbotham wrote two scholarly books on law and black citizens, *In the Matter of Color* and *Shades of Freedom*. In 1995, Higginbotham received the Presidential Medal of Freedom, the country's highest civilian honor.

J. Sydney Hoffman (1908-1998) was a senior judge in Pennsylvania Superior Court. Known for his keen legal mind and clarity of thought, he established the Accelerated Rehabilitative Disposition Program. He authored many dissenting opinions that became law in Pennsylvania. Hoffman had also served on the Family Court and Juvenile Court benches.

Joseph S. Lord III (1912-1991) was one of the lawyers to defend members of the Communist Party of Pennsylvania accused of plotting to overthrow the U.S. government, in violation of the Smith Act. Appointed to the federal bench in 1961, Judge Lord spent thirty years as a district judge, including ten years as chief judge. The list of his cases includes the Electrical Equipment Conspiracy Litigation, which he handled early in his tenure, and the suit to desegregate Girard College.

Dolores K. Sloviter was the first woman named to the Third Circuit Court of Appeals, in 1979.

Juanita Kidd Stout (1919-1998) became, at age sixty-eight, the first African-American woman to be a justice of any state's highest court. After service in the Philadelphia District Attorney's Office, Judge Stout was elected to the Philadelphia Court of Common Pleas and later was appointed to the Pennsylvania Supreme Court.

Charles Wright (1918-1993) used his position as judge to fight against the deliberate exclusion of African-Americans from jury duty as well as for racial balance in jury trials. In 1950, Judge Wright was one of the founders of The Barristers' Association of Philadelphia, Inc. In 1965, he became only the fourth African-American to sit on what is now the Philadelphia Court of Common Pleas.

AMERICAN BAR ASSOCIATION PRESIDENTS

Philadelphians who became presidents of the American Bar Association [years in bold] are:

Profiles excerpted from the Legends of the Bar Issue of the Philadelphia Lawyer Magazine (Winter, 2002).

Francis Rawle 1902-1903 was a founder of the American Bar Association in 1878. He held several positions in that organization, including treasurer and president. Rawle was an overseer of Harvard University, vice president of The Historical Society of Pennsylvania, and a reviser of *Bouvier's Law Dictionary* in 1883, 1887, and 1910.

Walter George Smith 1917-1918 was a lawyer, judge, President of the American Bar Association (1917), member of the American Committee for Armenian and Syrian Relief (1919), member of the U.S. Board of Indian Commissioners (1923), and prominent anti-divorce advocate. [Philadelphia Archdiocesan Historical Research Center]

Hampton L. Carson 1917-1918 served as Chancellor of the Philadelphia Bar Association from 1912 to 1914. He was a professor of law at the University of Pennsylvania and editor of its legal gazette. Carson also served as secretary of the Constitutional Centennial Commission of 1887.

Joseph Welles Henderson 1943-1944 The first non-Rawle family member of the Rawle firm, Joseph Welles Henderson, joined the firm in the summer of 1913, and became partner in 1917. In the 1920s, Mr. Henderson expanded the admiralty practice of the firm, a practice that the firm continues to this day. Henderson became the president of the American Bar Association in 1943 and served on the Board of Philadelphia City Trusts. [Rawle history website]

David F. Maxwell 1956-1957, an expert in corporate law, became well known in the courtroom as a combative litigator. In 1929, he became partner in the law firm of Edmonds and Obermayer (now Obermayer, Rebmann, Maxwell and Hippel). He chaired the American Bar Association's first post-World War II trip to London, where he was received by Queen Elizabeth II in Buckingham Palace.

Bernard G. Segal 1969-1970 argued nearly fifty cases in the U.S. Supreme Court. He was the first Jew to serve as Chancellor of the Philadelphia Bar Association and the first Jew to become president of the ABA. He reorganized the operations of the Philadelphia Bar Association, making it possible for many new members to excel within the Association. A long-time advocate of merit selection of judges, Segal is credited with having persuaded President Dwight D. Eisenhower to seek the views of the ABA on the qualifications of prospective candidates for the federal judiciary. In 1963, his leadership in civil rights activity led to the creation of the Lawyers' Committee for Civil Rights Under Law. President John F. Kennedy appointed Segal as one of the first co-chairmen of that committee.

Jerome J. Shestack 1997-1998 is a former partner and former head of the Litigation Department of the Philadelphia law firm of Wolf, Block, Schorr and Solis-Cohen. He was also a founding member and Chair of the Section of Individual Rights and Responsibilities, Chair of the Commission on Mental and Physical Disability Law, and Chair of the Standing Committee on Legal Aid and Indigent Defendants. He also initiated the first Women's Rights Committee in the ABA, the first ABA committee to support the Federal Legal Services program, and was an organizing member of the National Legal Services program and helped start the Legal Services Corporation. He was a founding member of the Lawyers Committee for Civil Rights Under Law in 1963. Under President Carter, Mr. Shestack was the U.S. Ambassador for Human Rights to the United Nations Human Rights Commission, and launched the U.N. Working Group to investigate disappearances under repressive regimes. He was the U.S. Alternative Representative to the U.N. General Assembly and to ECOSOC. Mr. Shestack also chaired the International Bar Association Standing Committee on Human Rights and founded its Human Rights Action program."[53]

After Governor George Wallace of Alabama said he would stand in the doorway of the University of Alabama so as not to allow black students admission despite a federal court order, Bernard Segal and Jerome Shestack prepared a letter asking Wallace to "refrain from defiance of a federal court order." Forty-six lawyers, including the then current and six prior Presidents of the American Bar Association, three former U.S. Attorneys general, and deans of various law schools signed the statement, which was published in the leading newspapers of Birmingham, Alabama. While Wallace did stand in the doorway, the statement was cited by U.S. Attorney General Nicholas Katzenbach as a key factor in getting Wallace to relent the next day. A few days later, Mr. Segal was asked by the White House to obtain a list of lawyers nationwide for a conference that resulted in the creation of the Lawyer's Committee for Civil Rights under law. Segal and New York's Harrison Tweed were named co-chairs.[54]

POLITICAL CHANGE

In 1951, a Home Rule Charter was adopted that gave the city (as opposed to the state) the authority of self-government including the power to impose taxes. William A. Schnader, Robert T. McCracken, Robert J. Callaghan, Abraham L. Freedman, Thomas B. K. Ringe, and Herbert E. Millen were lawyers on the Philadelphia Charter Commission. One of the main changes was redevelopment of the city's historical sector as well as provisions for low and middle income housing, new industrial sites, new parks and playgrounds, and conversion of blighted areas into university campuses (Temple, for one).

Another change was that Democrats, after decades of Republican leadership, were elected to the office of mayor. This new leadership was due to several factors such as embezzlement of city office-holders and growing black and immigrant populations who began to exercise their political muscle.[55]

It was in this environment that minorities and women began to require participation in many activities, including the legal profession, which had heretofore been the province of white men.

Profiles excerpted from the Legends of the Bar Issue of the Philadelphia Lawyer Magazine (Winter, 2002).

Richardson Dilworth (1898-1974) gained his legal reputation in his representation of Triangle Publications, which was owned by the Annenbergs. "He was elected to the offices of city treasurer, district attorney and mayor. During his mayoral term, the face of Philadelphia changed dramatically through a nationally recognized urban redevelopment program. Near the close of his career, Dilworth served for six years as president of the Board of Education." Dilworth argued for normalizing relations with China when he ran for governor in 1960. He lost. President Richard Nixon would normalize relations about fifteen years later.

Joseph Sill Clark (1901-1990) "was elected city controller in 1949 and was elected mayor in 1951." He was elected to the U.S. Senate five years later, and re-elected in 1962. Clark was a floor leader in the effort to secure passage of the Civil Rights Act of 1964 and helped in the passage of Headstart, a program to aid children in getting pre-elementary school education.

Abraham L. Freedman "although perhaps best known for his time on the trial and appellate federal bench, also played a prominent role in the watershed reform period of the early 1950s when the Democratic Party displaced the Republican Party that was dominant since the Civil War era."

OTHER CHANGES/ACHIEVEMENTS

In the twentieth century, large firms started to dominate the legal arena. Morgan, Lewis & Bockius LLP, the largest firm with an office in Philadelphia, has more than 1,400 lawyers worldwide (according to their website) dedicated to a variety of practices. Dechert LLP is the largest Philadelphia-based law firm with over 900 worldwide, as of 2006.[56]

Other attorneys belong to boutique firms or are sole practitioners. The age of specialization began with lawyers committing themselves early to one or just a couple of related fields, such as corporate taxation, mergers and acquisitions, human rights issues, mass tort litigation, and a variety of other specialties. The big firms have the principal advantage of having an ability to network within their firm. Big firms claim an ability to handle the tougher cases. Solo attorneys claim to give more personal attention and that they have their own network of attorneys and experts.

These new lawyers are not aristocrats who studied with other lawyers. They were trained in law schools like the University of Pennsylvania, Temple, Villanova, Widener, and nearby Dickinson. Also many of these new lawyers are from various races and ethnicities and are of both genders.

NEW AREAS OF PRACTICE

The twentieth century saw the emergence of new areas of practice due to a variety of new businesses like E-commerce, new possibilities like space travel, new rights like the American Civil Disabilities Act, and new strategies like Class Actions that enable a class of citizens who have been wronged to file suit against the wrongdoer. Philadelphia's lawyers have played a major part in developing these new practices.

GIVING BACK

Many attorneys, like Gerald Litvin, have helped the members of the Philadelphia Bar. Litvin organized the Academy of Advocacy, a nonprofit institute in Pennsylvania, created to improve trial skills and enhance the quality of litigated justice; that program (now part of Temple Law School) is frequently referred to in Eastern Pennsylvania as "Litvin's boot camp for trial lawyers." Before Litvin, Wilfred R. Lorry and John R. McConnell had well known advocacy programs at Temple. James E. Beasle Sr. gave generously to Temple Law School, which is now named in his honor.

Stephen J. Harmelin, managing partner at Dilworth Paxson LLP, is engaged in various civic and charitable activities. He founded the Philadelphia Constitution Foundation, which owned one of the world's most extensive libraries on international constitutions. Projects of the foundation included supporting the exhibition of an original Magna Carta in Philadelphia as well as providing guidance to the Constitutional Commission of the Russian Republic. He serves on the Board of the Barnes Foundation, which houses the most important collection of French Impressionist paintings outside of France, and is general counsel to the National Constitution Center, a $200 million project that opened in Independence National Historical Park on July 4, 2003. He is also chair of the Thomas Skelton Harrison Foundation.

Arlin Adams: Mr. Adams is counsel to the law firm of Schnader Harrison LLP. He served as a U.S. Court of Appeals judge from 1969 to 1987 He has handled numerous complex litigation matter including class action litigation and punitive damage matters. Susquehanna University created the Arlin M. Adams Center for Law and Society at Susquehanna to honor his many achievements. The University of Pennsylvania Law School and the Annenberg Foundation established the Arlin M. Adams Professorship on Constitutional Law in his honor in 2005. Schnader Harrison LLP website (www.schnader.com)

The service of the above to the community is just a sample of the many members of the Philadelphia Bar Association who give back to the community. Still others—like Stephen A. Cozen took a boutique firm of a few attorneys and expanded it into a firm, Cozen O'Connor, of 450 attorneys with twenty offices—give back by serving on numerous educational and philanthropic boards. Joe Gerber, a partner of Cozen O'Connor, said that many first-generation firms (firms where the original founders still practice) were the sons and daughters of immigrants. When excluded by the big firms because they didn't have the right "name" credentials, these new lawyers began their own firms focusing on some of the newer practice areas like personal injury and class actions. Many of the "blueblood" firms have seen the light and have begun to judge new hires based solely on merit. Mr. Gerber noted that the culture of these first-generation law firms is one that emphasizes family, education, and community pride, showing that many Philadelphia first-generation lawyers take pride in giving back to the community through various voluntary programs.

PORTRAITS

Philadelphia, through its bar association and libraries, has had some notable portraits of its lawyers and judges done throughout the centuries. The artwork is spread throughout the city and can be viewed at Jenkins Law Library, the University of Pennsylvania Law School, and the Free Library, among other sites. Artists of Philadelphia legal figures have included:

Henry Inman – Chief Justice John Marshall and William Rawle – located at the Bar Association building.

John Neagle (a pupil of Gilbert Stuart and the son-in-law of Thomas Sully, one of the city's best know portraitists) – George Sharswood, David Paul Brown, and a copy of William Tilghman (original by Rembrandt Peale), and a copy of William Lewis (original by Gilbert Stuart).

Thomas Sully – John Sergent, Horace Binney, and several others.

Robert W. Vonnoh – John C. Bullit, Samuel Dickson, and Richard C. Dale.

E.D. Marchant – James Thompson, Eli K. Price, and James D. Kent

Robert Susann (a graduate of the Pennsylvania Academy of Fine Arts. – William Schnader and William Gray.[57, 58]

Bernard Segal by Boris Kublanov. Courtesy of University of Pennsylvania Law School

CASES – CIVIL LIBERTIES

In the 1950s the fear of Communism hit many United States cities, including Philadelphia. As author Sherman Labovitz, of *Philadelphia Red*, explains, many supposed Communists were being targeted by the Federal Government for violation of the Smith Act.[59] What put Philadelphia on the legal map was the way it handled the defense. In particular, the Philadelphia Bar Association, under the chancellorship of Bernard Segal took an active role in insuring that those charged would have a defense – an unpopular decision in the 1950s.

Philadelphia was a good setting for taking an active role for several reasons. In 1952, it elected Joseph Clark mayor and Richardson Dilworth district attorney. Both were liberal, reform minded Democrats. Philadelphia has had local chapters of the ACLU and other organizations dedicated to helping the less fortunate. It also had a history, from the time of Andrew Hamilton, of defending those accused for freedom of speech issues. The city had a number of attorneys from the Main Line who, according to Labovitz, were comfortable enough that they could afford to assist in an unpopular cause – the defense of those charged, nine men, in 1953, with violation of the Smith Act.

Mostly, Philadelphia had good lawyers. The Philadelphia Bar Association leaders met and decided, at the request of Thomas McBride and willingness of the first Jewish Chancellor of the Bar, Bernard Segal, to enlist the aid of the best lawyers in the city. These attorneys included: Thomas McBride who would go on to become a Supreme Court justice; Joseph Lord, who would go on to become a federal judge and decide the Stephen Girard will/race case; David Cohen, who would go on to be a veteran city councilman; Lou McCabe, a top trial attorney; Edmund Spaeth, who would become a Pennsylvania Supreme Court justice; Benjamin H. Read; Henry W. Sawyer III, a top civil rights lawyer; John Rogers Carroll, Charles C. Hileman; Joseph N. DuBarry; and William J. Wolston.

The defense team, instead of focusing on the Communist Party as a whole, focused more on the right of individuals to free speech especially if "No action" is associated with that speech. Though the verdict was guilty the defense team was able to show to the public that the suit had little merit. The judge gave lenient sentences and ultimately the Smith Act, the basis for the charges, was held to be unconstitutional by the United States Supreme Court. Two members, William Douglas and Hugo Black, said it violated the First Amendment. The majority held that it was "ambiguous."

CASE MOST OFTEN MISQUOTED

Schenck v. U.S. (249 U.S. 47, 1919) Schenck v. United States is probably the most misquoted case in United States history. The United States prosecuted Charles Schenck, who was the general secretary of the Socialist Party in Philadelphia, Elizabeth Baer, who was its recording secretary, and other Party members. In 1917, a jury found them guilty of attempting to cause insubordination of World War One draftees because they had distributed leaflets urging draftees not to "submit to intimidation" by fighting in a war being conducted on behalf of "Wall Street's chosen few." In short, they were found guilty of influencing soldiers to resist the draft.

Justice Oliver Wendell Holmes, who wrote the Supreme Court Opinion, noted that nothing in the pamphlet suggested that the draftees should use unlawful or violent means to oppose conscription: "In form at least [the pamphlet] confined itself to peaceful measures, such as a petition for the repeal of the act" and an exhortation to exercise "your right to assert your opposition to the draft." Many of its most impassioned words were quoted directly from the Constitution.

Justice Holmes wrote, "the character of every act depends upon the circumstances in which it is done." And to illustrate that truism he went on to say, "The most stringent protection of free speech would not protect a man in falsely shouting fire in a theater, and causing a panic. It does not even protect a man from an injunction against uttering words that may have all the effect of force." Justice Holmes then upheld the convictions in the context of a wartime draft, holding that the pamphlet created "a clear and present danger" of hindering the war effort while our soldiers were fighting for their lives and our liberty.

Scholars like Alan M. Dershowitz argue that Holmes's reasoning was incorrect because Schenck's writings were protected speech and that the analogy is incorrect because yelling fire isn't really speech – it's more like the equivalent of an alarm going off.

But Dershowitz and Holmes would agree that the word "falsely" is required. After all if there is a fire in a theater people should know. Most people who want to support their argument that one just can't say anything (there are limits) use the phrase "you can't yell fire in a theater." That's wrong. The word falsely is required.

CASES – CIVIL CASES

Famous Estate Cases
Benjamin Franklin's Will

George Wharton Pepper wrote in his biography, *The Philadelphia Lawyer*, about a suit in which he represented Benjamin Franklin's heirs in a suit against Philadelphia over a trust that Franklin established in his will. The trust was to give the City 1,000 pounds sterling [about $5,000], which was to be used to make interest-bearing loans to "deserving artisans." Franklin estimated the trust would be worth $655,000 by 1890 and directed a distribution of $500,000 to be spent on "public works" and the rest to be reinvested and distributed in 1990 to the government of Pennsylvania and the "inhabitants of the City of Philadelphia" when the funds were projected by Franklin to be worth $19 million.[60]

Unfortunately, the trust was only worth $100,000 in 1890 and Franklin's heirs sued. Pepper's main argument on behalf of the heirs, who were trying to overturn/end the trust was whether the extending of the loans was a "charitable" activity. Senator Pepper and the heirs lost. After the Orphans' Court ultimately denied jurisdiction, the Common Pleas Court held that the loans were an act of charity and as Senator Pepper put it "Charities cover a multitude of sins."

In 1908, the distribution that was supposed to have been made in 1890 was spent for the Franklin Institute ($128,190.95).

According to Gerard J. St. John, the idea for the interest-bearing account came as a result of a parody of *Poor Richard's Almanac* written by French mathematician Charles-Joseph Mathon de La Cour in 1785.

In 1993, Gerard J. St. John, a partner (now retired) at Schnader Harrison Segal and Lewis LLP was appointed master to handle the 200-year distribution, which had accumulated to $2,256,952.05 (Franklin had predicted it would be worth four million pounds sterling, about nineteen million dollars).

Philadelphia honored Franklin's will which required loans to:
 Young married artificers [tradesmen] as have served apprenticeships in said town.

The loans were not to exceed sixty pounds sterling, not to exceed ten years, and not to exceed five percent. Franklin had been a tradesman/printer and the loans were to help these tradesmen start their own businesses.

Because tradesmen were replaced with large businesses, due to the Industrial Revolution, the loans were changed to home mortgages.

On recommendation of Mr. St. John and approval by the Orphans Court Judge, Frank O'Brien, the money in Franklin's trust was divided between the Franklin Institute and the Benjamin Franklin Foundation – a community foundation designed "to assist students or recent graduates of Philadelphia high schools…to gain additional training in a trade, craft, or applied science." An oversight committee will meet every decade or so to determine whether the Benjamin Franklin Fund still meets the intentions of the bequest.

Franklin's will also established an identical trust for Boston. The Boston trust accumulated about five million dollars by 1993, twice the amount of the Philadelphia trust. Boston likes to argue it managed their trust better. The difference is that Philadelphia honored Franklin's will through the loans to average citizens. Boston invested the money in commerce thereby maximizing their return.[62]

John Graver Johnson's Will and the Philadelphia Museum of Art

When Johnson practiced, lawyers took extended vacations in the summer when courts were closed. So Johnson traveled to Europe where he acquired an extensive art collection. Johnson's will dictated that his paintings be housed in a gallery he owned in his house at 510 Broad Street.

When Johnson died, his will and codicil became the subject of a court case about how Johnson's art should be treated. Judge Charles Klein, in 1959, agreed that Johnson's house was in disrepair and in an unsuitable neighborhood (Edmund Norwood Bacon, Director of the Philadelphia City Plan-

ning Committee, was one of the witnesses who so testified). But Judge Klein was angry that the artwork had been moved in 1933 without court approval at a time when funds could have been used to repair the house. With witnesses, including William George Constable, the curator of the Museum of Fine Arts in Boston, testifying to the good condition of the artwork in the museum, Judge Klein reluctantly agreed to a ten-year lease of the collection to the Philadelphia Museum of Art. Subsequently the collection was sold to the Philadelphia Museum of Art.[63]

The Barnes Foundation

The Barnes Foundation was created by Dr. Albert Barnes in 1922 "to promote the advancement of education and the appreciation of art." Barnes hired Owen J. Roberts (who later served as associate justice of the United States Supreme Court) to prepare the trust paperwork.

The collection includes 180 Renoirs in addition to 69 Cezannes, and 60 Matisses, 44 Picassos, 18 Rousseaus, 14 Modiglianis as well as the works of Monet, Manet, Van Gogh, and Pippin.

In 1923 Barnes' art was shown at a four week exhibition at the Pennsylvania Academy of Fine Arts. The show was panned by the Philadelphia critics, who were not receptive to Barnes' modern tastes. Barnes had particular disdain for the Philadelphia Museum of Art and

Albert Barnes by Alfred Bendiner.
Courtesy of University of Pennsylvania
Architectural Archives

its first director, Fiske Kimball. The foundation opened its doors in 1925. [For more on the artwork please see the art section].

Barnes's will (Barnes died in 1951) dictated the initial trustees and who could appoint subsequent trustees. Barnes changed his will so that instead of the University of Pennsylvania and the Pennsylvania Academy of Fine Arts having control over the majority of trustees – Lincoln University would have control. Among the notable graduates of Lincoln University are Langston Hughes and Thurgood Marshall, who would also serve as associate justice of the United States Supreme Court.

The Foundation has been involved in litigation. As a result of one series of lawsuits, the Barnes Foundation was opened to the public on Fridays and Saturdays (by appointment only).

As a result of additional court action, the 2,500 piece collection had a three-year (1993-1995) world tour. The tour raised $16 million for renovations and exposed the collection to five million people, including close to half a million in Philadelphia. (**For more on litigation involving the Barnes Foundation please see –** *Art Held Hostage* **by John Anderson. W.W. Norton and Company, NY © 2003**)

When funding again became an issue a number of charitable institutions like the Pew Charitable Trusts agreed to help fund the Barnes but only if the work would be moved into the city.

In December 2004 Judge Stanley Ott, a Montgomery County judge, ruled that the Barnes art could be moved to the city. Then Mayor, John Street, decreed that that the new Barnes Foundation building would be on the Benjamin Franklin Parkway – near the Rodin Museum and near the Philadelphia Museum of Art.

The move to the Parkway still engages as opponents to the move argue that the Barnes was so much more than just a warehouse for showing the art. They argue that the details of how the art was displayed, its relation to the horticulture Barnes created and its value as an educational resource make any move wrong. They say the money could have just as easily been spent to keep the art where it is and that the real purpose of the move is just to make money.[64]

Business

While most non-lawyers think of trial lawyers when they hear the phrase "lawyer," and when they think trial lawyers they usually think of criminal and personal injury law – the reality is different. Many of the top lawyers in the city are involved in aiding businesses in a variety of non-trial concerns including tax advice, corporate planning, mergers and acquisitions, compliance with a host of governmental regulations, employee benefits, and more. These lawyers rarely see a courtroom. Many of the lawyers who are in court are there because of litigation over business concerns from antitrust and contract issues to intellectual property and patent litigation.

Philadelphia lawyers have been involved in the development of virtually every building and every nonprofit and for-profit institution in the city and a variety of business ventures across the world. A few important business cases are discussed in other chapters. The merger and dissolution of the Penn Central is in the business section. The purchase by Comcast of AT&T's broadband, patent litigation over the ENIAC computer, and Philo T. Farnsworth's creation of the cathode ray tube for television are reviewed in the science section.

To take advantage of the growing intellectual property field, Drexel University has a new law school specializing in intellectual property, entrepreneurship and health care.

Religion
School District Of Abington Township, Pennsylvania, Et Al. v. Schempp Et Al. 374 U.S. 203 (1963)

This case, heard by the Supreme Court on Appeal from the Eastern District of Pennsylvania (in Philadelphia), held that requiring school students to listen to mandatory prayer readings was a violation of the First Amendment in that it constituted an "establishment of religion."

The Schempp family, which was of the Unitarian Faith, objected to a Pennsylvania law that required that "At least ten verses from the Holy Bible shall be read, without comment, at the opening of each public school on each school day. Any child shall be excused from such Bible reading, or attending such Bible reading, upon the written request of his parent or guardian."[65]

The Schempp case was heard in conjunction with a case brought by atheist Madeline Murray, whose son was required to listen to the reading of a passage from the Bible or the recitation of the Lord's Prayer during the school's opening exercises.

As a result of the Schempp decision, the Court created the "secular purpose" and "primary effect" tests for interpreting the Establishment Clause – What are the purpose and the primary effect of the enactment? If either is the advancement or inhibition of religion, then the enactment exceeds the scope of legislative power as circumscribed by the Constitution.

Lemon v. Kurtzman[66]

Churches have often vied for "state" money, often in the area of education. In an oft-cited case that originated with a Philadelphian, Alton T. Lemon, the Supreme Court developed the Lemon test. It's a three-prong test used to determine whether the aid to the state is secular or religious. "First, the statute must have a secular legislative purpose; second, its principal or primary effect must be one that neither advances nor inhibits religion; finally, the statute must not foster 'an excessive government entanglement with religion'."

Chief Justice Burger, who wrote the decision in 1971, was worried that acceptance of public money would curtail religious freedom: "Government grants ... have almost always been accompanied by varying measures of control and surveillance." The case was argued on Lemon's behalf by Henry W. Sawyer III.

Locally, the test was used by U.S. District Judge Stewart Dalzell in 2003 in ordering that a 1920 plaque containing text and commentary on the Ten Commandments be removed from a West Chester courthouse wall.[67]

In 2005, the United States Supreme Court, in two decisions, changed the way in which the Ten Commandments issue can be viewed. Judge Dalzell's reasoning no longer applies. The courts have wrestled with the standards set forth in Lemon and new cases are sure to arise.

The meaning and parameters of Schempp have been contested and litigated since. Issues have included saying prayer at school football games, distributing religious literature, holding religious extracurricular meetings, and most recently whether the words "Under God" in the pledge of allegiance are proper.

Henry W. Sawyer III, the legendary Philadelphia civil-rights attorney, argued the case for the Schemps.

CASES – CRIMINAL CASES

Philadelphia has been no stranger to its share of criminal stories that have made the headlines from organized crime killings to the trial of Joey Coyle for scooping up money when a Brinks truck's door opened to the flight of Ira Einhorn who was successfully brought back from France to be convicted of murder charges. One of the most important criminal cases, though, went straight to heart of the legal process:

Roofers Union

In a major scandal in the 1980s more than ten judges were given cash by the Roofers Union Local 30-30B.

One attorney familiar with the investigation said most of the cash changed hands at Christmas." "I understand it's all at Christmas," the attorney said. "They were in Christmas envelopes. They were Christmas presents." "Several judges," the source said, "explained that the contributions were to help pay off debts incurred during the 1985 judicial campaigns." "Roofers Union Local 30-30B has long been a powerful and controversial force in Philadelphia politics and organized labor. Its political-action committee (PAC) contributed thousands of dollars in last year's primary and general elections to candidates for public office throughout Philadelphia."[68]

The gifts were enough, however, to generate one of the biggest corruption scandals in Philadelphia history, to send two judges off to federal prison and to prompt the removal or resignation of thirteen judges implicated in the federal investigation, some of whom were reinstated later. The scandal was an embarrassment to the city's judiciary.[69]

Eastern State Penitentiary

The Eastern State Penitentiary opened in 1829 as part of a controversial movement to change the behavior of inmates through "confinement in solitude with labor." It quickly became one of the most expensive and most copied buildings in the young United States. It is estimated that more than 300 prisons worldwide are based on the Penitentiary's wagon-wheel, or "radial" floor plan.

Some of America's most notorious criminals were held in the Penitentiary's vaulted, sky-lit cells, including bank robber Willie Sutton and Al Capone. After 142 years of consecutive use, Eastern State Penitentiary was completely abandoned in 1971, and now stands, a lost world of crumbling cell blocks and empty guard towers. The penitentiary was Alex de Tocqueville's main incentive for coming to Philadelphia. Eastern State Gargoyles.

Text reprinted with permission of Ruth Savitz.

Defense Lawyers

Many criminal defense attorneys have defended the referenced cases and handled the large caseload of lesser known clients. The Philadelphia Public Defender's office, now run by Ellen Greenlee, represents indigent defendants. Some of the many notable criminal defense attorneys included:

Profiles excerpted from the Legends of the Bar Issue of the Philadelphia Lawyer Magazine (Winter, 2002).

Martin Vinikoor (1918-1976) was noted as one of Philadelphia's finest criminal defense lawyers. He was active in politics and became head of the Defender Association of Philadelphia. He obtained the first large grant from the city to support that association. He became an assistant district attorney and later a professor at Temple Law School.

Louis Lipschitz (c.1904-1993) was recognized as one of the bar's finest criminal defense lawyers. A scholarly and successful attorney, he was honored by the Philadelphia Bar Association's Criminal Justice Section in 1982.

Thomas D. McBride (1902-1965) served with distinction as Pennsylvania attorney general and later as a justice of the Pennsylvania Supreme Court. He was a respected criminal defense attorney in Philadelphia. He fearlessly provided counsel for unpopular causes, including the defense of eight Communists charged with conspiracy to overthrow the U.S. government. He was Chancellor of the Philadelphia Bar Association from 1956 to 1957.

Mr. Lipshitz described McBride's education in an article in *The Shingle*, on McBride's passing by noting that McBride was famous for driving a cab and marking papers for a logic course and talking and drinking at a few of his favorite speakeasies. He only came to class on days it rained, which meant he rarely came in until the semester was near an end.

"He knew many lawyers and had many potential free clients among the rebels who agreed with him on Ireland, prohibition, impeachment of Governors and court-martials. "If he did not know what the law was he did feel what it should be and usually persuaded judges and juries that he was right."

Prosecution Lawyers

Philadelphia has had a number of successful district attorneys. At least two have used the office as a stepping-stone to a political career.

Arlen Specter, who grew up in Kansas, was a Philadelphia district attorney and a lawyer on the Warren Commission investigation of the assassination of President Kennedy. Specter is credited for the "single bullet" theory to explain the assassination. He has been a U.S. Senator since 1980 (switching from Republican to Democrat in 2009). He was Chairman of the Judiciary Committee from 2005-2008.

He has written several criminal laws including the Terrorist Prosecution Act, the Armed Career Criminal Act and is co-author of the Second Chance Act. In earlier confirmation hearings he had the courage to cross party lines in opposing Judge Bork and disagreeing with conventional wisdom in supporting Justice Thomas after dissecting the contradictory and highly charged testimony.. As chairman of the Veterans Committee, he has pushed for just treatment for veterans after his father, Harry Specter was wounded in World War I and denied his bonus by the U.S. Government which broke its promise. (http://specter.senate.gov)

Ed Rendell, another former D.A., was a popular Philadelphia mayor for eight years in the 1990s. Many credit Rendell with saving the city from severe financial crisis and reinvigorating the city. He inherited a huge deficit, but turned it into a surplus by cutting city spending, shifting some public jobs to the private sector, and forcing the municipal unions to accept cuts. Most would agree that he brings a trademark enthusiasm and an ability to schmooze with anyone to any job he tackles. He was the National Democratic Party chairman in 2000. He was elected governor of Pennsylvania in 2002 and re-elected in 2006.

The current Philadelphia District Attorney is **Lynne Abraham** who recently brought about the return and conviction of Ira Einhorn. Before becoming the city's district attorney, she served as a Municipal Court Judge and then Common Pleas Court judge.

Richard A. Sprague, the founder and senior member of Sprague & Sprague, graduated from the University of Pennsylvania Law School in 1953. He worked for 2 ½ years as a Voluntary Defender in the Defender Association of Philadelphia and then had a distinguished career as First Assistant District Attorney of Philadelphia, Pennsylvania.

Mr. Sprague also served as Special Prosecutor for Washington, Allegheny, Philadelphia and Delaware Counties, in Pennsylvania, and as special counsel to the Pennsylvania Supreme Court Judicial Inquiry and Review Board.

He was Chief Counsel and Director of the United States House of Representatives Select Committee on Assassinations investigating the murders of President John F. Kennedy and Dr. Martin Luther King, Jr.

His work includes civil practice in addition to his criminal work. He is a teacher and a member of the Pennsylvania Judicial Conduct Board, the Pennsylvania Continuing Legal Education Board, the United States Senate Judicial Nominating Commission, and currently serves as President Judge Emeritus of the Pennsylvania Court of Judicial Discipline, formerly President Judge. (Sprague and Sprague website)

F. Emmett Fitzpatrick and Ron Castille were two other recent D.A.s. Mr. Fitzpatrick is now in private practice where he also defends clients. Mr. Castille is now Chief Justice Castille of the Pennsylvania Supreme Court.

A murder defendant (the nation's first serial killer) is shown in various stages of his trial. H.H. Holmes (aka Herman Webster Mudget) was America's first serial killer. The trial here is for the murder of local Philadelphian Ben Pitizel. Pitizel took out life insurance on himself for $10,000, naming Holmes as beneficiary. Pitzel was just supposed to disappear, but Holmes killed him and three of the five Pitezel children. Holmes claimed to have killed twenty-seven people. The drawing is from the Philadelphia Press, October 1895. Holmes can be seen defending himself.

Mudget Trial Scene (1890s). Original from Philadelphia Press – Public Domain

*the*PHILADELPHIA MERCHANT

*John Wanamaker
(1890s) by Unknown.
Original from
Philadelphia Press –
Public Domain*

John Wanamaker

*"Half the money I spend on
advertising is wasted; the trouble
is I don't know which half."*
John Wanamaker, owner of
Wanamaker's
old department stores

MERCHANT

PHILADELPHIA BUSINESS

NOTABLE STYLES
Family Run
Parallel The City's Fortunes
Set the Tone for the City's Styles
Voluntary Associations
Charity

Contents

PHIA MERCHANT

THE PHILADELPHIA MERCHANT

In the early 1700s and 1800s Philadelphia business was defined by its location. Penn chose it because of its potential as a seaport.

Philadelphia's early businesses were shipping and all the trades that were affected by shipping. Philadelphia's ports gave it access to the rest of the world. Because Philadelphia was a center of the colonies it was an ideal place for the first stop of goods from the South to the rest of the North and Philadelphia was a partner with parts of the North that did not have Philadelphia's and Pennsylvania's resources.

Transportation subsequently produced other major Philadelphia businesses. In part this was due to its resources; oil and steel, (in the outer bound areas) and, in part, again because of its location – a link to the North, the South, and the West. Carriages, trolleys, trains, car parts, trailers, and helicopters have all been built in and about the City.

Philadelphia was known as The Cradle of Finance. From Robert Morris who helped finance the Revolutionary War, Stephen Girard who helped finance the Second World War, the Union League which helped finance the Civil War, Philadelphians have played a major part in financing United States history. Its capitalists like the Drexel family have continued Philadelphia's major role in the economy. Philadelphia's central location helped make it a natural home of the Bank of North America and of the First and Second National Banks of the United States. In 1792 Philadelphia became home to the country's first United States Mint.

Philadelphia's other moniker was Workshop to the World. Steven Conn in his *Metropolitan Philadelphia* wrote, "Virtually anything made in a factory in the early twentieth century was probably made somewhere in Philadelphia."[1]

Philadelphia businesses have been first in many arenas. Benjamin Franklin began the Philadelphia Contributorship an insurance association designed to protect against fires in 1752. A competitor, the Mutual Assurance Company (a.k.a. the Green Tree competitor) began in 1784 by insuring homes with trees in the front yard, which the Contributorship would not. Green Tree closed in 2004 according to the *Philadelphia Business Journal.* (12/15/2004)

Many of the businesses that Philadelphians treasure have risen from the small and various neighborhood trades of the artists and craftsmen, welders and carpenters, clothiers, etc, to become citywide, region-wide, and national and international businesses.

Direct offshoots of William Penn's plan for the city are the businesses targeted to the city's various neighborhoods. Each neighborhood has its own set of businesses within its geographical area. Food stores, cleaning stores, restaurants, etc. Within each neighborhood the opinions of the neighbors can be found and still are found in media outlets from pamphlets and newspapers to radio. Over time these outlets have combined or expanded with other neighborhoods, but each media outlet is one way of defining Philadelphians. Which paper one reads (*The Philadelphia Inquirer, The Philadelphia Daily News, the City Paper, the Tribune, The Jewish Exponent,* and on and on), which radio station one listens to, is often reflected in the traditions and values of the neighborhoods that Philadelphia comes from.

Remarkably many Philadelphia businesses and professions have stayed in family hands. Some of the more prominent Philadelphia business names are Norris, Wharton, Morris, Ingersoll, Meade, Rush, Penrose, Roberts, Pepper, Meigs, and Wood. The money and aristocracy of these families did, though, help to create social divides in the City. The laborers are not known for their family names. Perhaps because of this, the laborers identify with fictional characters like Rocky Balboa and people like many of the "lunch pail" athletes that play for the local teams. One of the most notable places for laborers was the Philadelphia Navy Yard, a Philadelphia institution for centuries.

One profession that has a definite Philadelphia label is architecture where the "Philadelphia" school of architecture emphasized a more personal, sensitive design philosophy.

Philadelphia's business leaders have been notable for their charitable contributions from the Drexel family who helped create Drexel University and a network of missions, to the Pew Memorial Trust, the Wharton School of Economics, and Sidney Kimmel's Center for the Performing Arts. At the beginning of the twenty-first century, many of the richest Philadelphians include people who made their wealth in traditional industries – Publication (Leonore Annenberg), Clothing (Sidney Kimmel), Food (the Campbell Soup Heirs), and in new industries like Cable (The Lenfest Family and the Roberts family). All have contributed by giving back to charities in and about the city.

It took Franklin to help make Penn's plan work.[2] Franklin, through the force of his personality, theories about business, the practice of his own businesses and his many contributions to the city paved the way for much of the way business has been and is now conducted in and about Philadelphia.

The South East Prospect of the City of Philadelphia ca 1720 by Peter Cooper. Courtesy of The Library Company of Philadelphia

TRANSPORTATION

Shipping and the Naval Yard

Philadelphia, under the influence of William Penn and the Quaker religion, which stressed peace, did not start out like many of the other colonial seaports in that it avoided the making of ships for defense purposes. Rather it focused on the commercial side of building. But this trend ended with the onset of the French and Indian War and later the Revolutionary War. Philadelphia built its first warship in 1762, *The Hero*, which became a model for other war frigates.

From then on, Philadelphia saw the birth of the United States Navy and the Marine Corps and outfitted the first American fleet in 1775. A 44-gun frigate, *The United States*, was the first American warship to be launched under the naval provisions of the Constitution.

The Philadelphia Naval Yard kept pace with technology – steam, screw propellers, radio, and the steam turbine engine.

It was the first line of coastal defense during the Civil War and by World War II one of the most modern shipbuilding plants in the world.

The Naval Yard moved in 1876 to League Island and helped build the largest U.S. battleships, *New Jersey* and *Wisconsin*. Following the war, the Naval Yard helped the United States keep a large reserve fleet by refinishing ships built elsewhere.[3]

Sadly, in 1996, the Naval Yard was closed in cost cutting measures by the Government.On March 2, 1994, Senator Arlen Specter personally argued the case of Dalton versus Specter before the Supreme Court of the United States to protest alleged violations of the law in the closing of the Shipyard by the Base Realignment and Closure Commission. He lost.

CHARLES HENRY CRAMP,
Ship Builder of War and Merchant Vessels.

On October 21, 1997, Pennsylvania Governor Tom Ridge and Philadelphia Mayor Rendell signed an agreement with Kvaerner to renovate and modernize the publicly owned yard.

"Kvaerner will design and manufacture container and tanker ships using the world's most advanced robotics and software technology. Kvaerner is Europe's largest commercial shipbuilder, and an international engineering and construction company widely recognized as a world leader in high-tech."[4]

William Cramp and Sons Ship and Engine Building Company was another well known builder of naval vessels.

Carriages

Before motorized transportation, carriages did a thriving business in Philadelphia as the Currier and Ives lithograph of Girard Avenue Bridge in Fairmount Park shows and the Rodgers Coach Factory image shows.

Streetcars

Many businesses came to life during the Industrial Revolution. Philadelphia with its nearby natural resources of steel and oil took advantage in a variety of new businesses, from those in the transportation industry, to mining, textiles, and bottling, and many more.

Theodore Dreiser immortalized in literature (*The Financier*) Charles T. Yerkes. Yerkes was born in 1907 in Philadelphia. He began his career as a broker, which ended when he had to serve time in prison for stealing funds from the City. He was pardoned and moved to Chicago where he built his public transportation empire.

Peter A. B. Widener and William L. Elkins began buying up street car lines in Philadelphia until they had a monopoly, at which time they turned to buying up streetcars in New York, Chicago, and elsewhere. "Widener and Elkins dominated City Hall and also became part of the Quay machine of Pennsylvania."[5, 6]

Elkins Park is named after Elkins. Elkin's son helped fund Abington Hospital and his daughter helped fund Temple's Tyler School of Art.[7]

The Widener family has been a major contributor in Philadelphia. Widener University, Widener Memorial Hall, and the Widener Building are named after Widener.

Trolleys were subsequently replaced by the automobile and bus. Only a few trolley lines in Philadelphia survive.

Ship Image (1890s). Original from Philadelphia Press – Public Domain

1907 Railway Post Office (Philadelphia Trolleys Exhibition). Courtesy of Free Library of Philadelphia

Girard Avenue Bridge Fairmount Park ca 1860 by Currier and Ives.
Courtesy of The Library Company of Philadelphia

Wm. D. Rogers' Coach Manufactory Sixth and Brown St. Philadelphia by Alfred M. Hoffy.
Courtesy of The Library Company of Philadelphia

Trains

Baldwin Locomotives

Matthias W. Baldwin (1795-1866) began as a jeweler and silversmith. He then set up his own printing shop. In 1825, he began his own machine shop. It was in 1831 that he began his way toward fame with the creation and introduction of his first steam engine. His success led to the creation of Old Ironsides, the first steam locomotive.[8] Soon after, he launched Baldwin Locomotive Works, which built over 1500 steam locomotives. Baldwin was an abolitionist who helped build a school for black youth. His abolitionist stance led to a boycott by some Southern railroads, before the Civil War.

The plates shown here include the Observation end of the Penna. Limited on Horseshoe Curve and a Pullman Car.

Philadelphia and Reading/Reading Railroad

Passenger railroad service began in Philadelphia in 1832 with the Germantown and Northeast Railroad which used wood-burning steam engines built by Baldwin Locomotive Works.

The oldest train station in the United States, dating to 1834, is Shawmont station in the Shawmont section of Roxborough. The station not only had a stationmaster but a "waiting room, baggage room, post office, and living quarters...."

In 1838 the Philadelphia and Reading Railroad began construc-

Observation End of Pa. Limited on Horseshoe Curve 1891 by William Herman Rau. Courtesy of American Premier Underwriter's Inc.

An early engine used on the railroad line of the Philadelphia and Reading was imported from England. Called the "Rocket" it is on display in the Franklin Institute.

A Philadelphia firm, Eastwick and Harrison, built the next engine, the Gowan & Marx, which in 1842 was the most powerful locomotive in the US and ran between Pottsville and Philadelphia on the Philadelphia and Reading. It averaged twenty-five miles per hour, but could pull forty times its own weight.[9]

William H. Rau's Photographs

Philadelphian William H. Rau was commissioned by the Pennsylvania Railroad to take photographs (463 were taken) of the scenes along the route the Pennsylvania Railroad traversed. He had his own car for this task, which was designed to help advertise the Pennsylvania Railroad.

Rau along with other photographers like Edwin Wilson who edited the *Philadelphia Photograph* and Frederick Gutekist captured Philadelphia and the surrounding areas during the late 1890s.[10]

tion on rails that would give it freight and passenger service from Philadelphia to Pottsville.

Successive work on the railroad by the Philadelphia and Reading led to destinations in Harrisburg, Gettysburg, Allentown, Wilmington, and New York.

"It was a major distributor of anthracite coal from nearby regions in the Lehigh Valley and connected to other big railroads like the New Jersey Central, Lehigh Valley, Baltimore & Ohio, and New York Central. By the 1870s, the Philadelphia and Reading Railroad was the largest corporation in the world, with a capital of $170,000,000."

The combined lines became known as the Reading Railroad. The Reading Terminal was built in 1893. The entire system comprised about forty small railroads. The Boardwalk Flyer to Atlantic City broke worldwide speed records.

Even when Amtrak took over independent railroads throughout the nation in 1970, the Reading Railroad's passenger service remained independent, until taken over by Conrail in the late '70s and then by SEPTA in the 1980s. The line created between 1838 and 1842 is still heavily used for freight between the coal regions and Philadelphia by Norfolk Southern (the current owner).[11]

The Reading Terminal has been remodeled as part of the Pennsylvania Convention Center.[12]

Pennsylvania Railroad

The Pennsylvania Railroad was a leading provider of service to the Midwest. Like the Philadelphia and Reading it tried to service the coal regions.

One of the purposes of the line was to combat the advantages that New York had with the building of the Erie Canal. For decades the owners of the Pennsylvania Railroad lived in luscious estates on

Merger of two failing companies

Both the Pennsylvania Railroad and the New York Penn Central were failing before the merger, which formally took place on February 1, 1968. So lesson one is that failing companies shouldn't merge together.

Ten years to complete the merger

The beginning of the book shows that the merger itself took about ten years to complete. There were a variety of legal challenges to the merger, including one by Pennsylvania's Milton Shapp, a local cable owner. When Shapp ran for Governor in 1966, one of his campaign features was his opposition to the merger. Walter Annenberg, who ran

Bay Window, Parlor Car (Interior) by William Herman Rau. Courtesy of American Premier Underwriter's Inc

Philadelphia's Main Line.

In the 1950s the fortunes of the railroad began to decline.

Collapse of the Pennsylvania Railroad

Peter Binzen, a business columnist for the *Bulletin* and the *Philadelphia Inquirer,* and Joseph R. Daughen analyzed the merger of the Pennsylvania Railroad into the Penn Central and the bankruptcy of the Penn Central in their book, *The Wreck of the Penn Central.*[13]

Some of the best known names in business from J.P. Morgan to Cornelius and William Vanderbilt were involved with the New York Central.

The book discusses a number of reasons for the failure and draws lessons for future mergers.

the *Philadelphia Inquirer* at the time, was a friend of the Pennsylvania Railroad owners. According to Binzen and Daughen, Annenberg and his *Philadelphia Inquirer,* along with the railroad owners helped to defeat Shapp's 1966 bid. [Shapp would win in 1970 and 1974]. There were also a number of governmental regulations and obligations to carry some passenger traffic that had to be met. But the bottom line was that during the ten year time frame for the merger, the general times (for example the state of the economy) and the conditions of the companies had deteriorated, making a successful merger less likely. Automobiles and trucks had taken away many of the railroad lines customers.

Too many outside investments

According to the authors, the merged rail-line, Penn Central, held investments in a number of companies that that little or nothing to do with running a railroad. This meant that the energies of the people running the company were spread too thin.

Different cultures

The cultures of the workers and mostly the owners of the two main railroads, the Pennsylvania Railroad and the New York Central, were very different. New York Central was run by Alfred E. Perlman, a New York Jew who was not a joiner of clubs and by a number of Harvard MBAs. They focused on innovation, sometimes at the expense of knowing the basics. Pearlman had dealt mostly with failing companies.

The Pennsylvania Railroad Management team, headed by Stuart T. Saunders, hired from within its own ranks, and had a history of belonging to the best clubs in the city, like the Merion Cricket Club and the Philadelphia League. They knew the inner workings of railroads but were resistant to change.

Add to the above mix a lack of government support, a terrible winter in 1970, and the merger, the biggest of its day, failed in less than three years. It went into bankruptcy under Judge John Fullam. It ultimately survived bankruptcy but only after its railroad business had been taken over by CONRAIL. Today it survives as an insurance company under another name.

Old Maids

One of the more famous rail lines is the Paoli Local. To memorize the stops passengers recite the mnemonic – Old Maids Never Wed And Have Babies Period. The first letters of each word stand for the stops – Overbrook, Merion, Narberth, Wynnewood, Ardmore, Haverford, Bryn Mawr, and Paoli. The acronym needs work, as there are more stops between Bryn Mawr and Paoli. Several of the stops, Wayne, Wynnwood, and Paoli were exported to Oklahoma when citizens, who moved from the Pennsylvania Main Line to Oklahoma, wanted to remember their hometowns.

More Transportation

During the over three centuries since Penn founded his "Country Towne" in 1682 along the Delaware and the Schuylkill, transportation has undergone many transformations. "Steam replaced sails; the flow of petroleum silenced the rumble of coal; bridges replaced ferries; changes in climate and industrial effluvia eliminated ice-choked rivers; railroad, and then motor vehicles, replaced excursion steamers."[14]

Budd and Car Parts

For years the Budd plant (founded by E.G. Budd) in Huntingdon Valley made car parts, including using metal presses to make doors, roofs, fenders, and side panels for a number of car manufacturers. It recently closed, as have the doors of many manufacturers in the city.

Helicopters

While Boeing is based in Seattle, the Ridley Boeing plant just outside of Philadelphia manufactures helicopters.

Pennsylvania Railroad Art

The Pennsylvania Railroad had its own calendar, where wonderful artists like Grif Teller, Harold Brett, Frank Reilly, Alexander Leydenfrost, and Dean Cornwall showed their latest art. The Army-Navy game for years was played in Philadelphia's Municipal Stadium (later named JFK Stadium and later still demolished in 1992). The Pennsylvania Railroad had thirty-six trains to take fans to and from the game.

Left from top:
Philadelphia Old and New by Rob Lawlor.
Courtesy of Rob Lawlor

Main Line of Commerce 1951 in Visions of the Pennsylvania Railroad Featuring the Paintings of Grif Teller. Copyright 1992. Courtesy of the Penn Central Corporation

Mass Transportation 1955 in Visions of the Pennsylvania Railroad Featuring the Paintings of Grif Teller. Copyright 1992. Courtesy of the Penn Central Corporation

TEXTILES

Betsy Ross was an early seamstress. The creation of the loom and other tools to speed the production of clothes paved the way for new industries to make the clothes and bigger stores to house and sell them.

Charles Oakford

Legend has it that "Holy St. Clement whilst performing a pious pilgrimage, eased his weary feet by placing loose fur in his shoes; he discovered at the end of his journey that the hair had become felted into a regular cloth by the motion, heat, and perspiration, and that from thence he deduced the inference that wool and furs might be felted into bodies – from which invention arose the art of making hats"

After renting space for a short time, Charles Oakford set up shop in his mother's kitchen for making hats and rented another shop for preparing the furs. By the next month he had a small "front shop."

CHARLES OAKFORD & SONS MODEL HAT STORE
Nos 826 & 828, Chesnut Street, Continental Hotel, Philadelphia
HATS, CAPS & FURS, WHOLESALE & RETAIL.

Charles Oakford & Sons Model Hat Store ca 1860 by Ibbotson & Queen. Courtesy of The Library Company of Philadelphia

A year later, he moved to 30 Lombard St. where he employed two apprentices. His reasons for success included, "never hold a penny so close to your eyes as to lose sight of a dollar."

In 1830 he received an order for $10,000 worth of hats from a neighbor and a neighborhood merchant who had been watching him. They had discovered a large export market to Mexico. Oakford completed the order in six weeks, two days ahead of schedule. By 1833, he started making brush hats of fine Russian fur. The hats were light and peculiar in appearance but sold many. In 1847 he opened up "the" Philadelphia hat store at a cost of $3,000.

By 1850, Oakford was selling the "Oakford" hat wholesale throughout the entire county. By the time he died in 1862, Oakford set the standard for making a small business big, moving westward, and never being too important for his customers.[15]

Stetson Hats

As a youth, John Batterson Stetson was sent to Colorado for health reasons.

While in the West he was impressed with the local style of a ten-gallon hat. In later years the manufacture of "The Boss of the Plains," as he called his version, was his signature hat.

Like Charles Oakford, Stetson started small – in a one-room store on the northeast corner of 7th and Callowhill Streets and as his hats took hold, he moved to 4th Street above Chestnut "and in no time his hats were being sold in most of the retail establishments in Philadelphia." His novel idea of using traveling salesmen in 1869 created the need for more space to manufacture more hats. Another novel idea of his, to move his factory to the quiet northeast area of the city, gave him the space he needed. Eventually those twelve acres held five- and six-story hat factory buildings and the Stetson Hospital.

His aim "to do good work at fair prices" as well as his taking good care of his employees, their families, and the factory neighborhood non-employees, separated this man from the usual manufacturers of the time.

His buildings had the latest safety equipment, including automatic sprinkler systems and fire extinguishers on every floor.

He then set up one of the most liberal apprenticeship programs of that day. Mr. Stetson paid above scale wages and bonuses tied to attainment levels. He provided quite a few rooms in his factory for his employees to use for their religious, social, and other activities. Later, one room was expanded and opened to neighborhood people as well. It is reported to have had a fine organ and space enough to accommodate 2,000 people. There was also a library and parlor for evening socials. Professional entertainment and a 111-piece orchestra were provided every Saturday night.

In fact, there was activity every night of the week. Because of Mr. Stetson's patriotic bend, he organized a military company of young male employees. He had them outfitted and trained and even set up an armory.

Stetson built a dispensary for his employees and a free hospital on the land adjacent to his factory building. Another major assistance he provided for his workers was to establish the John B. Stetson Building Association, which gave them below-market rate loans...The plant was closed in 1971.[16]

Stetson text reprinted with permission of Cheltenham Township.

Fabric Row

In the early 1900s, many Jewish immigrants found their way to South Philadelphia. It is there between 3rd and 7th streets that many of them set up shop. Many opportunities were closed to Jews because of anti-Semitism, so the Jews, like others, found that beginning their own businesses was the way to succeed. Many of them opened a variety of clothing related shops where one could buy the fabrics, the sewing equipment, and the finished goods. The area became known as "Fabric Row." It still survives today. The shops of "Fabric Row" are now located on South 4th Street between Bainbridge and Queen Streets.

1865

1965

Where it began: the first Stetson "factory" - 1865

Stetson Hats. Courtesy of Cheltenham Twp

Sidney Kimmel

Though Mr. Kimmel is now known for his contributions to the new arts center – the Kimmel Center that bears his name – Mr. Kimmel made his fortune in clothing, specifically through his Jones Apparel. The Store manufactures and sells a number of brand-name fashions.[17] Mr. Kimmel is now planning to help fund the National Museum of American Jewish History in Philadelphia with a $25 million dollar donation (it is due to open in 2010) and helps with other worthwhile institutions and charities.

John Wanamaker and Department Stores

Like many early merchants, John Wanamaker learned about business by working his way up the ladder. He started as a handy-boy, then salesmen, and then he, along with a partner, Nathan Brown, purchased an existing clothing retail business. Wanamaker believed in the principal of advertising and for years no one, no company, in the city spent more for ads. More importantly, Wanamaker introduced the idea of trust. Before he started "Suits were never guaranteed, neither were they returnable, and the price was determined by the bargaining skill of the purchaser." Wanamaker advertised "One price only" and "Your money back if not satisfied." "Other principals included welcoming people 'back to the store without urging them to buy' and to plainly mark the price of each article of merchandise."

Opposite Page:
Wanamaker Eagle by Ruth Savitz.
Courtesy of Ruth Savitz

After several moves Wanamaker renovated an old freight station into the world's first department store, known from when it was built in 1876 Wanamaker's day as "The Grand Depot." "The next move, in 1911, was to the Main store near City Hall. It took nine years to build. The opening was attended by President William Howard Taft. Mr. Wanamaker was honored as "America's greatest merchant." Wanamaker purchased a New York clothing business and established foreign branches; one of which, the Paris branch, was run by his son, Rodman."[18]

The Grand Court is in the middle of the store. It has a dome 150 feet high and is surrounded by Ionic and Corinthian columns. It could hold 25,000 people. It's most notable treasure is the Eagle. When Philadelphians wanted to know where to meet the answer was always the same – let's meet at the Wanamaker Eagle. The Eagle weighs 2,500 pounds and is made of bronze. Wanamaker purchased it for $10,000 from the German Exhibition of Arts at the St. Louis Exposition in 1904.

Wanamaker's has the largest organ in the world. It began with close to 18,000 pipes. It now has 28,500 pipes. The organ was first heard in 1911.[19, 20, 21] More specifically, it was first heard in Wanamaker's on June 22, 1911, at the exact moment when England's King George was crowned in Westminster Abbey. President Taft heard the organ later that year when the store was dedicated. To enhance the sound Wanamaker's opened a private pipe organ factory in the store.

The pipes range in size from a quarter-inch to 32 feet.. There are six ivory keyboards and 729 color-coded stop tablets. There are 168 combination buttons and 42 foot controls. The finest organists have performed on the Wanamaker organ. It is now a National Historic Landmark. The pipe work encompasses the resources of three symphony orchestras.[22]

Other notable features included the Christmas light shows, a monorail in the toy section and the Crystal Tea Room on the top floor.

The Wanamaker Store, Philadelphia, Pa, Strawbridge, and Lits

"Wanamaker's was known as the Protestant department store. Strawbridge and Clothier owned by Isaac H. Clothier and Justus C. Strawrbridge was the Quaker store, and Gimbel Brothers along with Lits Brothers was the Jewish store."[23] Strawbridge and Clothier, in addition to its floors of merchandise, "perfected" shopping by mail. Artists made illustrations of the items for sale.[24]

While the Lits Store no longer operates, the building was an architectural wonder. It was renovated in the 1990s and today a variety of stores do business inside.

Isaac Clothier. Original from Philadelphians in Cartoons – Public Domain

BANKING

Philadelphia was known as the "Cradle of American finance." One of its earlier financiers was Robert Morris. Other bankers included Stephen Girard, who first made his fortune in the shipping business, Nicholas Biddle who was president of the Bank of the United States during Philadelphia's most prominent banking era, and Francis Drexel and his sons Tony and Anthony who led Philadelphia in private banking – worldwide.

Robert Morris (1734-1806)

Robert Morris was born near Liverpool, England, in 1734, but left for America at age thirteen. Morris apprenticed under Charles Willing and became a partner to Thomas Willing. He became involved in the West India Trade and then worked in banking plantations. By 1775, he was one of the city's richest merchants. Willing and Morris helped finance the Revolutionary War. In 1781 Morris became American Superintendent of Finance.

"Robert Morris discovered one of the basic rules of economy, the principle that credit is based on confidence and that a government, even though bankrupt, was indeed able to create trust."

The Bank of North America opened in 1782 as the first private commercial bank in the United States bank. It was successful and other commercial banks were soon chartered in other states. Eventually the Bank of North America was re-chartered as a Pennsylvania bank and was later taken over, in 1929, by a life insurance company.

ISAAC F. CLOTHIER,
Capitalist.

Morris's successes didn't last. The Jefferson Republicans, who feared a strong central government in the hands of Northern merchants, opposed him. His efforts to institute taxes through a poll tax, a land tax, a house tax, and an excise tax failed to yield the necessary revenues. So in 1783 he resigned.

He returned to the shipping business where his ship, *The Empress of China*, is believed to be the first American ship to do business with China. His business dealings were dedicated to investments in city real estate and western land. Sadly, his investments were too speculative and he was forced into bankruptcy and debtor's prison. After his release he lived on a pension he obtained with the help of his namesake – Gouverneur Morris.[24a]

Girard was known to be rather tight-fisted during his life. He would call in merchant's loans whenever he needed to support his bank. So it was a great surprise to see how kind he was in his Will, which established Girard College among other philanthropies. After death, he was given credit for his lifetime deeds including personally caring for the dying at Bush Hill hospital, during the yellow fever epidemic of 1793 in Philadelphia.[28]

Nicholas Biddle (1786-1844)

After graduating from Princeton at fifteen, Nicholas Biddle traveled Europe, studied law, handled several posts such as secretary of legislation to London, many of the details of the Louisiana Purchase,

Girard's Bank, Late the Bank of the United States, in Third Street Philadelphia 1828 by William Birch. Courtesy of The Library Company of Philadelphia

Stephen Girard (1750-1831)[25, 26]

Stephen Girard, born in France, made his early money in cider, wine bottling, and groceries. He made his fortune in the shipping business building vessels, which he named after great French writers and philosophers like Jean Jacques Rousseau.

Through artful dealing and political shrewdness Girard was able to use the assets of the First Bank of the United States to create the premier bank in the country—Girard Bank. Along with John Jacob Astor and David Parish, Girard helped finance the War of 1812. With the help of former Philadelphia lawyer and Secretary of the Treasury, James Dallas, Girard later helped create the Second Bank of the United States. He left over seven million dollars for the city of Philadelphia, canal construction, and the creation of Girard College."[27]

and helped edit the works of Lewis and Clark.

In 1816, Congress chartered the Second Bank of the United States. After five years of disorder, President Monroe appointed "his friend" Nicholas Biddle to head it in 1823.

He was "czar of American finance" for more than a decade. But with the election of Andrew Jackson in 1832 Biddle's fortunes changed. Jackson saw the U.S. Bank as an enemy of the states and the country. The existence of the bank was the main issue in Jackson's campaign against Henry Clay. Philadelphians wanted the bank and 50,000 people turned out in March 1833 to support it – at Independence Square. But in 1833 President Jackson ordered Biddle's bank to withdrawal its deposits.[29]

Philadelphia had lost out the capitol seat to Washington D.C. in 1800. In 1825, the opening of the Erie Canal withered its commercial dominance. In 1836, when the Second Bank's charter was ended, Philadelphia was no longer the financial capitol.

America, drunk with new democracy, suffered an "era of wild cat finance," which resulted in the panic of 1837, causing the decline of Philadelphia as a banking center and the fortunes of Mr. Biddle.[30]

The Drexels

The founder of the Drexel fortune, Francis Drexel began as a painting apprentice in Europe. He left for America at the age of twenty-six and settled in Philadelphia where he continued as a painter. On a three-year trip to South America, he had hoped to emulate Philadelphia's Gilbert Stuart and his painting of Washington by painting Simon Bolivar of Venezuela. Unfortunately, he painted Bolivar just at the time when popular sentiment turned against Bolivar.

While in South America, he began to appreciate the movements of currency.[31] When the Second Bank of the United States failed, he was able to capitalize on this understanding. Back in the United States he founded a currency brokerage firm in Louisville. In 1847, back in Philadelphia, he changed the name of his firm to Drexel and Co. and brought in his two sons, Tony and Anthony J., as partners. In 1848, the California gold rush helped make the United States attractive to foreign investors. In the 1850s the railroads required a lot of capital to start. Drexel helped furnish the capital and helped trade with foreign investors by establishing branch offices in other locations through a series of mergers.[32] Along with Jay Cooke, the Drexels helped finance the Civil War for the Union.[33]

In 1864, the Drexels, along with George Childs (the successful owner of a book publishing business), purchased the *Public Ledger* newspaper. In 1836, when the Ledger started newspapers were being sold for 5-6 cents. The *Ledger* sold for a penny and with the help of new technology and a perception of independence form political parties rose to be a prominent Philadelphia paper. But the penny cost and technology created debt allowing the 1864 purchase. Childs ran the newspaper and helped it become the second largest paper in the country behind the *New York Herald*. Childs also gave the financial community favorable press (as did many newspapers through the early 1900s).[34]

Self-Portrait with Wife, Catherine, and Daughter, Mary Johanna c. 1854 by Francis Martin Drexel. Courtesy of The Drexel Collections – sm – Drexel University, Philadelphia Pa

After the Civil War, Anthony J. Drexel initiated a meeting (which Dan Rottenberg details in his book, *The Man who Made Wall Street*) with J.P. Morgan who "controlled the fate of railroads and corporations." The meeting led to a partnership where Drexel was able to use Morgan's European connections and Morgan Drexel's money and experience. Drexel chose Wall Street for his New York office and helped start several business trends, which continue today:

• "Trading national currencies
• Guaranteeing credit for citizens abroad
• Rewarding workers based on individual initiative
• 'Sweat Equity' to deserving Employees"[35]

The interests of Tony and Anthony Drexel and J. P. Morgan helped to finance the rest of economic development in the United States through the rest of the nineteenth century and beyond.[36]

In the twentieth century, J.P. Morgan separated from the Drexels. The Philadelphia Drexel company helped finance PECO, PSE&G, the University of Pennsylvania Palestra, and Franklin Field. The vast amounts of wealth the Drexels left allowed subsequent generations of Drexels to live comfortably, though only a few became known for new creations.

Some of the Drexel money left helped found Drexel University. Tony Drexel's daughter, Katherine, was canonized by Pope John Paul II in 2000. St. Katherine used her inheritance to finance a series of missions she developed along business lines similar to the network of firms the Drexels created.

Drexel and Co. merged several times. By 1959 the Drexel money was no longer involved, only the name. By 1973 the firm became known as Drexel Burnham Lambert, which Wharton grad, Michael Milken, would lead.

Milken invested heavily in junk bonds, creating large fortunes in the 1980s and bankruptcy in the 1990s. Milken then devoted himself to helping charities for education and medical research.[38a]

Other Banking Interests

Other Philadelphia banks included the Philadelphia National Bank, The Consolidation National Bank, Mechanics National Bank, the National Bank of the Republic, Chestnuts Street National Bank, Market Street National Bank, The Land Title and Trust Company, and the Corn Exchange National Bank.[38]

Today no major banks are headquartered in Philadelphia, though many banks finance Philadelphia monetarily and through support of a variety of charitable interests.

United States Mint
Text Reprinted with permission of Independence Hall Association

The First Mint: Who Will Make The Money?

The United States' first mint — indeed the first structure sanctioned by the United States government — was erected in 1792, just two blocks from the present site. Many citizens of the new nation were deeply suspicious of federal power. They were accustomed to using coins issued by their own state banks, along with various forms of foreign currency. The suggestion of a single federal mint producing a uniform coinage was disturbing.

A coalition championed by adamant federalist Alexander Hamilton prevailed in these debates. The result was both the First Bank of the United States and a United States Mint. The First Mint was completed in the fall of 1792 in the capital city of Philadelphia. As a new capital city was being built along the banks of the Potomac, it was expected that the Mint would move there. Yet in 1800, when Washington, D.C., was ready, the government did not have the money to replace what was already an efficient operation. An Act of Congress in 1828 ensured that the Mint would remain permanently in Philadelphia.

The Second Mint: Need More Space

By the late 1820s the original Mint lacked the space and capacity to keep up with the demand for coinage. A new Mint designed in the classic style favored by the federal government of Andrew Jackson's era was finished in 1833. It was located on Broad Street, about a half mile west of its current location.

The Third Mint: A Roman Temple

Again, a larger Mint was needed. The third Mint, built in 1901, still stands (it now houses Philadelphia Community College). It is a block long and has a Roman temple's facade. Marble is ubiquitous. Massive Ionic columns lead to a lobby with vaulted ceilings, which were bejeweled with seven Tiffany glass mosaics. The mosaics depicted ancient Roman methods of coinage. Two of the mosaics are seen today at the current Mint.

The Fourth and Present Mint: What's There Now?

Once more, a larger Mint was needed — but also one with better access to highways and with more sophisticated security.

There are today four United States mints: Philadelphia, Denver, San Francisco, and West Point. The bullion depository at Fort Knox is also part of the Mint system.

The Philadelphia facility is the largest mint in the world.

EARLY NINETEENTH CENTURY BUSINESSES

An example (the lithograph is by Nicholas Wainwright) of a business in the nineteenth century and early twentieth are shown.

Hartley and Knight's Bedding Warehouse 148 South Second Street, Philadelphia, ca 1845, 39 x 31 cm. (15.25 x 12.25 in.). Courtesy of The Library Company of Philadelphia

ARTISANS

Betsy Ross (1752-1836)

Text reprinted with permission of Independence Hall Association (source: ushistory.org)

According to tradition – "Betsy would often tell her children, grandchildren, relatives, and friends of the fateful day when three members of a secret committee from the Continental Congress came to call upon her. Those representatives, George Washington, Robert Morris, and George Ross, asked her to sew the first flag. This meeting occurred in her home, some time late in May 1776. George Washington was then the head of the Continental

General Washington showed her a rough design of the flag that included a six-pointed star. Betsy, a standout with the scissors, demonstrated how to cut a five-pointed star in a single snip. Impressed, the committee entrusted Betsy with making our first flag.

Betsy Ross lost two husbands to the Revolutionary war and had her house confiscated by the British. Yet she managed to weave cloth pouches, which were used to hold gunpowder for the Continentals. On June 14, 1777, the Continental Congress, seeking to promote national pride and unity, adopted the national flag. 'Resolved: that the flag of the United States be thirteen stripes, alternate red and white; that the union be thirteen stars, white in a blue field, representing a new constellation'.[39]

The Birth of Our Nation's Flag by Charles H. Weisgerber. Courtesy of Independence Hall Association

Army. Robert Morris, an owner of vast amounts of land, was perhaps the wealthiest citizen in the Colonies. Colonel George Ross was a respected Philadelphian and also the uncle of her late husband, John Ross.

Betsy was also acquainted with General Washington. She had embroidered ruffles for his shirt bosoms and cuffs, and it was partly owing to his friendship for her that she was chosen to make the flag.

After a mix-up (Loyalists, supporters of Britain mistook the flying of a Grand Union flag hoisted by Washington after a victory by the Continental Army in Boston), Washington decided that a new flag was required

According to Betsy Ross's dates and sequence of events she was a widow struggling to run her own upholstery business (which she operated for several decades after the war). 'Upholsterers in colonial America not only worked on furniture but did all manner of sewing work, which for some included making flags'.

Jeweler's Row

Two streets of special interest to shoppers are Jeweler's Row and Antique Row. Jeweler's Row is the country's oldest Diamond District (begun around 1851) and one of the biggest. There are hundreds of jewelry stories on the brick paved streets that run on Sansom Street between Seventh and Eighth and between Chestnut and Walnut Streets. Many Philadelphia wedding rings were purchased on Jeweler's Row.

Mummers[40, 41]

While not a business, per se, the Mummers Parade does produce a lot of money for the city each New Year's. A lot of money and love goes into their costumes.

The Mummers march down the main streets of Philadelphia every New Year's Day. Early Mummers were from Southwark and Kensington and of English and Scotch-Irish descent. "The idea of the parade seems to have come from H.B. McHugh."[42]

Every band that plays in the parade comes from identifiable neighborhoods like South Philadelphia, Kensington, and even Bucks County.

"The Mummers are a fixture of the ethnic communities in South Philadelphia, and organized in a number of social clubs principally located on 2nd Street. There is a Mummers Museum dedicated to the history of Philadelphia Mummers at the corner of Washington Avenue and 2 Street.

About 15,000 mummers perform in the New Year's Day parade each year. The seven-mile-long parade up Broad Street to City Hall starts early in the morning and lasts until it is done. Thousands of Philadelphians line the route and visit open house parties. The clubs participating in the televised parade are judged, and several hundred thousand dollars in the past were awarded in prize money.

The Mummers are organized into four distinct types of troupes: Comics, Fancies, String Bands, and Fancy Brigades. All Mummers dress in elaborate costumes.

Comics start the Mummer's parade. Many Comic skits are based on current events and can be sophisticated, satirical or exuberantly sloppy.

Fancies have spectacular costumes, often huge and covered in ostrich feathers.

The String Bands are large marching bands composed of saxophones, banjos, violins, string basses, drums, glockenspiels, and accordions with dancers and backdrops.

The Fancy Brigades only perform indoors. They perform a complicated dance routine with elaborate backdrops to prerecorded music at the Pennsylvania Convention Center. [Source – Wikipedia]

INDUSTRY

Joseph Newton Pew (1848-1921)

The discovery of oil in Titusville, Pennsylvania, led to the rise of the Pew family fortunes. Joseph Newton Pew married Mary Anderson whose family members were early pioneers in the oil industry in Titusville. In 1880, Pew founded Sun Oil Company. When Joseph Pew died in 1912, his sons continued in the business.

Their legacy, the Pew Memorial Trust, is a major donor to various causes.

Other local oil refining companies included Standard Oil, Atlantic Refining Company, and Quaker City Oil Company.

Joseph Wharton (1826-1909)

Born in 1826, Joseph Wharton was one of ten children. His father was a descendant of Thomas Wharton who came to America in 1683. While Joseph Wharton came from a family of good financial standing, he resolved to make it on his own. He started in a dry-goods house of Waln & Leaming. He soon became manager of a zinc mine. Through experimentation in the production of metallic zinc and spelter, Wharton added to his wealth.

He then manufactured nickel in Camden, New Jersey, across the river from Philadelphia. Wharton invested in the Bethlehem Iron Company. When the Secretary of the Navy wanted a company to manufacture armor plate, the newly named Bethlehem Steel company was asked to help. Joseph Wharton went to France and England where he bought the rights to various patents and helped Bethlehem make gun forgings, armor plates, and ships for the Navy.

The Bethlehem Steel company works was sold to one Charles M. Schwab, founder of a large investment firm. But Wharton still held large interests in iron and steel and foresaw the 1900s development in this area. He was also a scientist and philanthropist.

He founded the Wharton School of Finance and Commerce of the University of Pennsylvania and the Wharton library at Swarthmore. He helped manage and contributed to both schools as well as to many other charities.[43]

Mummers on Broad Street by Howard N. Watson. Courtesy of Howard N. Watson

UNIONS and BUSINESS CLUBS

Carpenters' Hall

The Carpenters' Company, founded in 1724, is not a union. Rather, it was originally an association of master builders who erected Independence Hall, their own meeting place at Carpenters' Hall, and many of Society Hill's mansions. Today's membership of nearly 200 men and women comprise the region's leading architects, building contractors, and structural engineers.

Because the Hall could be rented, it became the home of many new institutions: the First Continental Congress, the First and Second Banks of the U.S., the American Philosophical Society, and the Franklin Institute.

Real unions – in addition to pay, benefit, and working condition issues – became involved in local politics. While these trends were national in scope, they have strongly applied to Philadelphia. Most every business discussed here – transportation, textiles, newspapers, and the rest of the media – depended on workers in various unions.

The success of various Mayors depends on their achieving the right balances between union interests and those of business. Not an easy task in 1877 when the workers on the Pennsylvania Railroad went on strike and not an easy task more recently when union help was a major concern regarding the current Pennsylvania Convention Center.

BUSINESS CLUBS

The Greater Philadelphia Chamber of Commerce

This organization, led in 2006 by Ex Governor Mark Schwieker, is (per their website) "dedicated to supporting and encouraging the continued growth of each of its nearly 6,000 member companies, and the business community at large."

World Affairs Council

The Worlds Affair Council of Philadelphia is devoted to informing the public about national and international matters.

Social Clubs

Some of the early clubs were formed along professional or common interest lines.

Carpenter's Hall Photo. Courtesy of Michael Penn

American Philosophical Society

This society, founded by Benjamin Franklin in 1743, is the nation's oldest learned society. It promotes useful knowledge in the sciences and humanities through excellence in scholarly research, professional meetings, publications, library resources, and community outreach.

Members are elected in the following disciplines:
◊ Mathematical and Physical Sciences
◊ Biological Sciences
◊ Social Sciences
◊ Humanities
◊ The Arts, Professions, and Leaders in Public & Private Affairs

The Society promotes research through the giving of grants and through its various publications.

The Franklin Inn club is for artists and writers.

Other clubs were also formed along social lines. These well known clubs included the Philadelphia Club, Philadelphia's first modern city club, founded by George Cadwalader, a yachtsman and duck hunter; the Acorn club, a female counterpart to the Philadelphia Club; the Rittenhouse Club (founded in 1888 and closed in 1993), and the Union League.

The Union League[44]

The Union League, Reprinted with permission of the Union League (source: email communication)

The Union League of Philadelphia was organized on December 27th, 1862 as a patriotic social society. According to its Articles of Association approved at that meeting, "*The primary object of the association shall be, to discountenance and rebuke by moral and social influences, all disloyalty to the Federal Government, and to that end, the associators will use every proper means in public and private.*" Furthermore, "*The condition of membership shall be unqualified Loyalty to the Government of the United States and unwavering support of its efforts for the suppression of the rebellion.*"

Within a year of its founding, the League attracted 1,000 members to its cause, and 1,500 by the end of the war. They were English, German, Irish, and Italian; Protestant, Quaker, Catholic, and Jewish; industrialists, businessmen, financiers, and artists. They formed committees to fulfill their mission: Military; Publications; Employment for Disabled Soldiers & Seamen; Soldiers Claim & Pension Agency; and Employment for Widows & Orphans. Most importantly of all, the Philadelphia League spawned a national movement that would see over 700 Union Leagues established from Maine to California by the war's end. Beginning in June 1863, the League's Military Committee raised nine army regiments and additional companies, totaling 10,000 men. The Military Committee raised over $100,000 from the members to support its efforts. Also in June, the League received permission from Secretary of War Edwin M. Stanton to raise black regiments. The Supervisory Committee on Enlistment of Colored Troops would raise eleven regiments totaling 11,000 men. Several League members donated land in Cheltenham Township to create Camp William Penn, the first training camp for African-American soldiers in US history. A Board of Publication of the Union League was created in February 1863. Its purpose was to "disseminate patriotic literature" in the form of pamphlets, newspapers, posters, broadsides,

Union League. Courtesy of Union League

and lithographs. All of its funds, in excess of $50,000, were raised by voluntary subscription from members. By the end of the war, over two million pieces of literature had been printed and distributed throughout the entire country.

Today, the League is the largest club in the city, both in terms of its clubhouse and membership, which currently numbers over 3,000. The brick and brownstone Broad Street building opened May 11, 1865. The architect was John Frazer. The Middle and Fifteenth Street sections of the clubhouse, dated 1911 and 1910 respectively, were designed by the architect Horace Trumbauer. Since its founding, the League has hosted American Presidents, heads of state, American and international politicians, and dignitaries, industrialists, and entertainers. Its membership reflects the demographic diversity of Philadelphia and the surrounding Delaware Valley region. For additional information, visit the League's website, www.unionleague.org

BUILDING AND ARCHITECTURE

One constant area of new business has been architecture. Throughout its history, the skyline and street lines of Philadelphia have constantly changed.

While Philadelphia didn't go the way of New York with skyscraper after skyscraper so that one could barely see the sky – it did see new buildings and new styles from the building of Penn Center and Society Hill to the PSFS building which was considered a marvel of architecture at the time of its construction. Other expansion included the buildings along the Benjamin Franklin Parkway, the Academy of Music, and the University of Pennsylvania.

The architects who designed these buildings and their styles and those of their predecessors are for another book. Their firms though have to be counted when summarizing the businesses in the city since the shaping of the skylines and the level eye-views certainly affected how Philadelphians think of themselves and non-locals think of the City.

In the 1800s Philadelphia's Architecture covered a variety of styles. The dominant one was "Greek Revival." Benjamin Harry Latrobe designed the Bank of Pennsylvania. Addison Hutton designed the Ridgeway branch of the Library Company in the 1870s. Architects like William Strickland and Thomas U. Walter made their marks with this style. Strickland's design included the Second Bank of the U.S., the Naval Hospital, and the Merchant's Exchange building. Walter designed Founders' Hall of Girard College, and the dome and some wings of the United States Capitol in Washington, D.C.

Other prominent styles of the nineteenth century included Gothic and historical periods such as Egyptian and Italian and French architecture with buildings like John Notman's Philadelphia Athenaeum, Strickland's Independence Hall, Napoleon Lebruns' Academy of Music, John McArthur's City Hall, and Thomas W. Richards' College Hall for the University of Pennsylvania.

Universities in the last quarter of the nineteenth century began establishing architectural programs based on the Ecole des Beaux-Arts in Paris.

Prisons saw change to embody the new views on penology and many prisons from the Eastern State Penitentiary to Moyamensing's Count Prison were built in the late 1800s.

An understanding of new structural materials and methods helped Philadelphia become a leader in building bridges.

Many architectural drawings and paintings are housed in Philadelphia's Athenaeum, itself a marvelous work of local architecture. The Athenaeum website includes many of the buildings and architects made famous in Philadelphia.[46]

Minerva Parker Nichols

Ms. Nichols was the first woman architect in Philadelphia and earned a national reputation.

Julian Abele. Courtesy of Free Library of Philadelphia

She drew on local colonial traditions using her inventiveness to create new works. These works included factories, foundries, schools, private clubs, inns, and homes in Germantown, Narberth, and Rolling Hill Park.[47]

Horace Trumbauer and Julian Abele

Text reprinted with permission of the Free Library of Philadelphia (source: www.library.phila.gov)

[Horace] Trumbauer and his talented designers, designed the high-rise Adelphia Hotel for the northeast corner of Thirteenth and Chestnut Streets. The next year, he and his staff designed the Stock Exchange on Walnut Street west of Broad… Two years later, Trumbauer employed innovative cast concrete ornamentation for his elegant, French classical Widener Building on South Penn Square. Not long before the United States entered the World War, Trumbauer and his designers planned the impressive, classical Beneficial Savings Fund Society building (1916) at Twelfth and Chestnut Streets.

To the east, Trumbauer built two major buildings, the Georgian style Public Ledger Building (1923), a headquarters for the important daily newspaper, at Sixth and Chestnut Streets and the enormous Ben Franklin Hotel (1925) at Ninth and Chestnut Streets. To the west, in addition to completing the Philadelphia Museum of Art, Trumbauer and his staff erected several buildings, including the sleek Le Chateau Hotel (1928), a skyscraper with Gothic ornament at Nineteenth and Locust Streets on Rittenhouse Square…. Toward the end of his career, in the late 1920s and early 1930s, Trumbauer experimented with a modern style based on the soaring vertical lines of Gothic cathedrals and popularized by illustrator Hugh Ferris, who sketched enigmatic, booming skyscrapers. Relaxing his steadfast commitment to historical styles, he designed two major hospital buildings in Center City in this modern, vertical style, the Hahnemann Medical College building (1927, now called the South Tower) at 230 North Broad Street and the Jefferson Hospital Curtis

Fisher Fine Arts Building. Courtesy of University of Pennsylvania Architectural Archives

Clinic (1930) on Walnut west of Tenth Street. The Trumbauer firm is best remembered for its elegant, dignified buildings in revival styles, especially an eclectic style based on a Beaux-Arts reinterpretation of the classical vocabulary.[48]

Trumbauer, in 1906, hired Julian Abele, a black architect, who worked for Trumbauer for thirty years as the chief designer. Abele helped designed the Widener Library, the Free Library of Philadelphia and Museum of Art, and various buildings on Trinity College (later renamed Duke University) among other projects. Abele became president of the firm after Trumbauer died. He was the first major black architect in America.[49]

Frank Furness (1839-1912)

Frank Furness was a veteran of the Civil War. After the war, Furness applied a Victorian Gothic approach to his buildings, which numbered over 650 and included Philadelphia Zoo Gatehouses, the Pennsylvania Academy of Fine Arts, the Merion Cricket Club, and numerous banks, hospitals, railroad stations, and private residences. Frank Furness is considered by some to be the grandfather of this Philadelphia School of Architecture.

Philadelphia School of Architecture

The Philadelphia School of Architecture was coined by Jan Rowan in an article he wrote in the April 1961 issue of *Progressive Architecture*. While there was no formal school and probably no collaboration among designers there was a commonality among a variety of designers and teachers who trained in Philadelphia, mainly at the University of Pennsylvania, in the late 1950s and early 1960s. The School included an emphasis on understanding the relationship between "place, community, and landscape" through "the use of light and attention to building materials."[50] The hallmarks of this "Philadelphia School" were:

Urbanistic. Weaving old and new like Ed Bacon did in the redevelopment of Society Hill

Real [not slick]. Muscular, commercial, big-boned.

Planned Space flowed properly. "Architecture begins with the making of a room." "The Philadelphia School adopted Kahn's stupendously intelligent diagonal-at-the-corner to solve the classical planning problem of 'turning the corner'."

Modern. "Relentless attention to visual detail and the unflagging confidence that shape, line, and texture could touch the soul."

Socially Responsible

Historical[51]

Louis Kahn (1901/1902 - 1974)

Louis Kahn was trained in the Beaux-Arts tradition at the University of Pennsylvania under Paul P. Cret. One of his influences was the scientist Buckminster Fuller.

Louis Kahn's work, beginning with the Richards Laboratories in 1958, and his lectures at the University of Pennsylvania, emphasized a new vision in modern architecture – a sense of order and a reason for being, "a more personal and sensitive design philosophy." His pupils and faculty members – people like Ehrman ("Bud") Mitchell Jr., Romaldo ("Aldo") Giurgola, Robert Venturi, Robert L. Geddes (former dean of the School of Architecture at Princeton), and other young architects – emerged to become part of what was known in the 1960s as the "Philadelphia School" of architecture.

"Kahn infused his buildings with monumentalism, richness, sweeping ideals, and Jungian archetypes. His guiding light was always the question: "What does the building want to be?" His design for the Salk Institute (1959-1965) realigned architecture with a seemingly eternal ideal."

One of Kahn's themes is the emphasis on function.

Other disciples of the Philadelphia school included Ed Bacon (who headed the Philadelphia City Planning Commission), Robert Geddes (the Pender Laboratory (1953-2003) on Penn's campus, Holmes Perkins (dean of the graduate school of fine arts at Penn, Louis Sullivan (who marked is mark in Chicago) and Aldo Giurgola.

Tom Devaney wrote on the feisty Mr. Bacon's death of the following exchange that occurred when Mr. Bacon spoke at the Kelly Writers House of the University of Pennsylvania.

Question by Michaela Majoun (MM)
MM: Of all your projects in Philadelphia, which one are you the most proud?
EB: Philadelphia.
MM: Yes, Mr. Bacon, which part?
EB: THE WHOLE GODDAMN CITY!
Text from http://www.writing.upenn.edu/wh/bacon.html10/15/05

Architects at Penn also talk of an earlier "Philadelphia School" in the early 1900s, which included Wilson Eyre (The University Museum at Penn) and Frank Miles Day (Houston Hall at Penn).

Louis I. Kahn. from Heinz Ronner, with Sharad Jhaveri and Alessandro Vasella [*Louis I. Kahn: Complete Works 1935-74*. p111, 114.]

Venturi, Scott Brown & Associates, Inc.

Text – Reprinted with permission of Venturi, Scott, Brown & Associates, Inc. © 2006 (source: www.vsba.com)

Robert Venturi and his partner Denise Scott Brown are two of the leading Philadelphia architects working today. Their work ranges from Philadelphia and nearby locations to venues across the world

Franklin Court

This project, a museum and memorial to Benjamin Franklin, is on the site of the home Franklin built for himself, set back from Market Street in the historic Old City in Philadelphia. The museum needs to fit into its context, but maintain a distinctive identity of its own. It is to serve educational and memorial purposes, stimulate its visitors' imaginations, convey a rich history, and reflect Franklin's spirit as well as tell the story of his life and accomplishments.

The response to these multiple challenges departed from the usual museum and memorial architecture by placing the main exhibit area underground and designing a steel "ghost" structure to represent the original house. This preserved as open space the site of Franklin's garden. Viewing ports are provided to allow visitors to see the few archaeological remains of the house uncovered during earlier research on the property. Quotes from Franklin's letters to his wife during the house's construction are engraved in the paving. The five historic houses that had faced Market Street were reconstructed; two are archaeological exhibits, the

Franklin Court by Mark Cohn. Courtesy of Venturi, Scott Brown and Associates, Inc.

Benjamin Franklin Bridge by Matt Wargo for VSBA. Courtesy of Venturi, Scott Brown and Associates, Inc.

others house administrative offices and a shop. As in Franklin's time, they enclose the garden beyond. The entry to the memorial through a passageway under these houses has a sense of discovery and drama. The inner court's landscaping recalls an eighteenth century garden. It has comfortable accommodations for visitors and is sturdily designed for intense use.

Benjamin Franklin Bridge

Unlike conventional bridge and architectural lighting, which tends to emphasize large structural elements such as piers and roadbeds, this design highlights the suspension cables themselves from below to create a glowing curtain of light across the river.

PSFS Building

Alfred Bendiner, the architect and artist, described the PSFS building as one of Philadelphia's best buildings, even though it could only be entered off the side entrance as the first floor was reserved for a dress shop (at least in Bendiner's day).

The PSFS building was the nation's first fully air-conditioned building and the first modern skyscraper. It was built in 1932. The Building today is a Lowe's Hotel.

Liberty Place. Courtesy of James. J. Kelly

Willard Rouse and Liberty Towers

In the late twentieth and early twenty-first century, the leading developer in the city was Willard Rouse whose One and Two Liberty Place structures broke the old rule that no building could be higher than William Penn's hat.

Rouse was involved in a number of city ventures including the Kimmel Center, the Philadelphia Stock Exchange Building and the Great Valley Corporate Center in Malvern

NOTHING MORE MODERN

THE PHILADELPHIA SAVING FUND BUILDING
TWELVE SOUTH TWELFTH STREET

PSFS Building. Courtesy of U.Penn.Architectural.Archives

*the*EXPERIMENTAL PHILADELHIAN

Benjamin Franklin – by Tim Ogline.
Courtesy of Tim Ogline

Picture – Benjamin Franklin

"Can the spring be fairer than in and around Philadelphia when wisteria blossoms on every wall and the coating is white with dogwood?"
Elizabeth Pennell, Writer

*the*EXPERIMEN

HILADELPHIAN

PHILADELPHIA SCIENCE

NOTABLE STYLES
Experimental Over Deductive
Philadelphia Firsts
Voluntary associations
Self-starters
Innovators

CONTENTS

AL PHILADELPHIAN

THE EXPERIMENTAL PHILADELPHIAN

While scientists do not have an equivalent to the phrase "Philadelphia Lawyer" or the "Philadelphia Sound," Philadelphia can make claim to being the most scientific city in America. This rich scientific history begins, not with Benjamin Franklin, but with William Penn. Penn's "Holy" Experiment, in which a variety of religions were allowed to exist in the same locale, independent of each other, was radically new. It had never been tried before – in America or in the rest of the world. Even two religions in the same region had given rise to many wars. Numerous religions in one location. The great philosopher Voltaire remarked how extreme a notion that idea was.

The second experiment begun in Philadelphia was just as radical. The Declaration of Independence and the writing of the United States Constitution. A Democracy of the People, by the People, for the People. That had never been tried in modern times. One has to go back to ancient Greece and Rome to find anything similar and there the military often had the final say.

The variety of neighborhoods that Penn fostered and the freedom to exercise one's religions, one's rights, within those neighborhoods are two key ingredients to experimentation in all fields: science, the creative arts, politics, etc. For identity and freedom within a neighborhood gives citizens in the neighborhood the confidence to try, to experiment with, new ideas. This is true whether the neighborhoods are Penn's regions of a city or American's states.

Franklin's voluntary associations, which began with his Junto organization, only enhanced experimentation. Voluntary associations had two practical consequences. The first was to allow the citizens of each neighborhood exposure to other neighborhoods where they could test their ideas and where they could adopt or learn from the other neighborhoods. The second consequence was to emphasize the practical side of science – that it should help in the common good. This combination of exposure and practicality meant a greater likelihood that ideas would not only be shared but would be useful – thus creating better experiments, and better products.

Add to the mix Franklin's examples of the self-starter in forming a newspaper or flying his kites to prove the flow of electricity and the stage was set for Philadelphia's originality.

In his day Franklin's voluntary associations led to the creation of many institutions in the scientific realm like the Philosophical Society, the Free Library, the Fire Department, and many other groups designed to help those within the group help those beyond the group. His inventions were aimed to help people in their daily lives, whether it was seeing with bifocals or keeping warm and safe with the Franklin stove and the lightning rod. Due to Franklin, Philadelphia's scientists, businessmen and creators became famous for a number of scientific "firsts" that the world has adopted.

Since Penn and Franklin, magazines found their home in Philadelphia and America through *The Ladies Home Journal* and *The Saturday Evening Post*, both published by Philadelphia's Curtis Publishing. Television and the computer were invented in Philadelphia. Commercial advertising and cable have their roots in Philadelphia. The first movie mogul, Siegmund Lubin, was based in Philadelphia. Lubin also helped invent some of the instruments used to project films. The Langenheim brothers (William and Frederick) of Philadelphia mastered the daguerreotype process necessary for photography. Atwater Kent made many of the nation's radios. Philadelphia could rightly be called America's Media Innovator. The ENIAC computer was the first all-purpose general computer. It was invented at the University of Pennsylvania.

The Fairmount Waterworks was an engineering marvel of the nineteenth century. Chemistry and manufacturing included and still include a variety of innovations based in Philadelphia.

Philadelphia has been and still is a leader in medicine with some of the best teaching hospitals and pharmaceutical developers in the world. Botany got its start with John Bartram and William Barton and continues with the Philadelphia Flower Show and Longwood Gardens among other "greene" contributions to the city's beauty. The city is home to numerous Nobel Prize and Franklin Award winners, discoveries, and inventions.

The roots for this experimentation, this love of new ideas, were set long ago, by Penn and Franklin. The crucible of letting ideas bubble up from the bottom, self-starting, sharing of ideas, the freedom and encouragement to experiment, and the financial backing of the city have made Philadelphia and will continue to make Philadelphia a leader in not only scientific and technical innovation but all professions and walks of life.

PHILADELPHIA FIRSTS

During the 1700s and 1800s, Philadelphia's firsts included the creation of various institutions and schools including:

"The Philadelphia Hospital, the oldest in America, was established in connection with the Philadelphia Almshouse." 1732

"The American Philosophical Institution, the first institution devoted to science in North America, was founded at Philadelphia by Benjamin Franklin, John Bartram, Dr. Thomas Bond, Thomas Godfrey and others." 1743

"The Pennsylvania Hospital, the first establishment in North America devoted to the relief of the sick and suffering, was chartered by the Assembly of Pennsylvania, at the solicitation of Benjamin Franklin, Dr. Thomas Bond, Rev. Richard Peters and others." 1751

"The first school of anatomy in North America was opened in Philadelphia by Dr. William Shippen in 1762."

"The first United States flag on record, was made here on Arch Street, by Elizabeth Ross." 1777

"The first agriculture society on this continent was 'The Philadelphia Society for Promoting Agriculture', formed by Dr. Rush, Robert Morris, Richard Peters and others in 1785."

"The Philadelphia Water Works, the first of the kind in the country, were commenced, and the water first sent through the pipes January 21, 1801."[1]

Benjamin Franklin founded the first medical school in America at the College of Philadelphia (now the University of Pennsylvania).

"The Philadelphia Zoo opened to the public on July 1, 1874. 1938 saw the country's first baby petting zoo and 1957 the first children's zoo. In 2003, the Zoo was home to over 1600 animals including the blue-eyed lemur, first exhibited at the Philadelphia Zoo. Other animals first exhibited at the Philadelphia zoo include the first births of cheetahs, the first white lions and the first chimpanzee birth at a zoo."[2]

James P. Bagian (M.D., P.E.) NASA Astronaut
[from the NASA website]

Dr. Bagian, a graduate of Philadelphia's Central High, Drexel University, and Thomas Jefferson Medical School was the first astronaut to treat another astrounaut space-motion sickness in outer space.

Dr. Bagian became a NASA astronaut in July 1980. One of his areas of expertise is Shuttle search and rescue planning.

Dr. Bagian first flew on the crew of STS-29, which launched from Kennedy Space Center, Florida, aboard the Orbiter Discovery, on March 13, 1989. His flight experiments included treating Space Motion Sickness with the drug Phenergan by intramuscular injection. This treatment method became a NASA standard.

On June 5, 1991, STS-40 Spacelab Life Sciences (SLS-1), the first dedicated space and life sciences mission was launched from the Kennedy Space Center, Florida, on June 5, 1991. SLS-1: It was a nine-day mission during which crew members performed experiments which examined how the body responds to microgravity.

"Other experiments of Dr. Bagian examined the causes of space sickness, and changes in muscles, bones, and cells which occur in humans during space flight, and experiments designed to investigate materials science, plant biology and cosmic radiation."[3]

Dignity by Ruth Savitz. Courtesy of Ruth Savitz

BOTANY

John Bartram (1699-1777)

Text reprinted with permission of John Bartram Association (www. bartramsgarden.org)

An unassuming Quaker farmer with a rudimentary education, John Bartram became widely known in America and Europe as an eminent botanist. Famed Swedish botanist Carolus Linnaeus called him 'the greatest natural botanist in the world' and his work is still held in high regard today.

Bartram traveled the wilds of the American colonies in search of curious seeds and plants to bring back to his garden. His goal was to document all the native flora of the New World.

Bartram's most famous discovery is the Franklinia alatamaha tree, which he is credited with saving from extinction.

William Bartram (1739-1823)

John's son, "William Bartram" was America's first native born naturalist/artist and the first author in the modern genre of writers who portrayed nature through personal experience as well as scientific observation. Bartram's momentous southern journey took him from the foothills of the Appalachian Mountains to Florida, through the southeastern interior all the way to the Mississippi River. His work thus provides descriptions of the natural, relatively pristine eighteenth-century environment of eight modern states: North and South Carolina, Georgia, Florida, Alabama, Mississippi, Louisiana, and Tennessee. William Bartram published an account of his adventure in 1791. It quickly became an American classic and *Bartram's Travels* has been described by one scholar as "the most astounding verbal artifact of the early republic."

Bartram's book became an immediate success in Europe where it influenced the romantic poets and armchair travelers who savored the descriptions of exotic, sub-tropical Florida as well as the relatively unexplored southeastern interior. Particularly enlightening and appealing were Bartram's accounts of the Seminole, Creek, and Cherokee Indians. During the first quarter of the nineteenth century William Bartram became the grand old man of American natural science, advising and mentoring the first generation of naturalists who were beginning to explore the new territories being added to the young nation.

The Bartram Trail Conference, Inc., founded in 1976, has sought to identify and mark Bartram's southern journey and works to promote interest in developing recreational trails and botanical gardens along the route. The BTC also seeks to encourage the study, preservation, and interpretation of the William Bartram heritage at both cultural and natural sites in Bartram Trail states.

The Franklinia Story

The exquisite Franklinia alatamaha tree, which boasts late summer blossoms, striking fall foliage, and an extraordinary history, is the most famous discovery of American botanists John and William Bartram.

The father and son explorers discovered a small grove of this unknown tree growing along the Altamaha River in Georgia in 1765. On a later trip, William gathered seeds to propagate at their Philadelphia garden. They named the tree Franklinia alatamaha in honor of John Bartram's great friend, Benjamin Franklin.

The tree was never again seen in the wild after 1803, but fortunately, because of the Bartrams, Franklinias still do exist. All Franklinias growing today are descended from those propagated and distributed by the Bartrams, who are credited with saving it from extinction.

The Franklinia tree is gaining an increased popularity among gardeners enticed by its delicate beauty, marvelous story of survival, and even perhaps its reputation as a challenge to grow![4]

Like many intellectuals of his era, Bartram was interested in all things philosophic and scientific. He studied the medicinal uses of plants and sometimes treated neighbors who could not afford medical care. He became a member of the Library Company and founded the American Philosophical Society with his friend, Benjamin Franklin.

The homestead of John Bartram (1699-1777), America's first botanist, co-founder of the American Philosophical Society, and a towering figure in colonial Philadelphia's scientific community, today is America's oldest living botanical garden. The 45-acre site on the Schuylkill River in Southwest Philadelphia features Bartram's eighteenth century home and farm buildings, historic botanical garden, wildflower meadow, water garden, freshwater wetland, parkland, river trail, and a museum shop. The house was named a National Historic Landmark in 1963.

Bartram and his heirs lived in the stone house over a period of 125 years. The garden continued to flourish under Bartram's descendants, who accomplished another first – publishing the new nation's first catalogue of American plants in 1783.

In the mid-1800s the Bartram homestead and garden were purchased by Philadelphia industrialist Andrew M. Eastwick, who resolved to preserve the Bartram legacy. In 1891 the City of Philadelphia bought the property as a public park and historic site. The non-profit John Bartram Association formed in 1893 to assist the City with care of the site.

Today the John Bartram Association operates Bartram's Garden as a house museum and botanical garden in cooperation with the Fairmount Park Commission and welcomes some 30,000 visitors annually. The Continental Congress adjourned a session specifically to visit John Bartram's garden.[5, 6]

Batram's Garden. Courtesy of John Bartram Association

Franklinia. Courtesy of John Bartram Association

William Barton (1754-1817)

Text Reprinted with permission of Academy of Natural Sciences (source: www.ansp.org)

Another early botanist was William P.C. Barton who taught at the University of Pennsylvania. His *Flora (published by Matthew Carey and illustrated by his wife) shows the work of early botanists.* "As was the case with many early botanists, Barton was also a physician, and served as a surgeon in the United States Navy. In the text with his drawing of Liriodendron tulipifera (tulip tree), he writes, "This magnificent tree may be considered not only as the pride and ornament of the American forest, but as the most superb vegetable of the temperate zones" and that "the bark of the tulip-tree is considerably stimulant." In his 1818 Philadelphia flora, he says it is "On the borders of rich woods, and in fields; common." Today it is the dominant forest tree in Fairmount Park.

Alexander Wilson (1776-1813)

Text Reprinted with permission of Academy of Natural Sciences

Alexander Wilson is considered by many to be the father of American ornithology. Born in Scotland he emigrated to the U.S. in 1794, at the age of twenty-eight. Wilson was a self-taught artist, and studied masters such as Mark Catesby. In 1804, when Wilson decided to create American Ornithology, he started accumulating material for his work in the Niagara area. Departing from Philadelphia in 1809, Wilson set out on a walking trip that was to take him to New Orleans. His purpose was to collect further material for his volumes and to sell subscriptions. On this trip he met John James Audubon in Louisville in 1810.

Wilson's American Ornithology portrayed more than three-fourths of the American birds known to have existed at that time. The engraving and coloring of Wilson's work was done in large part by Scottish-born Alexander Lawson, a Philadelphia engraver who specialized in subjects of natural history. Wilson died in 1813 during the production of American Ornithology, which was completed from Wilson's notes and sketches assembled by George Ord, a founder of the Academy of Natural Sciences of Philadelphia.

John James Audubon (1785-1851)

John James Audubon was born in Saint Domingue (now Haiti), the illegitimate son of a French sea captain and plantation owner and his French mistress. He was raised by his stepmother in Nantes, France. In 1803, aged eighteen years, his father sent him to American, in part to escape the Napoleonic Wars. He lived on the family-owned estate at Mill Grove, near Philadelphia. It was here that Audubon first began drawing and studying birds.

He traveled the Mississippi to learn more about birds that he had to shoot first in order to be able to study them. He used fine shot and learned how to wire the birds back together after he shot them so they would look like they did when they were alive.

He set sail for London to earn more money with his drawings. The British loved the Backwoods American and Audubon was able to raise enough funds to publish Birds of America, 435 life-size prints made from engraved plates. He followed up Birds of America with Ornithological Biographies, histories of each species written with Scottish ornithologist William MacGillivray.

In 1842, he published an American version of *Birds of America*. The National Audubon Society is named in his honor.[7]

Alexander Wilson and Alexander Lawson. "Roseate Spoonbill," Plate LXIII in American Ornithology, Volume VII. Philadelphia: Bradford and Inskeep. Courtesy of The Library Company of Philadelphia

Philadelphia Flower Show
Rich in History and Tradition

All Flower Show text reprinted with permission of the Pennsylvania Horticultural Society (source: www.philadelphiaflowershow.com)

Philadelphia, as William Penn envisioned with his parks and plan for a greene country towne, has been home to America's first horticultural society in 1827, and the nation's first flower show in 1829.

The first exhibition "brought together a variety of exotic and native plants that included magnolia, peonies from China, an India rubber tree, the Coffee Tree of Arabia, and sugar cane from the West Indies." "Under the direction of the Society's president, Jane G. Pepper, the Philadelphia Flower Show has blossomed into the leading show of its kind in the nation."

The spectacular gardens created by local nurseries and florists, exhibitors from around the world with their splendid offerings of sculpted gardens and floral artistry that have become the hallmark of the Philadelphia Flower Show. With its global recognition, the Show is the nation's most looked-to event for landscape and floral design ideas.

"The Flower Show has had homes at Masonic Hall on Chestnut Street, Convention Hall, the Civic Center, and now the Pennsylvania Convention Center. With its 1996 move, the Flower Show Today is the largest indoor Flower Show in the world entertaining crowds of nearly 300,000 people annually."[8]

Ernesta Drinker Ballard (of the famous Drinker Family and a Republican feminist) was one of the pioneers who helped the Philadelphia Flower Show, Philadelphia Green, and the Fairmount Water Works grow.

Philadelphia Flower Show-CF Bourb. Courtesy of © Pennsylvania Horticultural Society

Philadelphia Green

One of the successful programs of the Pennsylvania Horticultural Society (PHS) is the Philadelphia Green program, which is dedicated to helping make gardens grow in a number of vacant city lots, helping maintain city landscape, and giving youth an appreciation of horticulture. The proceeds from the Flower Show, as well as the contributions of many businesses like PNC Bank and charities like the Pew Charitable Trusts, help many neighborhoods regain their dignity by bringing beauty and a sense of community to vacant or blighted neighborhoods.

The style of the PHS involves an exhausting process that includes a lot of planning before topsoil is trucked to the community. The person credited with moving the PHS into such a "civic" force was Ernesta Ballard. She, along with Jane Pepper President, Blaine Bonham Jr. Executive Vice President, and numerous volunteers confirm Franklin's ideals of people working together for the common but practical good.[9]

Philadelphia Flower Show by Danielle Liss Blackham. Courtesy of Danielle Liss Blackham

Philadelphia Flower Show by Danielle Liss Blackham. Courtesy of Danielle Liss Blackham

Philadelphia Flower Show by Danielle Liss Blackham. Courtesy of Danielle Liss Blackham

Philadelphia Flower Show. Courtesy of Pennsylvania Horticultural Society

Philadelphia Flower Show – Waterloo.
Courtesy of © Pennsylvania Horticultural
Society

Philadelphia Flower Show by Danielle Liss
Blackham. Courtesy of Danielle Liss Blackham

Philadelphia Flower Show. Courtesy of
Pennsylvania Horticultural Society

Azalea Garden.
Courtesy of ©
Pennsylvania
Horticultural Society

Chanticleer by
Larry Albee.
Courtesy of
Chanticleer

Chanticleer

786 Church Road Wayne, PA
Text reprinted with permission of Chanticleer
(source: www.chanticleer.org)

Chanticleer is indeed a pleasure garden, offering an escape from the rush of every day life and a place where one can feel like a personal guest of the Rosengarten family. Chanticleer was the estate of Christine and Adolph Rosengarten, Sr., head of the pharmaceutical company Rosengarten and Sons. Their son Adolph Jr. left the property to be enjoyed as a 35-acre public garden. The garden has been open to the public since 1993. The *Washington Post* called Chanticleer "...one of the most interesting and edgy public gardens in America." The garden focuses on plant combinations, containers, textures, and colors, often relying on foliage more than flowers. Tens of thousands of bulbs clothe the ground in spring, followed by orchards of flowering trees with native wildflowers blooming in the woods. A vegetable garden complements a cut-flower garden. Courtyards are a framework for unusual combinations of hardy and tropical plants. Vines grow in nooks and crannies, trailing and twining. A serpentine of cedars, boulders, and agronomic crops undulates through a mown hillside. A woodland garden carpeted with Asian groundcovers and full of rarities leads to a water garden surrounded by exuberant perennials. A ruin plays with indoor/outdoor relationships and contrasts the light and dark sides of gardens. Sculptural, homemade seats, benches, wrought iron fences, and bridges highlight the uniqueness and personal nature of the garden.

Morris Arboretum

100 East Northwestern Avenue, Philadelphia, PA

The Penn-owned Morris Arboretum in Chestnut Hill is home to some 13,000 plants of 2,500 varieties from twenty-nine countries (including healthy specimens of Japanese camellia and a stately Engler beech that Wilson likely collected). It owes its varied inventory to plant exchanges and collecting trips that began in the late 19th century.

Before the University of Pennsylvania took them over in 1933, the grounds belonged to the estate of John and Lydia Morris. Unmarried siblings whose father had owned what was later named the Port Richmond Iron Works, the Morrises were true Victorian collectors. They collected Chinese pottery, Roman glass, Mediterranean coins, garden styles, and many plants. "They were really interested in the world around them," says Meyer, "and one way they expressed this interest was through these collections." (They also had the vision that their plant collections would be used as an educational tool for others one day.)

The siblings were not exactly rough-and-tumble adventurers—Lydia traveled with her tea set, and they stayed with rajas and other royalty when possible. But "relative to their life here in the United States, they were roughing it," given the state of travel lodgings at the time, Gutowski says. They also exchanged specimens with Harvard's Arnold Arboretum and Wilson (who later joined that institution from England's Veitch Nursery), among others.

Penn's botany department ran the Morris Arboretum from 1933 until 1975, at which point it became a multidisciplinary research center of the University. After decades of almost no plant exploration, the arboretum sent Paul Meyer (then curator) to Korea in 1979. Since then, the arboretum staff has taken more than a dozen collecting trips—all in collaboration with other institutions.[10]

Text reprinted with permission of the Morris Arboretum and the University of Pennsylvania

Morris Arboretum. Courtesy of University of Pennsylvania

Scott Arboretum of Swarthmore College

500 College Avenue, Swarthmore, PA
Text reprinted with permission of Scott Arboretum (source: www.scottarboretum.org)

It is a garden of ideas and suggestions. Encompassing more than 300 acres of the Swarthmore College campus and exhibiting over 4,000 kinds of ornamental plants, the Arboretum displays some of the best trees, shrubs, vines, and perennials for use in the region. The Arboretum is a living memorial to Arthur Hoyt Scott (Swarthmore Class of 1895).

Kohlberg Hall provides a dramatic backdrop for this garden which features plants with gold and purple foliage. Trees, shrubs, perennials, bulbs, and groupings of bold containers adorn low rock walls and vine covered pillars.

Scott Outdoor Amphitheater by Rebecca Robert. Courtesy of Scott Arboretum

Other Gardens:

Additional wonderful Philadelphia Gardens include the Japanese Garden in Fairmount Park, the Zoologicial Gardens, and the Wyck Gardens in Germantown.

Fairmount Park

Reprinted with permission. Independence Hall Association http://www.ushistory.org/

Fairmount Park (4,180 acres) is the largest landscaped park in the U.S. We can walk, bicycle, rollerblade, or drive along Kelly and West River Drives today and feel ourselves deep in the country. In the depths of the Wissahickon Ravine and at other points in the park, the city's tall buildings are not visible over the treetops, and if it were not for the hum of traffic on the Drives, we could be in the pastoral world that Thomas Eakins painted. It was Eakins who immortalized the scullers on the Schuylkill — some of these paintings such as "The Biglen Brothers Practicing" are exhibited today at the Philadelphia Museum of Art. The "Mount" for which the park was named is the rise on which the museum stands.

Fairmount Park was the site of the Centennial Exposition of 1876, and several buildings from that earlier fair still stand, notably Memorial Hall. One of the world's largest municipal parks, Fairmount contains several million trees; the oldest zoo in the U.S.; Boathouse Row; cherry blossoms to rival those along D.C.'s Potomac Basin; Robin Hood Dell, an outdoor venue for soul-filled summer singers; the Mann Music Center, the Philadelphia Orchestra's (and others') summer amphitheater; picnic areas; tennis courts; miles of bicycle paths; bridle paths; an azalea garden; hundreds of statues and monuments; and two dozen or so eighteenth- and nineteenth-century buildings, which comprise an unusual historical patrimony.

Many of the homes in Fairmount Park were country estates for some of the city's leading citizens. Perhaps the most famous is Lemon Hill [please see the art section for a painting of Lemon Hill]. This estate was the home of Robert Morris who signed the Declaration of Independence and was a major financier of the Revolution. Unfortunately, he went broke and Henry Pratt, a Philadelphia merchant picked up the home at a sheriff's sale in 1799. The home, as it now stands, was built in 1799. It became known as Lemon Hill because Pratt planted lemon trees. Eventually Fairmount Park took over Pratt's home and many of the other famous homes. Today the following homes and architectural wonders can be seen in Fairmount Park.

- Belmont Mansion
- Belmont Water Works
- Boathouse Row
- John Bolsen House
- Car Barn
- Cedar Grove
- Chamounix
- Fairmount Park
- Hatfield House
- Horticulture Center
- Landsdowne
- Laurel Hill
- Lemon Hill
- Letitia House
- Lighthouse
- Memorial Hall
- Mount Pleasant
- Ohio House
- Ormiston
- Philadelphia Museum of Art
- Pine Breeze
- Ridgeland
- Rockland
- Sedgeley
- Solitude
- Strawberry Mansion
- Sweetbriar
- Woodford

Text Reprinted with permission of Independence Hall Association

Shofuso by Ruth Savitz. Courtesy of Ruth Savitz

Longwood Gardens
Route 1, PO Box 501
Kennett Square PA

Text reprinted with permission of Longwood Gardens (source: www.longwoodgardens.org)

Longwood Gardens was originally inhabited by the native Lenni Lenape Tribe. William Penn acquired the land and later sold it to a Quaker family named Pierce. The farm was purchased in 1906 by Peirre du Pont so he could preserve the trees, and from 1907 until the 1930s Mr. du Pont created most of what is enjoyed today. In 1946, the Gardens were turned over to a foundation set up by Mr. du Pont, and after his death in 1954 Longwood's first director was hired. Since that time Longwood Gardens has matured into a magnificent horticultural showplace.

Exquisite flowers, majestic trees, dazzling fountains, opulent conservatory, starlit theatre, thunderous organ—all describe the magic of Longwood Gardens, a horticultural showstopper where the gardening arts are encased in classic forms and enhanced by machine-age technology.

Pierre du Pont was the great-grandson of Eleuthère Irénée du Pont (1771-1834), who arrived from France in 1800 and founded the DuPont chemical company. Pierre turned the family business into a corporate empire and used his resulting fortune to develop the Longwood property.

Longwood owes its present-day success to fortuitous circumstances. The Pierces, who planted the trees, actively pursued a Quaker interest in natural history. The site was known by 1850 as one of the finest collections of trees in the nation, and by that time its aesthetic qualities were as important as its botanical significance...

At the age of thirty-six, Mr. du Pont bought the Peirce farm and began creating what would become Longwood Gardens. He followed no grand plan; rather, he built the gardens piecemeal as the mood touched him, beginning with the 600-foot-long Flower Garden Walk in 1907. Although his later gardens would draw heavily on Italian and French forms, this early effort reflected what he termed an "old-fashioned" influence, with nostalgic cottage-garden flowers, exuberant shrubs, rose-laden trellises, and even a shiny gazing ball. The scale was grand, the accessories quaint.

The springtime effect of the Flower Garden was so successful that in June of 1909 Mr. du Pont hosted the first of many garden parties. These fêtes became the highlight of the summer social season and encouraged Pierre to look for ever more wonderful ways to delight his guests...The massive Conservatory opened in 1921, a perpetual Eden sustained by twentieth-century fuel oil. It would be hard to imagine a more theatrical setting for the indoor display of plants, unless it would be to the music of a massive

Christmas Display. Courtesy of Longwood Gardens

pipe organ, which he added in 1921 and replaced with one three times as large in 1930.

With the Conservatory a reality, Pierre turned his attention to another great love—fountains. Never mind that Longwood didn't have an abundant water supply; with electricity, anything was possible.... At the Open Air Theatre, he replaced the old waterworks with 750 illuminated jets. His hydraulic masterpiece was the Main Fountain Garden in front of the Conservatory: 10,000 gallons a minute shot as high as 130 feet and illuminated in every imaginable color....

Who could resist eternal spring in the midst of a cold Pennsylvania winter? Or outdoor entertainment under the stars followed by gushing torrents of rainbow-hued water? Mr. du Pont had devised a permanent world's fair of plants enriched by engineering and technology for the enjoyment of family, friends, and the public alike.

...When Pierre died in 1954 at the age of eighty-four, he left Longwood with a well-established horticultural tradition, experienced businessmen (his nephews) as trustees, and a sizeable endowment...

A picnic area and a plant nursery were established in 1956, the same year that an orientation center opened and guide maps were printed. A Desert House and thirteen outdoor water lily pools were constructed in 1957. New greenhouses devoted to tropicals opened in 1958. A plant breeding program was initiated in 1960, and, two years later, a new Visitor Center with a shop, auditorium, and 1,000-car parking lot on the former golf course showed a major commitment to the public....

Since DuPont's death, the Gardens have constantly been expanded and evolved.

Longwood's foremost influence on American horticulture has been through its educational programs, in keeping with Mr. du Pont's desire to establish "a school where students and others may receive instruction in the arts of horticulture and floriculture." For the past three decades, as many as 5,000 students a year have attended Continuing Education classes designed for both amateur and professional gardeners and nurserymen....

Longwood's extensive performing arts program is a logical outgrowth of Pierre du Pont's interest in music and theatre and takes advantage of the many performance spaces he created.

Spectacular fireworks and fountain displays attract 5,000 spectators on summer evenings, and more than 200,000 visitors come to see 400,000 lights outdoors at Christmas. Longwood combines the gardening arts with technology, and the results are unforgettable.

MECONOPSIS
East Coast anomaly blooms at Longwood Gardens
Meconopsis 'Lingholm'

"Once in a blue moon, you may see a blue poppy on the East Coast – one or two at the Philadelphia Flower Show perhaps, or a prized specimen nurtured in a private greenhouse. But to see masses of blue poppies in bloom, you needed to travel to the lands of cool summers: Scotland, Alaska, the Himalayas. Not anymore. Longwood Gardens has successfully produced a crop of blue poppies that, in February & March, are on display in the Conservatory's Exhibition Hall.

After several years of research and experimentation, Longwood has developed a strategy that works. In October, Blue Poppy Nursery in Alaska ships young plants to Longwood, where the production greenhouse facility becomes the poppies' interim home. The greenhouses' state-of-the-art technology enables Longwood to simulate the environmental conditions of a Himalayan summer. By early March, the plants are in flower and ready to go on display in the Conservatory, never having experienced the sultry temperatures of summer in the Mid-Atlantic."

Meconopsis. Courtesy of Longwood Gardens

RENASSAINCE MEN

BENJAMIN FRANKLIN'S DISCOVERIES AND INVENTIONS

Text reprinted with permission of the Franklin Institute (source: www.fl.edu)

Franklin was not a professional scientist. Franklin, in the classical tradition of Philadelphia scientists, worked on problems that were practical and useful. They were meant to solve problems. Franklin applied the old adage – "Necessity is the mother of all inventions."

Bifocals

Franklin solved his frustration of having to constantly switch between glasses for near-sightedness and far-sightedness by cutting the lenses of each in half and putting them in one frame. Today bifocals are used by many, especially the elderly.

Franklin Stove

In Franklin's day many homes were made of wood. Fires were built inside which kept people warm but had the hazard of causing fires. Franklin's solution was to build an "iron furnace stove, also know as the Franklin Stove. The appliance allowed people to warm their homes less dangerously and with less wood.[11]

Lightning Rod

Franklin spent the summer of 1747 conducting a series of groundbreaking experiments with electricity. He wrote down all of his results and ideas for future experiments in letters to Peter Collinson, a fellow scientist and friend in London who was interested in publishing his work. By July, Ben used the terms positive and negative (plus and minus) to describe electricity, instead of the previously used words 'vitreous' and 'resinous'. Franklin described the concept of an electrical battery in a letter to Collinson in the spring of 1749, but he wasn't sure how it could be useful. Later the same year, he explained what he believed were similarities between electricity and lightning, such as the color of the light, its crooked direction, crackling noise, and other things. There were other scientists who believed that lightning was electricity, but Franklin was determined to find a method of proving it.

By 1750, in addition to wanting to prove that lightning was electricity, Franklin began to think about protecting people, buildings, and other structures from lightning. This grew into his idea for the lightning rod. Franklin described an iron rod about eight or ten feet long that was sharpened to a point at the end. He wrote, 'the electrical fire would, I think, be drawn out of a cloud silently, before it could come near enough to strike...' Two years later, Franklin decided to try his own lightning experiment. Surprisingly, he never wrote letters about the legendary kite experiment; someone else wrote the only account fifteen years after it took place.

In June of 1752, Franklin was in Philadelphia, waiting for the steeple on top of Christ Church to be completed for his experiment (the steeple would act as the "lightning rod"). He grew impatient, and decided that a kite would be able to get close to the storm clouds just as well. Ben needed to figure out what he would use to attract an electrical charge; he decided on a metal key, and attached it to the kite. Then he tied the kite string to an insulating silk ribbon for the knuckles of his hand. Even though this was a very dangerous experiment, (you can see what our lightning rod at the top of the page looks like after getting struck), some people believe that Ben wasn't injured because he didn't conduct his test during the worst part of the storm. At the first sign of the key receiving an electrical charge from the air, Franklin knew that lightning was a form of electricity. His twenty-one-year-old son William was the only witness to the event.

Two years before the kite and key experiment, Ben had observed that a sharp iron needle would conduct electricity away from a charged metal sphere. He first theorized that lightning might be preventable by using an elevated iron rod connected to earth to empty static from a cloud. Franklin articulated these thoughts as he pondered the usefulness of a lightning rod:

May not the knowledge of this power of points be of use to mankind, in preserving houses, churches, ships, etc., from the stroke of lightning, by directing us to fix, on the highest parts of those edifices, upright rods of iron made sharp as a needle...Would not these pointed rods probably draw the electrical fire silently out of a cloud before it came nigh enough to strike, and thereby secure us from that most sudden and terrible mischief!

Franklin began to advocate lightning rods that had sharp points. His English colleagues favored blunt-tipped lightning rods, reasoning that sharp ones attracted lightning and increased the risk of strikes; they thought blunt rods were less likely to be struck. King George III had his palace equipped with a blunt lightning rod. When it came time to equip the colonies' buildings with lightning rods, the decision became a political statement. The favored pointed lightning rod expressed support for Franklin's theories of protecting public buildings and the rejection of theories supported by the King. The English thought this was just another way for the flourishing colonies to be disobedient to them.

Franklin's lightning rods could soon be found protecting many buildings and homes. The lightning rod constructed on the dome of the State House in Maryland was the largest 'Franklin' lightning rod ever attached to a public or private building in Ben's lifetime. It was built in accord with his recommendations and has had only one recorded instance of lightning damage. The pointed lightning rod placed on the State House and other buildings became a symbol of the ingenuity and independence of a young, thriving nation, as well as the intellect and inventiveness of Benjamin Franklin."

(Text reprinted with permission of the Franklin Institute)

For his efforts, Benjamin received honorary degrees from Harvard College, Yale College, and the College of William & Mary. The prestigious Royal Society in London recognized Franklin with a gold medal in 1753 and inducted him as a member in 1756. Such an honor was rarely bestowed upon an individual from fledgling colonial America, where scientific research had not yet been fully developed. What made the achievement even more remarkable was the fact that Franklin had no formal education in the sciences, relying purely on his personal intellect and curiosity. Despite the accolades, Franklin remained modest. He even refused to patent the lightning rod or attempt to profit from it.[12]

DOCTOR BENJAMIN RUSH (1745-1813)

Dr. Benjamin Rush was the only doctor to sign the Declaration of Independence. Merriweather Lewis, of Lewis and Clark exploration fame, consulted Dr. Rush before the expedition. Dr. Rush gave Mr. Lewis a variety of herbs and other health-related items.

The first chemistry text in the United States was prepared by Dr. Rush, who helped found the University of Pennsylvania – School of Medicine, of Dickinson College, and of Franklin College, precursor to Franklin & Marshall.

Dr. Rush's work included a humane approach to physical illness. He wasn't without critics. He supported blood-letting as a treatment for some diseases, a popular theory in his day. President George Washington died, "probably from excess blood-letting for a throat infection." Dr. Rush would die from the disease of typhus.

President John Adams appointed Dr. Rush Treasurer of the United States, a post he held until his death in 1813. The friendship with President Adams would prove useful as Dr. Rush helped two enemies, President John Adams and President Thomas Jefferson, put aside their differences and communicate, through letters, with each other. David McCollough, the historian, used those letters in his wonderful biography *John Adams*.[13]

David Rittenhouse (1732-1796)

David Rittenhouse was self-taught. His most famous astronomical instruments were "two orreries he constructed for the Colleges of New Jersey (now Princeton University) and Philadelphia (now the University of Pennsylvania). These orreries show the solar and lunar eclipses and other phenomena for a period of 5,000 years either forward or backward.

He would go on to become president of the prestigious American Philosophical Society (Franklin preceded him, Thomas Jefferson followed him) and served as a legislator, administrator, financier, state treasurer, and the first director of the United States Mint. He was also an astronomer, mathematician, instrument maker, and one of the nation's leading scientists at the time (with the exception of Benjamin Franklin).

His surveys included work on the Mason-Dixon line between Pennsylvania and "Ellicott's Line," the western boundary of Pennsylvania. Among other tools he used the Vernier compass (which he arguably invented) for his surveys. He wrote a number of important papers on astronomy, including "a paper putting forth his solution for locating the place of a planet in its orbit." He was a leader in the scientific comunity's observance of the transit of Venus in 1769, which won him broad acclaim. Rittenhouse wrote similar mathematical papers and experimented with magnetism and electricity.

"He was elected a member of the American Philosophical Society in 1768, serving over the years as curator, librarian, secretary, vice president, and, from 1791 to 1796, its president. He was elected to its committee to observe the transits of Venus and Mercury in 1769 based on plans he had made. Over the years he received a number of honorary degrees, including those from the Colleges of New Jersey and Philadelphia. In addition he was elected a member of the American Academy of Arts and Sciences, and a fellow of the Royal Society of London."

Rittenhouse used his skills to aid the American cause of the Revolution – first on the scientific side by helping improve rifles and in the selection of gunpowder mills. Later in the 1770s he served in a variety of political capacities including as a member of the Pennsylvania Constitutional Convention of 1776, and the Board of War. From 1779 to 1787 Rittenhouse was Treasurer of Pennsylvania, and from 1792-1795 he served as Director of the U.S. Mint. He served as a Professor of Astronomy and as a trustee of the University of Pennsylvania.[14]

William Penn's "Southwest Square," now Rittenhouse Sqaure was also renamed in his honor.

Philadelphia's inventive role in the movie industry (the part played in inventing film and the movie projector) is covered in the film section.

NEWSPAPERS
Franklin's Business – Printing
Most citizens know that Benjamin Franklin left Boston to live and work in Philadelphia. While Franklin was noted, along with Thomas Jefferson, for being a true "Renaissance Man," it was his printing operations that were his first viable venture of note.

His most famous publications were a newspaper called *The Pennsylvania Gazette* and his annual *Poor Richard's Almanack*. "He believed in the power of the press, using his printing press as a way to bring the news to all people. He used cartoons and pictures so that everyone could understand the news, even people who had not learned to read." In 1731, he founded America's first circulating subscription library.[15]

The Pennsylvania Gazette was a paper that expressed a full range of viewpoints and was open to all. This helped it become successful financially.

While working with his brother, James, in Boston, Franklin used names such as Silence DoGood, Cecilia Shortface, Anthony Afterwit, and Alice Addertongue who penned letters to the editor that Franklin actually wrote.[16] He would use his wit to get his points across in Philadelphia, as well. When he was criticized for mistakenly allowing an advertisement in his paper that offended many, he wrote the following parable to point out that try as one might you can never please everybody:

"A certain well-meaning man and his son were traveling towards a market town, with an ass which they had to sell. The road was bad, and the old man therefore rid [rode], but the son went afoot. The first passengers they met asked the father if he was not ashamed to ride by himself and suffer the poor lad to walk along through the mire: this induced him to take up his son behind him.

He had not traveled far when he met others, who said they were two unmerciful lubbers to both get on the back of that poor ass, in such a deep road. Upon this the old man gets off and lets the son ride alone.

The next they meet called the lad a graceless, rascally young jackanapes to ride in that manner through the dirt while his aged father trudged along on foot: and they said the old man was a fool for suffering it.

He then bid his son come down and walk with him, and they traveled on leading the ass by the halter; but then met another company, who called them a couple of senseless blockheads for going both on foot in such a dirty way when they had an empty ass with them, which they might ride upon. The old man could bear it no longer.

My son, he said, it grieves me much that we cannot please all these people. Let us throw the ass over the next bridge, and be no further troubled with him."

Franklin then explained that in his case, as editor of *The Pennsylvania Gazette*, he would never throw the ass over the bridge (would never refrain from printing something) just to please everyone.[17]

While *The Pennsylvania Gazette* did try to be objective, Franklin did not hesitate to use his *Poor Richard's Almanac* to give his views. *The Almanac* was coined after Richard Saunders who actually was a real person who did have an almanac. Saunders had died by the time Franklin began his publication.

The Almanac (shorthand for the phrase "All Man's Knack") was a popular book in Franklin's day and Franklin used it for a number of purposes, including dispensing his own personal advice. [These pearls of wisdom are reviewed in the Humor Section along with Franklin's *Drinker's Dictionary* and other writings].[18]

One of the most notable writings in the *Almanac* was actually a hoax that Franklin copied from the legendary satirist Jonathan Swift. Franklin did have a rival almanac publisher by the name of Mr. Titan Leeds. In Franklin's almanac, Franklin's penname – Richard Saunders – predicted Mr. Leeds' death in 1733. Mr. Leeds protested that he was alive and wrote a 1734 Almanac to prove his point.

Franklin responded by saying that the 1734 *Leeds' Almanac* could not have been written by Mr. Leeds since it included a number of aspersions and assaults on Franklin's good name, and knowing that Mr. Leeds was a good and honorable man, it must have been somebody else who had set forth those aspersions and assaults.

When Mr. Leeds finally did die in 1739, *Poor Richard's Almanac* responded by saying, what a shame it was that the publishers of the Leeds almanac had kept the truth of Mr. Leeds' failure to die in 1733 alive for six years.[19]

Humor aside, *Penn's Gazette* was devoted to commenting and helping the business of the day. Advertisements promoted local concerns.

Franklin nationalized his *Gazette* when he allowed relatives throughout the colonies to print it. He helped circulate his paper through his work as postmaster. In short, Franklin was America's first media mogul.

Other notable publishers follow: A summary of the reporters and lead stories would take volumes.
Matthew Carey and Henry Charles Lea
Born in Dublin in 1760, Matthew Carey's father said you can choose among twenty-five professions and Carey, to his father's dismay, chose printer/bookseller. Carey wrote a pamphlet on the necessity of repealing the penal code against the Roman Catholics. The advertisement announcing this treatise was "spicy and sensational." The Irish parliament denounced it and sought Carey's arrest. Carey's father sent him to Paris where he became acquainted with Franklin and Gilbert du Motier de La Fayette.

Carey returned to Ireland where his continued attacks on the British government led to his arrest. After imprisonment, but still essentially on parole, he fled to Philadelphia.

Lafayette, who was in Philadelphia on Carey's arrival, sent for Carey and loaned Carey $400 to start a newspaper – *The Philadelphia Herald*, first published on 1/25/1785. Carey managed to be severely wounded in a duel with a rival owner of *The Independent Gazette*. He then started up a serial magazine called the *Columbian*. The costs were too high and Carey started *The American Museum*, which published for six years.

Carey then quit to become a printer, bookseller, and stationer. In 1802, Carey wrote essays on the propriety of uniting the booksellers and printers of the U.S. He was one of the first to call for more tax on personal property in proportion to real property. His best work was "The Olive Branch, or Faults on Both Sides," which summarized the problems on both sides of the War of 1812.

Between 1819 and 1833 he wrote fifty-nine pamphlets on the protection of American industry. His businesses devolved to his two sons (as was the trend for many early and even later Philadelphia businesses) who did a large business as publishers and booksellers.[20]

The Henry Charles Lea family, according to Digby Baltzell's *Philadelphia Gentlemen* carried on the tradition of pamphleteering. Henry Charles Lea was "proper Philadelphia's most profound scholar, ardent reformer, and successful publisher." One of the early members of the Union League, he eventually resigned when that bastion of conservatism refused to throw its weight on the side of municipal reform. He organized several reform associations, including the committee of 100 – a leading reform group today. Retiring in 1880, Lea devoted the rest of his life to philanthropy and the writing of history. His "History of the inquisition of the middle ages," published in 1888, is the definitive work on the subject of his day.[21]

Joshua Bertram Lippincott

Born in 1857, Lippincott founded the family publishing house – Bibles, prayer books, *Lippincott's Pronouncing Gazeteer*, *Lippincott's Magazine* and *The Medical Times* among other publications. While Vice President of the J.B. Lippincott Company at No. 229 South Sixth Street. Mr. Lippincott was also V.P. of the Wharton Steel Company, President of the Hibernia mine railroad, V.P. and Director of the Wharton and Northern Railroads, and a Director of the Farmers and Mechanics National Bank. He was a patron of the arts, a University of Pennsylvania Trustee, a member of the Union League and various clubs, including the Art, University Corinthian Yacht, Franklin Poor Richard, and Huntingdon Valley clubs. His son – Craig Lippincott – was President of J.B. Lippincott.[22]

Philadelphia Newspapers

The Philadelphia Inquirer (first called the *Pennsylvania Inquirer*) began in 1829 as a strong supporter of Andrew Jackson's principles. The *North American* began in 1839. *The Public Ledger* was the first "penny" paper, after printing presses made publication easier. It started in 1836 and changed the way newspapers got the news. Instead of waiting for the news to be reported to the paper's main desk by organizations involved in or related to the news, the *Ledger* sent out reporters to gather the news and report back. The *Ledger* also started the tradition of having newsboys sell the papers in addition to having the paper mailed to subscribers.[23]

In the late 1800s, there were over a dozen Philadelphia newspapers. *The Ledger* was the largest, followed by the *Times*. Other papers included the *Press*, the *North American* and the *Bulletin*.[24] *The Public Ledger* (morning and evening); the *Inquirer*, and the *Bulletin* were all Republican. David Stern's, *The Record*, was a Democratic challenger. There were plenty of ethnic papers from the black *Philadelphia Tri-*

J. B. Lipincott. Original from Philadelphia in Cartoons – Public Domain

George W. Ochs. Original from Philadelphia in Cartoons – Public Domain

bune (founded by Christopher Perry in 1884), to the Jewish *Exponent*, the Catholic *Standards, Patryota* (a Polish journal), *Nord Americka* (a German one), the *Germantown Courier*, the *Kensingtonian*, the *South Philadelphian*, the *Union Labour Review*, and others.[25]

Sadly, a number of papers began to expire. *The Public Ledger* and the *Evening Ledger* were gone by 1942. *The Record* died because of longtime labor supporter Stern's indignation at a bitterly fought strike a few years earlier ("How could they do it to me?" [a long time supporter of Unions], Stern asked.") The largest paper to end was the *Evening Bulletin*, which William Lippard Mclean and his sons ran. The *Evening Bulletin* had the catch-phrase "Nearly Everybody Reads The *Bulletin.*" The afternoon *Bulletin* lost out to the morning *Inquirer* when the nationwide trend of cities towards one paper hit Philadelphia.[26]

The owner of *The Philadelphia Inquirer* in the early 1920s was Moses Annenberg (by way of Chicago). Annenberg also owned *The Miami Tribune*, but he made his fortune through his ownership of the *Daily Racing Form*. Moses Annenberg owned a wire service to bookmakers, racing and gambling papers in New York, among other ventures. He was tried for tax evasion, pled guilty, paid millions in back taxes and interest, and was sentenced to three years in prison. Some say the indictments were payback for *The Philadelphia Inquirer's* opposition to FDR's New Deal.[27]

Moses left *The Philadelphia Inquirer* and his other publication interests (in the new name of *Triangle* publications) to his son Walter Annenberg, who ran the newspaper until 1969 when he sold *The Philadelphia Inquirer* and the *Philadelphia Daily News* to John Knight. Annenberg's *Triangle* publications also included a radio and television station, *WFIL, TV Guide, Seventeen Magazine*, the *Morning Telegraph*, and *TV Guide*.

Annenberg, who served as U.S. Ambassador to the Court of St. James and was knighted by the Queen of England, was best known for his charitable contributions. He established the Annenberg School of Communications at the University of Pennsylvania and brought in Kathleen Jamieson to run it.

He donated Annenberg Hall to Temple, gave the United Negro College Fund a $50 million dollar grant, gave over $350 million to the University of Pennsylvania and made substantial charitable contributions to the arts and a host of other interests.[28, 29] The Annenberg Center for the Performing Arts at the University of Pennsylvania is also named after Walter Annenberg.

In 2002, Walter Annenberg died. His widow was recently listed as the richest Philadelphian.[30]

In 2006, The Philadelphia Media Holdings, headed by local marketing executive Brian Tierney, brought the *Philadelphia Inquirer* and the *Philadelphia Daily News* back under local management.

MAGAZINES
Curtis Publishing

Another successful publisher about the time of Lippincott was Curtis Publishing founded by Cyrus Hermann Kotzschmarr Curtis (1850-1933). Curtis Publishing was located in the Curtis Building on Independence Square. One of Curtis's first magazines was the *Ladies' Home Journal* – the leading woman's magazine of its day. The *Journal* provided "advice on clothes, food, house, decoration, manners, and morals" to the "entire middle-class female populace of the United States."

The male counterpart was *The Saturday Evening Post. The Post* included wonderful fiction, "colorful advertising," and covers by illustrators like Norman Rockwell. Its run was halted not by other magazines but by the "advent of television after World War II."[31]

"Other writers included Rudyard Kipling, Theodore Dreiser, Sinclair Lewis, G. K. Chesteron, H. G. Wells, Arnold Bennett, John Galsworthy, Gilbert Parker, and Stephen Crane.

George Horace Lorimer held conservative views and this was reflected in the articles he published in the magazine. Upton Sinclair wrote that the material in *The Saturday Evening Post* was as "standardized as soda crackers; originality is taboo, new ideas are treason, social sympathy a crime, and the one virtue of man is to produce larger and larger quantities of material things." However, Lorimer did employ the radical David Graham Phillips, who wrote over fifty articles criticizing the rich and power. By December 1908, Lorimer was able to announce in the *Saturday Evening Post* that for the first time the journal was selling over a million copies a week.

In March 1916, Lorimer agreed to meet Norman Rockwell, a twenty-two year old artist from New York. When Lorimer saw his work, he immediately accepted two front covers Rockwell had produced and commissioned three more. This was the start of his long-term relationship with the magazine that was to last over forty-five years. Other illustrators who produced front covers during this period included Joseph Leyendecker, Charles Marion Russell, and Walter Everett."[32]

As for the presses and magazine publishers in 2008, there's *Philadelphia Magazine*, which turned 100 in 2008, three University Presses – Temple, Penn, and St. Joseph's – and only two medium-sized independent Presses – the Running Press and Camino Books. There are a few smaller presses but the rise is in television, cable, and the Internet, not the written word.

*Triple Self Portrait by Norman Rockwell. Collection
of the Norman Rockwell Museum, Stockbridge,
Massachusetts. Courtesy of John Rockwell*

Television And Philo Taylor Farnsworth

Text reprinted with permission of the Franklin Institute and Paul Schatzkin (Author, The Boy Who Invented Television, http://farnovision.com)

Philo Taylor Farnsworth was born in Utah. It was there that he came up with the fundamental idea that would launch television's creation. To pursue his dream, Farnsworth moved to Philadelphia, where he joined forces with Philco (the Philadelphia Battery Storage Company), who agreed to fund Farnsworth's venture.

According to the organization Broadcast Engineers, Farnsworth, in 1933, installed one of the first TVs, where his "… son watched 'Steamboat Willy' a Mickey Mouse cartoon over and over again."

In 1933 Farnsworth struck out on his own running of his venture out of his home in Wyndmoor, just outside of Philadelphia.

In 1934, at the Franklin Institute, Farnsworth demonstrated the first full scale demonstration of electronic television anywhere in the world. Residents lined up around the block to see the demonstration which ran for twenty days." To entice people to come, Farnsworth's camera would allow visitors to see their own image on the screen. Other early actors for Farnsworth's television experiment at the Franklin Institute were Joan Crawford and W.C. Fields. Also appearing were members of Farnsworth's family and the Philadelphia's skyline.

Farnsworth's company also built the first electronic video switcher, which allowed for cutting from one camera to another.[33]

Farnsworth's main competition in the development of television was RCA, run by David Sarnoff. RCA had made a fortune in the radio business and was using its money and clout to win the patents for the television idea. Philco was paying large radio royalties to RCA and their initial invitation to Farnsworth was in part to get a leg up on RCA. Philco was so anxious to have Farnsworth succeed they wouldn't even let him take time off to bury his son back in Utah. That's when Farnsworth left.

Photograph of Philo T. Farnsworth, et al. *Philo T. Farnsworth with his wife Pem and two unidentified individuals with his experimental television camera and monitor on the steps of his Mt. Airy home in Philadelphia, ca. 1935. Courtesy of The Historical and Interpretive Collections of The Franklin Institute, Inc., Philadelphia, PA.*

RCA claimed that their employee, Vladimir Zworkin, invented the key element "an electrical image which is the key step in the process of converting light into electricity" in 1923. They claimed that Farnsworth's claim, filed in 1927, was interfering with their prior invention. Farnsworth claimed that he had the idea back in 1922 while he was still in high school. RCA wondered how a teenager could have come up with the idea but were surprised when Farnsworth's high-school science teacher, Justin Tolman, verified Farnsworth's story by producing from memory a sketch of the idea (an Image Dissector) that Farnsworth had shown him in 1922.

Farnsworth's claim read as follows:

An apparatus for television which comprises means for forming an electrical image, and means for scanning each elementary area of the electrical image, and means for producing a train of electrical energy in accordance with the intensity of the elementary area of the electrical image being scanned.

In April of 1934, the U.S. Patent office found in favor of Farnsworth. They ruled that both Farnsworth's 1922 idea and Zworkin's 1923 version were not valid, but that the 1927 idea of Farnsworth's was.

RCA waited until the last day of the eighteen month appeal period to appeal.

Meanwhile Farnsworth struggled for funds. The likely backers were radio companies who were already paying royalties to RCA and couldn't risk angering RCA. Adding to the competition to profit off of television, the newly created Federal Communications Commission had yet to set "signal standards." Like computers in the 1990s, this created compatibility problems. People with Farnsworth sets could only listen to Farnsworth stations. Ditto RCA, Zenith, and the other competitors. An added factors in the competition was that A.T. and T. owned the right to the "coaxial cables needed to network the television signals from city to city and investigations by the FCC into monopoly practices of A.T. and T. and RCA, among others.

A.T. and T., in order to deflect attention from the FCC investigation, agreed to enter into a cross-license agreement with Farnsworth where A.T. and T. would have access to Farnsworth's main patent (as well as a host of related ones) and Farnsworth would have access to the cables. The two together could have launched commercial television. Farnsworth's other patents also defeated new initiatives by RCA. Farnsworth's investors took note and together they moved his lab to Indiana.

In December of 1939, Farnsworth and RCA also entered into a cross-license agreement requiring RCA for the first time to pay royalties to someone else – Farnsworth (actually Farnsworth's company – Farnsworth Television and Radio). The Company was acquired soon after the war ended by International Telephone and Telegraph (ITT). Farnsworth remained with ITT, where he concentrated on other ideas, like nuclear fusion, until his retirement in 1967.[34]

The Aftermath

As for television in Philadelphia, it attracted new performers and new shows. Philadelphia now has three local television affiliates and several cable affiliates. Local newscasters Larry Kane (recently retired) and James Gardner have been stalwarts at the anchor desk for decades. Kane moved to New York for a short period but, like many of the Philadelphia lawyers who preferred a local profile, Kane moved back a short time later. One of the few newscasters to make a national splash was Jessica Savitch, who tragically died in an automobile accident several years after she made her switch. The first female on air anchor in a prime-time major market was Philadelphian Marciarose Shestack.

Television stars ranged from Sally Starr to David Morse. "American Dreams" was set in 1960s Philadelphia with "American Bandstand" as the mainstay of the program.

One person who began on radio and made the transition to television was John Facenda who was a news anchor at WCAU-TV for twenty years beginning in 1948.

Facenda was WCAU's first announcer. He had a remarkable ability to connect with the audience and a perfect voice for any medium. It was his warmth though that made him a legend. To calm his nerves he placed a picture of his mother nearby. At the end of each broadcast he would use his famous tagline, "Have a nice night tonight and a good day tomorrow. Goodnight, all." He developed the tagline while with WIP radio.

According to *The Philadelphia Inquirer*, "Facenda received a letter of encouragement when he first used the tagline. The letter suggested that he continue with the tagline because there were a lot of people alone who could use the good cheer the tagline gave. In the 1950s and 1960s, Facenda often had more viewers than the other two competitors combined." [Broadcast Pioneers]

Facenda was also the voice of NFL football films. He was replaced by another Philadelphia legend, Harry Kalas.

Cable

Cable television was born out of necessity: People in the rural areas couldn't easily get television signals. To solve this problem, John Walson, who sold local televisions in Mahanoy City, in the mountains of Philadelphia, in the 1940s, put an antenna on top of a large utility pole nearby. The signal was sent down to his store. In this CATV, Community Antenna Television, was born – using coaxial cable and "self-manufactured 'boosters' (amplifiers)."

Milton Jerrold Shapp (who later became governor of Pennsylvania) figured out how to "consolidate" all the plethora of antennas that had matured by the 1950s – even in the city. He used a master antenna (MATV) – which was able to carry multiple signals at once. Nearby, an appliance store salesman, "Robert (Bob) Tarlton," used Mr. Shapp's system for his hometown – thus beginning cable television, similar to its use today. Originally designed to enhance reception, people like Mr. Walson and others figured out how to use microwave to bring in signals from different cities, expanding the range of channels for viewers. Originally free, cable owners figured out how to make money – charge for the usages. The first company to do this was HBO, Home Box Office, in November 1972 out of Wilkes-Barre, Pennsylvania. HBO's signal is now carried by satellite, allowing it to service millions of viewers.

Text Paraphrased from Federal Communications Commission – History of Cable Television

Philadelphia Skyline (showing Comcast Building) Photo. Courtesy of Michael Penn

Comcast

Comcast was founded by Ralph Roberts, Daniel Aaron, and Julian Brodsky in 1963 with the purchase of a 1,200 subscriber cable system in Tupelo, Mississippi. The company was renamed Comcast Corporation from American Cable Systems and incorporated in Pennsylvania in 1969. It grew through a series of acquisitions, including partial or full purchases of Westinghouse's Group W. Cable, Barry Diller's QVC, Storer Communications, American Cellular Network Corporation, E.W. Scripps cable systems, and a variety of other cable related purchases.

In 2000, Comcast acquired the interests of Lenfest Communications. H.F. "Gerry" Lenfest "built Suburban Cable, a billion-dollar empire" over three decades. Gerry Lenfest was a house lawyer for Walter Annenberg's Triangle Publications. He is one of the city's major philanthropists.

Currently, Comcast Corporation is the nation's leading provider of entertainment, information, and communications products and services with 24.4 million cable customers, 15.3 million high-speed Internet customers, and 6.8 million Comcast Digital Voice customers. "Comcast is principally involved in the development, management, and operation of broadband cable systems and in the delivery of programming content." (as of 5/26/09)

Products include Digital Cable, High-Speed Internet, and Digital Voice services.

Comcast's content networks and investments include E! Entertainment Television, Style Network, Golf Channel, VERSUS, G4, PBS KIDS Sprout, TV One and ten Comcast SportsNet networks, and Comcast Interactive Media, which develops and operates Comcast's Internet businesses, including Comcast.net and Fancast.com.

Comcast also has a majority ownership in Comcast-Spectacor, whose major holdings include the Philadelphia Flyers NHL hockey team, the Philadelphia 76ers NBA basketball team and two large multipurpose arenas in Philadelphia.

Comcast also delivers its video, high-speed Internet, and voice services to small businesses through its Business Class service.

With its headquarters at the new Comcast Center in Philadelphia, PA, Comcast services customers in thirty-nine states and the District of Columbia. (as of 3/31/09)

Parts of the Comcast profile paraphrased from the Comcast website – www.comcast.com

Radio
Atwater Kent (1873-1949)
Text from the Atwater Kent Museum History (source: www.atwaterkent. info)

Atwater Kent made his mark in the automotive, telephone, and radio manufacturing industries. His automotive work included a "revolutionary ignition system" used by a dozen other car manufactures.

"In 1921 the company received an order for 10,000 headsets. Kent realized that with some retooling his company would be in a position to capture part of the growing market for radios. In 1922 Kent produced his first radio components and in 1923 his first complete radios. By 1924 the company had outgrown its Stenton Avenue campus and moved to a new $2 million plant on Wissahickon Avenue. This plant, constructed in sections, would eventually cover thirty-two acres. In 1925 the Atwater Kent Manufacturing Company became the largest maker of radios in the nation. Supporting the manufacture of radios was the "Atwater Kent Hour," a program broadcast throughout the country in the mid-1920s. The show featured top entertainment and became one of the most popular and acclaimed regular radio programs of the era. In 1929 the company reached its peak performance with over 12,000 employees manufacturing nearly one million radio sets. The plant itself was an architectural sensation and received hundreds of visitors annually.

At this time Kent downplayed the table models for which the company was known and focused on more expensive cabinet models. But he had misjudged the buying public. By 1931 the country was in the midst of the Great Depression. Because of the general economy and competition from other manufacturers, the average cost of a radio had been reduced from a high of $128 in 1929 to $78. Those companies that concentrated on more affordable models, such as Philco, soon captured the market. With declining sales, the Atwater Kent Manufacturing Company closed in 1936. When he died in 1949, Kent held ninety-three patents for improvements in automobile ignition systems and electronics.

The Atwater Kent Museum of Philadelphia was founded in 1938 by well-known radio manufacturer, A. Atwater Kent, at the request of Mayor S. Davis Wilson and local cultural leaders. Kent agreed to purchase the old Franklin Institute Building and reopen it as a museum and library of city history in honor of the 150th anniversary of the signing of the Constitution of the United States. Opening in 1939, the Atwater Kent Museum holds 100,000 objects and images of Philadelphia history spanning 300 years and including the famed wampum belt received by William Penn from the Lenape Tribe, George Washington's presidential desk used when Philadelphia was capital of the United States, and other significant objects of city history.[37]

Radio Stations

Radio broadcasts began in Philadelphia in February in 1922 with the licensing of WGL. Since then a variety of radio stations have caught the ear of most Philadelphians.

Most of these stations were and are typical businesses. Some were set up in local homes and later became worth over one-hundred million. Others were established to promote other ventures such as Lits Departments Stores and Gimbels, and to promote local newspapers. A number of radio stations were engaged in head-to-head competition with each other until one was left standing, forcing the other to change formats.

EARLY AM STATIONS – WCAU [Many radio stations are covered in the music chapter]

WCAU – William Durham began the radio station in 1922 at 1936 Market Street. In 1927 William Paley bought United Independent Broadcasters. Paley used $500,000 of his family's money to purchase the network, which he renamed Columbia Broadcasting System (CBS). WCAU was the network's flagship station. WCAU moved to new facilities at 1622 Chestnut, the first building in the country constructed expressly for radio use.

The Chestnut Street location had seven studios and a sound workshop for Leopold Stokowski. One studio was large enough to hold the entire Philadelphia Orchestra, which played live over the CBS Radio Network from WCAU. Two in-house bands played for WCAU.

Some of the many people listeners could hear on WCAU included Jack Benny, Eddie Cantor, Edgar Bergen, Bing Crosby, Frank Sinatra, Kate Smith, Red Skelton, Guy Lombardo, the Dorsey Brothers, Will Rogers, Arthur Godfrey, Burns and Allen, Fred Allen, and Edward R. Murrow, just to name a few.

Local personalities included Bill Dyer, Taylor Grant, Norman Brokenshire, Alan Scott, Bob Menefree, and columnist Jack McKinney. "Stan Lee Broza's Horn" & "Hardart's Children Hour" was a popular show.

Two newspapers, *The Philadelphia Record* and *The Philadelphia Evening Bulletin*, took over ownership in the 1940s. CBS acquired WCAU, in 1958, for fifteen million six hundred thousand dollars. Since the 1960s talk radio has been the format with such hosts as Larry King, Frank Rizzo, Dominic Quinn, Steve Fredericks, and Harry Gross, among others.[38]

Eniac and The Development Of The Computer
Text reprinted with permission of the Rare Book & Manuscript Library, University of Pennsylvania (source: ww.library.upenn.edu)

John W. Mauchly (1907-1980) worked at the Moore School of Electrical Engineering between 1941 and 1946. Mauchly, along with J. Presper Eckert (1919-1995), helped in the creation of the first general purpose computer, the ENIAC. Mauchly conceived of the idea while Eckert brought it to life.

Built at the University of Pennsylvania's Moore School of Electrical Engineering, in 1946, ENIAC is an acronym for "Electronic Numerical Integrator and Computer." The ENIAC demonstrated that high-speed digital computing was possible using the then-available vacuum tube technology.

The First Plan

Mauchly drafted a memo during the summer of 1942, outlining the first large-scale digital electronic computer designed for general numerical computations.... A budding association with J. Presper Eckert, who had been the laboratory assistant for the course that Mauchly had taken during the previous summer, provided valuable technical support. Indeed, Mauchly and Eckert together discussed what it might entail to build a large electronic computer.

The memo was carefully drafted to bring together the various interests that would justify an electronic computing project. This included the ability of such a computer to produce ballistics tables—a task on which the Moore School was falling increasingly behind. It also drew attention to the engineering expertise of the Moore School.

Most important, Mauchly laid out the design as a general purpose digital computer. …

Mauchly's memo became the basis for a formal proposal submitted the following year. At this point, the impetus came from Lt. Herman Goldstine of the Ballistics Research Laboratory. Having received a Ph.D. in applied mathematics from the University of Chicago…Goldstine encouraged both the Moore School and the Ordnance Department to support the project. An official proposal was submitted in April of 1943, and the resulting contract, Project PX, gave birth to the ENIAC computer. All together, the U.S. Army provided approximately $500,000 for the ENIAC's development.

Mauchly was never officially a researcher on Project PX. Given his designated duties as an instructor, he was permitted only to act as a consultant to the project. In his spare time, however, Mauchly worked closely with Eckert and others to realize the ENIAC computer. [Project PX: The ENIAC Project, 1942-1946. John W. Mauchly and the Development of the ENIAC computer.]

The ENIAC Computer – Innovations

The ENIAC was a large-scale, general purpose digital electronic computer. Built out of some 17,468 electronic vacuum tubes, ENIAC was in its time the largest single electronic apparatus in the world. There were two fundamental technical innovations in the ENIAC.

[Capable of handling numerous calculations.]

The first had to do with combining very diverse technical components and design ideas into a single system that could perform 5,000 additions and 300 multiplications per second. Although slow by today's standards—current microprocessors perform 100 million additions per second—this was two to three orders of magnitude (100 to 1,000 times) faster than existing mechanical computers or calculators.

The sheer speed of the machine and its limited, but sufficiently versatile, programming mechanisms allowed the ENIAC to demonstrate that electronic computing could be applied to some of the nation's most pressing problems, such as the development of the hydrogen bomb. The significance of electronic computing to national security was an important factor in the birth of the modern computing industry.

[Reliable even with so many vacuum tubes.]

The second, and equally impressive, technical achievement was the machine's reliability. Many others working on large-scale precision machinery, such as electronic fire control systems and differential analyzers, considered the possibility of electronic computation before either Mauchly or Atanasoff. These scientists, however, rejected digital electronic computing, because they felt that a system large enough to do useful computations would require too many vacuum tubes to provide reliable operation.

As the main project engineer for the ENIAC, J. Presper Eckert proved to be an outstanding engineer who overcame the most difficult technical challenges in building the ENIAC. The rigorous vacuum tube reliability studies that he oversaw and the cautious reliability design methods adopted by the entire ENIAC project

Mauchly and ENIAC. Courtesy of University of Pennsylvania – Rare Book and Manuscript Library (John Mauchly Collection)

team made it possible to operate the ENIAC, with all of its vacuum tubes, within a comfortable margin of reliability.

[First public display]

The ENIAC was officially unveiled to the public on Valentine's Day, 14 February 1946. Press releases from the War Department and articles that appeared in popular magazines, such as *Newsweek*, attest to the widespread attention that ENIAC received upon its public dedication. [The ENIAC John W. Mauchly and the Development of the ENIAC computer.]

The ENIAC was divided into thirty autonomous units, twenty of which were called accumulators. Each accumulator was essentially a high-speed ten-digit adding machine that could also store the results of its calculations…

The ENIAC was controlled through a train of electronic pulses. Each unit of the ENIAC was capable of issuing a control pulse that would initiate computation in one or more of the other units. This meant that a 'computer program' on the ENIAC consisted principally of manually wiring the different units of the machine so that they would perform their operations in the desired sequence. A typical program on the ENIAC thus consisted of a nest of wires interconnecting the various units of the machine. Special wiring trays gave some semblance of order to these wires, but programming the ENIAC was nevertheless a difficult affair.

[The programming was sophisticated for the time. The ENIAC was probably the first electronic machine to support the conditional branch instruction, what programmers call the If-then-else instruction.]

Several other units rounded out the basic functions of the ENIAC. A unit known as the 'cycling unit' produced the basic pulse patterns used throughout the machine…IBM punch card readers and printers were employed to deliver data into and out of the machine. [Technical Description of the ENIAC. John W. Mauchly and the Development of the ENIAC computer.]

[Private Uses for Computing. The 1950 Census.]

"Mauchly and Eckert ultimately formed the Electronic Controls Company in downtown Philadelphia. Eckert assumed the task of designing a new computer system, more or less along the lines laid out in von Neumann's report. Mauchly, meanwhile, took on the more general task of identifying the uses of electronic computers. This duty was important, because as a private venture the Electronic Controls Company had to sell its machines if it were to survive. The company's first client was the U.S. Census Bureau." [Out on their Own. 1946-1951. John W. Mauchly and the Development of the ENIAC computer].

Legacy: Commercial Computers

The ENIAC's legacy was larger than just the UNIVAC computer built by the Eckert-Mauchly Computer Corporation. …

MEDICINE and HOSPITALS

Seeing the potential in electronic digital computation, other private firms, including Engineering Research Associates and IBM, soon entered into the business of digital electronic computers. … The first UNIVAC computer was delivered to the Census Bureau in June 1951. …. [The UNIVAC and the Legacy of the ENIAC. John W. Mauchly and the Development of the ENIAC computer.]

Modern-day Philadelphia is the second largest medical research and education center in the United States. The Philadelphia region has more than 120 hospitals and clinics, including 20 teaching hospitals and 6 medical schools; more than 70 manufacturers of medical instruments; more than 60 biomedical research firms and 40 pharmaceutical companies; as well as nearly 10,000 physicians.

Many of these institutions can trace their roots back to a number of firsts, set in Philadelphia. The current status of the medical profession – its leading doctors, discoveries and institutions are material for many more books.

Physicians in Philadelphia formed, in 1774, the Society for Inoculating the Poor, the first benevolent association designed to relieve the horrors of small pox.

The Philadelphia Dispensary for the medical relief of the poor the first of its kind in the United States was established, in 1786, by Dr. Benjamin Rush.

Philadelphia physicians have leant their talents to aiding those who suffered from a variety of diseases from yellow fever epidemics to Legionnaire's Disease.

Current hospitals include:

- Albert Einstein Healthcare Network
- Fox Chase Cancer Center
- Frankford Hospital
- Graduate Hospital
- Hahnemann Hospital
- Jefferson Hospital
- Methodist Hospital
- Pennsylvania Hospital which was founded in 1751 by Benjamin Franklin and Dr. Thomas Bond
- Presbyterian Medical Center
- St. Christopher's Hospital for Children
- Temple University Hospital
- The Medical College of Pennsylvania Hospital
- University of Pennsylvania
- Will Eye Hospital
- And a host of community hospitals

Many of these hospitals are ranked, in various specialities, as some of the best in the country.

Two early medical organizations were:

The College of Physicians of Philadelphia[39]

Located at 19 South 22nd Street, Philadelphia PA 19103
www.collegeofphysicians.org
Text reprinted with permission of The College of Physicians of Philadelphia (www.collegeofphysicians.org)

Take Two Aspirin and See Your Electrician by Bruce Johnson. Courtesy of Bruce Johnson

The College of Physicians of Philadelphia is a not-for-profit educational and cultural institution dedicated to advancing the cause of health while upholding the ideals and heritage of medicine. The College of Physicians of Philadelphia was founded in 1787 by twenty-four prominent Philadelphians, including John Redman (1722-1808), elected first president of The College; John Morgan (1735-1789), founder of America's first medical school; and Benjamin Rush (1745-1813), a signer of the Declaration of Independence and vigorous advocate of many humanitarian and social causes.

The College, according to its constitution, was founded "to advance the Science of Medicine, and thereby lessen human misery, by investigating the diseases and remedies which are peculiar to our country" and to promote "order and uniformity in the practice of Physick." Dr. Rush, the primary mover behind the founding of the institution, further articulated these aims when he declared in a speech to the newly-formed College that it should collect and publish medical observations and inquiries on health-related topics, hold regular meetings, cultivate a botanical garden, and create a medical library. Developing a national dispensatory and advising government bodies on matters pertaining to the health of American citizens were also goals Rush articulated. Though not all of Rush's aims were immediately carried out, all of them have been achieved in the long history of the College

The Library was founded in 1788 when John Morgan donated sixteen of his own books to the College. Other members followed

suit and, soon, they determined to collect books, provide an adequate place to keep them, and regularize borrowing procedures. The first librarian was appointed in 1792. Books, journals, manuscripts and other material accumulated gradually. The greatest benefactor of the Library to date has been Dr. Samuel Lewis (1813-1890), a true bibliophile, who donated thousands of books to the College, including medical incunabula and a rare first edition of William Harvey's De Motu Cordis (1628).

The Historical Medical Library now collects only in medical history and related fields. Our retrospective collection development policy is designed to improve the Historical Medical Library's capabilities as one of the world's leading resources for the history of western medicine through the late twentieth century.

In the history of medicine, The College is a renowned center for study as well as a prestigious repository. The Francis Clark Wood Institute for the History of Medicine, founded in 1976 to make better known to the scholarship community the rich historical resources of the Library and the Mütter Museum of The College of Physicians of Philadelphia, provides money for short-term fellowships and a year-long scholar in residence program. Conferences have also been held, including one whose theme was "'A Melancholy Scene of Devastation': The Public Response to the 1793 Philadelphia Yellow Fever Epidemic (1993).

Today, over 1,500 Fellows (elected members) continue to convene at The College and work towards better serving the public. Our outreach programs include PhillyHealthInfo.org, a neutral

PHARMACEUTICALS

Philadelphia has been and is home to numerous pharmaceutical companies and innovators. The most famous was Albert Barnes, the noted art collector. Glaxo Smith Kline, Wyeth, and Bristol Meyer Squibb in Princeton, and other companies, all helping out the medical profession, are all nearby – though many have, like other prominent Philadelphia businesses, been acquired by or merged with businesses outside of the city.

CHEMICAL COMPANIES
Dupont

Dupont, based in nearby Wilmington, Delaware, was founded as an explosives manufacturer. In 1902, Pierre S. Dupont and two other cousins helped transform the company to a modern corporation involved in the production of synthetic textile fibers, paints, varnishes, plastics, and heavy chemicals.

Other products it has or is involved with include Lucite, Freon, Nylon, x-ray films, pharmaceuticals, and diagnostic instruments.[41]

Pierre S. Dupont opened his carefully cultivated estate, Longwood Gardens, to the public.

Physician. Original Image from Philadelphia Press – Public Domain

A. M. HANCE,
Hance Bros. & White, Chemists.

A.M. Hance (Philadelphians in Cartoons). Courtesy of Philadelphians in Cartoons – Public Domain

health resource for the Delaware Valley. The public is invited to attend the many lectures, workshops, and conferences the College offers. Our programs reflect our reverence for the past, our commitment to the present, and our vision for the future of medicine and health.

The Wistar Institute[40]
University of Pennsylvania
Text reprinted with permission of the University of Pennsylvania (source: www.wistar.org)

The Wistar Institute, founded in 1892, is named after Caspar Wistar, a respected Philadelphia physician who was the author of the first American anatomy textbook. It is the nation's first independent medical research facility.

Along with William Homer and Dr. Joseph Leidy, Dr. Wistar collected and preserved a variety of animal, fossil, and human specimens as tools for medical research which are part of the campus.

From the 1950s the Wistar Institute has been a leader in research – beginning with vaccine research led by Dr. Hilary Koprowski and Leonard Hayflics PhD which led to vaccines against rubella, or German measles, and rabies. In the 1970s, cancer was the main research topic of the Wistar Institute. With the help of the Fox Chase Cancer Research Center, Philadelphia is one of the leaders in finding cures for this disease. Today, The Wistar Institute focuses on cures for AIDS, cancer, and a variety of other autoimmune diseases.

Rohm and Haas

Rohm and Haas Company was founded in 1907 by Otto Rohm, a chemist, and Otto Haas, a businessman. It is one of the world's largest manufacturers of specialty chemicals – technologically sophisticated materials that find their way into applications in a variety of major markets.

"Markets where extensive use is made of Rohm and Haas products include the paint and coatings industry, electronics, household products/ detergents/ personal care, water treatment, adhesives, plastics and salt."[42]

Chemical Heritage Foundation (CHF)
Text from their website – www.chemheritage.org

The Chemical Heritage Foundation (CHF) [founded in the 1980s] serves the community of the chemical and molecular sciences, and the wider public, by treasuring the past, educating the present, and inspiring the future. CHF maintains a world-class collection of materials that document the history and heritage of the chemical and molecular sciences, technologies, and industries; encourages research in CHF collections; and carries out a program of outreach and interpretation in order to advance an understanding of the role of the chemical and molecular sciences, technologies, and industries in shaping society.

The Foundation's most prestigious award, The Othmer Gold Medal, is named after chemical engineer Donald Othmer.

Joseph Priestly (1733-1804)

The American Chemical Society's most prestigious award is named after Philadelphian Joseph Priestly.

Joseph Priestly's preachings about the purpose of government led the British to expel him. He settled in Philadelphia where he helped found the first Unitarian Society of Philadelphia in 1796.

Between 1772 and 1775 Priestley's chemical achievements include the isolation of oxygen and identification of its properties, as well as those of seven other gases.

He demonstrated the carbonation of water, advanced an understanding of the role of blood in respiration and his experiments would lead to the process of photosynthesis. Priestly made his discoveries and the methods behind them available to the public so that they could be replicated.

Text reprinted with permission of the Franklin Institute

FRANKLIN AWARDS[43]

Stockholm may have its Nobel Prizes but the Franklin Awards, named after Benjamin Franklin, are seventy years older, beginning in 1824, and cover a broader range of sciences.

Fields recognized today include Chemistry, Computer and Cognitive Science, Earth Science, Engineering, Life Science, and Physics. The Committee members represent academe, corporate America, and government; they evaluate the work of nominated individuals for its uncommon insight, skill, or creativity, as well as its impact on future research or application to benefit the public.

Through its awards program, The Franklin Institute seeks to provide public recognition and encouragement of excellence in science and technology. In 1998, the Institute's long-standing endowed awards program was reorganized under the umbrella of The Benjamin Franklin Medals.

The list of Franklin Institute laureates reads like a "Who's Who" in the history of nineteenth and twentieth century science, including Alexander Graham Bell, Pierre and Marie Curie, and Rudolf Diesel, who received Cresson Medals at the beginning of [the twentieth] century; as well as Thomas Edison, Niels Bohr, Max Planck, Albert Einstein, and Stephen Hawking, who received the equally prestigious Franklin Medal.

To date, 100 Franklin Institute laureates also have been honored with 102 Nobel Prizes, including 2003s Benjamin Franklin Medal Laureates in Physics, Dr. Raymond Davis, Jr. and Dr. Masatoshi Koshiba.

Through the years, numerous other medals have also been established. Two of the newest awards were made possible in 1988 by a $7.5 million bequest by Philadelphia chemical manufacturer Henry Bower. Mr. Bower, whose grandfather received the 1878 Cresson Medal, endowed the Bower Award for Business Leadership and the Bower Award and Prize for Achievement in Science. Both awards carry gold medallions, and the Science Award carries a cash prize of at least $250,000, making it one of the richest American prizes in science.

The Bower Award for Business Leadership. *From a bequest from Henry Bower, a Philadelphia chemical manufacturer, the Institute established The Bower Award for Business Leadership in 1990. Courtesy of The Historical and Interpretive Collections of The Franklin Institute, Inc., Philadelphia, PA. (Photograph by Charles Penniman.)*

MANUFACTURING and ENGINEERING

Fairmount Water Works
Philadelphia is home to marvelous civil engineering

Philadelphia's signature engineering achievement of the early 1800s was the building in 1815 of the Water Works behind what is now the Philadelphia Art Museum. "During the greater part of the nineteenth century, it was the second most popular tourist site in the United States after Niagara Falls."

In the 1790s yellow fever, which is spread by mosquitoes, became an epidemic in Philadelphia, killing nineteen percent of the Philadelphia population in just one year. Believing that dirty water was the source of the epidemic and wanting clean water for drinking and fighting fires Philadelphia sought to make the water safe. Like most cities, Philadelphia had drawn its water from wells and cisterns in the lowlands of the city.

A plan was developed by Benjamin Henry Latrobe to build a basin on the Schuykill, the bottom of which would be three feet below low water. With the use of steam pumps, this basin water would be lifted and brought by canal and tunnel along the line of Chestnut Street to Broad where another steam engine at Centre Square (now City Hall) would lift it to a reservoir thirty feet above ground where it would then flow throughout the city. For a variety of reasons a new plan was designed to use a reservoir at the top of Morris Hall (Fairmount).

The Fairmount Water Works originally also relied on steam pumping engines. But the steam boilers were costly and exploded so in 1822 waterworks and pumps were used including "double-acting" force pumps designed by Frederick Graff, Sr. Later water turbines were installed. The wooden mains and piping were replaced by iron ones.

"Gigantic water wheels, 16 feet in diameter, used water from a bay created by the Fairmount Dam. At the time of its construction, the dam, measuring 1,204 feet, was the longest in the world. As they turned, surprisingly soundless, the wheels operated pumps that sent water through a series of mains to the city's reservoirs."

The water-pumping machinery was housed in "buildings [neo-classical] that resembled a genteel country estate" making the science a pleasant sight for the eyes. Charles Dickens wrote:

"The Water-Works, which are on a height near the city, are no less ornamental than useful, being tastefully laid out as a public garden... The river is dammed at this point and forced by its own power into reservoirs, whence the whole city is supplied....at a very trifling expense."

During the functioning of the Water Works the Fairmount Park Commission also bought up many industrial mills which operated or fed pollutants into the Schuykill River.

"Over 1,800 acres were bought in 1868. Boathouse Row and East and West Fairmount Park were borne out of these purchases." Typhoid fever helped bring about the end of the Water Works. New water pumping stations had "sand filtration beds to purify the water." Graff became the leading expert on hydraulic engineering and was called in to help New York and Boston build their water systems.

The Water Works became a public aquarium and later a swimming pool. In the 1980s, some of the buildings were renovated. Much of the Fairmount Water Works has now been restored. Educational programs are run from the new building and plans for environmental uses are in progress. "According to Mr. [Ed] Grusheski, the reason full restoration has taken so long is that the environment along the Schuylkill River had to catch up to the preservationist's concepts. Thanks to the Federal Clean Water Acts of the 1970s, there has been 'an amazing turnaround in the quality of the river's water'."[44]

Text reprinted with permission of the Free Library of Philadelphia (source: www.library.phila.gov)

The Waterworks in Centre Square Philadelphia [1800] by W[illiam] Birch & Son. Courtesy of The Library Company of Philadelphia

Philadelphia Waterworks © 2003 by Nicholas P. Santoleri. Courtesy of Nicholas P. Santoleri

Philadelphia Waterworks, Oil on canvas, 24" x 30" © 2002 (private collection) by Elaine Moynihan Lisle. Courtesy of Elaine Moynihan Lisle

PHILADELPHIA WORLD'S FAIR

During the Centennial year of 1876, Philadelphia was host to a celebration of 100 years of American cultural and industrial progress. Officially known as the 'International Exhibition of Arts, Manufactures, and Products of the Soil and Mine', the Centennial Exhibition, the first major World's Fair to be held in the United States, opened on May 10, 1876, on a 285-acre tract of Fairmount Park overlooking the Schuylkill River.

The fairgrounds, designed almost exclusively by twenty-seven-year-old German immigrant Hermann J. Schwarzmann, were host to thirty-seven nations and countless industrial exhibits occupying over 250 individual pavilions. The Exhibition was immensely popular, drawing nearly nine million visitors at a time when the population of the United States was forty-six million. The most lasting accomplishment of the Exhibition was to introduce America as a new industrial world power, soon to eclipse the might and production of every other industrialized nation, and to showcase the City of Philadelphia as a center of American culture and industry.[45]

Significance

The fair was a response to the nation's inability to 'compete on a par' with earlier exhibitions. This Fair impressed foreign nations with America's growing industrial and commercial advantage. *The Times of London*, while noting America's home ground advantage observed, The Centennial fixed America in the minds of the outside world as a nation of inventors and mechanics instead of a nation of farmers…The Centennial ushered in an unprecedented era of invention as America moved from the age of steam to the age of electricity and the internal combustion engine.

"The main halls were the Machinery, Memorial, Agriculture, Horticulture Halls. In addition, there were Government Buildings and State Buildings that served as headquarters of the individual state Centennial commissioners and as reception rooms where visitors could sign a guest book….

"State exhibitions had a stipulation. No reference to the recent Civil War could be construed as political or offensive. Still, most southern states declined to participate. Some were still recovering financially from the War….

"Each state had its designated state day at the Centennial, which included parades along State Avenue, music, and speeches….

Women's Pavilion

When a group of women was denied permission to exhibit independently in the Main Exhibition Building, the result was one of the novel and more controversial exhibit buildings of the Centennial. The Women's Pavilion was the brainchild of Mrs. Elizabeth Duane Gillespie and her committee of thirteen Philadelphia ladies. Intended to showcase the abilities of women in all spheres of activity, the Pavilion displayed not only needlework, corsets, and household items, but new inventions such as emergency flares, model interlocking bricks, and a patent land

pulverizer. Mrs. Gillespie was adamant in her insistence that every item in the Pavilion be the work of women. Only the structure itself was designed by Schwarzmann, a woman architect from Boston having applied too late for consideration.

Mrs. Gillespie was careful not to align herself too closely with what was considered the radical element in the women's movement at the time. Women's suffrage was not mentioned, and no attempt was made to identify with the demonstration led by Susan B. Anthony on July 4 at the Independence Hall ceremonies. In a final insult, Women's Day at the Centennial was celebrated on November 7, Election Day because, it was argued, men would be at the polls and would not mind missing this event.[46, 47]

Foreign Participation

The eleven nations who erected buildings were: Brazil, Canada, France, Germany, Great Britain, Japan, Portugal, Spain, Sweden, Tunis, and Turkey. Other nations who participated: Austria, Belgium, Holland, Italy, Norway, Egypt, Denmark, Switzerland, Mexico, Venezuela, Russia, Chile, Peru, Argentine Confederation, Sandwich Islands [Hawaii], China, Australia, Greece, Bolivia, Nicaragua, Colombia, Liberia, Ecuador, Orange Free State, Guatemala, Honduras.[48]

Food and Concessions

Visitors could dine at any of nine restaurants, including The Great American Restaurant, Trois Frères Provencaux, Restaurant of the South, Lauber's German Restaurant, the French restaurant La Fayette, George's Hill Restaurant, The Dairy, The Vienna Bakery and Coffee-House, or the New England Farmer's Home of 100 Years Ago. Diners complained of the service and the prices at most of these establishments. For quick snacks there were stands selling popcorn, a novelty, as well a waffles, soda water, root beer, and other snacks. The Sons of Temperance erected a fountain serving ice water inside a wooden structure at the intersection of Fountain and Belmont Avenue. Prominent throughout the grounds were cigar stands, bootblacks, and public comfort stations.[49]

Music at the Fair

The main source of music during the Centennial was the Music Pavilion at the central transept of the Main Exhibition Hall, which was usually occupied by popular bands. In the same building were two immense organs, the Centennial Organ by Hook and Hastings of Boston, and the Roosevelt Organ by Hilborne L. Roosevelt of New York, which had a special 'electric echo' effect. A second Music Pavilion was located outdoors in Lansdowne Valley between Memorial Hall and Horticultural Hall.

Machinery Hall, of all places, was home to the Centennial Chimes, thirteen chimes representing the thirteen original colonies, played three times daily by a professor Widdows of Washington, D.C. There were daily concerts arranged by manufacturers of musical instruments.[50]

OUR CENTENNIAL—PRESIDENT GRANT AND DOM PEDRO STARTING THE CORLISS ENGINE.—From a Sketch by Theo. R. Davis.—[See Page 422.]

*Philadelphia Sesquicentennial World's Fair
(Centennial Exhibition). Courtesy of Free
Library of Philadelphia*

*Opposite:
Corliss Engine (Centennial
Exhibition Collection). Courtesy
of Free Library of Philadelphia*

VENUES

The Franklin Institute
222 North 20th St.

Ask any Philadelphian to respond to "Philadelphia Science" and most will say Benjamin Franklin and the Franklin Institute.

For many the Franklin Institute invokes childhood memories of walking through a large heart, seeing oneself in the Hall of Mirrors, and wondering about the meaning of Focalaut's Pendulum – the Pendulum that every so often knocks down some pegs and every twenty-four hours knocks them all down, thus showing that the earth rotates around its axis every twenty-four hours.

The full history of the Franklin Institute is set forth on their website...

Text reprinted with permission of the Franklin Institute (source: all Franklin Institute text, www.fi.edu)

On February 5, 1824, Samuel Vaughan Merrick and William H. Keating founded The Franklin Institute of the State of Pennsylvania for the Promotion of the Mechanic Arts. Located in the Philadelphia County Court House (known today as Independence Hall), The Franklin Institute's purpose was to honor Ben Franklin and advance the usefulness of his inventions.

Soon, the Institute moved to the east side of Seventh Street, between Market and Chestnut Streets, (today the home of the Atwater Kent Museum) where it remained for its first century.

In 1930, The Franklin Institute and the Poor Richard Club began to seek funds to build a new science museum and memorial hall. In just twelve days, the sum of 5.1 million dollars was raised, providing the means for construction to begin. In 1932, the cornerstone of the new Franklin Institute was laid at 20th Street and the Benjamin Franklin Parkway. In 1933, construction began on the Fels Planetarium, donated by Samuel S. Fels. It was to be only the second planetarium in America.

On January 1, 1934, The Franklin Institute Science Museum opened to the public. The Museum's hands-on approach to science and technology, combined with the Fels Planetarium, made the Institute a popular spot. As the end of the twentieth century drew near, major changes were beginning at the Institute. In May of 1990, The Mandell Center, Tuttleman Omniverse Theater (now known as the Tuttleman IMAX Theater), and Musser Theater opened, adding dramatically to the size and appeal of The Franklin Institute. The new exhibits, exciting Omnimax films, and interactive presentations continued the Institute's long tradition of making science and technology fun.

Today, one hundred and seventy five years after the Institute's founding, The Franklin Institute Science Museum continues to offer new and exciting access to science and technology in ways that would both amaze and delight Mister Benjamin Franklin.[51]

Exhibits

Two of the old exhibits that are popular at the Franklin Institute are the walk-through heart [updated with many new features about the heart in 2004] and Foucalt's Pendulum. The Franklin Air Show [opposite] was also recently updated. Mixed in with the old exhibits are frequent new exhibits including the *Titanic* in 2004.

Heart at the Franklin Institute[52]
Text reprinted with permission of the Franklin Institute

The Heart at the Franklin Institute is a child's delight. It is an educational tool that allows children to walk through an enlarged hear where it can learn about how the heart and the related parts work.

Newton's Dream is a kinetic sculpture at the Franklin Institute where you can watch dozens of golf balls shooting around metals tracks in a three-dimensional maze. There are ten different ways a ball can travel from the top of Newton's Dream down to the bottom.

The Giant Heart. *The Franklin Institute's "Giant Heart: A Healthy Interactive Experience," initially installed as a temporary exhibit in 1954 as The Engine of Life. Courtesy of the Historical and Interpretive Collections of The Franklin Institute, Inc., Philadelphia, PA. (Photograph by Charles Penniman.)*

Foucault's Pendulum. *The ubiquitous Foucault Pendulum, placed in the Institute's main staircase in 1934, to demonstrate that the earth is always in motion. Collections of The Franklin Institute, Inc., Philadelphia, PA. (Photograph by Charles Penniman.)*

Foucault's Pendulum

Text reprinted with permission of the Franklin Institute

The pendulum is the centerpiece of the original museum. It is located in the grand stairwell which leads to all floors of the museum.

Mr. and Mrs. Richard L. Binder donated the Foucault pendulum at the Franklin Institute. It was installed on 15 February 1934. Eleven men held the 85-foot wire that holds the bob in order to prevent kinks from tangling it. They did so throughout a Center City parade as they were guarded by mounted policemen.

M.L. Foucault was experimenting and noticed that a steel rod he had on a nearby lathe would oscillate in a plane that resulted from the initial force. This led Foucault to develop his famous pendulum experiment.

The theory is simple, given a perfect setting (e.g. no friction), a suspension pendulum will oscillate in a constant path. However, as the earth rotates, that path appears to change. In reality, what is changing is the world about the pendulum. After a twenty-four hour period, the pendulum would again appear to travel the path it first set.

This is significant. If the pendulum indeed travels in a straight path and we see changes, then we know the earth is actually spinning. Theoretically, after twenty-four hours, the pendulum will once again swing in the path it first began. The reality of the experiment is that it does not reach that path after twenty-four hours. Factors like gravity and friction play a part in variations to the twenty-four hour path. For other variables the answers are at the Franklin Institute.

The Franklin Air Show, opened October 18, 2003.

Text reprinted with permission of the Franklin Institute

In March of 2001 the 1911 Wright Model B was carefully removed from The Franklin Institute's Aviation Hall to be restored. The airplane returned to the Institute and was reassembled in late June and early July, 2003, and now hangs in its new location as a featured exhibit in The Franklin Air Show.

The Wright Model B was the first plane manufactured in quantity by the Wright Brothers. It was the first time Wilbur and Orville used a rear stabilizer. The plane has skids and wheels, allowing for take-off and landing on any level field. The Wright Brothers enforced a strict policy for those interested in acquiring one of their flying machines; in order to buy a plane from them, you had to first take flying lessons at their factory in Ohio. Wilbur and Orville shipped the plane to the customer only when they felt that person was capable of flying it. In 1911, a Model B biplane cost about $5,000. This particular Model B, purchased by a young Philadelphian named Grover Cleveland Bergdoll in 1912 and donated to The Franklin Institute in 1934, took to the skies for about 748 flights before being placed in storage.

Mutter Museum

Located at 19 South 22nd Street, Philadelphia, PA 19103
Text reprinted with permission of the Mütter Museum of The College of Physicians of Philadelphia (www.collegeofphysicians.org)

The Mütter Museum of The College of Physicians of Philadelphia was founded to educate future doctors about anatomy and human medical anomalies. Today, it serves as a valuable resource for educating and enlightening the public about our medical past and telling important stories about what it means to be human. The Mütter Museum embodies The College of Physicians of Philadelphia 's mission to advance the cause of health while upholding the ideals and heritage of medicine.

In 1858, Thomas Dent Mütter, retired Professor of Surgery at Jefferson Medical College, presented his personal collection of unique anatomic and pathological materials to The College of Physicians of Philadelphia★. Our collection now boasts over 20,000 unforgettable objects. These include fluid-preserved anatomical and pathological specimens; skeletal and dried specimens, medical instruments and apparati; anatomical and pathological models in plaster, wax, papier-mâché, and plastic; memorabilia of famous scientists and physicians; medical illustrations, photographs, prints, and portraits. In addition, we offer changing exhibits on a variety of medical and historical topics.

★ *The College of Physicians website (www.collegeofphysicians.org)*

Academy of Natural Sciences

1900 Benjamin Franklin Parkway
Text reprinted with permission of the Academy of Natural Sciences

The Academy of Natural Sciences of Philadelphia was founded in 1812 'for the encouragement and cultivation of the sciences, and the advancement of useful learning.'

The Academy's history mirrors the evolution of the relationship between the American people and the natural world. The oldest natural sciences institution in the Western Hemisphere, the Academy was founded when the United States hugged the Atlantic coastline, and Philadelphia was the cultural, commercial, and scientific center of the new nation. Classic expeditions to explore the western wilderness, such as those led by Stephen Long and Ferdinand Hayden, were organized at the Academy. These explorers brought back new species of plants and animals, which were studied and catalogued; they formed the foundation of the Academy's scientific collections which now contain over 25,000,000 specimens.

The Academy opened its doors to the public in 1828. Here, the mysteries of nature were revealed, its chaos organized and labeled in Latin and Greek. By the turn of the century, Academy expeditions were ranging farther afield, to the Arctic, to Central America, and later to Africa and Asia. Plants and animals collected during these excursions were incorporated into the Academy's magnificent dioramas, many of which were constructed in the 1920s and '30s. In 1948, long before water pollution and environmental degradation became topics of public concern, the Academy established the Environmental Research Division."

Joseph Leidy (1823-1891) was one of the leading American scientists of the nineteenth century. He was the Father of American Vertebrate Paleontology, the Founder of American Parasitology, a leading teacher in human anatomy and Natural History and an expert in a wide range of fields.[53]

The Remarkable Nature of Edward Lear

Text reprinted with permission of the Academy of Natural Sciences

Known the world over as the author of 'The Owl and the

Joseph Leidy at Desk. Courtesy of Academy of Natural Sciences

Macaw by Edward Lear Courtesy of Academy of Natural Sciences

Pussycat' and other 'nonsense poems' for children, Edward Lear (1812-1888) was also an extraordinarily accomplished natural history painter, ranked by many contemporaries—and subsequent art historians—as an artist on a par with John James Audubon.

In the decade of the 1830s, Lear was the unofficial artist in residence at the London Zoo, illustrating dozens of natural history publications for others as well as his own spectacular monograph on parrots, Illustrations of the Family of Psittacidae, or Parrots (1832).

Just as he was achieving an international reputation for his scientific illustration, Lear abruptly terminated this part of his career in order to devote himself full-time to landscape painting and travel.

Fortunately, his scientific illustrations endure. The Ewell Sale Stewart Library of The Academy of Natural Sciences owns copies of virtually every one of the dozens of now rare books that Edward Lear illustrated.

Eagle Owl by Edward Lear Courtesy of Academy of Natural Sciences

PHILADELPHIA ART

**Picture – Dr. Albert Barnes
The Philadelphia Artist**

"If Pennsylvania Painters are the democrats of our art then Boston painters are its aristocrats."
Guy Pene Du Bose
Art Critic

PHILADELPHIA ART
NOTABLE STYLES
Realism
   Families
      Private Collections

CONTENTS

PHILADELPHIA ART

Philadelphia's early painters were portrait artists like Gilbert Stuart (who did the famous portrait of George Washington), Thomas Sully, and Charles Willson Peale. Later many artists worked for local newspapers, magazines or created ads for local businesses to support their private art.

Philadelphia's importance in the art world stems in large part to its teaching institutions beginning with the Pennsylvania Academy of the Fine Arts. Founded by Peale, the institution helped educate Thomas Eakins, Maxfield Parrish, N.C. Wyeth, and Mary Casssatt and helped spawn several art movements including the Ashcan movement and Pennsylvania Impressionism.

Other art institutions include the Moore College of Art (formerly the Philadelphia School of Design), which helped female artists like those of the "Philadelphia Ten" create art which rivaled and influenced those of their male counterparts.

Many of the artists trained in these schools helped make famous a number of mediums from engraving, etching, and oil paints to illustrations and photography. The most famous female artist was Mary Cassatt, who grew up in Philadelphia and studied at the Pennsylvania Academy of the Fine Arts before moving to France where she, along with Berthe Morisset, were two of the most famous well-known Impressionist artists. William Glackens helped Albert Barnes accumulate his legendary Impressionism collection.

Others artists like the Calder family established their own identity in sculpting. And yet others, like the many African American artists (Humbert Howard and Dox Thrash among others), found work through the kindness of the Works Progress Administration and the support of the Pyramid Club and the Barnes Foundation.

The most famous Philadelphia art includes the collections of a number of private collectors, including Albert Barnes, who collected impressionist and African American Art and displayed it in Lower Merion's Barnes Foundation. Other notable collections of Philadelphia artists include the art of John Graver Johnson, the Pennsylvania Impression of the Lenfests at the James Michener Museum, and Charles Blockson's African American collection at Temple University. Bill Cosby's collection of African-American Art, including that of Philadelphian Ossawa Tanner, has toured the country.

The Philadelphia Museum of Art is notable for its collections from far reaches of the world, its notable photography collections, new exhibits of famous artists; the building is the gateway to the City's reach to Fairmount Park, which is home to the largest display of sculptures in the country.

Recently Philadelphia's museums showed their voluntary spirit when they each made a contribution on a common theme to the Institute of Contemporary Art. The theme was Nothingness.

Philadelphia Murals are a way for the various neighborhoods to identify their neighborhood in colorful and eye-catching ways.

William Birch's engravings show an early picture of the city while *The Philadelphia Bulletin's* Alfred Bendiner's drawings show a more recent architectural and social Philadelphia look.

Paintings of Boathouse Row and the Philadelphia skyline have attracted artists across neighborhoods, as do the Wyeth paintings of Chadds Ford and the numerous Pennsylvania Impressionism artists who made Bucks County one of their favorite regions to landscape.

Today popular painters like Joe Barker, Charles Cushing, Rob Lawlor, Elaine Moynihan Lisle, Perry Milou, William Ressler, and Nicholas P. Santoleri, and new artists from the learning institutions mentioned above and other schools like the Tyler School of Art and the University of the Arts are continuing to lead Philadelphia to new visions.

With the court ruling that the Barnes Foundation Art will be moved to the Benjamin Franklin Parkway – the stage is set for the Parkway to be a Miracle Mile of great Philadelphia art along the most beautiful street in America. At one end will be the Pennsylvania Academy of the Fine Arts. At the other end the Pennsylvania Museum of Art. In-between there will be the Barnes Foundation, the Rodin Museum, and the Moore College of Art.

PAINTERS

One of the earliest persons to depict Philadelphia was William Birch, who made a number of engravings of the city.

William and Thomas Birch

Text reprinted with permission of Independence Hall Association (source: www.ushistory.org/birch)

WILLIAM RUSSELL BIRCH was born in Warwickshire, England, April 9, 1755. He studied at Bristol and London and frequently exhibited in London. In 1794, he immigrated to America with his family and settled in Philadelphia. He is best known for his miniature and enamel portraits and this series of Views of Philadelphia which he worked on with his son Thomas and published in 1799-1800. "THOMAS BIRCH, William's son, was especially recognized for his paintings of the War of 1812 naval engagements and for his marine and winter scenes."

Several exhibitions of Birch's Views were collected by S. Robert Teitelman and were displayed in various exhibitions at the Philadelphia Free Library of Philadelphia. Mr. Teitelman has also taken his own photographs of the Birch Locations in 1960 and 2000. The exhibit with more detailed commentaries of the paintings-sites can be viewed on the website noted in the footnotes.[1]

Library and Surgeon's Hall, in Fifth Street, Philadelphia (The City of Philadelphia, in the State of Pennsylvania; as it appeared in the Year 1800 by William Russel Birch.) Courtesy of The Library Company of Philadelphia

Charles Willson Peale and Family (Charles Willson Peale 1741-1827)

Perhaps the leading painter of famous Americans in colonial America was Charles Wilson Peale (1741-1827). Many of these early paintings, being before photography, were the only way of knowing what some of these Americans looked like.

Peale was known as the "Artist of the American Revolution." His subjects included George Washington, Thomas Jefferson, Alexander Hamilton, and miniatures of officers in the Colonial Army, where Peale rose to the rank of Captain.

To have a home for many of these early paintings Peale established a museum at Independence Hall. Peale, with the help of sculptor William Rush, also helped found the Pennsylvania Academy of the Fine Arts in 1805. It is the oldest art museum and art school in the nation.

In 1801 he led, with the aid of the American Philosophical Society and Thomas Jefferson, the first United States scientific expedition to upstate New York where the bones of mastodon were exhumed.[2]

Peale then created a museum to hold his artworks and his natural history artifacts. "By the second decade of the nineteenth century, Peale had increased the museum's collections to more than 100,000 objects, including 269 paintings, 1,894 birds, 250 quadrupeds, 650 fishes, more than 1,000 shells, and 313 books in the library."

"Two of his seven sons were artists: Raphaelle (1774-1825) and Rembrandt (1778-1860). His brother, James (1749-1831), was a noted miniature painter in Philadelphia. Two of James's daughters, Anna Claypoole (1791-1878) and Sarah Miriam (1800-1885), were among the earliest professional women painters in America."[3]

Peale's estate is now part of LaSalle University. Much of the museum artifacts were sold to P.T. Barnum and Moses Kimball.

Benjamin West (1738-1820)

Benjamin West studied art in Philadelphia and Italy. He was England's most famous Neoclassical painter. King George III named him England's royal painter after he painted an historical scene in modern dress rather than costume. The British treated him well, even during the Revolutionary War. When he supported Napoleon, though, he was asked to leave.[4, 5] Benjamin West influenced younger American artists, including Charles Willson Peale, Gilbert Stuart, and John Singleton Copley.

West was modern for the times because he painted people in current dress instead of the dress from antiquity. His painting of Benjamin Franklin is in the science section.

Edward Hicks (1780-1849)

Edward Hicks was a Quaker preacher in nearby Bucks County. His painting conflicted with his beliefs. Quakers emphasized plainness and Hicks himself said that God created the best painting – the World. All other paintings, including his own, paled in comparison.[6]

Hicks began painting in midlife to supplement his preaching. Beginning as a painter of signs and coaches Hicks expanded his craft to paint pictures on commission. Typically, Hicks painted in oil on wood or canvas, specializing in Biblical scenes, especially Peaceable Kingdoms inspired by Isaiah, as well as history paintings and panoramas of Bucks County farm life. His style was naive, rendering animals and human figures in realistic detail, while handling perspective awkwardly.

"Although Hicks lacked formal training as an artist, he taught himself in the same manner favored by many academies, copying earlier paintings or etchings. Indeed, most of Hicks's paintings were based on engravings. Due to the discovery, during the twentieth century, of many of Hicks's paintings, his stature as an artist has increased tremendously, so that today he is regarded as the greatest American naïve painter."[7]

Peaceable Kingdom comes from Chapter 11 of Isaiah, which says "The wolf also shall dwell with the lamb, and the leopard shall lie down with the kid, and the calf and the young lion and fatling together; and a little child shall lead them." His nephew, Thomas Hicks, was also a well known painter.

Thomas Eakins (1844-1916)

Text reprinted with permission of the Philadelphia Art Museum (source: all Philadelphia Museum of Art text, www.phila.museum.org)

Eakins was among the first generation of American artists who flocked to Paris for artistic training. Unlike his contemporaries, however, he was determined to apply Beaux-Arts techniques to subjects that were distinctly American and reflected his own experience. Eakins's preoccupation with athletics is reflected in his famous scenes of rowing, sailing, fishing, and boxing, among other sports. Some of the finest and most celebrated of these include Max Schmitt in a Single Scull, Starting Out After Rail, Shad Fishing at Gloucester on the Delaware River, and Between Rounds, among others.[9]

"Thomas Eakins was an American realist painter – one of the foremost of the nineteenth century. Working independently of contemporary European styles, he was the first major artist after the American Civil War (1861-1865) to produce a profound and powerful body of work drawn directly from the experience of American life.

"Born in Philadelphia on July 25, 1844, Eakins studied drawing at the Pennsylvania Academy of the Fine Arts from 1861 to 1866. His concurrent study of anatomy at Jefferson Medical College led to a lifelong interest in scientific realism. He was strongly influenced by seventeenth-century masters, particularly the Dutch artist Rembrandt and the Spanish painters Josepe de Ribera and Diego Velazquez. These masters impressed him with their realism and psychological penetration. He returned to Philadelphia in 1870 and lived there the rest of his life.

"Eakins's paintings depict scenes and people observed in the life around him in Philadelphia, particularly domestic scenes of his family and friends. He exercised his scientific inclination in paintings of sailing, rowing, and hunting, where he delineated the anatomy of the human body in motion. He painted several large and powerful hospital scenes, most notably The Gross Clinic (1875, Jefferson Medical College, Philadelphia), which combined sharp realism—a depiction of an operation in progress—with psychological acuity in the portrayal of the surgeon, Doctor Gross.

"As director of the Pennsylvania Academy of the Fine Arts, Eakins introduced an innovative curriculum, including thorough study of anatomy and dissection as well as scientific perspective, which revolutionized the teaching of art in America. His insistence on study from the nude scandalized the school's authorities, however, and he was forced to resign in 1886. During the later part of his career, Eakins's scientific interests were overshadowed by his preoccupation with psychology and personality, and in his art he concentrated prin-

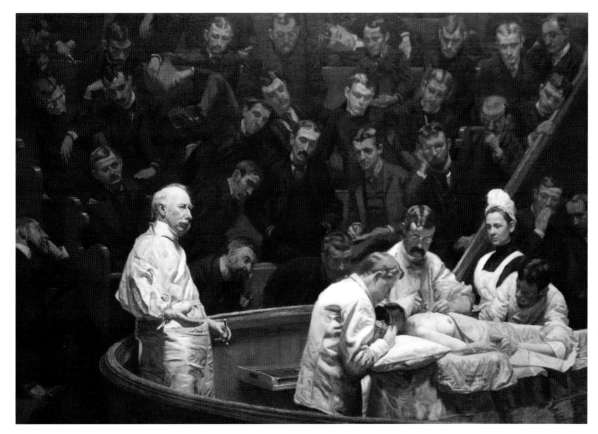

The Agnew Clinic by Thomas Eakins. Courtesy of University of Pennsylvania Art Collection

cipally on portraiture—studies of friends, scientists, musicians, artists, and clergymen. In addition to their masterly evocation of personality, these portraits are characterized by uncompromising realism and by a sculptural sense of form, which is evident in the strongmodeling of the sitters' heads, bodies, and hands. Typical of his full-length portraits is The Pathetic Song (1881, Corcoran Gallery of Art, Washington, D.C.), with the standing figure of a singer in a rich silk gown silhouetted against a dimly lighted music room.

"Although none of his paintings brought him financial or popular success, Eakins had a profound influence, both as a painter and as a teacher, on the course of American naturalism. His realistic approach to painting was ahead of his time. He died in Philadelphia on June 25, 1916."[10, 11]

Mary Cassatt (1844-1926)

Mary Cassatt was part of another famous Philadelphia family. Her father was a wealth merchant. Her family lived in France, for a time, before moving to Philadelphia. Impressed by what she had seen in Europe, Mary strove to become an artist- a difficult enough task for men, an uphill battle for the women of her day.

Her brother Alexander was a President of the Pennsylvania Railroad and helped build the tunnels that let people travel straight through to New York City instead of having to take the ferry.

At 16, she began studies at the Pennsylvania Academy of the Fine Arts. She left for Europe where she lived most of her life in Paris. France. Cassatt thought that Europe was more open to women being successful.

One of her non-Impressionism influences was the Italian master Correggio. She was commissioned by the archbishop of Pittsburgh to copy two of his works. The commissions helped her European career.

Ordinary women and children, in ordinary scenes, were her favorite topics. Her paintings showed a love for children though she never had any of her own. Cassatt got her break in 1892, when she received a commission for a mural for the Woman's Building at the Chicago World's Fair.

Cassatt was also a noted printmaker. She helped influence the Impressionism school by buying some of their art or having wealth Americans but the art. (http://www.artelino.com/articles/mary_cassatt.asp)

As the Moore College of Art described her work (in an exhibit with Alice Neel and Karen Kilimnk – two successive Philadelphia woman artists of note)

"Cassatt's paintings give the nineteenth-century French middle class a simple grandeur. Often engaged in everyday activities and in moments of quiet intimacy, her sitters are given an iconic stature."[12]

She helped a number of Philadelphians, including Henry C. Gibson, the Wideners, the Elkins, John G. Johnson and her father acquire French paintings in the latter 1800s.

The Letter (1890-1891) is part of the collection of the Philadelphia Museum of Art.

Family Group Reading, Oil on Canvas, 22 1/4 x 44 1/4 inches (56.5 x 112.4 cm), c. 1901, Gift of Mr. and Mrs. J. Watson Webb, 1942 by Mary Cassatt. Courtesy of Philadelphia Museum of Art

Henry Ossawa Tanner (1859-1937)

Henry Ossawa Tanner was another of the many students who learned painting under Thomas Eakins. Tanner studied in Philadelphia (at Robert Vaux Consolidated School and at the Pennsylvania Academy of the Fine Arts). He opened his own studio in Philadelphia in 1885, but moved to Altanta in 1889.

The Banjo Lesson, is a realistic study of black life, which he painted in Philadelphia. After Atlanta he settled in Paris where discrimination against African Americans was perceived by Tanner to be less intense. His subject matter included blacks from America as well as Africa and the Middle East. By the mid-1890s, Tanner shifted from painting African American genre scenes to religious paintings.

"Although Tanner remained active until 1936, he did not adjust his expressive style to the period's artistic movement. He also resisted periodic attempts of African American leaders to enlist him as a spokesman, preferring to concentrate on artistic rather than racial issues. Nonetheless, his commitment, spiritual motivation, and international acclaim have inspired generations of African American artists."[13]

Maxfield Parrish (1870-1966)

Maxfield Parrish was originally born Frederick Parrish in 1870 into a Quaker family. His father Stephen was a well known artist. He was a student at the Pennsylvania Academy of the Fine Arts in the 1890s. He also was taught by Howard Pyle of the Drexel Institute of Art, Science and Industry (now Drexel University). He later moved to Cornish, New Hampshire – home of a well-known artist's colony.

Parrish became one of the country's best known illustrators for magazines such as *Harper's Bazaar*, the *Century*, *Scribner's*, *Collier's*, the *Ladies' Home Journal*, and *Life* and for books like *Edith Wharton's Italian Villas and their Gardens* (1904), and a children's collection of the Arabian Nights tales (1909). In addition to his private paintings, Parrish painted for a variety of businesses. His advertisements and business calendars became an art form. According to the National Museum of American Illustration – Parrish was best known for his use of a variant of the color blue called lapiz lazuli and his idyllic images of women in classical settings

"Other images had scenes embellished with billowing clouds in a fairytale ambience of maidens and knights lying under porticoes and these were equally harmonic, idealistic, and loved."

By 1925 Parrish had become one of the most popular artists in America.[14]

Calder Family
The Grandfather, Alexander Milne Calder (1846-1923)
Alexander Milne Calder is the designer of the statue of William Penn atop City Hall. The William Penn Statue is the tallest statue on any building in the world.

The Father, Alexander Stirling Calder (1870-1945)
Logan Circle is one of Penn's original five squares (Northwest Square). In olden days it was used as a burial ground and a place for public executions.

In 1825 it was renamed for James Logan and seventeen years later it was a punishable offense to take a cow, horse, cart wagon or carriage into the square. Eventually the graves, mounds, and hillocks were removed or leveled.

It is now one of the most beautiful spots in the city. The square has become a circle, the Swann Memorial Fountain. The statues in the circle are by Alexander Stirling Calder."[15]

The Son, Alexander Calder (1898-1976)
Alexander Calder obtained a mechanical engineering degree but it is his unique mechanical mobiles and art that have made him famous. After work as an illustrator Calder moved to Paris where he "created his Cirque Calder, a complex and unique body of art. The assemblage included diminutive performers, animals, and props he had observed at the Ringling Brothers Circus. Fashioned from wire, leather, cloth, and other found materials, Cirque Calder was designed to be manipulated manually by Calder.(c) 2006 Calder Foundation, New York/Artist Rights Society (ARS), New York

In the fall of 1931, a significant turning point in Calder's artistic career occurred when he created his first truly kinetic sculpture and gave form to an entirely new type of art. The first of these objects moved by systems of cranks and motors, and were dubbed "mobiles" by Marcel Duchamp, for in French mobile refers to both motion and motive. Calder soon abandoned the mechanical aspects of these works when he realized he could fashion mobiles that would undulate on their own with the air's currents. Jean Arp, in order to differentiate Calder's non-kinetic works from his kinetic works, named Calder's stationary objects "stabiles."

Calder concentrated his efforts primarily on large-scale commissioned works in his later years."[16, 17]

Text reprinted with permission of the Calder Foundation, New York/Artist Rights Society (ARS), New York © 2006 (source: www.calder.org).

LITHOGRAPHS

Nicholas B. Wainwright Lithographs
The Collection of early lithographs at the Library Company of Philadelphia includes many like the following by Nicholas B. Wainwright.

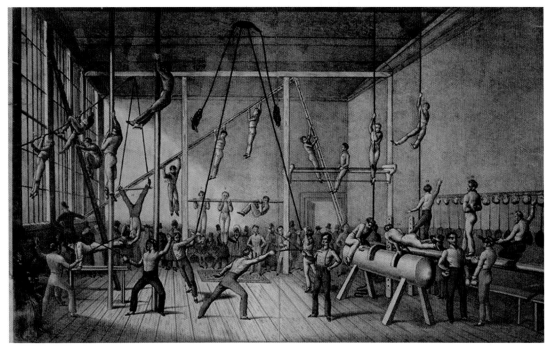

Clockwise, from top:
Commissioners Hall,
Northern Liberties,
Philadelphia: ca. 1852 by
Kuchel, Charles Conrad
Lith., Thos M. Scott Pinxt.
Courtesy of The Library
Company of Philadelphia

Souvenir of the coldest
winter on record. Scene
on the Delaware River at
Philada. during the severe
winter of 1856 by Queen,
James Fuller. Courtesy of
The Library Company of
Philadelphia

Public Baths. Thos. E. J.
Kerrison's Arcade-Baths
1847 by Rease, W. H.
lithographer. Courtesy of
The Library Company of
Philadelphia

Roper's Gymnasium ca 1831
by Clay, Edward Williams.
Courtesy of The Library
Company of Philadelphia

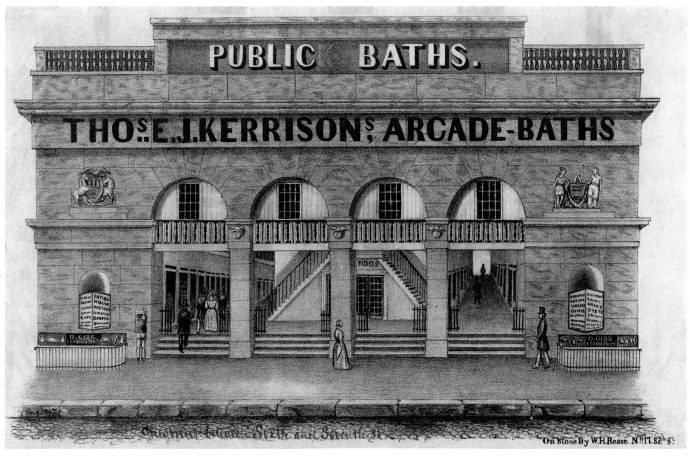

WATERCOLORS

Some selected oil paintings of Philadelphia in the collection of the Library Company of Philadelphia are shown on these pages.

Benjamin R. Evans painted hundreds of views of Philadelphia in the mid- to late 1800s; most are original works. Some are copies of earlier photographs or drawings. Evans' primary patron was a Mr. Ferdinand J. Dreer; most of these works published came from his estate.

Taylor "Views of Old Philadelphia," 1861
Winterthur Library

In 1861, Philadelphia was undergoing new construction. To capture the buildings before they were torn down, an artist made pencil and wash sketches of a number of Philadelphia locations. The patron for the artwork was Ferdinand J. Dreer ((1812-1902). It is not known who the artist was. While there is some though that it might have been Frank Hamilton Taylor (1846-1946). The current prevailing thought is that it was another Taylor, James E. Taylor (1839-1901). The sketches were of pencil and wash. (www.brynmar.edu)

Winterthur, located in the Brandywine Valley of Delaware is the former home of Henry Francis du Pont (1880-1969). DuPont and his father, Henry Algernon, designed Winterthur after the style of 18th and 19th century European homes. DuPont added his horticulturalist touch. (Winterthur website)

Lemon Hill, 1857 by Benjamin R. Evans. Courtesy of The Library Company of Philadelphia

Valley Green, Wissahicon Above Red Bridge, c. 1869 by Benjmain R. Evans. Courtesy of The Library Company of Philadelphia

Taylor, Sketchbook 1861, Philadelphia, Pa. Page 12 Sketch. North Side of Liberty Street. Courtesy of Winterthur Library: Joseph Downs Collection of Manuscripts and Printed Ephemera

ILLUSTRATORS

Some of the many notable illustrators who worked in Philadelphia include:

Joseph Pennell (1857-1926)

Joseph Pennell was born in Philadelphia. Pennell trained at the Pennsylvania Academy of Fine Arts and at the Pennsylvania School of Industrial Art. He married Elizabeth Robins in 1884 Pennell was the painter, though he had a journalist's eye for a story and Elizabeth was a writer [some of her writings appear in the preface]. The two honeymooned in Europe where they took a tandem bicycle ride where he sketched what he saw and Elizabeth wrote about the sights. The combination made enough of an impression to entitle the Pennells to a showing at the Exhibition of the Society of Painters-Etchers in 1885.

His next work was to illustrate a series of articles by George W. Cable on New Orleans. Based on the New Orleans Etchings, Joseph Pennel was asked to illustrate articles by William Dean Howells in Italy.

Pennel made his plates, in addition to using them for prints. Later he worked with James McNeil Whistler (of "Whistler's Mother" fame). Where he used lithography. Pennell founded the Senefelder Club in London to bring lithographers together and hold exhibitions of their prints.

Another series was the "Wonder of Work" art where Pennell focused on factories including those in the Panama Canal. "Joseph Pennell's pictures of War Work in England," was another European project.

Pennell also worked in the United States, most notable San Francisco. After World War he taught etching at the Arts Students' league in New York, wrote several books, served as an art critic on the Brooklyn Eagle, and helped run the New Society of Sculptors, Painters & Engravers. He died in 1926.

His book of sixty-four lithographs of the City of Philadelphia (Joseph Pennell's pictures of Philadelphia) is a must read.

"Pennell is considered to have done more than any other one artist of his time to improve the quality of illustration both in the United States and abroad and to raise its status as an art. He produced more than 900 etched and mezzotint plates, some 621 lithographs, and innumerable drawings and water colors."
(http://www.czbrats.com/Builders/pennell.htm – cz as in the Panama Canal Zone)

Augustus Kollner

Augustus Kollner illustrated how one could, in the 1800s, make a living as an illustrator. His art included trade cards, labels for drugstores and manufactures, billheads and invitations, and other commercial art. This allowed him the opportunity to etch and later use watercolor for his views of many American and Canada cities. His most noted work is his fifty-four views (done in watercolor and later transferred into lithographs) of American cities.[19]

Earl Horter (1881-1940)

Earl Horter, born in 1881 in Germantown, Pennsylvania, was known for his realistic etchings of urban scenes, though he was also an illustrator and painter. As a teenager, he engraved stock certificates. He was essentially self-taught. He had an early one-man show in 1916 in New York at the Frederick Keppel and Company gallery. Horter moved back to Philadelphia in 1917, where he lived until 1940. He worked as art director for the N. W. Ayer advertising firm from 1917-1923.

Horter loved modern art and acquired a collection of European and American modern art, African sculpture, and Native American artifacts. The Philadelphia Museum of Art put on an exhibition of his collection (which was dispersed before his passing) in 1999. The exhibit was called "Mad for Modernism." The Philadelphia Museum of Art wrote of the collection that it reveals the dynamic and creative energies at work among a circle of contemporary artists and their friends in Philadelphia during the 1920s and '30s. The exhibit included "some 50 paintings, sculptures, drawings and prints by the seminal European figures in early modern art such as Picasso, Braque, Duchamp and Brancusi, as well as Horter's American colleagues such as Charles Sheeler and Arthur B. Carles. A group of 20 African sculptures and Native American artifacts represent other important components of Horter's collection."

"Horter was also a teacher in Philadelphia at the Stella Elkins Tyler School of Art; Graphic Sketch Club (now the Fleisher Art Memorial); and the Philadelphia Museum School of Industrial Art (now the University of the Arts)." (askart.com and Philadelphia Museum of Art website)

Philadelphia Sketch Club[20]

Text reprinted with permission of Philadelphia Sketch Club (source: www.sketchclub.org)

The Club is located at 235 S. Camac St. between 12th & 13th, Locust & Spruce Sts.

The history of the Philadelphia Sketch Club dates back to November 20, 1860, when six students and former students of the Pennsylvania Academy of the Fine Arts decided to form an illustration group to hone their skills in illustration. The group quickly expanded to include artists who worked in a variety of media. Public programs encouraging the making and appreciation of art date back to the organization's earliest days.

Today the Philadelphia Sketch Club provides an environment where a wide range of visual artists can interact with one another and involve themselves directly in public arts programming, thereby becoming part of a community with a common focus.

The Philadelphia Sketch Club's low cost, open enrollment workshops attract a large number of participants, and the atmosphere encourages development of one's own approach to making art rather than dictating a particular method or style. In presenting exhibitions,

Tea in the Afternoon by Joseph Pennell. Courtesy of Free Library of Philadelphia

the PSC strives for variety in terms of subject, approach, and medium which we feel presents the best opportunity to educate those who attend our exhibitions. The PSC has a number of ongoing programs aimed at young artists to include an annual exhibition of works by students from the School District of Philadelphia and a portfolio review program for college art students.

The membership of the PSC has included many noted artists including Thomas Eakins, Thomas Anshata, Thomas Moran, Daniel Ridgway Knight, Joseph Pennell, H. Lyman Sagen, N.C. Wyeth, and Earl Horter.

The PSC also retains a permanent collection of art, artifacts, and documents. The PSC's facility, a Federal Period triple row house, blends the quaintness and parochial flavor of the art world of the past with the excitement and regional focus of the art world today.

SARTAIN FAMILY

John Sartain (1808-1897)

Born in London, England, in 1808 John Sartain introduced from London the art of mezzotint engraving – a process which helps turn oil paintings into prints. Engraving was a process to translate color originals into black and white reproductions.

"Mezzotint engraving involves rocking a spiky roulette wheel or other similar gravers' tool across a metal plate (either copper or steel) in different directions until the plate is covered with tiny burrs of raised metal. If inked and printed at this point, the plate will print completely black. The engraver, by burnishing or scraping away the fragile burr, is able to produce degrees of shadow from black to white without the lines common to etching or line engraving. This process most closely resembles and best recreates the effects rendered in oil paintings."[21]

John Sartain is thought to have engraved over 1500 prints during his career. Many of these were illustrations commissioned by the leading magazines of the day, including *Godey's Lady's Book*, *Graham's Magazine*, the *Eclectic* and *Nineteenth Century*. Sartain also tried producing his own magazine (with the help of William Sloanaker) – the *Union Magazine of Literature and Art*. Writers included Longfellow and Poe. The magazine, which had its first issue in 1849, failed in 1852 and Sartain spent years paying off the debts."

"Three of his children with wife Susannah – Emily, Samuel, and William gained their own prominence in the art world."[22]

BRANDYWINE ILLUSTRATORS

Howard Pyle (1853-1911)

In the last fifteen years of his life Howard Pyle taught some of the best artists of a generation the art of illustration. Rebuffed by the Pennsylvania Academy of the Fine Arts, illustration wasn't considered to be a "fine art," Mr. Pyle set up his teaching shop at Drexel Institute in Philadelphia in 1894. Wanting to work with the best illustrators he decided to set up shop in Wilmington, Delaware, and taught summer classes in Chadds Ford, Pennsylvania (the geographical area encompassing these two locations is known as Brandywine Valley).

Pyle's teaching expertise included composition – a picture had to tell a story.

Pyle began as a writer. He also worked as an illustrator for Harper & Brothers and their variety of publications including *Harper's Weekly and Monthly* and *Harper's Bazaar*. It was those dual skills that allowed him to know which parts of various writings needed illustrations. He crafted his compositions like actors on a stage. His illustrations of Pirates, the American Revolution, and the Civil War have become standards.

Among his students were Newell Convers Wyeth, Harvey Dunn, Dean Cornwall, Phillip Russell Goodwin, and Frank Earle Schoonover.[23, 24] These artists are known as the artists of the Brandywine School, as are their disciples. The subject matter of the artists included (but wasn't limited to) the beautiful farmland environs of the Brandywine River Valley.

Pyle's art can be seen at the Delaware Museum of Art (formerly the Wilmington Society of Fine Arts) in Wilmington, Delaware and the Brandywine River Museum in Pennsylvania. Mr. Schonover helped launch the Wilmington Society of Fine Arts and was a lifetime director.[25]

N.C. Wyeth and Family[26]

After a year and a half of Pyle's instruction, N.C. Wyeth's work began to appear in national publications such as *Colliers*, *Harper's*, *Scribner's*, and the cover of *The Saturday Evening Post*.

Wyeth's western travels gave him plenty of material for his art. Back east, in 1911, he purchased eighteen acres of land in Chadds Ford, in the heart of the Brandywine River Valley. He and his family have stayed there since.

N.C. Wyeth worked with Scribner's to illustrate some of best known adventure classics: *Treasure Island*, *Kidnapped*, *The Yearling*, *The Boy's King Arthur*, *The Black Arrow*, *Robin Hood*, and the *Last of the Mohicans*.

In addition to his illustrations, N.C. Wyeth gained inspiration from the beautiful nature around Chadds Ford. His son Andrew and grandson James became famous painters. His other children were successful in a variety of arts.

He died early, in 1945.[27, 28, 29]

Andrew Wyeth

Andrew Wyeth, the son of N. C. Wyeth, is one of America's most famous realist painters. He was born on July 12, 1917.

His early paintings were in oils and watercolors. The focus of his subjects are "the quiet corners of existence" and the "minutia of nature" around him. In addition to paintings of his hometown, Chadds Ford, Andrew Wyeth's paintings also include the surrounding area of his summer home in Cushing, Maine. His portraits tend to be of people he knows – "family members, neighbors, drifters, and misfits."[30]

Perhaps his most famous painting is that of Christina Olson, a friend of his wife Betsy James Wyeth. The painting is Christina's World (Museum of Modern Art, 1948, New York). Other celebrated works include those of a model – Helga Testorf and Kuener's farm, the farm of his friends Anna and Karl Kuener.

"Wyeth's brother-in-law, Peter Hurd, introduced the young artist to egg tempera, the medium that would allow Wyeth to achieve the superb textural effects that distinguish his work. It was quick drying and had a fresco-like surface when dry. Those characteristics appealed to Wyeth, who has commented to Richard Merryman in *Andrew Wyeth:*

A Secret Life that, 'Oil is hot and fiery, almost like a summer night, where tempera is a cool breeze, dry, crackling like winter branches blowing in the wind. I'm a dry person, really. I'm not a juicy painter. There's no fight in oil. It doesn't have the austere in it'."

His paintings are spread throughout the world. The largest homes are the Brandywine River Museum in Chadds Ford, Pennsylvania; the Farnsworth Museum of Art in Rockland, Maine; and the Greenville County Museum of Art in Greenville, South Carolina.

James Browning Wyeth

The third generation of the Wyeth family of painters included James Browning Wyeth (b. 1946), the nephew of Carolyn Wyeth who served as his teacher. Andrew Wyeth is his father. While Andrew disliked oils James chose oil as his main medium though he works in a variety of mediums including what he calls "combined mediums" which "primarily consists of watercolor and gouache painted with thick impasto layered with selective varnishes, but can include anything, and has even included three dimensional-elements such as 19th-century whale bone letters adhered to paper." (Eat, 1999) *(http://www.farnsworthmuseum.org/james-wyeth)*

James paintings have more of an urban influence. "In New York he was mentored by New York City Ballet founder Lincoln Kirstein, whose portrait he painted, and later he worked in the studio of his friend Andy Warhol, whose portrait he also painted."

Subject matters, in addition to Chadds Ford, have included John F. Kennedy, the participants in the Watergate trials and congressional hearings (he was commissioned by *Harper's Magazine*), and NASA in the late 1960s and 1970s. Maine and Monhegan Island have been favorite sources. Famous paintings include Portrait of a Pig, Newfoundland (1971) and The Raven (1980).[30, 30a, 31, 32]

Brandywine River Museum[33, 34]

The Brandywine River Museum, in Chadds Ford, a renovated nineteenth-century brick gristmill, houses "hundreds of illustrations, landscapes, still-lifes, interiors, portraits and nude figure studies."

Some of the work of the Wyeths is housed in the Museum, including Henriette Wyeth's portraits of her sister Carolyn and of Andrew and Betsy Wyeth and Carolyn Wyeth's Dark Shore (1933) and Deep Summer (1956) and her portrait of the Wyeth homestead, Up from the Woods (1974).[35, 36]

The Brandywine River Museum's emphasis is on American illustration. "Among the hundreds of illustrators represented are early twentieth-century giants such as Edwin Austin Abbey, Winslow Homer, Howard Chandler Christy, Charles Dana Gibson, Rose O'Neill, Maxfield Parrish, and Rockwell Kent; late twentieth-century cartoonists, such as Al Hirschfeld, Charles Addams, Edward Gorey, and Charles Schultz; and other illustrators such as Theodor Geisel (Dr. Seuss), Charles Santore, and Nancy Eckholm Burkert."

"The collection also includes the art of Reginald Marsh, George Bellows, and Frederic Remington."

ASHCAN SCHOOL

Robert Henri (1865-1929)

Robert Henri (born Robert Henry Cozad until his family changed their name) was born in Ohio. Eighteen years later the family moved to Atlantic City. Henri studied at the Pennsylvania Academy with Thomas Anshutz from 1886 to 1888. Henri then left for Europe where he studied at the Académie Julian and Ecole des Beaux Arts in Paris. He returned to Philadelphia in 1891 where he began teaching professionally at the Philadelphia School of Design for Women (now Moore College of Art) in 1892.

"During this time, Henri met and befriended a group of young artists and newspaper illustrators who admired him for his talent and the fact that he was one of few artists in Philadelphia to have studied in Paris. Henri invited these men to his studio for weekly discussions on art, ethics, literature, music, and politics, which, consequently, created a dynamic artistic environment. More importantly, however, he lectured on the role of artists in the United States. Henri firmly believed that serious artists should develop their own means of expression, and not be pressured into following - and perpetuating - aesthetic conventions."

Four of the friends (Henri wasn't that much older) were newspaper illustrators, William Glackens, George Luks, Everett Shinn, and John Sloan, who, collectively, were known as the "Philadelphia Four." Although three of the four had studied at the PAFA, they did not aspire to be serious artists. Henri, however, encouraged them to paint. Henri encouraged them to "Paint what you feel. Paint what you see. Paint what is real to you."

Henri believed that before Philadelphia would accept his work and that of his students, their work had to be accepted in Paris. Some were so accepted. In 1990 Henri and the "Philadelphia Four" also moved to New York where Henri took a teaching position at the New York School of Art.

Henri became involved with the various art juries, including the relatively conservative National Academy of Design. While his works were accepted there, those of his students were not. The differences cam to a head. In 1908 Henri arranged for a separate exhibition of Eight artists at the MacBeth Gallery in New York The "Eight" as they came to be known, were Henri, Glackens, Luks, Shinn, Sloan, Arthur B. Davies, Ernest Lawson, and Maurice Prendergast).

"The exhibition, which opened on February 3, 1908, was an immediate success, not only because of its publicity, which was provided for by the "Philadelphia Four," but also because the works were more accurate and livelier representations of life in the United States than anything selected for exhibition by the Academy." The critics reviews were mixed. The ones who liked the art liked the creativity and truthfulness The exhibition encouraged other progressive artists.

Henri left the New York School of Art and opened his own schools. His students included Patrick Henry Bruce, Stuart Davis, Edward Hopper, Rockwell Kent, and Yasuo Kuniyoshi. Henri's notes and criticisms were published, in 1923, in his book, The Art Spirit. *(Resource Library Magazine (www.tfaoi.com) and the Minnesota Museum of American Art)*

William Glackens (1870-1938)

William Glackens and John Sloan both attended Central High School. Both served as illustrators for the local Philadelphia newspapers of their day and along with other artists moved to New York and joined the Ashcan movement.

Many years later, after 1910, Glackens advised [Albert] Barnes in forming his famous collection of modern art. Glackens also worked as an illustrator for *The Saturday Evening Post*.

"Glackens had an incredible visual memory, frequently going out on assignment without pencil or paper and producing accurate drawings when he returned. The implications of this intensive visual training for the future members of the so-called 'Ash Can' school should be obvious; in a sense, they learned to observe before they learned to paint, and they captured movement and gesture in their work before being schooled in 'correct' drawing in the academic sense." [37]

John Sloan (1871-1951)

Sloan painted in New York, as well as other sites. His New York paintings included one of his best – Recruiting in Union Square were displayed at the Pennsylvania Academy of the Fine Arts. [38]

Much of Sloan's work can be seen at the Delaware Museum of Art.

Herbert Pullinger (1878-1961)

According to the Philadelphia Print Shop – "Herbert Pullinger was a lifelong resident of Philadelphia and popular teacher at the old Philadelphia Museum School of Industrial Arts from 1923 to 1958," He worked as a painter, printmaker, and commercial illustrator.

He was also part of the Ashcan School.

Tea in the Afternoon by John Sloan. Original image from Philadelphia Press – Public Domain

PENNSYLVANIA IMPRESSIONISM

Text reprinted with permission of University of Pennsylvania Press and Brian Peterson from Pennsylvania Impressionism (source: www.upennedu.pennpress)

Many artists like the Wyeth family left the city for more rural pastures where they set up artist colonies to support each other.

One of the best known of these colonies formed in 1898 on the banks of the Delaware River north of Philadelphia, centered in the picturesque village of New Hope, Bucks County. Known as the Pennsylvania impressionists, this group of artists played a dominant role in the American art world of the 1910s and 1920s, winning major awards and sitting on prestigious exhibition juries. Their work was celebrated for its freedom from European influence, and was praised by the noted painter and critic Guy Pene du Bois as "our first truly national expression." Many of the Pennsylvania impressionists both studied and taught at the Pennsylvania Academy of the Fine Arts in Philadelphia, and their stylistic roots hearkened back to the "academy realism" practiced by Thomas Eakins and his followers.

Edward Redfield was the generally acknowledged stylistic leader of the New Hope painters; his vigorously realistic, unsentimental brand of impressionism influenced several generations of artists associated with the group. However, what most characterized Pennsylvania impressionism was not a single, unified style but rather the emergence of many mature, distinctive voices: Daniel Garber's luminous, poetic renditions of the Delaware River; Fern Coppedge's colorful village scenes; Robert Spencer's lyrical views of mills and tenements; John Folinsbee's moody, expressionistic snowscapes; and William L. Lathrop's deeply felt, evocative Bucks County vistas.

Pennsylvania impressionist artwork is now widely collected, and many works in private hands are shown here, as well as the holdings of the James A. Michener Museum, recognized as the most extensive public collection.[39] Many Pennsylvania Impressionism works were purchased by Gerry and Marguerite Lenfest and given for the James Michener Museum in Bucks County which houses a Pennsylvania Impressionism collection.

Edward W. Redfield CRAFTSPERSON, PAINTER

BORN: December 18, 1869, Bridgeville, Delaware
DIED: October 19, 1965, Center Bridge, Pennsylvania

The Pennsylvania school born in the Academy at Philadelphia or in the person of Edward W. Redfield is a very concise expression of the simplicity of our language and of the prosaic nature of our sight. It is democratic painting—broad, without subtlety, vigorous in language if not absolutely in heart, blatantly obvious or honest in feeling. It is an unbiased, which means, inartistic, record of nature.

—Guy Pene du Bois

Text reprinted with permission of the James Michener Museum (www.michenermuseum.org)

Among the New Hope impressionists, Edward Willis Redfield was the most decorated, winning more awards than any American artist except John Singer Sargent. Primarily a landscape painter, Redfield was acclaimed as the most "American" artist of the New Hope school because of his vigor and individualism. Redfield favored the technique of painting en plein air, that is, outdoors amidst nature. Tying his canvas to a tree, Redfield worked in even most the brutal weather. Painting rapidly, in thick, broad brush strokes, and without attempting preliminary sketches, Redfield typically completed his paintings in one sitting. Although Redfield is best known for his snow scenes, he painted several spring and summer landscapes, often set in Maine, where he spent his summers. He also painted cityscapes, including, most notably, Between Daylight and Darkness (1909), an almost surreal tonalist painting of the New York skyline in twilight. Blessed with a long life, Redfield painted until the age of 84, when he began to lose the vigor he needed for his physically demanding artistic practices.

Daniel Garber PAINTER, PRINTMAKER

BORN: April 11, 1880, North Manchester, Indiana
DIED: July 5, 1958, Cuttalossa, Lumberville, Pennsylvania

[O]ut of the realism of the Bucks County countryside [Garber] created an ideal, almost mystical world. – Lauren Rabb, Pennsylvania Impressionists: Painters of the New Hope School

Daniel Garber was one of the most important painters of New Hope's second generation. Born of Old German Baptist farming stock in Indiana, Garber moved east as a teenager to pursue his dream career as an artist. After studying at the Pennsylvania Academy of the Fine Arts and in Europe, Garber settled down to painting in his home, Cuttalossa, in Lumberville. Garber's style combines realism and fantasy, precise draftsmanship and decorative technique, emblazoning all in vibrant, shimmering colors. A landscape artist, Garber was best known for his paintings of Bucks County woods and quarries. To a greater extent than many of his New Hope colleagues, Garber also achieved recognition as a figure painter. A leading instructor at the Pennsylvania Academy of the Fine Arts for over forty years, Garber influenced younger generations of painters, as well.

BUCKS COUNTY
MODERNISTS

The Modernists led by artists working from the art enclave of West Mechanic Street in New Hope, were fed up with the conservativism of the Impressionists.

The modern artists working in New Hope included such masters as: Lloyd (Bill) Ney, Adolph Blondheim, Charles Evans, Peter Keenan, Ralston Crawford, Charles F. Ramsey, B.J.O. Nordfeldt, Charles Rosen, Louis Stone, Elsie Driggs, and Lee Gatch.

SCULPTURES AND
STATUES

Text reprinted with permission of Public Art in Philadelphia website

Philadelphia is blessed with a number of marvelous sculptures and statues, commemorating heroes, popular leaders, "patriotic ideals, and historic events." From Lazzarini's marble figure of Benjamin Franklin to Pinto's Fingerspan in Fairmount Park, from Laurel Hill Cemetery's celebrated sculpture garden to Lipchitz's controversial Government of the People...public art has continued to enhance, define, and challenge Philadelphians' perception of their city.

The armchair tourist, for example, can visit Dickens and Little Nell in Clark Park, the John Wanamaker's Eagle, the All Wars Memorial to Colored Soldiers and Sailors in Fairmount Park, or the Julius Erving Memorial on Ridge Avenue, among many others.[40]

Many of the best known statues are visible by walking down the Benjamin Franklin Parkway or are in buildings along the Parkway.

Buds and Blossoms by Daniel Garber. 1916 Oil on Canvas. Courtesy of Philadelphia Museum of Art: Promised gift of Margaerite and Gerry Lenfest

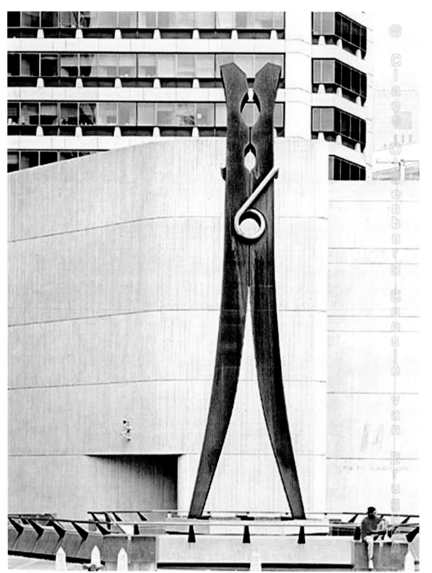

Clothespin, 1976, Cor-Ten and stainless steels, 45 ft. x 12 ft. 3 in. x 4 ft. 6 in. (13.7 x 3.7 x 1.4 m), Centre Square Plaza, Fifteenth and Market streets, Philadelphia, Photo by Attilio Maranzano, Sculpture by Claes Oldenberg. Courtesy of Claes Oldenburg

Holocaust Sculpture. Sculpture to the Martyrs.

By C. Natan Rapoport (1964).

This tribute to the victims of the holocaust shows humanity scrambled together trying to reach out for survival. It is in memory of the six million Jewish martyrs who perished at the hands of the Nazis between 1933 and 1945. It is a powerful statement of struggle and agony. Among the striving figures can be discerned the torah, an old scholar wearing his prayer shawl, and an arm holding a sword for freedom. [Inscription]

Viewable at the corner of 16th and Arch Street.[41]

Government of the People

By Jacques Lipchitz, 1976. In front of the Municipal Services Building.

Northwest corner, Broad and JFK

This sculpture was completed after Jacques Liphchitz died and after some controversy over the funding of it. Private donations were needed when the city terminated its option.

Clothespin

Claes Oldenberg

Oldenburg's sculptures depicting normal every day items in large scale size are many. The clothespin sculpture is forty-five feet high. His large broken button adorns the University of Pennsylvania Campus.[42]

MUSEUMS

The University of Pennsylvania Museum of Archaeology and Anthropology

3620 South Street

Text from the website (http://www.museum.upenn.edu/new/about/index.php) of the University of Pennsylvania Museum of Archaeology and Anthropology

Penn Museum, founded in 1887, "seeks to advance understanding of the world's cultural heritage." The Museum has sent more than 400 archaeological and anthropological expeditions to all the inhabited continents of the world. "Three gallery floors feature materials from Egypt, Mesopotamia, the Bible Lands, Mesoamerica, Asia, and the ancient Mediterranean World, as well as artifacts from native peoples of the Americas, Africa, and Polynesia."

The Rodin Museum

Benjamin Franklin Parkway at 22nd Street

The Rodin Museum, at 21st and Callowhill Streets, was donated by Jules Mastbaum, the theatrical magnate. Mastbaum commissioned Paul Cret and Jacques Garber, two French Neoclassical artists, to build the museum and a garden.

The Rodin Museum, which opened to the public in 1929, houses 124 sculptures, including bronze casts of the artist's greatest works: *The Thinker*, perhaps the most famous sculpture in the world; *The Burghers of Calais*, his most heroic and moving historical tribute; *Eternal Springtime*, one of the most powerful works dealing with human love; powerful monuments to leading French intellectuals such as *Apotheosis of Victor Hugo*; and the culminating creation of his career, *The Gates of Hell*, on which the artist worked from 1880 until his death in 1917.

The reflecting pool in the garden courtyard evokes calm and echoes the cool beauty that the visitor will experience within the building.[43]

African American Museum

701 Arch Street

Text from the AAMP website.

Founded in 1976 as the Afro-American Historical and Cultural Museum in celebration of the nation's Bicentennial, the Museum was the first institution funded and built by a major municipality to preserve, interpret, and exhibit the heritage of African Americans. Throughout its evolution, the Museum has objectively interpreted and presented the achievements and aspirations of African Americans from pre-colonial times to the current day. The African American Museum in Philadelphia currently houses four galleries and an auditorium, each of which offers exhibitions anchored by one of the Museum's three dominant themes – the African Diaspora, the Philadelphia Story, and the Contemporary Narrative.

Pennsylvania Academy of the Fine Arts

118 N. Broad Street

Text reprinted with permission of PAFA (source: www.pafa.org)

HISTORY

The Pennsylvania Academy of the Fine Arts was founded in 1805 by painter and scientist Charles Willson Peale, sculptor William Rush, and other artists and business leaders. It is the oldest art museum and school in the nation. The Academy's museum is internationally known for its collections of nineteenth and twentieth century American paintings, sculptures, and works on paper. Its archives house important materials for the study of American art history, museums, and art training.

A concerted effort is made to represent women and culturally-diverse artists in the collections and exhibitions...

Some of the many museums not covered in detail but definitely worth a visit include:

American Helicopter Museum
American Swedish Historical Museum
Atwater Kent
Carpenters Hall
ChildVenture Museum
Congress Hall
Declaration House
Delaware Museum of Natural History
Eastern State Penitentiary
Edgar Allan Poe National Historical Site
Elfreth's Alley Museum
Fabric Workshop and Museum
Fireman's Hall
Fonthill Museum
Franklin Court
Garden State Discovery Museum
Independence Seaport Museum
Insectarium
Institute of Contemporary Art
Japanese House and Garden
Mercer Museum
National Liberty Museum
National Museum of American Jewish History
Philadelphia Doll Museum
Please Touch Museum
Polish American Cultural Center
Rosenbach Museum and Library
Taller Puertorriqueno
Winterthur

Pennsylvania Academy of Fine Arts Campus. Photograph by Tom Crane. Courtesy of Pennsylvania Academy of Fine Arts, Philadelphia, PA

THE BUILDINGS

The Academy's historic landmark building opened in 1876. The building, designed by the Philadelphia firm of Frank Furness and George Hewitt, is generally considered to be primarily the work of Furness who finished the project after the partnership dissolved in 1875. Furness had been a pupil of Richard Morris Hunt, who introduced him to the esthetics of the modern Gothic revival. This included John Ruskin's appreciation of the richly colored designs of fourteenth century Venice, Owen Jones's and Christopher Dresser's Eastern influenced ornament, and Viollet le Duc's use of foliated decoration combined with cast-iron architecture. The building is considered one of the finest surviving examples of Victorian Gothic architecture in America. It was carefully restored in 1976.

The Academy opened the Samuel M.V. Hamilton Building, which houses additional studios and classrooms for the school and post-World War II art, opened to the public in 2005, during the Academy's 200th anniversary celebration. The nearly 300,000-square-foot building, originally built for the Gomery-Schwarz automobile company, was acquired by the Academy from the federal government in 1999.

SCULPTURE

Sculpture has been an intrinsic part of the Academy since its founding in 1805. William Rush, one of the three artists connected with the formation of the Pennsylvania Academy of the Fine Arts, was also one of the nation's first sculptors, representative of the American craft tradition aspiring to European fine arts.

The Academy holds several notable works by Rush, including a masterful self-portrait.

The kind of art tradition Rush sought to emulate is represented in the collection by his contemporary, Jean-Antoine Houdon, a French sculptor who memorialized several of America's Founding Fathers, and by later nineteenth century American sculptors working in a neoclassical style, including Hiram Powers, William Wetmore Story, Randolph Rogers, and Joseph Alexis Bailly. Bailly was the first of the Academy's notable sculpture instructors now represented in the collection. Others include Thomas Eakins, Charles Grafly, Albert Laessle, and Walker Hancock.

With more than 300 works ranging from 1780 to the present, the Academy's sculpture collection is particularly notable for its portrait busts, neoclassical marble sculpture, French-inspired bronze figures, direct carvings in stone and wood, and the overall variety of materials and techniques represented. Other major artists represented in the sculpture collection include Augustus Saint-Gaudens, John Quincy Adams Ward, A. Stirling Calder, Gaston Lachaise, Alexander Calder, Chaim Gross, Isamu Noguchi, David Smith, Leonard Baskin, Louise Nevelson, George Segal, Mary Frank, Red Grooms, Siah Armajani, and Nancy Graves.

PAINTINGS

With a collection of nearly 2,000 paintings, the Pennsylvania Academy owns some of the most important and recognizable works in American art. Benjamin West's Penn's Treaty with the Indians (1771-72), Gilbert Stuart's George Washington, Charles Willson Peale's The Artist in His Museum (1822), and Winslow Homer's The Fox Hunt (1893) are only a handful of such major works.

The paintings collection is renowned for its holdings from the Federal period, including works by the Peale family, numerous portraits by Gilbert Stuart and Thomas Sully, and a fine collection of portrait miniatures.

Works from the late 19th century, when American artists began working in a more international style, constitute one of the high points of the Academy's collection. Paintings by William Merritt Chase, James McNeill Whistler, John Singer Sargent, Mary Cassatt, John Twachtman, Theodore Robinson, Childe Hassam, Henry O. Tanner, Cecilia Beaux, and Thomas Eakins are among the most significant examples. In the early twentieth century, the Academy collected works by some of its famous alumni, including Robert Henri, John Sloan, William Glackens, Everett Shinn, and George Luks, all of whom were connected with the Ashcan School.

Twentieth century developments in abstraction are documented in the collection by artists such as Arthur B. Carles, Florine Stettheimer, Stuart Davis, Georgia O'Keeffe, Ben Shahn, Jack Levine, Mark Rothko, Jacob Lawrence, Richard Diebenkorn, Adolph Gottlieb, and Leon Golub.

As a school synonymous with the figurative tradition, the Academy's collections also are rich in the works of twentieth-century representational artists such as Edward Hopper, Guy Pène du Bois, Reginald Marsh, Isabel Bishop, Thomas Hart Benton, Alfred Leslie, Philip Pearlstein, Andrew Wyeth and Bo Bartlett, Alex Katz, Alice Neel, and Vincent Desiderio.

FAMOUS ACADEMY ARTISTS

Many of America's greatest artists have been affiliated with the Pennsylvania Academy of the Fine Arts, either as founders, students, faculty, exhibitors, or with works now part of the permanent collection.

Some Pennsylvania Academy stars:

Thomas P. Anshutz	Cecilia Beaux
Alexander Stirling Calder	Arthur B. Carles
Mary Cassatt	Thomas Eakins
Frank Furness	Daniel Garber
William Glackens	Charles Grafly
Robert Henri	John Marin
Violet Oakley	Maxfield Parrish
Charles Willson Peale	Rembrandt Peale
William Rush	The Sartain Family
Morton Schamberg	Everett Shinn
John Sloan	Henry O. Tanner
Benjamin West[44]	

The Incense Burner by Thomas P. Anshutz. Oil on Canvas, Ca. 1905, 64 x 40 in. Acc. No. 1940.11. Courtesy of the Pennsylvania Academy of Fine Arts, Philadelphia, PA Henry D. Gilpin Fund

Philadelphia Museum of Art

Text reprinted with permission of Philadelphia Museum of Art website

26th Street and the Benjamin Franklin Parkway

The Philadelphia Museum of Art is described in the city section, as one of the buildings along the Parkway. A few additional items to consider about the museum are:

The Museum was built with the help of a number of architects, including Horace Trumbauer and the firm of Zanizinger, Borie, and Morday. The two side pavilions were built first to insure city funding for the completion. It was built in response to the Centennial Exposition of 1876.

The Building

Echoing the design of a Greek temple but of more massive Roman proportions, the Museum building is considered one of the crowning achievements of the "city beautiful" movement in architecture in the early part of the twentieth century. It is constructed of pure Minnesota dolomite, with glazed blue roof tiles embellished with polychrome finials and pediments. Covering ten acres of ground, it contains over 200 galleries.

Of special interest on the exterior of the building is the group of polychrome terracotta sculptures in the tympanum of the pediment on the North Wing, which was designed by sculptor C. Paul Jennewein and installed in 1933. This marked the Museum as the first major building in over 2,000 years to adapt polychromy in this manner. In ancient Greek architecture, however, the architectural ornament and sculpture in terracotta and stone were painted with perishable pigments, while those of the Museum are of ceramic glazes. The completed tympanum encompasses ten free-standing figures, mythological Greek gods and goddesses signifying sacred and profane love. Executed in brilliant colors and gold glazes, the tympanum is seventy-feet wide at its base above the supporting columns, rising to twelve feet in height at the center. It is an outstanding example of ceramic art in color.

Jennewein also modeled the bronze doors of the elevators inside the Museum, while the octagonal bronze basin for the great fountain on the East Terrace, with bas-reliefs depicting Courtship, was designed by the Philadelphia sculptor Henry Mitchell (1915-1980) and installed in 1958. The acroteria of the roof are adorned with bronze griffins, seated with one paw outstretched or standing watchfully. This mythological creature, traditionally a guardian of treasure, has served as the symbol of the Museum since the 1970s.

Inside, the Great Stair Hall is awesome in its magnitude and provides a fitting setting for the thirteen magnificent tapestries from the Palazzo Barberini in Rome (a gift of the Samuel H. Kress Foundation), "Diana" at the top of the stairs whose poised figure once graced – as a weathervane – the first Madison Square Garden in New York (Gotham, likely, would like to have it back), and "Ghost," a mobile by the present-day Alexander Calder, son of the sculptor of the Logan Circle fountain and grandson of the man who created William Penn on the top of City Hall.

Early History – 1920s

It was during this important period in the Museum's history that the distinguished architectural historian Fiske Kimball (1888–1955) was appointed Director, in 1925. Under his leadership the Museum forged ahead to the front ranks of art institutions in the United States. In his capable hands was placed the responsibility not only for the architectural development of the interior plan, but also the acquisition of collections that would be worthy of the building and of the city.

Kimball lost no time in devising a unique plan for the installation of the Museum. On the second floor, the principal exhibition area, would be a series of galleries arranged in historical sequence, encompassing a selection of masterpieces in painting and sculpture along with architectural elements, furniture, and other objects of their time. This arrangement would, in Kimball's words, 'enable the visitor to retrace the great historic pageant of the evolution of art.' Where possible, these masterpieces were to be installed in actual interiors of the appropriate period. At once, Kimball set about acquiring many of the Museum's period rooms and finding donors to purchase them, sending his curators to Japan, China, France, England, and Holland.

Collections Overview

One of the nation's great artistic and historic resources, the Museum houses more than 225,000 objects spanning the creative achievements of the Western world since the first century A.D. and those of Asia since the third millennium B.C.

Highlights of the Asian collections include paintings and sculpture from China, Japan, and India; furniture and decorative arts, including major collections of Chinese, Japanese, and Korean ceramics; a large and distinguished group of Persian and Turkish carpets; and rare and authentic architectural assemblages such as a Japanese teahouse, a Chinese palace hall, and a sixteenth century Indian temple hall.

The European collections, dating from the Medieval era to the present, encompass Italian and Flemish early Renaissance masterworks; strong representations of later European paintings, including French Impressionism and Post-Impressionism;

sculpture, with a special concentration in the works of Auguste Rodin; decorative arts; tapestries; furniture; the second largest collection of arms and armor in the United States; and period rooms and architectural settings ranging from the façade of a Medieval church in Burgundy to a superbly decorated English drawing room by Robert Adam.

The Museum's American collections, surveying three centuries of painting, sculpture, and decorative arts, are among the finest in the United States, with outstanding strengths in eighteenth and nineteenth century Philadelphia furniture and silver, rural Pennsylvania furniture and ceramics, and the paintings of Thomas Eakins.

Holdings of modern art include extraordinary concentrations of work by such artists as Pablo Picasso, Marcel Duchamp, and Constantin Brancusi as well as American modernists, making the Museum one of the best in world in which to see modern art. The expanding collection of contemporary art includes major works by Cy Twombly, Jasper Johns, and Sol LeWitt, among many others. In addition to these collections, the Museum houses encyclopedic holdings of costume and textiles as well as prints, drawings, and photographs that are displayed in rotation for reasons of preservation.

The collections in the Museum are comprised of:

Philadelphia History
Crafts – hand and machine.
World Interiors – Japan, China, England, and others.

There are collections from families such as Thomas Eakins, John G. Johnson [McIlheny], Marey Adeline Williams, and others.

The Galleries
American Art
Arms & Armor
Asian Art
Costume & Textiles
Dutch Ceramics
European Art 1100-1500
European Art 1500-1850
European Art 1850-1900
Modern & Contemporary
Prints, Drawings & Photographs

The most recent long-tenured Museum Director was Anne D'Harnoncourt The Philadelphia Museum of Art recently celebrated its 125th anniversary.

COLLECTORS

Philadelphia had many art collectors in the nineteenth and twentieth centuries. The Widener Collection was donated to the National Gallery of Art.

Other collections included those of George and William Elkins, and Henry P. McIlhenny.

Albert Barnes and John G. Johnson. Two of the best known collectors were Albert Barnes and John G. Johnson. Another noted collector was Peter Widener, who donated his artwork outside the city.

The legal disputes of the Barnes Foundation and the life of attorney Johnson are discussed in the law chapter.

The John G. Johnson collection is on display at the Philadelphia Museum of Art.

The Barnes Foundation

Albert Coombs Barnes was born in 1972 in the white working class neighborhood of Kensington. He attended Central High School, one of the leading public secondary schools of his day. At Central, Barnes developed a friendship with William Glackens, who later would become a renowned painter with the Ashcan Eight Movement. Barnes received a medical degree from the University of Pennsylvania, where he helped to support himself through tutoring and boxing.

Discovering that he didn't like the practice of medicine, Barnes went back to school in Berlin – where he studied chemistry and physiology. While he Berlin, Barnes recruited Herman Hille, a pharmacologist to help create an antiseptic silver compound called Argyrol. Hille, who had invented the compound and Barnes who marketed it, formed a firm. In 1907, Barnes, with the aid of Philadelphia lawyer and

Charles Laughton Visits Dr. Albert C. Barnes.
Courtesy of Temple University Archives

art collector John Graver Johnson, bought out Hille, who was obligated to disclose to Barnes the secret formula. Through his new business Dr. Barnes amassed a fortune. The workforce was racially-integrated and included both genders.

Barnes reunited with Glackens and gave Glackens the green-light to begin buying some of the new Impressionist paintings. Barnes also befriended Leo Stein (the brother of the writer Gertrude Stein), who helped Barnes with the buying of additional modern artwork. Barnes worked with a number of Parisian art dealers in expanding his collection.

Barnes enlisted Paul Phillipe-Cret to build a home for the art (next to Barnes' personal home) in Merion. Cret built a French chateu housing twenty-three galleries. Cret is credited for being the architect of the Benjamin Franklin Bridge and the Rodin Museum. The Barnes Foundation was also established to "promote the advancement of education and the appreciation of the fine arts." The collection is one of the largest collections of Impressionist, Post-Impressionist, and early Modern paintings. The location also included an Arboretum. Barnes' wife, Laura, in 1940, established the Arboretum School where students could learn horticulture, botany, and landscape architecture under the guidance of first-rate faculty.

Barnes, who grew up in a working class environment, was never one to warm to the high-society world. When he was young he attended African American camp revival meetings (Barnes and many African Americans were Methodists). From this early age Barnes became friendly and appreciative of many African Americans. He would later require that nearby Lincoln University, a pre-eminent African American University of its day, have control of nominating the Trustees for his Foundation after he died. His friendship also led him to collect and support the art, culture, and rights of African Americans. One of the notable students of the Barnes Foundation was local Philadelphia artist Horace Pippin.

Barnes was not just interested in collecting art. With the aid of John Dewey (a professor at Columbia University), George Santayana, and William James (philosopher and brother to the writer Henry James), Barnes developed his own theories about art education. He wanted the workingman to appreciate and study art. It was this appreciation for the workingman that led Barnes to create the Barnes Foundation in 1922, with Dewey as the Foundation's first director of education.

The Barnes collection is notable for the way it is displayed. The art isn't arranged by period or by artist. Rather each room is arranged for its aesthetics.

The Barnes art is now in the process of being moved back into Philadelphia, near the Philadelphia Museum of Art. The hope of some Philadelphians is that along with the Pennsylvania Academy of Fine Arts, the Rodin Museum, and the Philadelphia Museum of Art that the addition of the Barnes art on the Benjamin Franklin Parkway will create a "Miracle Mile" of great others. The hope is balanced by the frustration of many who believe that Barnes wish to keep the art in Merion should be respected and that the experience and education of viewing the art in the Merion location will be lost on the moving of the art.

The Charles L. Blockson Afro-American Collection
Text reprinted with permission of Charles Blockson, Temple University

Charles L. Blockson spent more than forty years amassing one of the of nation's largest private collections of items relating to Black history. In 1984, he donated his collection to Temple University in Philadelphia.

The collection includes over 200,000 items (books, pamphlets, prints, drawings, posters, sheet music, statues, busts, and artifacts) spanning three continents and nearly four centuries.

Mr. Blockson served as chair of the Underground Railroad Advisory Committee and directed the National Park Service's resulting studies, including the Official Map and Guide of the Underground Railroad.

His latest book is *Damn Rare: The Memoirs of an African American Bibliophile*, published in 1998.

Photograph: Members of several famous Philadelphia African American Families are shown standing inside a Philadelphia church in 1944.
First row: Gertrude Bustill, Paul Robeson's Aunt (with scarf), Attorney Sadie Mossell Alexander with her daughter Mary
Second row: Marian Robeson Forsythe (Paul Robeson's sister), Paul Robeson, Gertrude Bustill Cunningham (with white hat) and Dr. Nathaniel Mossell
Third row: Far right – Arron Mossell, Nathaniel's brother
The other people are not identified

Philadelphia African American Families. Courtesy of Charles Blockson and Temple University

AFRICAN-AMERICAN
ARTISTS

Humbert Howard and the Pyramid Club

The Pyramid Club was formed in November 1941 by Dr. Walter F. Jerrick of South Philadelphia. It was recognized as Philadelphia's leading Negro Social Club. While the Pyramid Club supported musicians and other creative endeavors the most important and memorable enterprise was the annual art exhibition. Humbert Howard was responsible for the annual art exhibition and arranged to have the art of Philadelphians and New Yorkers and artists from other locations exhibited at the Pyramid Club. Howard called himself an integrationist, meaning that while the club only had black members, it did show the work of white artists – as long as the subject matter was black. Dox Thrash was also a member. The Pyramid Club was located at 15th and Girard. It no longer exists.

Howard was educated at Howard University, the University of Pennsylvania (though not a graduate), and the Barnes Foundation, in Merion, Pennsylvania. The Works Progress Administration (WPA) helped provide employment for many black artists, including Howard, who was the first black member of the Philadelphia Art Alliance.

One of the few art dealers who would handle the art of blacks was Robert Carlen. Howard was one of his clients. Howard painted many Philadelphia scenes. He credits the Barnes Foundation for helping develop his style.

Public Domain. Oral history interview with Humbert Howard, 1988 Oct. 26, Archives of American Art, Smithsonian Institution. Interview with Humbert Howard. Conducted by Marina Pacini at the Artist's home in Philadelphia, Pennsylvania October 26, 1988.

African Dancers, 1973, watercolor and chalk on paper, 22 ½ x 29 ¾ inches (Philadelphia Museum of Art), Gift of Isabella E. Walter, 1973. Courtesy of Philadelphia Museum of Art

Horace Pippin (1888 – 1946)

Born and raised in West Chester, Pennsylvania, Horace Pippin worked several jobs and joined the army in 1917 before adopting an art career. Upon his return from service, he was badly injured in his right arm. Because of this difficulty Pippin devised a method of using a hot iron poker for gouging out composed creations into wood panels. He then filled the panels with colorful paints. He began painting in 1929 and never received any formal training though he was offered training. He refused it to have control over his own style

He was one of America's top "primitive" painters, often begin compared to Henri Rousseau. His subject matter ranged from his early depictions of trench warfare (The End Of The War: Starting Home – which is part of the Philadelphia Museum of Art collection) to historical, religious, and genre paintings. "Giving Thanks" is part of the Barnes Foundation collection.[47]

(World Wide Arts Resources (http://wwar.com/masters/p/pippin-horace.html)

Dox Thrash (1893-1965)

Dox Thrash was born in Georgia and trained as an artist a the Art Institute of Chicago. He found his fame in Philadelphia where he moved in 1925. "Dox Thrash achieved his greatest fame working with the Federal Art Project from 1936-1939. It was here that he first worked on and invented the process of carborundum mezzotint with the help of Mesibov at the Fine Print Workshop in Philadelphia."

Defense Workers by Dox Thrash, c. 1941, carborundum mezzotint over etched guidelines. Philadelphia Museum of Art: Federal Works Agency Works Projects Administration long term loan to the Philadelphia Museum of Art from the Fine Arts Collection, U.S. General Services Administration, 1943. Courtesy of Philadelphia Museum of Art

Dox Thrash and Claude Clark in Fine Print Workshop, Philadelphia Federal Art Project by Myron Krajaey, c. 1940, 3" x 10", Federal Work Projects Administration, on deposit at the Philadelphia Museum of Art. Courtesy of Philadelphia Museum of Art

The Carborundum Mezzotint Process was a new art medium, the first real printmaking breakthrough since Alois Senefelder discovered lithography. The Work Progress Administration (WPA) gave him the chance to experiment. He took advantage. "I got some of the carborundum powder they used in grinding lithograph stones and rubbed it into a copper plate with an old flatiron. I got a queer rough surface. Well, this fellow Mesibov looks over my shoulder, and says, 'Hey, I bet you could work lines in that.' I took a burnisher (a knife-like tool) and sketched a nude." – Dox Thrash in the *Philadelphia Record* October, 1940.

Dox Thrash used this carborundum print process as his primary medium in paying portrayals of African-American life in the mid-twentieth century. He also influenced other black artists. He was posthumously honored with a show at the Philadelphia Museum of Art in 2002 entitled, *Dox Thrash: An African-American Master Printmaker Rediscovered.*[48] *(http://library.griftec.org/dox_thrash.htm- Griffin Technical College, Georgia)*

NOTABLE FEMALE ARTISTS

Cecelia Beaux (1855-1942)

Text reprinted with permission of Pennsylvania Academy of the Fine Arts

Cecilia Beaux, a native of Philadelphia, received her first instruction in drawing from a former Pennsylvania Academy student and distant cousin of her uncle Will Biddle, Catherine Ann Drinker. From 1876 to 1878, Beaux studied briefly and irregularly at the Pennsylvania Academy of the Fine Arts (but avoided working with Thomas Eakins). Her most important Philadelphia arts professor was William Sartain with whom she studied in a private class from 1881 to 1883.

In 1885 Beaux won a prize at the Pennsylvania Academy for a double portrait of her sister and first-born nephew (Les Derniers Jours d'Enfance, 1883-85), and thereafter became a rising star in the Philadelphia art world. In 1888 and 1889, Beaux completed her art training in Paris.

During her lifetime Beaux was regarded as one of the country's leading portraitists. In 1895, Beaux became the first woman critic at the Pennsylvania Academy and headed its portrait classes until 1915. After World War I, the American government selected Beaux as part of a team commissioned to paint official portraits of Europe's war heroes.

Alice Neel

Text paraphrased from the Alice Neel website and Moore College of Art & Design, 160 Years and Beyond (Arcadia Press, 2008)

Alice Neel was born in 1900 near Philadelphia. She was trained at the Philadelphia School of Design (now the Moore College of Art and Design) in the 1920s. Neel left for New York where she painted for the Works Progress Administration. Neel was "never fashionable or in step with avant-garde movements. Sym-

Alice Neel – Self Portrait by Alice Neel. Courtesy of Moore Galleries

pathetic to the expressionist spirit of northern Europe and Scandinavia and to the darker arts of Spanish painting, she painted in a style and with an approach distinctively her own."

Her paintings were influenced by her liberal beliefs which included support of black activists and the women's movement. In the 1960s she painted a series of dynamic portraits of artists, curators, and gallery owners, among them Frank O'Hara, Andy Warhol, and the young Robert Smithson.

She was described in her *New York Times* biography as "the quintessential Bohemian."

Moore College of Art & Design
Text paraphrased from the Moore College of Art & Design, 160 Years and Beyond (Arcadia Press, 2008)

The Moore College of Art & Design began in 1848 as the Philadelphia School of Design for Women. It was founded by philanthropist Sarah Peter to "educate women in the design arts and provide opportunities for employment." Moore graduates include the first woman to design a US postage stamp, to master the art of mezzotype, to serve as director of an American advertising agency, to design fabric for an automobile interior, and to be a registered general contractor with the Carpenter's Union.

Additional influences include the Red Rose Girls and the Philadelphia Ten. The Red Rose Girls were Jessie Wilcox Smith, Elizabeth Shippen, and Violet Oakley. They were named the Red Rose Girls by their mentor, Howard Pyle, because they lived and worked in a country inn, called the Red Rose Inn, near Villanova.

History Of The Plastic Club
247 South Comac Street
Prepared by Barbara MacIlvaine (www.plasticclub.org)
Text reprinted with permission of the Plastic Club and Michael Guinn (source: email communication)

In the late 1800s women artists began to meet to exchange ideas and show their work. Emily Sartain hosted the organization of the "Plastic Club" in 1897. Art clubs for men already existed in the city. They didn't allow women. The term "Plastic" in the name, suggested by Blanche Dillaye who later was elected the first president, refers to the state of any unfinished work of art. ...

The club had several locations including 10 S. 18th St. and the current location at 247 South Camac Street. It holds exhibits that display artwork in a variety of mediums.

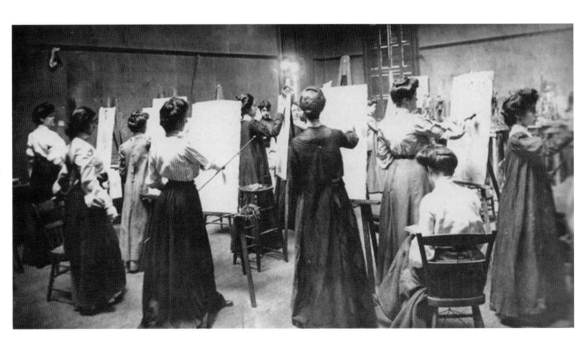

Women – 1900. Courtesy of Moore Galleries

Some of the leading male artists of the day lectured and showed their work at the Plastic Club. Howard Pyle and William Merritt Chase were among the clubs greatest supporters and teachers.

The members also helped support World Wars I and II in a variety of ways. In addition to painting and graphic arts, the other disciplines supported included:

Professional photographers Mary Carnell, Mathilde Weil, Eva Watson;
Sculptors Beatrice Fenton, Katherine Chen, Florence Tricker, Margaret Welsh. ...
Stained glass designers Violet Oakley, Paula Himmelsbach Balano;
Bookbinding, Florence Fulton;
Jewelry design, Miriam T. Smith, Esther A. Richards;
Silhouette artist Katherine Buffam;
Muralists Marianne Sloan, Anne Chuse Richardson, Margaretta E. Hinchman, and Violet Oakley; and the multi-talented Sarah Crumb-Weaver, jewelry designer, puppeteer.

The members of the Plastic Club also support the other arts institutions throughout the city, including the Philadelphia Art Alliance.[49, 50] The club still thrives.

The Philadelphia Ten

The Philadelphia Ten was a group of women painters and sculptors, who showed their work together between 1917 and 1945 in Philadelphia, as well as in other major East Coast and Midwest cities.

All members of the group (a total of thirty, the group began with ten) studied art in the schools of Philadelphia, primarily the Philadelphia School of Design for Women [which later would become the Moore College of Art] and the Pennsylvania Academy. Among the best known of the group are Fern Coppedge, M. Elizabeth Price, and Harriet Frishmuth. A book accompanies a traveling exhibition of the same name.[49, 50]

THE MURAL ARTS PROGRAM

The City of Philadelphia Mural Arts Program is one of the largest public art initiatives in the nation. Its mission is to engage in community art collaborations and art education, increasing public access to art. Since its inception, the Mural Arts Program has produced more than 3,000 murals and educated more than 20,000 underserved youth in neighborhoods across Philadelphia. The murals have become a source of tremendous pride and inspiration to millions of residents and visitors to the city and have earned Philadelphia international praise as the "City of Murals."

History

The Mural Arts Program began in 1984 as an element of the Philadelphia Anti-Graffiti Network, an effort spearheaded by then Mayor Wilson Goode to abate the graffiti crisis plaguing the city. The Anti-Graffiti Network hired muralist Jane Golden to engage graffiti writers and redirect their destructive energies into positive ones.

Jane befriended the graffiti writers, immersing herself in their subculture. What she found was an awe-inspiring amount of raw artistic talent. Recognizing their creative force, Jane began to provide opportunities for them to channel their talent into mural-making. Painting murals provided a support structure for these young people to refine their artistic skills while empowering them to take an active role in their neighborhoods. The murals themselves transformed a city dilapidated from years of economic distress and population loss, adding color, beauty, and life to neighborhoods and communities in need.

In 1996, then Mayor Ed Rendell formalized the Mural Arts Program and made Jane its director. Congruently, Jane established the Philadelphia Mural Arts Advocates, a nonprofit organized to raise funds and provide support to the nationally recognized program. Today's Mural Arts Program is a successful public/private partnership encompassing both the city agency and the nonprofit.

Community

As visually striking as the murals are, what they represent is much more powerful. Each mural is the product of a collaborative grassroots process that empowers neighborhood residents to tell their individual and collective stories, pass on culture and tradition, and foster leaders within the community. The Mural Arts Program works with more than 100 communities each year to co-create murals that serve the needs of neighborhoods, stabilizing abandoned lots, revitalizing open spaces, and inspiring civic pride. The organization's street-level approach to mural-making involves block captains, neighborhood associations, schools, community development organizations, and several city agencies in the struggle against blight and economic underdevelopment.

Education

The Mural Arts Program's mural-making process engages thousands of children, youth, and adults each year, enabling them to find their artistic voice, develop their self-confidence, and discover new ambitions while creating murals.

The Mural Arts Program's award-winning art education programs annually serve nearly 2,000 youth at neighborhood sites throughout the city. These programs, which are targeted to at-risk youth and offered free of charge, use mural-making as a means to engage youth through an intensive curriculum that teaches transferable life and job skills such as taking personal responsibility, teamwork, and creative problem solving.

It is the Mural Arts Program's belief that if young people are equipped with a strong sense of self, knowledge of their potential, and a connection to the world around them, they will be better prepared to make wise decisions and choose positive paths throughout their lives.

Redemption

The Mural Arts Program has become a national leader in arts and criminal justice programming, offering educational outreach programs in local prisons and rehabilitation centers in an effort to use the restorative power of art to break the cycle of crime and violence in communities. The Mural Arts Program provides an array of mural-making programs for adult men and women at correctional facilities in the Philadelphia Prison System and at the State Correctional Institution (SCI) at Graterford. Re-entry programs for ex-inmates allow them to assist in mural projects. The Mural Arts Program also provides art-making and rehabilitation programs for adjudicated youth at local detention centers and residential placement facilities.

Vision

The success of the Mural Arts Program is in large part due to its faith in three simple words that Jane Golden herself uses as a personal and professional mantra: Art Saves Lives. It is with this conviction that the Mural Arts Program looks forward to enhancing its existing programs and embarking on new initiatives that will continue to challenge and inspire the many individuals whose lives are touched by Philadelphia's murals.

The Mural Arts Program has grown exponentially since 1984. Today it offers stable employment to hundreds of local artists; its acclaimed art education and prison programs now serve as an international model. Tens of thousands of visitors each year come to Philadelphia to tour the world's largest outdoor art gallery and muralists from around the world come to Philadelphia to be trained in mural-making. The Mural Arts Program has made Philadelphia synonymous with murals.

Mural Tours

The Mural Arts Program offers public and private mural tours – a uniquely Philadelphia cultural experience – to provide both residents and visitors with an opportunity to learn more about the murals.

For more information, visit www.muralarts.org/tours or call 215.685.0750.

Peace Wall – Grays Ferry (1988), by Zane Golden and Peter Pagast. Photo by Jack Ramsdale.

CONTEMPORARY ART

Other Contemporary Art Galleries

The Philadelphia Museum of Art is committed to contemporary art. Fiske Kimbell began collecting Picasso and Brancusi for the Museum and Henry Clifford, a curator for the museum from 1941-1965, continued the tradition.

The Newman Galleries, among many other sites including the Pennsylvania Art Alliance, host contemporary art by local artists. Several follow:

Woodmere Art Museum

9201 Germantown Avenue – Philadelphia, PA 19118
Corner of Germantown Avenue and Bells Mill Road in Chestnut Hill
www.woodmereartmuseum.org
Woodmere text reprinted with permission of Woodmere Art Museum

Concentrating on the art and artists of the Philadelphia area, Woodmere's Permanent Collection includes over 2,600 objects, including works by Daniel Garber, Thomas Pollock Anshutz, Edward Moran, Violet Oakley, Nelson Shanks, Benjamin West, and N. C. Wyeth. Their impressive collection of works on paper includes prints and drawings by Earl Horter, Arthur B. Carles, Robert Riggs, Julius Bloch, Jessie Willcox Smith, and Herbert Pullinger.

One of the artists who has exhibited at the Woodmere is Bill Scott, a local contemporary artist.

Bill Scott

The playful and exuberant nature of Garden Fireflies belies the serious nature of the artist's intent and the depth of knowledge, experience, and hard work that is buried beneath the surface ebullience. In fact, this is the trademark of works by William (Bill) Scott, a Philadelphia artist who has distinguished himself not only as a painter but also as a gifted writer on the arts and an ardent advocate of his fellow Philadelphia artists. All his works are about color, and from an early age he was enthralled by artists' use of

Garden Fireflies, 1993. Acrylic on paper; 38 1/4" x 31 1/2", Gift of the artist, 1993 by Bill Scott. Courtesy of Woodmere Art Museum, Philadelphia

color, in particular its use by French artist Berthe Morisot. Later, the influence of Morisot would be joined by that of American expatriate artist Joan Mitchell and Philadelphia artist Jane Piper, with whom Scott developed a close personal relationship. Garden Fireflies typifies Scott's recent work, which has moved away from a purely abstract, gestural approach to one that hints at representation.

The Rosenfeld Gallery

113 Arch Street
www.therosenfeldgallery.com

(As per their website) The Rosenfeld Gallery has a very inclusive aesthetic, representing a broad range of approaches from realism, interpretive realism, and expressionism, through non-objective abstraction. The gallery also exhibits a broad range of media including paintings in oils, acrylics, watercolors, encaustic, pastel as well as sculpture in metal, glass, clay, and wood.

Gross McCleaf

27 S Sixteenth Street, Philadelphia, Pennsylvania 19102, 215-665-8138

www.grossmccleaf.com

A number of images of Gross McCleaf artists are represented in this book.

Gross McCleaf Art Gallery represents over forty artists, painting landscapes, city scenes, still life, and interiors in a wide range of styles. With rotating exhibitions in three galleries, an extensive inventory, and thirty years experience, Gross McCleaf provides a unique opportunity to collectors interested in Philadelphia's grand realist tradition. The Gallery is located on Sixteenth Street, between Walnut & Sansom Streets in Center City, Philadelphia.

Two of these artists are Bertha Leonard and Celia B. Reisman

Ms. Leonard is a local woman with degrees from local institutions – Tyler School of Art, Temple University, Bachelor of Fine Art, Graduate School of Tyler School of Fine Art, and the Barnes Foundation. Her art is shown in the Food section.

Ms. Reisman left home for the Kent State Blossom Art Program, Carnegie Mellon University, and Yale University.

The Philadelphia Art Alliance is the oldest multidisciplinary arts center in the United States. It was founded in 1915 to promote visual art as well as literary and performing art by theater aficionado and philanthropist Christine Wetherill Stevenson (1878-1922) and has been located since 1926 in the historic Wetherill mansion on Rittenhouse Square in Center City Philadelphia. The Alliance hosts a variety of exhibitions and lectures by noted artists.[52]

Penn's Institute of Contemporary Art is a showcase for its title's subject – Contemporary Art.

There are now scores of art galleries in and about the city hosting a variety of exhibitions in a variety of styles – all promoting scores of new and upcoming artists. The artists shown are just a sampling.

Untitled by Mary Nomecos. Courtesy of The Rosenfeld Gallery

Signs of Fall, oil on canvas, 36 x 52 inches, by Celia B. Reisman. Courtesy of Gross McCleaf Gallery

*Bartram's Bridge ©
2008 by Nicholas P.
Santoleri. Courtesy of
Nicholas P. Santoleri*

Nicholas P. Santoleri

www.santoleri.com
Text reprinted with permission of Nicholas Santoleri

Nicholas P. Santoleri grew up in a rural area of Chester County, Pennsylvania, where he developed a fascination with the landscape and colonial architecture found there. Through his paintings, Santoleri hopes to evoke a sense of nostalgia blended with his belief that the past must be permitted to intertwine with the present. Best known for the rich detail and realistic style of his watercolor paintings, Nick has broadened his creative vision through expanding his media and subject matter. The artist's portfolio includes landscapes, still life, and portraits in watercolor, oil, pencil, and pen and ink. Nick is a member of the Philadelphia Sketch Club and continues to develop his artistic talent with classes at the Pennsylvania Academy of Fine Arts.

Nick has established a national reputation through twenty years of publishing fine, limited edition prints from his original paintings.

Santoleri's popular Philadelphia prints have been used on the sets of a number of movies and TV shows shot in the Philadelphia area.

Several of his pieces have been published by a Japanese firm for exclusive distribution in Japan and the fine art publisher New York Graphic Society has published reproductions of Santoleri's artwork for international distribution.

Rob Lawlor

www.lawlorgallery.com
Text reprinted with permission of Rob Lawlor (source: email communication)

Born and raised as a Philadelphian with a background that includes some minor league baseball, years of joy on the musical stage, a career in newspaper cartooning, and a love of painting, all gracious gifts from God. Robert works primarily in oils, and his love of color leads him to paint landscapes and cityscapes with an impressionistic palette.

His art can be seen in the law chapter and the back jacket.

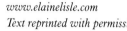

Rittenhouse Square Purples by Rob Lawlor. Courtesy of Rob Lawlor

Elaine Moynihan Lisle

www.elainelisle.com

Text reprinted with permission of Elaine Moynihan Lisle (source: email communication)

Elaine Lisle is a Philadelphia painter known for her lively and colorful street scenes. Her work has been described as "the exuberant expression of people engaged in life." Her work spans a variety of subjects from traditional en plein air landscapes to carefully constructed compositions involving figures and complicated architectural elements. Her landscapes and cityscapes are rendered with crisp bold brushwork and delight the viewer with light and color as well as a sense of intimacy.

Lisle's work can be found in private and corporate collections around the globe. She is represented in the Philadelphia area by Artists' House Gallery. Her paintings can also be found at the Artworks gallery at the Philadelphia Museum of Art. She is also affiliated with galleries in London and New York.

Lisle received a Bachelors degree in Fine Arts from the University of Pennsylvania and she also did post-graduate work at the Pennsylvania Academy of Fine Arts. She is on the faculty of the Main Line Art Center in Bryn Mawr, Pennsylvania, where she teaches en plein air painting and large composition.

Fall on Chestnut Street, Oil on Canvas, 36" x 48", © 2007 (private available) by Elaine Moynihan Lisle. Courtesy of Elaine Moynihan Lisle

Charles Cushing

www.charlescushing.com
Text reprinted with permission of Mr. Cushing
(source: email communication)

Charles Cushing has lived and worked in Philadelphia for over thirty years. He is a graduate of the Pennsylvania Academy of Fine Arts (1988). Over 500 of his original oil paintings are in public and private collections in the region, including the Union League of Philadelphia. In 2008, Cushing was honored by the Philadelphia College of Physicians for his efforts in the campaign to keep Thomas Eakins' masterpiece "The Gross Clinic" in Philadelphia. His contribution included executing a life-size replica of that painting to help raise public awareness. This canvas is on display in the lobby of the Two Penn Center Building at 15th and JFK Boulevard.

Bellevue Hotel by Charles Cushing. Courtesy of Charles Cushing

Joe Barker

Joe Barker is from LaFayette, Alabama. He attended school at Manhattanville College in Purchase, NY but was kicked out to pursue an art career. He worked in Greenwich Village, New York where he sold his first work of art for one dollar and fifty cents. He also worked in Harlem, New York. He was commissioned by Mr. Nielson to do paintings of Langston Hughes' house and the street where Langston Hughes lived for the Arthur Schomburg collection. Mr. Schomburg's vast private collection, now housed in the Schomburg Center for Research in Black Culture (formerly the 135th Street branch of the New York Public Library), is one of the outstanding collections of materials concerning the history and culture of people of African descent.

Joe's sponsors included Adolph Primavera, Ed Bernstein and Howard Braitman .

In 1979 he moved to Philadelphia where he has been a sidewalk artist ever since. In 1990 he was commissioned to do a painting for each of the rooms in the Rittenhouse Hotel. For years he worked in water colors. He recently switched to oil.

Rembrandt's by Joe Barker. Courtesy of Joe Barker

Howard N. Watson

www.howardwat.com

Text reprinted with permission of Howard N. Watson (soruce: email communication)

Howard N. Watson, a resident of Wyncote, Pennsylvania, has become a nationally recognized watercolorist and illustrator. His work has been commissioned by former President Jimmy Carter, former Vice President Walter Mondale, President Bill Clinton, noted singer Perry Como, Hall of Fame basketball coach Jack Ramsey, sportscaster Tom Brookshier, and famous art collector Set Momjian. Mr. Watson is proud to present these Limited Edition Prints of popular Philadelphia scenes. Mr. Watson received his formal art training at the Pennsylvania State University, Temple University's Tyler School of Fine Art, and the University School of Arts (formerly the Museum School of Art).

He has performed painting workshops nationally and internationally. His workshops have been conducted at the New Jersey shore, Philadelphia County, Bucks and Montgomery Counties, and the famous Cape Cod in New England. He has also presented painting workshops in Austria, Switzerland, France, Scotland, Canada, Hawaii, and in Norway.

Mr. Watson is represented by the Carol Schwartz Gallery in Philadelphia. He is listed in *Who's Who in the East* and in *Who's Who in American Art*. He has served on Boards of the Port of History Museum, the Victorian Society, the Pennsylvania Council on the Arts, the Philadelphia Volunteer Lawyers for the Arts, the Philadelphia Committee to End Homelessness, and the Woodmere Art Museum.

Howard Watson has been the "Artist in Residence" at the White House during the Carter Administration and more recently has provided art for President Bill Clinton.

He has been made an Honorary Member of the Allied Artists of America (AAA) and the Philadelphia Watercolor Society (PWC). He has been an active member of the American Watercolor Society (AWS) since 1962, and the Philadelphia Watercolor Society since 1958, where he served as President for 10 years. Mr. Watson currently serves as Archivist for the Philadelphia Watercolor Society.

The Love Statue by Howard N. Watson. Courtesy of Howard Watson

Perry Milou

www.perrymilou.com

Text reprinted with permission of Perry Milou (source: email communication)

Milou's body of work has often been described as "alluring," "brilliant," "glamorous," and "vibrant." Milou is a graduate from the University of Arizona. In 1990 he was the first student ever to convince the Bachelor of Fine Arts program to incorporate an "Open Studio" major. He creates pop and contemporary art that is often a tribute to political figures, iconic sports players or notable celebrities.

Milou's current style is simply called "Rain," the spontaneous vertical running of his oils. This partnered with his incorporation of Swarovski Crystals is cutting edge and extremely unique to the artist himself! Milou employs a rich palette to create vibrant representational works in multiple genres. "My aesthetic today is about fantasy. "I want my work to evoke smiles and happy feelings in an easy way," he continues. His recent, "Lover Lip Series," is a collection of large iconic pop oils. Painted in Milou's most recent rain style, he illustrates both classic and contemporary puckers such as Sophia Loren, Brigitte Bardot, Angelina Jolie, and Jessica Alba. Another noteworthy series is his "Vegas Icon Playing Cards," a deck of ultra pop oils complete with Swarovski crystals and decoupage quoted borders.

(See concepts @ perrymilou.com)

In 2001 he was commissioned by the world-renowned Philadelphia Museum of Art to create two large oils. He portrayed the buildings' famous facades, in a Vincent van Gogh style with a Milou twist. In 2007 Milou was again commissioned by the Museum to create a portrait of founding father, Benjamin Franklin, to celebrate his 300th birthday.

Additionally, Milou was selected to participate in the 2007 International Art Show – Art Expo at the Jacob Javitz Center in New York City. In 2007, Cantor publishing Group exclusively selected his Marilyn Monroe series for the book, *Marilyn In Art*.

Milou is also involved in philanthropic and civic organizations including Co-Founder of the Philadelphia Art for ALS, an annual supporter of CVI, the Cardiovascular Institute of Philadelphia, the Susan B. Komen Breast Cancer Foundation, Wynnewood 36th Street Association, MOCA Shakers and Gen. Art. Most recently, he has begun collaboration with the Miami Children's Museum, where he will launch a series of fine art workshops called "Palette Kids" to begin on Saturdays in July through August.

Collectors of Milou's work include Sylvester Stallone, Julious Erving, the late Smarty Jones owner, Roy Chapman, Philadelphia Governor Edward Rendell, and attorney James Binns.

Critics and collectors have hailed his bold, vibrant palette over the past thirty years. Born and bred in Philadelphia, Milou opened his eponymous gallery at 17 NW 36th Street in Miami, Florida, in early May 2008. "I am constantly looking at the sky; it is the closest thing to watching GOD paint in the present moment!"

Ruth Savitz

www.photosofphiladelphia.com

Ruth's photos appear throughout the book. She is an award-winning photographer.

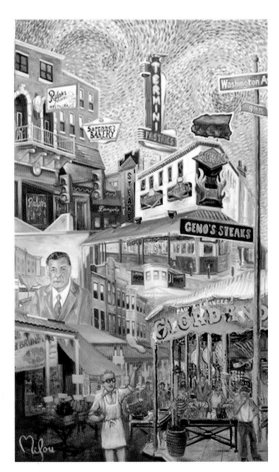

Numerous artists and photographers have gravitated to the scenic beauty of boathouse row, behind the Philadelphia Museum of Art and along the banks of the Schuylkill River in Fairmount Park. Schuylkill is a Dutch word meaning "hidden river." "500 years ago, Dutch immigrants gave it this name because of the point of confluence on the Delaware River was disguised by verdant wetlands."[53]

THE SCHUYLKILL NAVY was founded in 1858 by nine Philadelphia boat clubs. It is the oldest sports governing body in the US.

The Philadelphia Girls Rowing Club is the oldest building, built as a Skating Club in Italianate style in 1860. The present stone Italianate building was constructed in 1860 as a house for the combined Skating and Humane Societies, which merged in 1861. Other boathouses have been built in a variety of styles beginning with Victorian Gothic. Additional styles include Georgian Revival, Eastlake style, and Mediterranean style.

The clubs have been successful at the Thames Cup at Henley, various Olympic races, and other championship rowing events.

Possibly the best single sculler was Joe Burk, who rowed at the University of Pennsylvania under Rusty Callow. Joe rowed with a very unorthodox style at an extremely high short stroke of forty strokes per minute for the entire race. He was a four-time winner of the U.S. and Canadian Championships, and won the Diamond Sculls at the Henley in England in 1938 and '39, setting the course record in 1938.

Jack Kelly Sr. and Jr. (Movie section), two of the area's great rowers, are profiled in the movie section along with Grace Kelly, of the same family.

One of the most successful coaches was Ted Nash, who coached at the University of Pennsylvania from 1965 to 1983 and coached the Penn Athletic Club from 1983.

Notable Boathouse row artists include:

Charles Wilson Peale, William Groombridge, Count de Colbert Maulevier, William Birch, Geroge Parkyns, and William Rush.

The most famous artist is Thomas Eakins.

Thomas Eakins, a well known Victorian artist and a Philadelphia Barge club oarsman, immortalized the Biglin brothers in four rowing pictures, the Pair-Oared Shell, the Biglin Brothers Racing, the Biglin Brothers Turning the Stake, and John Biglin in a Single Scull. Eakins also produced several other rowing masterpieces. Eakins' most famous painting is of Max Schmitt in "The Championship Single Scull," with Eakins rowing in the background. This painting memorializes a championship race in 1870, in which Schmitt won by three lengths over four highly regarded competitors. "Eakins did not depict the race itself, but wanted to represent the sort of training that went into it, making the painting a tribute not just to Schmitt's victory, but also to the discipline that created it. This gives a pensive quality to the work, suggesting that the pain is brief but Victory is forever." (www.boathouserow.org and Joe Sweeney)

Opposite Page:
South Philadelphia by
Perry Milou. Courtesy
of Perry Milou

Misty Trees and
Railings by Ruth
Savitz. Courtesy of
Ruth Savitz

Top:
St. Patrick's Day by Melissa
Hernandez Hughes. Courtesy of
Melissa Hernandez Hughes

Boathouses in the Snow by Howard
N. Watson. Courtesy of Howard N.
Watson

Boathouse Reflections, Oil on canvas, 24" x 30", © 2007 (private collection), by Elaine Moynihan Lisle. Courtesy of Elaine Moynihan Lisle

Boathouse Row by James Kelly. Courtesy of James Kelly

Boathouse Row V, © 2000, by Nicholas P. Santoleri. Courtesy of Nicholas P. Santoleri

Boathouse Row #2 by Perry Milou. Courtesy of Perry Milou

Boathouse Row Sunset by James Kelly. Courtesy of James Kelly

PHILADELPHIA MUSIC

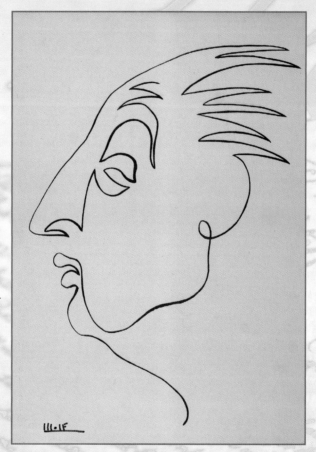

Leopold Stokowski (line drawing). Courtesy of University of Pennsylvania – Rare Book and Manuscript Library (Leopold Stokowski Collection)

Picture – Leopold Stokowski
Reprinted with permission of the University of Pennsylvania, Rare Book & Manuscript Library

THE PHILADELPHIA SOUND

"Boston is tougher, more independent. Nothing ever happens that isn't clear. The Philadelphia sonorities are less transparent … rounder and deeper and more human. They have a tactile quality too, like a skin you might touch. … Nowhere else is there such a string choir, one would like to stroke its tone, like pinky brown velvet."

Virgil Thompson, Music Critic

PHILADELPHIA MUSIC

NOTABLE STYLES
The Philadelphia Sound
Rock And Roll
Jazz/Opera
Great Venues

CONTENTS

THE PHILADELPHIA
SOUND

The phrase Philadelphia Sound brings to mind a number of styles, a number of neighborhoods, from the jazz of John Coltrane, Dizzy Gillespie, and Grover Washington, Jr. to the rap of Jazzy Jeff and Will Smith. It evokes gospel and folk and Patti Labelle; the operatic voices of Marian Anderson and Mario Lanza. There are rock and rollers; Philadelphia soul; jazz singers; blues singers; and lyrics for musicals and for the movies.

Mostly though, the phrase "Philadelphia Sound" is attributable to the "Phabulous" Philadelphians – the orchestral sound of the Philadelphia Orchestra. The sound began with the sweet string serenades of Leopold Stokowski and matured under Eugene Ormandy. The Orchestra has also matured – from playing in an Opera Hall and The Academy of Music to playing in Verizon Hall in the Kimmel Center for the Performing Arts. When not playing inside, the Orchestra plays under the stars in its summer venue – The Mann Music Center or one of its three summer venues.

The Philadelphia Sound is also the moniker for the soulful recordings that came out of Philadelphia since the 1960s and 1970s under the label and guidance of Kenneth Gamble and Leon Huff and also Thom Bell.

Philadelphia music also includes great composers like Samuel Barber and Rodgers and Hammerstein (Hammerstein's father helped start the Philadelphia Opera Company). Noted publishers include George Willig and Co. and Theodore Presser Company. Noted backers include Bernie Lowe's Cameo Records, Larry Magid, and Allen Spivak.

Philadelphia music has the most styles of all the Philadelphia professions.

Philadelphia has its own Hall of Music Fame that includes what this selection misses, such as Boyz II Men and the Oak Ridge Boys.

Philadelphia Sound: Virtually every American musical sound has a Philadelphia connection like the Philadelphia Folk Festival or the trained musicians from the Curtis Institute, the University of the Arts or the other schools in the city.

There's the Philly Pops and the music that supports various dance institutions like the Pennsylvania Ballet and Philadanco.

Philadelphia Sound: The styles, the varieties, the contributions are endless.

CLASSICAL

The Philadelphia Orchestra
Text reprinted with permission of the Philadelphia Orchestra (source: www.philorch.org)

Founded in 1900, the Philadelphia Orchestra has distinguished itself as one of the leading orchestras in the world through over a century of acclaimed performances, historic international tours, best-selling recordings, and its unprecedented record of innovation in recording technologies and outreach. The Orchestra has maintained unity in artistic leadership with only seven music directors throughout its history: Fritz Scheel (1900-07), Carl Pohlig (1907-12), Leopold Stokowski (1912-41), Eugene Ormandy (1936-80), Riccardo Muti (1980-92), Wolfgang Sawallisch (1993-2003), and Christoph Eschenbach (2003-08).

This rich tradition is carried on by Charles Dutoit, who was appointed chief conductor and artistic adviser of The Philadelphia Orchestra from the 2008-09 season through the 2011-12 season. Mr. Dutoit has a long-standing relationship with the Orchestra, having made his debut with the ensemble in 1980. As chief conductor and artistic adviser, he will lead the Orchestra in Philadelphia as well as at Carnegie Hall and on tour. He will continue his role as artistic director and principal conductor of the Orchestra's annual three-week residency at the Saratoga Performing Arts Center and will lead concerts when the Orchestra is in residence at the Bravo! Vail Valley Music Festival.

Leopold Stokowski Conducting the Philadelphia Orchestra Acadamey of Music – 1913. Courtesy of University of Pennsylvania - Rare Book and Manuscript Library (Leopold Stokowski Collection)

Throughout its history, The Philadelphia Orchestra has introduced an unprecedented number of important works as world or American premieres, including Barber's Violin Concerto, Mahler's "Symphony of a Thousand," Rachmaninoff's Symphonic Dances, Schoenberg's Gurrelieder, and Stravinsky's Rite of Spring. Its illustrious tour history includes a number of landmarks events. In 1936, the Orchestra became the first American orchestra to undertake a transcontinental tour; in 1949 it toured Great Britain as the first American orchestra to cross the Atlantic after World War II; in 1973 it became the first American orchestra to perform in the People's Republic of China; and in 1999 it became the first American orchestra to visit Vietnam.

The Orchestra also boasts an extraordinary record of media firsts: It was the first symphonic orchestra to make electrical recordings (in 1925); the first to perform its own commercially sponsored radio broadcast (in 1929, on NBC); the first to perform on the soundtrack of a feature film (Paramount's The Big Broadcast of 1937); the first to appear on a national television broadcast (in 1948, on CBS); and the first major orchestra to give a live cybercast of a concert on the internet (in 1997).

The Philadelphia Orchestra annually touches the lives of more than one million music lovers worldwide through its performances (more than 300 concerts and other presentations each year), publications, recordings, and broadcasts. A winter subscription season is presented in Philadelphia each year from September to May, including expanded education and community partnership programs. The Orchestra also appears annually at New York's Carnegie Hall and at the John F. Kennedy Center for the Performing Arts in Washington, D.C. Its schedule each summer includes an outdoor season in Philadelphia with concerts in local neighborhoods and at The Mann Center for the Performing Arts, an annual residency at the Bravo! Vail Valley Music Festival, followed by a three-week residency each August at the Saratoga Performing Arts Center in upstate New York.

Academy of Music – Audience by Alfred Bendiner. Courtesy of University of Pennsylvania Architectural Archives

Leopold Stokowski (1882-1977)

Leopold Stokowski came to America in 1905. Before serving as music director of the Philadelphia orchestra he served as organist and choirmaster at St. Bartholomew's in New York and as concertmaster for the Cincinnati Symphony Orchestra; although his contract was for five years, he obtained a release after three years in order to accept an offer from the Philadelphia Orchestra, in 1912.

"He conducted most of the repertoire by heart, an impressive accomplishment at the time. He emphasized the colorful elements in the music, and was the creator of the famous 'Philadelphia Sound' in the strings, achieving a well-nigh bel canto quality."[1]

As stated, Leopold Stokowski helped create what came to be known as the "Philadelphia sound." Critic Virgil Thompson wrote:

Boston is tougher, more independent. Nothing ever happens that isn't clear. The Philadelphia sonorities are less transparent …rounder and deeper and more human. They have a tactile quality too, like a skin you might touch. ... Nowhere else is there such a string choir, one would like to stroke its tone, like pinky brown velvet.

Boston [is] intellectually elegant and urbane. Philadelphia is where everything, even intellectual achievement and moral pride, turns luxury into a sort of sensuous awareness of sacred differences.[2]

[Leopold Stokowski. Fantasia: Animating Music. Courtesy University of Pennsylvania, Rare Book & Manuscript Library]

Stokowski led the Philadelphia Orchestra in a number of notable performances including Mahler's Symphony No. 8 (Symphony of a Thousand). The performance included an (augmented) orchestra of 110, two choruses of 400 each, a 150-member children's chorus, and eight soloists. There were eight performances at the Philadelphia Academy of Music and one later at New York's Metropolitan Opera House. Its success put Philadelphia and Stokowski on the classical music map.

"In the fall of 1937 Walt Disney suggested to Stokowski that they collaborate on an animated short of Paul Dukas' *The Sorcerer's Apprentice*. The final cost of the film, which was completed in January 1938, was so high that Disney was concerned about recouping his investment. His solution was to build additional segments around the

Dukas work and expand the project into a 'Concert Feature,' as it was then called, a proposal that Stokowski accepted enthusiastically. Many different storylines and accompanying musical works were discussed in meetings that included Disney, Stokowski, and the composer and commentator Deems Taylor, who would serve as *Fantasia's* narrator. By April 1939 the decisions on repertory were made, and a Disney crew traveled to Philadelphia to make the recordings.

The soundtrack was recorded on the Academy of Music stage on nine different channels using thirty-three individual microphones. *Fantasia* premiered in New York on 13 November 1940. *The New York Herald Tribune's* critic Virgil Thomson commented the next day that: "Leopold Stokowski, whatever one might think of his musical taste, is unquestionably the man who has best watched over the upbringing of Hollywood's stepchild, musical reproduction and recording. Alone among successful symphonic conductors, he has given himself the trouble to find out something about musical reproduction techniques and to adapt these to the problems of orchestral execution. Alone among the famous musicians who have worked in films he has forced the spending of money and serious thought by film producers and their engineers toward achievement of a result in auditive photography comparable in excellence to the results that the expenditure of money and thought have produced in visual photography. Musicians will thank him and bless his name."

[Leopold Stokowski. Champion of Modern Music. Courtesy University of Pennsylvania, Rare Book & Manuscript Library]

…Stokowski dedicated enormous energy to the performance of the music of his own time. Audiences and orchestra boards, however, did not always share his enthusiasm and his programming ideas were often resisted. In largely conservative Philadelphia, in particular, it was not unusual for a first hearing of a new work to be greeted with a noisy demonstration from the hall. In response, Stokowski was known to admonish his audience both from the stage and in the press.

Economic realities also conspired against the conductor's progressive concert plans, and the battles fought over budgetary support in Philadelphia echoed intermittently in later years. Stokowski, however, persevered and determinedly included new compositions in his programming, not necessarily as a challenge to his audiences, but as a manifestation of his artistic credo.

Eugene Ormandy and the Philadelphia Orchestra by Alfred Bendiner.
Courtesy of University of Pennsylvania Architectural Archives

Eugene Ormandy (1899-1985)

[Eugene Ormandy. From Prodigy to the Podium. Courtesy University of Pennsylvania, Rare Book & Manuscript Library]

Born Jenō Blau in Budapest on 18 November 1899, Eugene Ormandy was a child prodigy who received his early musical training from his father, an amateur musician. Ormandy began playing violin at age three, and at age five was the youngest member ever admitted to the Royal Academy of Music in Budapest. When he was nine, Ormandy began violin studies with the virtuoso Jenō Hubay (for whom he had been named), music composition with Zoltán Kodály, and harmony and counterpoint with Leó Weiner. He graduated at age fourteen and earned a diploma three years later that carried the title "artist violinist."

He toured Germany and Hungary in 1917 as soloist with the Blüthner Orchestra, and in 1919, when Hubay was named director of the Budapest Academy, Ormandy was appointed head of the violin department. During that time he also studied philosophy at Budapest University, receiving his degree in 1920. Later that year he left the Academy for a recital tour of France and Austria, and while in Vienna in 1921, he met two concert promoters. A promised United States tour of 300 concerts for $30,000 enticed Ormandy to New York, where he arrived on 2 December 1921. Unfortunately, the promoters proved to be insolvent; the expected contract did not materialize; and within two weeks the twenty-two-year-old violinist was virtually penniless.

While in New York, Ormandy auditioned for Ernō Rapée, conductor of the orchestra at New York's Capitol Theater movie palace. He was accepted and assigned a seat at the back of the second violin section but was moved to the concertmaster chair within the week. He made his conducting debut at the Capitol Theater in September 1924 with portions of Tchaikovsky's 4th symphony, when the orchestra's conductor fell ill. In 1926, when Rapée left the Capitol, Ormandy was appointed associate director.

[Eugene Ormandy. Ushering in the Ormandy Era. Courtesy University of Pennsylvania, Rare Book & Manuscript Library]

After successful guest appearances with the Philadelphia Orchestra and a five year tenure with the Minneapolis Symphony Orchestra, Ormandy became the music director of the Philadelphia Orchestra.

In December 1934 Leopold Stokowski made public his intention to resign as conductor of the Philadelphia Orchestra with an announcement that he would appear during only half of future concert seasons. During the following two years, Ormandy contributed to the steady stream of guest conductors at the Philadelphia Orchestra. Then, in the spring of 1936, Ormandy was formally appointed co-conductor of the Philadelphia Orchestra and released from his Minneapolis contract, which had one more year to run. For the next five concert seasons Ormandy and Stokowski shared the Philadelphia podium while maintaining a cordial, albeit distant, relationship. In 1938 Ormandy advanced one step closer to sole proprietorship of the Orchestra when the Board named him Music Director "in recognition of his splendid musical achievements that have made the last three years a succession of triumphs for conductor and orchestra alike." It was not until 1941, however, when Stokowski finally severed his ties to Philadelphia, that the "Ormandy Era" officially began.

[Eugene Ormandy. Orchestral Premiers. Courtesy University of Pennsylvania, Rare Book & Manuscript Library]

THE PHILADELPHIA SOUND

Ormandy inherited a virtuosic ensemble from Stokowski and continued to maintain a high artistic level throughout his tenure in Philadelphia. The changes he did make were accomplished over time and included a move from "free bowing" in the strings, which was favored by Stokowski, to the more traditional "uniform bowing"—with all strings simultaneously bowing in the same direction—while still preserving a seamless sound. Gradual changes in orchestra personnel also contributed to Ormandy's molding of his own orchestral sound, but an additional consideration is Ormandy's distinctive interpretations of the works he conducted. In this matter his influence extended beyond dynamics, phrasing, and tempi to the recomposition of the score itself.

Although not unique to Ormandy, the role of conductor as editor and arranger was clearly one that he adopted during his forty-two years as Music Director of the Philadelphia Orchestra. Contributing to the rich texture he achieved in performance was his practice of altering orchestrations by doubling one instrumental part by another. He also made cuts to works and often reworked the composer's conception of a particular rhythmic or melodic passage. While his critics complained loudly about the latitude he took in altering the compositions he conducted, Ormandy regularly employed this battery of techniques to achieve the sound ideal that earned him and Philadelphia considerable distinction.

[Eugene Ormandy. The Philadelphia Sound. Courtesy University of Pennsylvania, Rare Book & Manuscript Library]

Ormandy was responsible for bringing many new works to Philadelphia, including a number of important premieres. From his early years in the city through the 1960s and 1970s, the conductor continued to program the familiar along with the unknown. The result is a lengthy and impressive list of works by composers from both sides of the Atlantic, among them Samuel Barber, Béla Bartók, Benjamin Britten, David Del Tredici, David Diamond, Gottfried von Einem, Ernst Krenek, Bohuslav Martinu, Gian-Carlo Menotti, Darius Milhaud, Krzysztof Penderecki, Vincent Persichetti, Sergei Prokofiev, Sergei Rachmaninoff, George Rochberg, Ned Rorem, William Schuman, Roger Sessions, Dmitrii Shostakovich, and Virgil Thomson.

Ormandy made over 140 professional recordings.

David Kim is the current lead violinist and Concertmaster, who leads the Orchestra when the conductor is not present.

Ethel Lunenfeld was also a noted illustrator of the Philadelphia Orchestra.

OPERA

Marian Anderson (1897-1993)

Text reprinted with permission of Pennsylvania, Rare Book & Manuscript Library

Marian Anderson's musical education and performing experience were the product of personal, familial, and communal determination and faith. Through the financial support of her church—the Union Baptist at Fitzwater and Martin—and her community, she was able to take voice lessons in Philadelphia, first with soprano Mary Saunders Patterson around 1915, then with contralto Agnes Reifsnyder from 1916 to 1918, and finally with Giuseppe Boghetti in 1920. The latter was made possible through a benefit concert held on 14 May 1920 and sponsored by the Union Baptist Church. In the summer of 1919 she studied with Oscar Sanger at the Chicago Conservatory of Music. From 1914 Marian Anderson was performing in public concerts and by 1917 was giving solo performances. She even appeared as soloist in productions of Handel's *Messiah* and Mendelssohn's *Elijah* in Philadelphia and Boston.

[Marian Anderson. A Philadelphia Story. Courtesy University of Pennsylvania, Rare Book & Manuscript Library]

By the late 1920s Marian Anderson was convinced that the only way to develop her vocal acuity and expand her concert tours was to venture to Europe. Her manager at the time—Arthur Judson—had been persistently suggesting that she "switch" her training and work to that of a soprano: something that she knew would only shorten rather than augment her performing career... In addition to the training and experience received and the unprecedented success in Scandinavia, perhaps the most noteworthy—certainly the most famous—moment in all of Marian Anderson's tours of Europe was her performance in Salzburg, Austria, in 1935. Although she performed at the Salzburg Festival, her initial concert was not well publicized and was poorly attended. A second performance was given, however, one afternoon in the ballroom of one of the city's hotels. Conductor Arturo

Marian Anderson. Courtesy of University of Pennsylvania – Rare Book and Manuscript Library (Marian Anderson Collection of Photographs)

Toscanini attended this concert and is quoted as proclaiming that "a voice like hers is heard only once in a hundred years."

[Marian Anderson. The European Tours: England and the Continent. Courtesy University of Pennsylvania, Rare Book & Manuscript Library]

It was through the persistent efforts of Billy King, Marian Anderson's Philadelphia-born accompanist, that impresario Sol Hurok became aware of the contralto. ... Sol Hurok's management marked a quantum leap in experience and individualized attention to career development. The year 1935—the 1935/36 season—was the first for Hurok and Anderson, and he remained her manager for the rest of her performing career. In her autobiography Marian Anderson writes of her interest in Hurok because of "his reputation for daring and constructive management ... [and] the boldness with which he did things."

She had been represented by the Arthur Judson Agency, which, with its many clients, was unable to devote the kind of personal attention that was Hurok's trademark. Sol Hurok may be credited not only with shaping the course of Marian Anderson's career but also with providing the counsel and care that allowed her to concentrate on singing rather than issues of politics, race, finances, and related details that are necessary to a concert career but debilitating to the study and practice of song. Marian Anderson performed to critical and financial success into her sixties—a remarkable achievement for a vocalist performing works in the classical repertoire.

[Marian Anderson. Sol Hurok Presents: The First Decade. Courtesy University of Pennsylvania, Rare Book & Manuscript Library]

In February 1939, she became a center of national attention when the Daughters of the American Revolution refused to let her appear at Constitution Hall in Washington, D.C., citing the organization's rules of racial segregation. The resulting publicity only contributed to her success; Eleanor Roosevelt sent her resignation to the DAR, and the Secretary of the Interior, Harold L. Ickes, invited her to sing at the Lincoln Memorial. She was also one of the first black performers to sing at the Metropolitan Opera.

Mario Lanza (1921- 1959)

*[**Mario Lanza:** Text and Image reprinted with permission of Damon Lanza, Bob Dolfi and Marlene D'Attanasio (source: email communication)]*

Mario Lanza was born in South Philadelphia, Pennsylvania, as Alfredo Arnold Cocozza on January 31, 1921. Antonio Cocozza, Mario's father, was born in Filignano, Italy, and emigrated to the U.S. when he was just sixteen years old. Mario's mother, Maria Lanza, immigrated to America at the tender age of six months from a town not far from Filignano called Tocco da Casauria, in the Abruzzi region. This is how Mario decided on his name 'Mario Lanza', by taking the masculine form of his mother's maiden name. Maria and Tony met in South Philadelphia in 1919. They moved into their family home at 636

Mario Lanza. Courtesy of Robert Dolfi

Christian Street, South Philadelphia, where two years later "Freddie" was born.

Mario, then known as 'Freddie', was raised in an atmosphere of opera and Caruso recordings which were played mostly by his father on a daily basis at home. He eventually began to sing along with these records and the more he listened, the more he sang. William K. Huff, concert manager at the Philadelphia Academy of Music, arranged for an audition for Mario with the famed Serge Koussevitsky. Koussevitsky was so impressed that he immediately invited Mario to Tanglewood in the Berkshires where he had a music school for promising singers and musicians. This is where Mario sang his first student opera in the role of Fenton in Nicolai's *The Merry Wives of Windsor*. Mario received great reviews from the Metropolitan Opera people as well as from the music critics. While in the army, Mario auditioned for Peter Lind Hayes and was immediately accepted into his troupe that gave concerts at many army bases in the country. It was during this time that Mario joined the cast of *Winged Victory*, a musical put on by Moss Hart, which ran until May 1944. Through Sam Weiler, Mario began to study with the famed Enrico Rosati, who had earlier coached the famous Gigli. It has been said that upon hearing Mario's voice, Rosati looked up to the heavens and exclaimed, "I have been waiting for this voice to come along for many, many years."

While performing with Francis Yeend at the Hollywood Bowl on 28 August 1947, Mario impressed Louis B. Mayer, head of MGM motion picture studio, who was in the audience with Kathryn Grayson with whom he would make his first movie, *That Midnight Kiss*. Soon thereafter, Mario made his professional New Orleans opera debut as Pinkerton in *Madam Butterfly* with soprano Tomiko Kanazawa. Mario sang two performances of this opera, but sadly, this was to be the last full opera Mario would ever sing.

Mario went on to make five more movies, namely *Toast of New Orleans* (1950), *The Great Caruso* (Mario's favorite) (1951), *Because You're Mine* (1952), *The Student Prince* (featuring his singing only due to a dispute with MGM) (1954), *Serenade* (1956), *Seven Hills of Rome* (1958), and his last picture, *For The First Time* (1959).

In Mario's short but productive career, he managed to do many concerts and radio shows such as "Life With Luigi", "Great Moments in Music", replacing Jan Peerce in 1945, the famous "Coca-Cola Shows" 1951-52 and several more.

Anna Moffo (1932-2006)

Anna Moffo, born in Wayne, Pennsylvania, was educated at the University of Pennsylvania and the Curtis Institute. She started performing as a soprano in 1955 and performed in dozens of opera houses in a variety of roles.

Moffo made her American debut as "Mimi in *La Bohème*" at the Lyric Opera of Chicago in 1957, and made her Metropolitan Opera debut in 1959 as Violetta in *La Traviata*. She returned to the Met in the 1960-61 season to sing three new roles, Gilda in *Rigoletto*, Adina in Donizetti's *L'Elisir d'Amore*, and Liù in *Turandot* with Birgit Nilsson and Franco Corelli. She was especially popular in Italy where she hosted the "Anna Moffo Show" from 1960-1973.

[Wikipedia]

EARLY ROCK AND ROLL

In the late 1950s and early 1960s, "Philadelphia became the hub of the record business." "Philadelphia was just the most insane, most dynamic, the most beautiful city in the history of rock & roll and the world." Its energies "were just phenomenal."

The Philadelphia Sound involved three record producing companies at the time: Cameo-Parkway, Chancellor, and Swan. The songs were aimed at teenagers and sung by "dreamboat" stars. Cameo's stars included Chubby Checker and Bobby Rydell; Chancellor's included Fabian (who was picked by a talent scout because of his good looks) and Frankie Avalon.[3]

Bernie Lowe (1917-1993)

Bernie Lowe launched Cameo Parkway Records around 1957. One of the early signings by Parkway Records (an early offshoot) was Ernest Evans, otherwise known as Chubby Checker. Checker and Lowe, along with Kal Mann, helped Cameo/Parkway make Philadelphia a launching pad for early rock and roll. Other legends produced by Lowe and his team included Bobby Rydell, Dee Dee Sharp, The Tymes, The Orlons, and The Dovells.[4]

He wrote the song "Teddy Bear" for Elvis Presley and he started his career leading the orchestra on the Paul Whiteman TV Teen Club, an original Philadelphia production in the early 1050s (Marty Katz, nephew of Bernie Lowe).

American Bandstand

American Bandstand started locally, in Philadelphia, in 1952. It was the first network show dedicated exclusively to rock and roll. The initial host, Bob Horn, was replaced in 1956 by a local DJ Dick Clark. Broadcast for 90 minutes, "the show was picked up by 67 ABC affiliates, some for the full 90 minutes and others for just 60 or 30 minutes. The show was broadcast weekday afternoons and was given a primetime slot for 13 weeks in the fall of 1957."

Features included a weekly top ten review, featured performers who lip-synced their own songs and "Rate a Record" with a few teens chosen from the audience, giving the kids an opportunity to pass judgment on the latest single.

Philadelphia favorites who performed there and whose songs became huge hits because of the exposure included Frankie Avalon, Chubby Checker, Fabian, and Danny and the Juniors.

Dance was a key part of the show as the television story American Dreams, based on American Bandstand showed. Many teens would line up to be a part of the show and were often coupled. Fans would follow their fashions, their dance steps and what they could find out of their personal lives.

Some notable dance records played were The Twist and Pony Time by Chubby Checker, The Bristol Stomp by the Dovells, Wah-Watusi by the Orlons and The Mashed Potato by Dee Dee Sharp.

The show moved to Los Angeles where Clark hosted until 1989 (the last two years with USA network). It ran out of legs when it ended after a brief period when David Hirsch was the host of the show.[5, 6]

Frankie Avalon

A South Philadelphia native, Frankie Avalon became a matinee idol. Born Francis Thomas Avallone, Avalon teamed up early with Bobby Rydell in a group called Rocco and the Saints.

His break-though hit was "Venus." In Hollywood Avalon made "Grease," "Beach Blanket Bingo," "The Alamo," and "The Take." Avalon often teamed up with Annette Funicelloi.

American Bandstand with Dick Clark. Jerry Blavatt went on to be a famous Philadelphia DJ. Courtesy of Temple University. Urban Archives. Evening Bulletin Photo Collection.

Bobby Rydell

Bobby Rydell, nee Robert Ridarelli, was born in 1942.

Cameo Records, run by Bernie Lowe, produced his first hit record – "Kissin' Time." Other hits included "We Got Love," "Wild One," and "Swingin' School." He had thirty records on the charts with fifteen in the top twenty.

Other hits included "Volare" and "Sway." In addition to singing, Bobby Rydell has appeared in numerous films and television projects including *Bye Bye Birdie*. He still occasionally tours with other Philadelphia legends.

[Bobby Rydell's website].

Chubby Checker

Chubby Checker (born Ernest Evans) put the dance to the music with songs he recorded such as "The Twist" and "Pony Time," both of which became huge hits. Chubby Checker appeared on American Bandstand. Cameo-Parkway Records produced some of his songs.

Fabian

Fabian was a musical success in his teens with hits like "Turn Me Loose" and "Tiger." Like other Philadelphia Rock and Roll stars he appeared in television and film – including appearances with John Wayne, James Stewart, Jack Palance, and Tuesday Weld.[7]

SOFT ROCK

Hall and Oates

Text from their website – www.hallandoates.com

Daryl Hall and John Oates began working together in the 1970s and became one of the most successful duos in rock history. Their music is best known as rock 'n soul. They've had 8 #1 hit singles. Some of their best known songs include, "Do It For Love" released in 2002 and "Rich Girl," "Kiss On My List," "Maneater," "Private Eyes," "I Can't Go For That (No Can Do)," "Sara Smile," "She's Gone," and "One On One."

THE SOUND OF PHILADELPHIA

Kenny Gamble and Leon Huff – The Sound of Philadelphia

Text reprinted with permission of Gamble and Huff, from their website www.gamble-huffmusic.com

Kenny Gamble and Leon Huff have been songwriting and composing partners for over thirty years. They have brought to radios and record collections around the world a balance of passionate soul ballads and funky dance tracks that have become known as the Philly Sound. Their songs of peace, love, social conscience and turmoil, a sweet, sexy, stirring socially conscious music are also known as the Sound of Philadelphia.

In the 1950s and 1960s, Kenny Gamble worked for Georgie Woods and Jimmy Bishop and also operated his own record store in South Philadelphia. His own musical group "Kenny Gamble and the Romeos" had an early local hit with "Ain't it Baby, Part I." The Romeos lineup, which included songwriter Thom Bell and guitarist Roland Chambers have worked with Gamble and Huff through the decades. An early success was "I'm Gonna Make You Love Me," which was written for Dee Dee Warwick, became a hit with Diana Ross and the Supremes.

Leon Huff grew up in Camden, New Jersey, where he was influenced by his mother who played piano for the local church choir. He performed with several "doo-wop" groups. While performing as a pianist he found a mentor in Phil Spector. Encouraged by other musicians, Leon Huff began songwriting in the late 1950s. One of Gamble and Huff's early hits, sung by the Soul Survivors, was "Expressway to Your Heart," which was inspired by a traffic jam on the Schuylkill Expressway.

Their Rhythm and Blues (R&B) music was sung by some of the top performers, including Soul Survivors ("Expressway to Your Heart"), Archie Bell and the Drells ("I Can't Stop Dancin'"), Wilson Pickett ("Don't Let the Green Grass Fool You"), and Aretha Franklin ("A Brand New Me"). They had two Number One hits with Jerry Butler ("Only the Strong Survive" and "Hey, Western Union Man").

Gamble and Huff created Philadelphia International Records in 1971. The hits continued with the O'Jays ("Back Stabbers" and "Love Train"), Harold Melvin and the Blue Notes ("If You Don't Know Me By Now"), and Billy Paul whose song "Me and Mrs. Jones" won the label's first Grammy.

Along with the help and partnership of Thom Bell and distribution by CBS Records, the PIR label rose to the top levels of the record business. Gamble and Huff were able to tailor their songs for their stars which included songs for Lou Rawls, the Jackson Five, and their own house band MSFB (Mother Sister Father Brother) whose hit "The Sound of Philadelphia" became the theme song for the TV dance show "Soul Train." Their sound reflected Philadelphia from the freedom of Independence Hall and the vibrations of the Liberty Bell to the locomotive rhythm of a SEPTA train and the ebb and flow of Philadelphia's star athletes. Their album "Let's Clean Up the Ghetto," with songs by Teddy Pendergrass, the O'Jays, Lou Rawls, the Intruders, Dee Dee Sharp, and Archie Bell inspired young people to clean up their neighborhoods.

Kenny Gamble has invested his money and time in The Universal Companies – a business devoted to helping renovate South Philadelphia with affordable housing, jobs, schools, and the necessary ingredients for a good community. Other nonprofits helped by Kenny Gamble include research for cures for leukemia and cancer. He is on the Board of Directors of the Philadelphia Music Foundation, which honors Philadelphia's contributions to music.

Gamble and Huff continued writing for stars like Patti LaBelle, Phyllis Hyman, and McFadden and Whitehead. Today many of the leading R&B producers can trace their roots to Gamble and Huff.

In 1995, after writing or co-writing over 3,000 songs, Gamble and Huff were inducted into the National Academy of Songwriters Hall of Fame.

Thom Bell

Thom Bell worked with Gamble and Huff to produce the "Philadelphia Sound." "His smooth, lush, passionate arrangements helped the Delfonics with their hit Didn't I Blow Your Mind This Time? His first hit was the Delfonics' La La Means I Love You, in 1968

Bell, left the Delfonics to work another local group, the Stylistics. Along with songwriter, Linda Creed, and Russell Thompkins, Jr., the lead singer, the Stylistics made three albums with hits such as "I'm Stone in Love with You" and "Break Up to Make Up." Bell also helped produced albums with the Spinners whose hits, with Bell, include "Could it Be I'm Falling in Love.

He won a Grammy for Best Producer of the Year in 1975. In 2006, Bell was inducted into the Songwriter's Hall of Fame. [Wikipedia]
Sources: Al Hunter "Al Blues for Philly Jazz, City's Swing Thing Ain't What it Used To Be" Philadelphia Daily News 2/6/98 and explorePhiladelphihistory.com – Jazz Section.

JAZZ

Early twentieth century Philadelphia boasted the largest African-American population north of the Mason-Dixon Line. Educated, black, elite groups of caterers, skilled craftsmen, and personal service workers supported a rich musical culture, especially in the areas of classical and religious music.

Frank Johnson's band of the 1830s, with its "syncopated marches" was one of the early black Philadelphia musical acts. In the late 1800s, black Philadelphians, who learned their craft in church choirs, supported their own symphony orchestra and choral societies. In the early twentieth century black Philadelphia music, with a heritage in classical and religious music, began to be influenced by southern jazz. One of the singers to first give voice to this new generation was Ethel Waters from Chester, Pennsylvania, the first recording star of the African-American owned Black Swan Record Company. Early venues included the African-American owned Standard and Dunbar theaters on South Street.

Jazz influences came from a variety of groups, including Joe Venuti and Eddie Lang, two South Philadelphia Italians whose main jazz instruments were the guitar and the violin. West Philadelphia's Jan Savitt toured with his Top Hatters in the 1930s and early 1940s. Tunnell "became one of the first African-American vocalists to sing regularly with a prominent white band." Other early notables included "legendary teachers Adolph and Dennis Sandole, pianist Jimmy Amadie, Bebop trumpeter Robert "Red Rodney" Chudnick, and saxophonist Stan Getz.

The most early twentieth century notable white dance band was that of Howard Lanin. "Lanin orchestras helped start the careers of Red Nichols, Artie Shaw, the Dorsey brothers and other white jazz musicians."

In the 1940s and 1950s, legends like Dizzy Gillespie, John Coltrane, and the Heath Brothers navigated their way to Philadelphia. Other players included South Philadelphia's Bobby Timmons, Sam Reed, and Hen Gates. North Philadelphia also had Benny Golson and Lee Morgan. According to Leon Mitchell, who played sax and piano in the 1950s and was later the musical director of the Philadelphia Legends of Jazz Orchestra – bebop (the improvisational music of smaller less formal bands) was "cultivated" in Philadelphia. Along with the King, Dizzy Gillespie, there was Pianist Bud Powell and Charlie Parker played here too. Other jazz notables included Philly Joe Jones, Clifforn Brown, Wilbur Hare, and many others who played in the local club scene at places like "the Rendezvous, the Red Hill, the Blue Note, the Down Beat, the Show Boat, Pep's, Billy Krechmer's, the Cadillac Club, and Aqua Lounge."

"Saxophonist Odean Pope would go on to become one of the musicians who made up the next generation of Philly's jazz legacy, as were pianists McCoy Tyner, Kenny Barron, and Dave Burrell, trumpeters Lee Morgan and Ted Curson, bassists Jimmy Garrison, Reggie Workman, and Charles Fambrough, saxophonists Archie Shepp, Grover Washington, Jr., and Byard Lancaster, and drummers Rashied Ali, Albert 'Tootie' Heath, and Sunny Murray."

Other players of note include Christian McBride, Duane Eubanks, Byron Landum, Chris Lowery, Orrin Evans, Darryl Hall and Joey DeFrancesco, and more recently Mickey Roker, Trudy Pitts, Dave Burrell, Bobby Zankel, Charles Fambrough and Greg Osby, and Jamaaladeen Tacuma, Bobby Zankel, Uri Caine, and Ahmir Thompson.[8]

One composer/arrange of note was Sun Ra (born Herman Blount, in Alabama). Su Ra and his band, the Solar Myth Arkestra, played out of Philadelphia's Germantown section for a while.[9]

John Birks [Dizzy] Gillespie (1917-1993)

John Birks Gillespie was born in South Carolina in 1917 but moved to Philadelphia when he was eighteen. He began playing trumpet with Frankie Fairfax. After working with Cab Calloway and Duke Ellington Gillespie's unusual stylings began to be successful with Earl Hine's big band, which also featured Billy Eckstein and Charlie Parker.

Some of his successes included Gillespie's compositions like "Groovin' High," "Woody n' You," "Anthropology," and "A Night in Tunisia." "A Night in Tunisia" was one of the works that launched "bepop jazz," which was to become Gillespie's trademark.

Gillespie also worked to cultivate "Afro-Cuban" music.

He was a composer, band leader, and singer as well as a trumpet and trombone musician.[10, 11]

Dizzy Gillespie. Courtesy of Temple University Archives. Urban Archives. Evening Bulletin Photo Collection.

John Coltrane (1926-1967)

Born in North Carolina, in 1926, John Coltrane trained in Philadelphia at Granoff Studios and the Ornstein School of Music.

Early associations were with the Eddie "Cleanhead" Vinson, Jimmy Heath, and Dizzy Gillespie. Coltrane credits Miles Davis with the freedom to experiment with the "sheets of sound" approach – a method of playing multiple notes at once.

By 1960, he had formed his own quartet, the John Coltrane Quartet. That year he also recorded for Atlantic Records and won fame with his albums My Favorite Things, Africa/Brass, Giant Steps, and Impressions. His biggest hit was a testament to his faith and God – A Love Supreme.

Coltrane's music in 1965 reached a new synthesis of almost religious fervor, emotional force, and a nearly hypnotic tension. It was at this time that he also attained his greatest public acclaim, simultaneously winning the Hall Of Fame, Record of the Year, Jazzman of the Year, and tenor sax categories in the 1965 DB reader's poll. He died early, in 1967, yet his music influenced new generations of jazz musicians and can be heard in a variety of projects including movies like *Mr. Holland's Opus* and *Mo Better Blues* and television shows like "Cosby," "NYPD Blue," and "ER."

Coltrane's thirty-two minute "Love Supreme" is considered a canon of Jazz. According to Ashley Kahn, the author of a book about the album.

"Today, in addition to jazz fans, rockers and rappers, head-bangers and hip-hoppers all swear their allegiance to him. A Love Supreme is 'an unusually complete vision of one man's spirituality expressed through his art. Coltrane used the tools he had available and that he knew: a saxophone, a well-practiced quartet – even his own voice – to create music worthy of his creator'."[12, 13, 14]

Grover Washington, Jr. (1943-1999)

Smooth Jazz. That's probably the best way to describe saxophone great Grover Washington, Jr.

Over the years he created more than twenty albums.

The album that made him a great success was "Winelight" in 1980. Other successes, after that included: "The Best Is Yet To Come," "Strawberry Moon," "Then" and "Now" and "Time Out of Mind."

Grover Washington, Jr. often played the National Anthem at Philadelphia Seventy-Sixer games, the pro basketball team in Philadelphia. He gave back to the community in a variety of ways, including serving as chair for the Special Olympics, helping the homeless, the Variety Club, The Settlement Music School, and the United Negro College Fund. He died in 1999.

GOSPEL

Dixie Hummingbirds

The Dixie Hummingbirds began as the Sterling High School Quartet in South Carolina. The founder was James B. Davis. Baritone Ira Tucker and Willie Bob, a bass soon joined. Their fame grew in Philadelphia where Tucker would "run up the aisles and rock prayerfully on his knees." With the addition of Paul Owens the quartet honed a style called "trickeration," a kind of note bending distinguished by sensual lyrical finesse and staggering vocal intricacy. The quartet actually included five members, four-part harmony in support of the lead vocalists. They helped influence Jackie Wilson and a Philadelphia group – the Oak Ridge Boys.

They called themselves the Hummingbirds because "that was the only bird that could fly backwards and forwards, and that was how our career seemed to be going at the time," to quote then-leader James Davis.

The Hummingbirds played to packed houses in the South and "… on Philadelphia's WCAU under various titles like the Swanee Quintet and the Jericho Boys. The Hummingbirds recorded under the Apollo label as well as Gotham and Hob and later the Peacock label."[15, 16]

The father of Gospel, Thomas A. Dorsey (from the South) was inspired by a Philadelphian – Reverend Charles A. Tindley, who started singing around 1900.

Later additions included James Walker and guitarist Howard Caroll. Like Bessie Smith, many black performers before the 1960s had trouble recording with "white" labels.

Some of their best known songs included: 1952's "Trouble in My Way," 1953's "Let's Go Out to the Programs," 1954's "Christian's Testimonial," 1957's "Christian Automobile," and 1959's "Nobody Knows The Trouble I See". "After 1966 they essentially retired from the mainstream circuit to concentrate on performing in churches with one major exception. They backed up Paul Simon on his performance of 'Loves Me Like a Rock'."[17] Their best-known song was "I'll Overcome Some Day" which soon became "We Shall Overcome."[18]

Other gospel performers included the Angelic Gospel Singers led by Margaret Wells Atkinson.

OTHER STYLES

Folk Music

The 1960s saw the introduction of a number of new locations from the Gilded Cage to the Main Point and later the Khyber Pass. One of the early stars of folk music and one of the first performers at the Main Point was Jim Croce.

James "Jim" Croce (1943-1973)
Text reprinted with permission of Ingrid Croce (source: email communication)

Jim Croce began his career early singing in coffee houses, college concerts, local bars, and various universities, and later with his future wife, Ingrid, as a duo. He often sang at Villanova while a student; where he was a D.J. for the college radio station on Sunday nights.

Though Jim passed away at only thirty years old, his classic hits like "Time in a Bottle," "Bad, Bad Leroy Brown," "I'll Have to Say I Love You in a Song," and "Operator" continue to engage fans from around the world.

His sincere words and down-to-earth troubadour style told stories of the common man and crossed all borders, remaining timeless.

In 1972, the release of his album Life and Times yielded "Bad, Bad Leroy Brown" and several other hit recordings. The album reached the top of the national pop charts before it went Gold.

"Jim was humble, but when he sang, he touched us. The intimacy was so tangible and memorable that after decades people still light up when they share the enjoyment they hold of their first Jim Croce concert." —Ingrid Croce

Jim Croce died in a plane crash on September 20, 1973, in Natchitoches, Louisiana, at age thirty, one day before releasing his third ABC album, "I Got a Name." The posthumous release included three hits, "I Got a Name," "Workin' at the Car Wash Blues," and "I'll Have to Say I Love You in a Song." By December 1973, Jim Croce's first two albums, "You Don't Mess Around with Jim" and "Time in a Bottle" were in the top 10 albums for 1973 at the same time. Along with the many awards of recognition Jim Croce received for his music, he would have felt honored when he was posthumously inducted into The National Academy of Popular Music's Songwriters Hall of Fame and The Philadelphia's Music Foundation's Hall of Fame.

Wanting to honor and continue his legacy, twenty-five years ago Ingrid Croce opened Croce's Restaurant & Jazz Bar in the Historic Gaslamp Quarter in Downtown San Diego, California. Croce's offers Contemporary American cuisine, an award winning wine list, live music nightly, and true Croce hospitality.

Rap/Hip-Hop

Will Smith and DJ Jazzy Jeff (Jeff Townes) helped bring hip hop to Philadelphia. Their 1998 album "He's the DJ, I'm the Rapper" won the first Grammy for Hip-Hop. Smith combined his musical gifts with comedy and acting. His television show "The Fresh Prince of Bel-Air" was premised on a Will Smith persona moving from Philadelphia to the West, never forgetting his roots.[19] [For more on Will Smith see the film section].

Philadelphia Experiment

This style, a "fusion" of Philly Sound/Jazz and Hip Hop, was made popular by Christian McBride, jazz legends Uri Caine on keyboards and guitarist Pat Martino, along with McBride, and Roots/Questlove drummer Ahmir Thompson.[20]

Old Sounds
Frank Johnson

Johnson, an African American, was a composer, bandleader, fiddler, bugler, and orchestra director. Lafayette sponsored a European tour for him where he played for Queen Victoria. Another notable, James A. Bland, wrote over 600 songs, including "Oh, Dem Golden Slippers," the theme song of the Philadelphia Mummers. The Soap Box Club sang spirituals, ballads, and folk songs.[21]

New Sounds

A few of the new notables are Usiq, Bilal and Floetry, and Roots.[22]

FEMALE STARS

Bessie Smith (1894-1937)

Bessie Smith was born poor and orphaned young in Chattanooga, Tennessee, in 1894. Mentored by Ma Rainey, Bessie Smith began her singing career with Rainey's Rabbit Foot Minstrels. She perfected her blues style in clubs in and around Philadelphia and Atlantic City. She was one of the most successful black performers of her day.

Her first hit was "Down Heated Blues."[23, 24]

In a performance of Lady Day at the Emerson, the character of Billie Holiday, who was born in Philadelphia, credits Louis Armstrong and Bessie Smith for her inspiration. The role of Ms. Holiday was played by Cab Calloway's daughter. In the role, it is also noted that many of the white studios would not perform Ms. Smith's songs. Black studios and white studios which recorded A tracks by black performers would come much too late for Ms. Smith.[25]

Ethel Waters (1896-1977)

Born in Chester, Pa. in 1896 Ethel Waters became the first African American star helping to open the doors for many black performers. A star of the theater and film she launched her musical career with Stormy Weather and Dinah. She was the first black actress to receive an Emmy nomination. And won the New York Dram Critics Award for her performance in A Member of the Wedding by Carson McCollough. She also starred in radio with Jimmy Dorsey's Band.

Pearl Bailey (1918-1990)

Pearl Bailey won fame in Hollywood and Broadway. She combined her sultry voices with a humorous presence.

Her hits included "Baby It's Cold Outside" and "Takes Two to Tango."

She debuted on Broadway during 1946 in the musical St. Louis Woman.

She performed jazz as well. In addition to her singing and recording career (with Columbia and Coral records) she worked in the movies including the W.C. Handy biopic St. Louis Blues and the first filmed version of Gershwin's classic operetta Porgy and Bess.

Ms. Bailey won a Tony award for Hello, Dolly!, starred in her own television variety show, and still found time to work for the United Nations in 1976. She was awarded the Medal of Freedom in 1988.

Phyllis Hyman (1941-1995)

Phyllis Hyman was a jazz singer with a soulful touch. Her early hit songs included "Betcha By Golly Wow," "Loving You," and "I Don't Want To Lose You."

Pattie LaBelle
Text reprinted with permission of Patti LaBelle's website

Even as the melodic doyen of the legendary 1960s quartet, Patti Labelle & the Bluebelles, and the retro '70s trio, Labelle—Patti's kinetic performances and signature, four-octave instrument served as the group's torch. For more than forty years in the music business, the two-time Grammy-winning legend continues to solidify herself as a musical pioneer. Never resting on her laurels, Patti embarked on a new genesis with the release of her introspective masterpiece, Timeless Journey, in May 2004 and her exquisite collection of remakes, Classic Moments, in June 2005.

As she continues into her fourth decade of performing, the Philadelphia maven has returned to her roots with her latest project, The Gospel According to Patti LaBelle. "I was born gospel, so it's not like I'm coming back or trying to impress people with this new gospel project. I've always done this. I've never done a whole album. That's the only thing that's missing," observes the songstress. "I've come full circle where you can say it's a complete project." "Because of Bud's (longtime Musical Director and friend, Budd Ellison) situation, and I always wanted him to be involved with my gospel project because he was involved in all of my CD's, I said I better start now because he's slowly going away. That was my real reason for starting it." Sadly, Bud Ellison passed away from prostate cancer before the completion of the album. Patti has dedicated this album to his loving memory in addition to donating all the proceeds to a variety of cancer organizations.

Patti's artistic evolution has enabled her to be a chameleon without diminishing her edge, vocal prowess or legion of fans. "I'm always moving and trying to discover something new to entice me," explains Patti.

Although she's widely-known for classic moonstruck ballads such as the duet "On My Own" with Michael McDonald, "If Only You Knew," "You Are My Friend," and "If You Asked Me To," her diverse musical tastes have only enhanced her versatility. Today Patti continues to receive respect and admiration from a new generation of artists.

As a mother, author, actress, and activist, the Philadelphia native born Patricia Holte has transcended the music arena. As an author, she's written four best-sellers *Don't Block the Blessings: Revelations of a Lifetime*, *Patti Labelle's Lite Cuisine*, *Labelle Cuisine*, and *Patti's Pearls*. Finally, as an actress, she's starred in her own sitcom-series, "Out All Night," and numerous television shows and specials. Patti launched a lifestyle show, "Living It Up With Patti LaBelle," on the TV One Network in 2004 and has expanded her horizons into fashion with Patti LaBelle Clothing, available on HSN and at HSN.com.

Also a diabetic, Patti has been proactive in the fight against the very disease that claimed her dear mother's life. She serves as a spokesperson for the National Medical Association that administers a scholarship in her name, the National Minority AIDS Council's Live Long, Sugar campaign and the American Diabetes Association. Patti also serves on the Boards of the National Alzheimer Association and the National Cancer Institute and the University of Miami's prestigious Sylvestri Comprehensive Care Center dedicated a special research laboratory in her honor for her work on behalf of cancer awareness. In addition, Patti has three Honorary Doctorate Degrees from Cambridge University, Drexel University, and the Berklee School of Music, among a host of other accolades.

Patti LaBelle. Courtesy of Patti LaBelle/Pattonium

Jill Scott

Jill Scott's beautiful voice distinguishes her among Rhythm and Blues artists. Her platinum debut, *Who is Jill Scott? Words and Sounds* Vol. I, was a mix of jazz, R&B, hip-hop, and spoken word. It was released in 2000.

"She is the antithesis of every plastic pop singer out there, joining the ranks of India Arie and Erykah Bad as great songstresses with dreamy, original sounds and important, relevant lyrics."

Her recent albums include *Beautifully Human Words and Sound Vol. 2* (2004) and *The Real Thing: Words and Sounds Vol. 3* (2007).

She won a Grammy in 2005 for Best Urban/Alternative R&B Performance for "Cross My Mind." She is also an actress and a poet. [Wikipedia notes][26] She stars in the television series "No. 1 Ladies Detective Agency."

VENUES

Curtis Institute of Music

1726 Locust Street – Corner of Rittenhouse Square
Text reprinted with permission of the Curtis Institute of Music

Founded by Mary Louise Curtis Bok in 1924, the Curtis Institute of Music is one of the premier conservatories for the teaching of music in the world. Its alumni include Samuel Barber, Leonard Bernstein, and Anna Moffo. The current President/Director, Roberto Diaz (shown), is who replaced Gary Grafman in 2006. The faculty includes many of the premier musicians of the twentieth and twenty-first centuries. A [partial] timeline of the institute shows how influential the Institute has been and is still.

Curtis offers numerous and varied occasions for music lovers to hear the students through the Student Recital Series and performances of the Curtis Opera Theatre and the Curtis Symphony Orchestra.

1924 – To house the new conservatory of music, Edward and Mary Louise Curtis Bok purchased three buildings on the south side of Locust Street–the Romanesque home of the prominent Drexel family, the adjoining Sibley house, and the Beaux-Arts-style Cramp mansion.

From the beginning Mrs. Bok emphasized that the school would be best served by maintaining a small student body and a strong student-teacher relationship, with the result that students and faculty would each expect more from the other. Therefore, she assembled a faculty that would attract the most promising students. In the school's first years, instructors included Leopold Auer, Josef Hofmann, Anton Horner, William Kincaid, Wanda Landowska, Carlos Salzedo, Marcella Sembrich, Leopold Stokowski, Marcel Tabuteau, Isabelle Vengerova, and Efrem Zimbalist.

Today the school's faculty includes celebrated teachers and performing musicians such as Richard Danielpour, Leon Fleisher, Claude Frank, Pamela Frank, Gary Graffman, Jennifer Higdon, Ida Kavafian, Seymour Lipkin, Otto-Werner Mueller, Aaron Rosand, Joseph Silverstein, members of the Guarneri Quartet, and many current and distinguished retired members of the Philadelphia Orchestra.

1941 – Efrem Zimbalist, head of violin faculty, is named Curtis director, a position he holds for twenty-seven years.

1945 – Future Pulitzer Prize-winner George Walker becomes one of the first African-American students to graduate from Curtis, having studied both piano and composition.

1970 – Rudolf Serkin reinvigorates opera department with the appointment of Max Rudolf, formerly artistic administrator of the Metropolitan Opera under Rudolf Bing. Mr. Serkin also revives the conducting department, which had been suspended when Fritz Reiner left in 1941.

1977 – John de Lancie, oboist and Curtis alumnus, is named Curtis director, the first graduate to hold the position. During his tenure, the academic curriculum is formalized, leading to accreditation by the National Association of Schools of Music (NASM).

1986 – Alumnus and world-renowned pianist Gary Graffman is named artistic director of Curtis. In 1989 he becomes director

Roberto Diaz. Courtesy of Curtis Insitute

and in 1995, president, the first person to hold both titles. [27]

In 1979 Mr. Graffman's performing career was interrupted by an injury to his right hand. Since then, his concertizing has been limited to the small repertoire of concertos written for the left hand alone.

The Philadelphia Metropolitan Opera House

The Philadelphia Opera House was built by Oscar Hammerstein (the grandfather of the lyricist Oscar Hammerstein II) and opened in 1908. It competed with the opera performed at the Academy of Music. Opera didn't last at the Philadelphia Opera House. The Opera Company of Philadelphia, formed in 1975, performs opera at the Academy of Music and the Perelman Theater at the Kimmel Center.

Philadelphia is and has been home to a number of wonderful performing music venues.

Older venues included The Old Apollo Theater, a number of old jazz halls and several outdoor arenas (The Valley Forge Music Fair, Temple University Music Festival at Ambler Campus, and others). The Mellon Jazz Festival was also a Philadelphia tradition. Now Mellon sponsors individual concerts at the Kimmel Center.

Existing Centers include the new Kimmel center, the Academy of Music and the outdoor theaters – the Robin Hood Dell (now divided into East for jazz, pop, and voice and West (Mann Music Center) for more classical music.

Kimmel Center

260 South Broad Street
Text reprinted with permission of the Kimmel Center Inc.

Architectural History

The Academy of Music, which was originally built for opera, was built in 1857 and served as home to the Philadelphia Orchestra for the entire twentieth century. The Orchestra pushed for a new concert hall throughout its existence. Howe and Lescase, who designed the PSFS building, and Frank Lloyd Wright, were among the rejected architects.

Money, however, was the main problem in raising a new hall. Donations from the Pew Charitable Trusts and Sidney Kimmel were not enough. In 1996, at the urging of a group convened by Marjorie O. "Midge" Rendell, authority for a new building was given to a new arts authority.

A new design by Rafael Violy was revealed in 1998. The New York architect envisioned two buildings encased in a glass dome – an idea recycled from a performing arts center he designed for Baltimore that never got built....

With the new design's cello-shaped concert hall and 150-foot-high glass vault, Rendell and developer Willard G. Rouse 3d hoped it would spur donations. It did. With the aid of Stephanie W. Naidoff over $111 million was raised in four years....[28]

The Kimmel Center, [Mr. Kimmel's donations were accepted after all] includes a theater named after Ruth and Raymond G. Perelman in addition to the new concert hall, named Verizon Hall, after Verizon – a local phone company.

Philadelphia Sound

Russell Johnson, the acoustician, included equipment to help fine-tune the needs of the Orchestra and the Hall.

Kinetic Kimmel by Perry Milou. Courtesy of Perry Milou

Academy Of Music

Broad and Locust Streets
Text Source – Philadelphia Inquirer, Friday January 26, 2007. "On occasion of the Academy of Music's 150th anniversary." Section H.

The Academy of Music (known as the "Grand Old Lady of Broad Street") has been called the finest opera house in the country. Built by Napolean LeBrun and Gustav Runge, the Academy opened on January 26, 1858.

While orchestral music has been the prime art performed in the Academy of Music, early uses included theater, opera, vaudeville, political conventions (President Ulysses S. Grant was nominated for a second term there), debates, charity balls, and even a football game between Penn and Princeton.

Its simple Byzantine brick exterior is countered by its magnificent Victorian interior. Inside are magnificent sculptures and a trademark crystal chandelier.

The principal tenant until the building of the Kimmel Center for the Performing Arts was the Philadelphia Orchestra known for its lush Philadelphia sound created by conductor Leopold Stokowski and continued by Maestro Eugene Ormandy. Stokowski's magic included Mahler's Symphony No. 8, which is shown at the introduction to the music chapter, and numerous world premiers.

Performers and conductors over the decades have included music legends such as Arturo Tosanini, Enrico Caruso, Richard Strauss, Luciano Pavarotti, Marian Anderson, Edith Piaf, and Isaac Stern. Even Harpo Marx played the Academy of Music.

The Academy of Music is now home to the Pennsylvania Ballet and the Opera Company of Philadelphia.

Ginger Rogers, in the Philadelphia based movie *Kitty Foyle* hoped, one day, to be married to somebody who could take her to the annual charity ball, known as the Assembly. The ball is one of the last galas in the country to still require white tie and tails as opposed to tuxedos. Today it is known as the Academy Ball. Attendees for the 150th anniversary included the Royal Highness the Prince of Wales and the Duchess of Cornwall. Some ticket prices went for $2,500. The Ball is a fundraiser that raises, at least in 2007, over a million dollars. According to *Philadelphia Inquirer* architectural critic, Inga Saffron, The Academy's brick exterior is "boisterously three-dimensional. The bricks feel like they've been sculpted, rather than merely laid."

Academy of Music, Interior. A Century After. Picturesque Glimpses of Philadelphia and Pennsylvania 1875. Courtesy of The Library Company of Philadelphia

The Broad Street location was remarkably democratic. Opera halls in Europe were often in parks or set aside from the main street. The Academy is right on the street. It was the beginning of the numerous city enhancements that would extend Philadelphia from the Delaware River seaport to the Schuylkill.

The inside seats nearly 3000 people, more than the Verizon Hall in the Kimmel Center. Its wooden amphitheater tickets were often sold for a low price to those who couldn't afford subscriptions. It was a cheap way of being introduced to great music. The great Academy dome is "frescoed with images of the various arts." The glass chandelier, which has been adapted for electricity, is more than eighteen feet high. "In 1992 Martin Scorcese filmed the opening sequence of Edith Wharton's "The Age of Innocence" at the Academy of Music.

Robin Hood Dell
Robin Hood Dell East
Ridge Avenue & Huntingdon Drive

The City decided to build a concert amphitheater seating 10,000 in Fairmount Park. In 1930, the new amphitheater, Robin Hood Dell, was opened at Ridge Avenue and Dauphin Street. This location, in addition to being convenient to the regular public transit lines, was located near the terminal of the park trolleys which ran to the Woodside Park amusement park and West Philadelphia.

"The Robin Hood Dell East concerts have their roots in free summer concerts sponsored by the City of Philadelphia at the Lemon Hill Concert Pavilion in Fairmount Park. Concerts were held near 31st and Poplar Streets, seven nights a week, during the summer in the 1920s. A fifty-piece orchestra, composed mostly of members of the Philadelphia Orchestra, performed at the concerts, which attracted as many as 20,000 people. The crowds were too large to fit in the concert pavilion, and the overflow sat or stood on the grass around the pavilion, extending as far as the sounds of the orchestra could be heard." (http://beta.phil.gov/delleast/history.html)

The first concert at Robin Hood Dell took place on July 8, 1930. Even though Robin Hood Dell was much larger than the Lemon Hill Concert Pavilion, many who came to the concerts frequently found the amphitheater filled to capacity, and remained outside to listen to the music.[29]

The Mann Music Center
5201 Parkside Avenue
Text reprinted with permission of Philadelphia Orchestra.

The Mann Center opened as the summer home of The Philadelphia Orchestra in 1976, replacing the Robin Hood Dell stage, which had hosted Orchestra summer concerts since 1930. Originally known as Robin Hood Dell West, the center was renamed in 1978 after Fredric R. Mann, a longtime Philadelphia resident and tireless businessman, whose advocacy of summer concerts in Fairmount Park extended back for more than half a century.

It also is the stage for many pop and rock concerts.

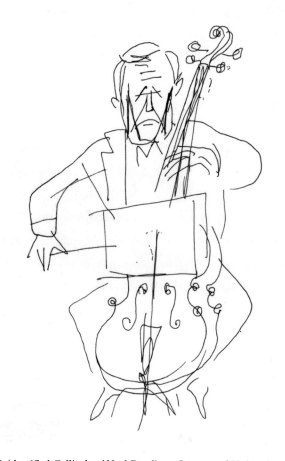

Unidentified Cellist by Alfred Bendiner. Courtesy of University of Pennsylvania Architectural Archives

Mann Music Center by Alfred Bendiner. Courtesy of University of Pennsylvania Architectural Archives

COMPOSERS/PRODUCERS

Samuel Barber (1910-1981)

Samuel Barber, born in West Chester, attended Curtis Institute in the mid-1920s, while still a teenager.

"Barber, who is generally regarded as a neo-Romantic composer, is admired for an extremely lyrical quality that permeates his compositions, works that are also characterized by a high degree of tonality."

Adagio for Strings is among his best known works. Toscanini introduced his "First Essay for Orchestra" and "Adagio for Strings" with the NBC Orchestra in 1938. It has been played at many somber occasions such as the funerals of Franklin D. Roosevelt, Albert Einstein, and Princess Grace of Monaco.

His operas included *Vanessa* which premiered at the Metropolitan at Lincoln Center in 1958. "That work won the first of two Pulitzer Prizes for Barber. He won a second Pulitzer along with a Music Critics Circle Award in 1962 for Piano Concerto No. 1, which had its premiere at the Avery Fisher Music Hall (then Philharmonic Hall) at the Lincoln Center." [www.musicianguide.com]

Richard Rodgers and Oscar Hammerstein, II

While not technically from Philadelphia, Rodgers and Hammerstein lived in nearby Bucks County. Many of their plays tried out in New Hope or Philadelphia before going to New York. The shows and songs they produced are some of the best musical theater ever. The grandfather of Oscar Hammerstein II helped build the Philadelphia Opera Company.

Oscar Hammerstein II (lyrics) and Richard Rodgers (composer) joined together in 1942 to create some of the most memorable Broadway American musicals. Their many hits included their first sensation, *Oklahoma*, and numerous others including *Carousel, Allegro, South Pacific, The King and I, Me and Juliet, Pipe Dream, Flower Drum Song*, and *The Sound of Music*. *The Sound of Music* was also made into an Oscar winning movie starring Julie Andrews. They also wrote *State Fair*, a musical for the movies and "Cinderella," a musical for television. They earned numerous Tony and Academy Awards and even the Pulitzer Prize award. "Collectively, the Rodgers & Hammerstein musicals earned thirty-four Tony Awards, fifteen Academy Awards, two Pulitzer Prizes."[30]

Harold Prince

Hal Prince attended the University of Pennsylvania in the 1940s. The Hal Prince Theater at the Annenberg Center on the University of Pennsylvania Campus is named after him, as is a new theater in Downtown Philadelphia. The Prince Music Theater (founded in 1983 by Marjorie Samoff as the American Music Theater Festival) is dedicated to the development and production of new musical-theater pieces.[31] Theater at the Prince Music Theater is also complemented by a film program, which tries to show films that complement the current theater production and films by other entities including the Gay and Lesbian Film Festival, and the Weekend Film Festival.[32]

Harold Prince received a Kennedy Center Honor and 19 Tony Awards for his Broadway musicals, which include *The Pajama Game, Damn Yankees, New Girl in Town, West Side Story, Fiorello*, and *Caba-*

ret. He later partnered with Steven Sondheim and helped produce *Company, Follies, A Little Night Music, Pacific Overtures*, and *Sweeney Todd*. Without Sondheim, Prince directed *Candide, On the Twentieth Century*, and *Evita*.

"Other Prince productions included *The Phantom of the Opera* with Andrew Lloyd Webber, *Kiss of the Spider Woman*, and *Showboat*. He also works in opera and has staged *La Fanciulla del West, Madama Butterfly, Turandot, Faust*, and other works at the Metropolitan Opera, Chicago Lyric, Houston Grand, and Vienna Staatsoper."[33]

Larry Magid & Allen Spivak

Larry Magid and Allen Spivak brought major musical talent to Philadelphia and opened one of rock music's first live venues in 1968, the Electric Factory.

Their productions include Live Aid which, in 1985, was produced from Philadelphia's JFK stadium and simulcast in Wembly Stadium in England raising "more than $75 million for famine relief, earning Magid and Spivak citations from the United States Congress and the City of Philadelphia."

"Other productions included: The Atlantic City Pop Festival, The Quaker City and many other Jazz Festivals, The Broadway Musical Upton, It's Hot starring Maurice Hines. A four year tour of *Phantom of the Opera, Song Of Singapore*, a number of plays, 1993's world tour of *Jesus Christ Superstar*; the Broadway and national production of *GREASE!*, and the touring production of the Broadway smash *Hello, Dolly!*. They also ran the Bijou Cafe which was considered one of the country's most influential showcase clubs."[34]

They also produced a 2005 version of Live Aid called Live 8. Philadelphia was one of the eight sights.

RADIO STATIONS

Profiles of many of Philadelphia's best music radio stations (old and new) can be seen on the website of Broadcast Pioneers of Philadelphia, a federally recognized, state chartered charity, made up of 325 area broadcasters.

Stations in Philadelphia have run the gambit, including:

Classical
WFLN
Jazz
WJJZ
WRTI Temple University's station.

A few summaries follow:[34]
WFIL was operated by *The Philadelphia Inquirer* and was a principal affiliate of the ABC Radio Network.

Some of the on-air talents included Phil "Uncle Philsy" Sheridan, Al Meltzer (later a local TV sportscaster for KYW, WCAU, and Comcast SportsNet), and Jim Gearhart.

WFIL played popular music around the clock, and then, in 1966, switched to Top 40 hits. On-air talents in this format included George Michael, Long John Wade, and Allen Stone.

Slogans like "WFIL Is Boss" and "WFIL Gets It Together" helped the station succeed with a younger audience.

ROCK AND ROLL

WMMR, Philadelphia's oldest "Rock and Roll" station includes popular disk jockeys Paul Barsky and Pierre Robert.[35]

MINORITY FOCUS

WDAS (formerly WIAD, then WELK): The WDAS call letters came from silk manufacturers, Dannenbaum & Steppacher. In the 1950s, under the ownership of Max M. Leon, the station played big bands, ethnic, and cultural shows. Leon, the founder and conductor of the original Philly Pops Orchestra, added an all-night classical music show.

Programming switched to black entertainment, jazz, and rhythm & blues with such on air talent as Georgie Woods, Jimmy Bishop, Carl Helm, Butterball Tamburro, Jocko Henderson, and Hy Lit.

Ed Bradley (of "60 Minutes" TV fame) was a feature reporter.

In the 1970s Georgie Woods' show moved from music to talk.

In 1988, the station switched to its current all gospel music and religious format.

EARLY FM STATIONS

WDVR was responsible for broadcasting in stereo twenty-four hours a day, seven days a week, and created the first big money giveaway in radio ($101,000) and the first professional TV spot to promote radio. In 1980, WDVR changed its call letters to WEAZ and started using the name "Eazy 101."

WHAT: *The Public Ledger* sold their station, in 1944, to Dolly Banks and her brother William Banks. One of the stars of the FM station was Sid Mark. While the station was known as a jazz station Mark became famous for playing Frank Sinatra only music on Fridays and Sundays.

SOME AM STATIONS

WURD: On-air talk talent included Frank Ford, Carol Saline, Maxine Schnall, and Ron Eisenberg and Peter Tilden. The station now is a black talk radio station.

WNTP, formerly WZZD, began, in 1924, as WIBG for "I Believe in God." On-air talent included Doug Arthur and Joe Niagara. WIBG, known as Wibbage, played Top 40 songs. Its printed list of the "Top 99" songs was the first radio station survey sheet distributed at local record shops.

Other on air talent included Don Wade, 'Dirty' Don Cannon, Tom Rivers, McClintock, Gary Brooks, Cat Martin, Doug James, Sean Casey, Bill Gardner, and 'Giant Gene' Arnold with his 'Giant Gene's Electric Scene' program.

Today, WNTP broadcasts syndicated news talk programs.

The Tweeter Center, across the river in nearby Camden, is a popular site where younger audiences can see Brittany Spears or the Dave Matthews Band.

PHILADELPHIA SONGS

Sports Songs

The "Fightin' Phils" Theme Song Lyrics by Bickley Reichnec and Eliot Lawrence.

"Sweet Little 16" by Chuck Berry has the line "Cause they'll be Rocking on Bandstand in Philadelphia P-A." The Flyers adopted this song in honor of their Number 16, Bobby Clarke, in his playing days for the Philadelphia Flyers

"God Bless America," while not about Philadelphia alone, became identified with the city when the Flyers asked Kate Smith to play it before important games. More often than not Kate Smith's and the song's magic worked their charms – resulting in a Flyers win. The song was played often during the 1970s when the Flyers twice became Stanley Cup Champions.

"Rocky Theme Song." Anytime an underdog needs a boost this is the song that is played. Recently, the Indiana Professional Basketball Team played it to boost their team. The only problem was that they were playing the Philadelphia 76ers. The irony was not lost on any Philadelphia fan and the 76ers won the game and the series.

"Let it Flow (Dr. J's Theme Song)" by Grover Washington, Jr. is a smooth jazz piece emulating Julius Erving's game and moves.

"Ain't No Stopping Us Now" written by Gene McFaddedn and John Whitehead and Jerry Cohen and sung by McFadden and Whitehead was a theme song for the Eagles

"Philadelphia Freedom" is the theme song for the Philadelphia Tennis Freedoms, a Professional Tennis team. It was written by Elton John for Billie Jean King when she decided to start a professional tennis league. The song has been played so often that listeners have forgotten its origin.

Local Songs

"South Street Saturday Night." While many people think of South Street as the province of the young and hip, African Americans have been living on South Street for over a century and a half. At one time an affluent section of town, the street resonated with jazz and laughter. L. Vassor Warde composed "South Street Saturday Night." African Americans William Gardener Smith and David Bradley wrote novels about the street with the same name—South Street.[36]

"South Street" was a popular song by the Orlons. It was written by Kal Man with music by David Appell about the fun of gathering on Philadelphia's South Street.

"Streets of Philadelphia" (music and words by Bruce Springstein) was part of the movie *Philadelphia*.

Several other Philadelphia classics include:

"Philadelphia Polka." A song sung by the Quaker City String Band for its Mummers parade.

"The Schuylkill River Boat Song."

PHILADELPHIA FOLK FESTIVAL

This festival takes place outside of Philadelphia in nearby Schwenksville in the summertime. It was founded by the Philadelphia Folksong Society. It has grown into the biggest folk festival in the country, maybe the world.

Gene Shay was a founding member and has been the MC for the event since it started. A new stage was built for the 40th annual festival, in 2001.

A variety of great folk performers are on hand from nationally known names likes Ani DiFranco, Ralph Stanley, and Mary Chapin Carpenter to many local talents as well.

For many it's a yearly way of keeping up with old friends. Many folk performers also can be seen each summer in Upper Merion Township in a series called "Under the Stars."

Other popular folk sites include "The Second Fret," "Tin Angel," "Khyber Pass," Penn's "Cherry Tree," and the "New" Point, which is just a few doors down from the old "Main Point."

PHILADELPHIA FILM

Picture – Grace Kelly

"The consistent theme in Philadelphia films from The Show Off through The Philadelphia Story through The Young Philadelphians through Trading Places and Philadelphia is that a blue collar type rubs up against or conflicts with a blueblood and both learn that they are more alike than not."

Carrie Rickey
Film Critic

Grace Kelly by Andy Warhol © 2008 The Andy Warhol Foundation for the Visual Arts Inc./ Artists Rights Society (ARS), NY. Courtesy of Andy Warhol Foundation and Artist Rights Society and Getty Images

PHILADELPHIA FILM

NOTABLE STYLES
Grace
  Underdog
    Neighborhoods

Contents

PHILADELPHIA
IN THE MOVIES

Philadelphians first saw themselves on the big screen in *The Show Off*, *Kitty Foyle*, and *Fantasia*.

The first well known actors from Philadelphia who made it to film were the irascible W.C. Fields; Larry Fine, one of the Three Stooges; Janet Gaynor; and the graceful Grace Kelly. Many of the actors were often successful in other fields before becoming a movie star.

Movies about Philadelphia tend to fall into two categories – those where the city itself is a central character and others where the city is background to the story. For movies with the central character theme, the central character is usually a neighborhood or the clash between two neighborhoods. The issue in the movie is – to what extent access to these neighborhoods are inclusive and to what extent these neighborhoods, these cultures, can coexist with other neighborhoods.

Most of these films tend to show the interaction and conflict where different neighborhoods or cultures collide. There are the high society types and regular folk in *The Young Philadelphians*, *Kitty Foyle*, and *Trading Places*; urbanites and rural people in *Witness*; heterosexuals and gays in *Philadelphia*; real people (the musicians) and animated people in *Fantasia*; Americans and foreigners in some of James Michener's films; and graduates who played four years of college ball and a neighborhood bartender in *Invincible*.

Some movies show that a peaceful exchange is hopeless. Others, that it's possible if only the different neighborhoods would open their eyes. Most show that prejudice is not inborn. It, like Michener's favorite song, has to be "Carefully Taught." (*South Pacific*)

Other films could have been shot elsewhere but for the producer's love of the city. Even here there are noticeable Philadelphia traits. Brian DePalma and David Lynch highlight the bizarre (ask anybody who follows Philadelphia sports). Charles Fuller, Marc Bowden, and James Michener are marvelous storytellers. The latter three made their reputations as writers/ playwrights before their stories made it to the silver screen.

Siegmund Lubin founded the world's first movie studio which made 2500 films from 1896 through 1923. Philadelphia since then has not had any major movie studios. It does, though, continue, with the aid of the Greater Philadelphia Film Office and the Philadelphia Film Society, to produce and show numerous films by and about Philadelphians.

The showcases today are not as glamorous as some of the old theaters like the Mastbaum, the Boyd or the Erlanger. The old single theaters like those in the *Last Picture Show* are a relic of the past. But there are a number of comfortable new ones like the Historic District's Ritz Theater, the first multiplex theater devoted to independent and "art" films, and the County Theater out in James Michener's hometown, Doylestown, that also shows some of the best art house and commercial films available. They're not only complete with cookies and cakes, in addition to popcorn, but they come with programs, discussion groups, memberships, and more.

Sharon Pinkenson, the Executive Director of the Greater Philadelphia Film Office, notes a practical side to making films in Philadelphia. Aside from the variety of neighborhoods and wonderful scenes, Philadelphia makes it easy to make films here. Whether it's providing two policemen for each shoot or the ease of getting parking licenses, the Greater Philadelphia Film Office invites local, national, and international filmmakers local to film here. The practical side is a two-way street as filming in Philadelphia has been a great boon to the region's economy.

A variety of educational programs allow Philadelphians to learn about the history of film and how to make and market their own films.

Even the critics are friendly. You can hear, read or question some of the City's critics and movie commentators, like the *Philadelphia Inquirer's* Carrie Rickey and WHYY's Patrick Stoner, who can tell you what you really saw.

PHILADELPHIA FILM SUPPORT

Greater Philadelphia Film Office: Making Philadelphia the Hollywood of the East

The Greater Philadelphia Film Office is dedicated to helping filmmakers choose Philadelphia as the place where they produce and direct their movies. The Greater Philadelphia Film Office helps filmmakers in a variety of ways, including:

◊ Production guide free to locally produced projects.
◊ One stop service for all city department requests.
◊ Location scouting and photo files for entire region.
◊ A complete digital database of locations and resources.
◊ Referrals and negotiations with businesses.
◊ Coordination with neighborhoods and owners of private property.
◊ Assistance with government permit or license requirements.
◊ Ongoing dialogue with organized labor.
◊ Philadelphia film crew hats, tee shirts, and umbrellas.
◊ Sponsor of the "Set in Philadelphia" screenwriting competition.
◊ Organize premieres of films made in Philadelphia.
◊ Support and promote local film festivals.
◊ Projects & events related to growth of the local film and video industry.
◊ Lobby for government incentives for film industry growth.

The Greater Philadelphia Film Office (GPFO) is a "film commission" representing southeastern Pennsylvania that officially serves the counties of Bucks, Chester, Delaware, Montgomery, and Philadelphia. It is a member of the Association of Film Commissions International (AFCI), and a founding member of Film US. GPFO, first established in 1985 as a part of Philadelphia city government, continues to reside within city offices. In 1992, it became a regional economic development office, incorporating as the Greater Philadelphia Film Office, a Pennsylvania non-profit corporation, in July 2000.

The Greater Philadelphia Film Office has had a significant impact on the region's economy. The economic impact of film and TV production in the regions, since 1992, exceeds two billion dollars. [For more on how the Greater Philadelphia Film Office helps promote Philadelphia films please see the bus tour section at the end of this chapter].

Film Series

Formed in 2001, The Philadelphia Film Society's mission is to engage the diverse communities of the region by producing major film events and other year-round programming. Among its most prominent activities are:

The Philadelphia Film Festival

Held for two weeks in early spring, the Festival brings the world's imagination to Philadelphia with screenings of nearly 300 features, documentaries, shorts, and animation from 50 countries for an audience of 61,000.

Festival programming is arranged into thematic sections, including World Focus, American Independents, Documentary Traditions, Cinema of the Muslim Worlds, New Korean Cinema, and the utterly unique and often alarming Danger After Dark, a celebration of genre film from around the world. The Festival also hosts a showcase of regional filmmaking, entitled Festival of the Independents, sponsored by City Paper.

In 2001, the Festival instituted a Juried Competition for Best Feature, Documentary, and Short Film, and it distributes ballots to all ticket holders to determine Audience Awards. The Festival also hosts the "Set in Philadelphia" screenplay competition in collaboration with the Greater Philadelphia Film Office.

Philadelphia International Gay & Lesbian Film Festival

Founded in 1995 by TLA Entertainment Group, the Festival presents a "rainbow" of GLBT film and video images from around the world. The festival screens as many as 200 features, documentaries, and shorts, and attracts an attendance of over 25,000, making it the largest gay and lesbian film festival in the Eastern U.S. For two weeks in April, the Festival presents as many as 300 works on film and video, ranging from star-studded studio features to daring experimental student shorts. Anywhere from 40-50 nationalities are represented, with the latest works from such standard-bearers as France and Italy screening alongside new voices from Estonia, Lebanon, South Africa, and beyond.

Philadelphia Jewish Film Festival

Entering its twenty-sixth year (in 2006), the festival brings to Philadelphia the diversity of Jewish experience through the magic of cinema.

Location: The Gershman Y • 401 South Broad Street, Philadelphia, Pa 19147

EARLY FILM

Eadweard Muybridge (1830-1904)

Text reprinted with permission of the Franklin Institute (source: www.fi.edu)

Eadweard Muybridge was born Edward James Muggeridge in Kingston-upon-Thames in 1830. He traveled to the United States in 1852 with the notion of someday changing his name to use the Saxon spelling (he eventually did by 1867). Muybridge worked as a commission merchant for American and English book publishers on the East Coast for a few years before moving to San Francisco. There he worked as a book dealer until 1860, offering finely illustrated American and English works. In that time, Muybridge was elected to the board of directors of San Francisco's Mercantile Library Association, a position of considerable honor.

Although he had worked with photographers in New York and San Francisco, Muybridge himself did not seriously take up the art until sometime between 1861 and 1866, when he was back in England recovering from a near-fatal stagecoach accident. The accident changed him dramatically, in person as well as profession. Treated by a physician known for his belief in "natural therapy"—rest and outdoor activity—Muybridge devoted himself to photography, concentrating on outdoor views as part of his natural therapy. He returned to San Francisco in 1867 as an "artist-photographer," and quickly became one of the foremost landscape and general view photographers on the West Coast.

Muybridge used the wet-collodion photographic process introduced by the Englishman Frederick Scott Archer in 1851. Besides being more light sensitive than other processes (allowing shorter exposure time), this process made fine detail possible. The prints looked almost like daguerreotypes on paper. His Scenery of the Yosemite Valley, of 1867, offered as the work of "Helios," was held in high regard and brought him much acclaim. Muybridge was commissioned to work on several photography projects, including an expedition of the Alaskan Territories and documentation of Pacific Coast lighthouses.

Muybridge repeatedly announced in his advertisements that, "Helios is prepared to accept commissions to photograph Private Residences, Views, Animals, Ships, etc., anywhere in the city, or any portion of the Pacific Coast." In 1872, former Sacramento governor and railroad builder Leland Stanford wanted a photograph of his racing horse Occident trotting at full speed. This collaboration led to Muybridge's first photographic analysis of motion.

Stanford had a theory that at some point in its stride, a trotting horse has all four feet off the ground at the same time. He had tried various ways of measuring the horse's footfalls, but none were successful. Muybridge was amazed by the proposition. In an excerpt from an anonymously published essay, he wrote:

...Mr. Muybridge therefore plainly told Mr. Stanford that such a thing had never been heard of; that photography had not yet arrived at any such wonderful perfection as would enable it to depict a trotting horse at speed. The firm, quiet man who had, over mountains and deserts and through the malignant jeers of the world, built the railroad declared impossible, simply said: "I think if you will give your attention to the subject, you will be able to do it, and I want you to try." So the photographer had nothing to do but "try."

Muybridge took the picture and Stanford was satisfied with it, but unfortunately, this and a few other early attempts were not published. In 1874, the two expanded their photographic experiments. Muybridge learned of an instrument called the Phenakistoscope or Zootrope, that presented a "series of successive images of persons or animals represented in various attitudes. When these attitudes are coordinated so as to bring before the eye all phases of movement, the illusion is complete; we seem to see living persons moving in different ways."

Photograph of Muybridge. *Photographic portrait of Eadweard Muybridge, photographer unknown, taken from his 1887 publication Animal Locomotion: An Electro Photographic Investigation of Consecutive Phases of Animal Movements, 1872-1885. Courtesy of the Historical and Interpretive Collections of The Franklin Institute, Inc., Philadelphia, PA. (Photograph by Charles Penniman.)*

Eadweard Muybridge photograph. *Eadweard Muybridge's motion picture sequence called "Jumping," Plate 640, from his 1887 publication Animal Locomotion: An Electro Photographic Investigation of Consecutive Phases of Animal Movements, 1872-1885. Courtesy of The Historical and Interpretive Collection of The Franklin Institute, Inc., Philadelphia, PA. (Photograph by Charles Penniman.)*

In early June of 1878, Muybridge made his first successful serial photographs of fast motion at Stanford's California stock farm. The photographs were of a horse running and another horse trotting; they were developed on the spot so as not to be accused of doctoring the images. Muybridge began traveling, giving lectures and demonstrations of his work around the world. In August of 1883, the University of Pennsylvania in Philadelphia decided to sponsor Muybridge's further experiments. This setting was quite suitable to him. Philadelphians Fairman Rogers (scientist and then head of the Pennsylvania Academy of Fine Arts) and Thomas Eakins (painter, sportsman, and student of anatomy) were both members of a university commission formed in 1884 to supervise Muybridge's work.

Up until 1886, Muybridge took thousands of photographs and redid more than 500 of them. He worked at the Zoological Garden, and also photographed many human models. Animal Locomotion was finally published in November of 1887, and contained 781 plates. Muybridge had created an encyclopedic anatomy of motion, depicting humans and animals in various stages of work, play, and rest. The photographs shown here are just a sample of the many Muybridges that The Franklin Institute has in its collections. Fortunately, "the photographer had nothing to do but try." Muybridge's work, equally valuable to artists, scientists, and photographers, is considered the birth of early motion pictures.

All images pictured here are from The Franklin Institute's Animal Locomotion collection. © 1887, Eadweard Muybridge.

Where Muybridge was able to freeze motion in his film, he did not do so at regular intervals. Thomas Eakins captures the regular intervals of a pole-vaulter at nine intervals. In addition to being more accurate photos like this one below helped Eakins better understand the human form so he could paint it better.[1]

The Birth of Film

After the Civil War, Philadelphia was a mecca for photographic innovators and inventors. In 1870, Henry Renno Heyl created a "phasmatrope," a projector flashing still images in such swift succession that it gave the illusion of movement. [gophila.com]

While there were experiments at using celluloid as a film backing done by others, the first to have success was Philadelphia's John Carbutt. The key was to make the celluloid film transparent. Carbutt's Keystone Dry Plate Works Company in combination with the Celluloid Manufacturing Co. was able "to produce a thin celluloid film which was sufficiently transparent. They did this by slicing a thin layer from a block of celluloid – this was then pressed between heated polished plates to remove the slicing marks." Carbutt's success is dated to 1888. He sold his celluloid film to Thomas Edison in Orange, New Jersey. [Plastics Historical Society website – www.plasticquarium.com]

Carbutt was the first President of the Photographer's Association of America. His invention of the aforesaid Carbutt dry plate was noted in his *New York Times* obituary. [7/29/1905. *New York Times*] Carbutt also used he dry-plate technology to make faster X-ray exposures.

While Carbutt's technology was useful, what ultimately led film on its way was the invention of roll film. In a dispute that went on for over a decade, Reverend Hannibal Goodwin (also of New York) was credited with its invention, though Eastman Kodak was the ultimate seller of the roll film.

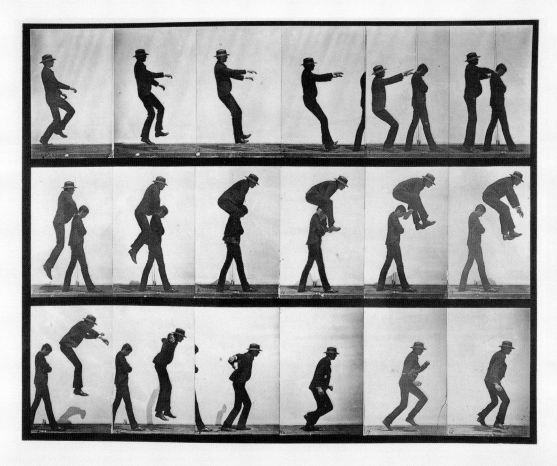

Eadweard Muybridge photograph. Eadweard Muybridge's motion study sequence photographs called "Leap Frog," Plate 169 from his 1887 publication of Animal Locomotion: An Electro Photographic Investigation of Consecutive Phases of Animal Movements, 1872-1885. Courtesy of The Historical and Interpretive Collections of The Franklin Institute, Inc., Philadelphia, PA. (Photograph by Charles Penniman.)

1884 Motion Study: George Reynolds, gelatin silver print. Courtesy of Philadelphia Museum of Art. Gift of Charles Bregler 1977

Lubin Poster (Self Inflicted). Courtesy of Philadelphia Free Library

Siegmund Lubin (1851-1923) The Nations' First Movie Mogul

Philadelphia has been home to a tradition of wonderful movie houses and venues but in the early 1900s it was most noted for the studios of Siegmund Lubin.[2]

Lubin, an immigrant from Europe, worked his way from a peddler to an optician to someone who experimented with cameras and projectors to a major movie producer with multiple studios. A tragic fire, in 1914, burned most of his films and he retired to being an optician again.

In the interim he helped create a lot of the equipment that sped film into the twentieth century. He collected films and made numerous movies of all sorts from westerns to comedy, drama and melodrama as well as history, science, and education films. Lubin manufactured and sold a patented projector he called the Cineograph. In 1899 "he became an exhibitor when, in Philadelphia, he constructed what was probably the first theatre built solely for the exhibition of motion pictures. Soon, he had over 100 theatres all along the East Coast."

For ten years he was involved with litigation with Thomas Edison over the rights to the manufacture and sale of movies. Edison hired husky spies to trail Lubin. Lubin hired fake crews to throw the spies off his trail. In 1908 they settled their differences and joined forces (in a arrangement called the Trust) with other firms to help set the standards for movie paper and help launch the distribution of films.

Lubin built a major block long studio at 20th and Indiana where five different films could be made simultaneously. He added another studio, Betzwood, near Valley Forge, a few years after opening the first studio. One of the players in his Florida studio was a young Oliver Hardy.

World War I cut off his access to foreign markets, a fire destroyed many of his films, the year-round sunny climate of California drew artists westward, and the breakup of the Trust – all led to the end of Lubin's studio.

Lubin was known for his charity. His employees had free lunches and he would often pay their medical and hospital bills.

Lubin helped a number of well known movie makers, including Sam Goldwyn, Jesse Lasky, Mark Dintenfass, and the Warner brothers. Lubin also used film to help fight anti-Semitism.[3]

ACTORS

Larry Fine (1902-1975)

Larry Fine was best known for his role as one of the Three Stooges. Born Louis Feinberg, Mr. Fine was born in 1902 in South Philadelphia. He worked as a musician and sang for local Philadelphia theaters while attending prestigious Central High School. He joined up with the stooges while working in vaudeville.

The trio, Moe, Larry, and Shemp, first opened on Broadway in *A Night in Venice* and later appeared in 20th Century-Fox's comedy *Soup to Nuts* (1930).

Fine and the other Stooges left for Hollywood where they worked for Columbia Pictures for twenty-four years, where they made some of the funniest short movies ever. They never did get to realize their dream of full-length films like their closest counterpart, the Marx Brothers.[4]

Ed Wynn (1886-1966)

Ed Wynn, like many others of his generation, began in vaudeville in New York. He was the Texaco Fire Chief on radio. He acted in film from 1957-1967 winning a Best Supporting Actor nomination for *The Diary of Anne Frank*. He was known for his fluttery voice and his expressive face. His son was the actor Keenan Wynn.

James Darren

James Darren worked in film, starring as a surfer Moondoogie, and in "Gidget." He starred in television's "Time Tunnel." He launched a successful singing career with the song "Goodbye Cruel World," "Angel Face," "Conscience," and "Her Royal Majesty," all of which were Top Ten hits.[5]

Rocky and Sylvester Stallone

If Grace Kelly is the actress most Philadelphians take pride in, *Rocky*, the story of a working class underdog who gets his big chance in a fight against the reigning champion, is the film most Philadelphians cherish. Sylvester Stallone, a Philadelphia native, wrote the script and then shopped it around until he could find a producer. The movie went on to win the 1977 Oscar Award and garnered numerous other Oscar nominations. Most importantly, for Stallone, it made millions and led to a number of sequels, including 2006's *Rocky Balboa*.

The movie is appealing on several levels to Philadelphians. There are many memorable scenes of the city. From the guys singing on the corner to the famous run up the Benjamin Franklin Parkway to the steps of the Art Museum. The hero, from South Philadelphia, is a down on his luck guy struggling to survive. The struggle is best captured in the scene where, instead of cooking his breakfast, he just pours a couple of broken eggs into a glass and swallows them raw.

The story takes place in 1976 which is a celebration of Philadelphia's most famous year, 1776, when the Declaration of Independence was written in Philadelphia.

The film has become so identifiable with the underdog that once the Indiana Pacers played the song in hopes of inspiring their team to a basketball playoff victory. The only problem was they were playing the team from Philadelphia – the Seventy-Sixers. Philadelphia fans noticed the irony. The Seventy-Sixers won the game.

Rocky Balboa by Perry Milou. Courtesy of Perry Milou

Kevin Bacon

Kevin Bacon grew up in Philadelphia. His father was Edmund N. Bacon, the noted City Planner who helped design Society Hill and Market Street East. Mr. Bacon first came to fame in Barry Levinson's movie, *Diner*, in which he played a seemingly quiet young alcoholic who revealed his wisdom by answering all the questions on a segment of "Jeopardy." Since then he has starred or acted in numerous films including: *Apollo 13, Footloose* (city boy charms country town with his dance moves), *A Few Good Men* (where he played an attorney), *JFK, Stir of Echoes, Mystic River, The Woodsmen,* and others.

Mr. Bacon is also a musician and has a band with his brother. His fame as an actor inspired the Six Degrees of Separation Game, which seeks to link people to each other through six intermediate contacts.

Will Smith. Courtesy of Will Smith

Will Smith

Text reprinted with permission of Will Smith (source: www.willsmith.com)

Will Smith was born Willard Christopher Smith, Jr. on September 25th, 1968, in Philadelphia, Pennsylvania. He attended Overbrook High School in Winfield, Pennsylvania, which is where he soon became known to his friends as "The Prince," for his charming antics. Little did he know that this nickname would still have meaning over thirty years later.

At the early age of twelve, Smith began rapping and developing his own style under the influence of hip-hop legend, Grandmaster Flash. Four years later, at only sixteen, he met Jeff Townes, also known as DJ Jazzy Jeff, who he eventually collaborated with under the title, Fresh Prince. The two produced a number of songs including the worldwide hit, "Girls Ain't Nothin But Trouble," and in 1989, the duo won their first Grammy for Best Rap Performance for "Parents Just Don't Understand." Shortly thereafter, they won another Grammy in 1991 for "Summertime." DJ Jazzy Jeff and the Fresh Prince continued to make music together until their final album, "Code Red," which was released in 1993. Even though this was the end for the rap duo, Smith re-emerged as a solo artist in 1997 with his debut LP, "Big Willie Style" and continues to make and produce music today.

Prior to his debut as a solo artist, Will Smith had already made a name for himself in the acting realm. In 1990, Will Smith was cast in the NBC sitcom, "The Fresh Prince of Bel-Air," which starred Smith as the "Fresh Prince," a young street-smart kid from Philly living in one of LA's wealthiest areas, Bel-Air. The family comedy proved to be a great success running for six years and giving Smith a name in the industry.

It wasn't long before the movie offers came rolling in. One of his first roles was in the film starring Whoopi Goldberg and Ted Danson, *Made In America*, in which Smith played the best friend of Goldberg's onscreen daughter. His next role in the Oscar-nominated film, *Six Degrees of Separation*, garnered him international respect after proving to the world that he could play more than the comical Fresh Prince. This eventually led to the 1995 box-office hit, *Bad Boys*, which was one of the first-ever action films to feature two black lead actors.

After *Bad Boys*, things only got better for Will Smith. He starred in over a dozen films including *Independence Day* (1996), *Men in Black* (1997), *Enemy of the State* (1998), *Ali* (2001), *I, Robot* (2004), *Hitch* (2005) and *The Pursuit of Happyness* (2006) to name a few. Over the span of his acting career, he's won twenty-eight awards and has been nominated for forty-nine others including two Oscar nominations for Best Performance by an Actor in a Leading Role for his role in *Ali* and in *The Pursuit of Happyness*.

After successfully conquering the music and film industries, Will Smith has taken on the new role as producer. With the help of partner James Lassiter, Smith recently launched Overbrook Entertainment, a film and television production company that also does artist management. Since its birth, Overbrook has produced several box office hits including *I, Robot*, *Hitch*, and the most recent, *The Pursuit of Happyness*.

Other notable Philadelphia connected actors include those mentioned elsewhere—Mario Lanza, Frankie Avalon, Bill Cosby, and W.C. Fields. Others include Eddie Fisher, Jack Klugman, Broderick Crawford (*All the King's Men*), George Reeves ("Superman"), Peter Boyle (*Joe, Young Frankenstein, Everybody Loves Raymond*), John and Lionel Barrymore, Dennis Christopher (*Breaking Away*), and Richard Gere. Bruce Willis from nearby Pennsauken, New Jersey, has appeared in Philadelphia films.

ACTRESSES

Grace Kelly (1929-1982)

Grace Kelly was one of the most successful Philadelphians in the movies. Her career was cut short due to her marriage to Prince Ranier of Monaco and any dream of a comeback by her untimely death in an auto accident.

Kelly had two characteristics that made her a star, aside from the acting ability she learned from acting in plays at the Bucks County Playhouse and in studying method acting. Grace Kelly was beautiful. Before making it to the screen she worked as a model. After her success she was on the cover of virtually every magazine that cared about film or beauty.

The second quality that audiences and directors loved was one described by Alfred Hitchcock while filming *Dial M for Murder*. "An actress like her gives the director certain advantages. He can afford to be more colorful with a love scene when it is played by a 'lady' than when it is by a hussy. Using one actress, the scene can be vulgar, but if you put a lady in the same circumstances she can be exciting and glamorous."[6]

Edward Liman of *Saga Magazine* wrote, "She was the opposite of sweater girls." "Grace Kelly is all the more exciting for her quality of restraint."[7] This lady-like quality, this quality of restraint was an image that most people thought of when thinking of the Main Line except that with the Main Line image there often is a concern about snobbishness. Kelly avoided that. She grew up with a famous father, Jack, a brother Jack, Jr., and with Uncle George in East Falls, which is closer to Philadelphia than it is to the Main Line.

Her father started as a bricklayer, but began his own bricklaying business, which became the "largest construction enterprise" on the East Coast.[8] Her father was also a rower, the best rower for the best club, the Vesper Club, on Boathouse Row on the Schuylkill. But because he was not "an English Gentlemen" he was not allowed to race at the Royal Henley Regatta in England. Fortunately, the Belgium Olympics of 1920 were a few weeks away. Kelly won the gold, besting Jack Beresford, the winner of the Henley Regatta. Kelly returned home a hero, where he became a City Councilman, ran for mayor (but lost a close election in 1935 to the Republican), and continued to run his business.

Jack Kelly, Jr. also won at the Olympics.

Uncle George won a Pulitzer Prize for *Craig's Wife* in 1925-26, a story of a compulsively tidy and controlling housewife, a play in which Grace performed and which was made a film three times, once with Joan Crawford.[9] Two other oft-performed plays of Mr. Kelly are *The Torch Bearers* and *The Show Off*. The latter, about a braggart who is humbled and an incompetent who makes good (both the same person) was also made into a film in 1946. Red Skelton starred as J. Aubrey Piper, the braggadocio and lovable incompetent.

Grace Kelly began her rise, after modeling and work at the Bucks County Playhouse on television where she starred in a number of dramas, melodramas, and soap operas with commercially sponsored names like Kraft Television and the Philco TV Playhouse

Her first major film was opposite Gary Cooper in *High Noon*. She played with many of the leading men of the day such as Ray Milland in *Dial M for Murder*, James Stewart in *Rear Window*, William Holden in *Bridge at Taki Ri*, and Bing Crosby in *Country Girl*. Kelly won the Oscar for her role in *Country Girl* besting Dorothy Dandridge, Judy Garland, Jane Wyman, and Audrey Hepburn.[10]

She also starred with Cary Grant in *To Catch a Thief*. Her last major film before leaving for Monaco was *High Society*, a musical remake of the famous *Philadelphia Story*. Kelly sang two songs in the film and appeared with Bing Crosby, Frank Sinatra, and Louis Armstrong.

Grace Kelly and Cary Grant. Courtesy of Temple University Archives. Urban Archives. Evening Bulletin Photo Collection.

Janet Gaynor (1906-1984)

Janet Gaynor, nee Laura Gaynor, was born in Philadelphia on October 6, 1906. After working in menial day jobs, Janet Gaynor tried silent films. She won the 1927 Academy Award for her cumulative work in *Seventh Heaven*, *Sunrise*, and *Street Angel*.

She made the successful transition to talking films where she starred in the 1937 movie *The World's Sweetheart*. In that same year she starred in the classic film *A Star Is Born*, where she was nominated for another Oscar.[11]

Jeanette MacDonald (1903-1965)

A childhood star, Jeanette MacDonald first made her mark at West Philadelphia High School as a singer. When Ira Gershwin said her "silky soprano voice wasn't quite right for jazzy Broadway musicals" she left for Hollywood.

Her prime year was 1927. She worked with French star Maurice Cheavlier before teaming and singing with Nelson Eddy. She also did get to work on Broadway, radio, opera, television, and made recordings and gave concerts.

Credits include *Love Parade*, *Vagabond King*, and *Monte Carlo*. She co-starred with such greats as Spencer Tracy and Clark Gable.[12]

Blythe Danner

Born in Philadelphia, Danner graduated from The George School in Bucks County. Her father was the President of a bank, but loved to sing and was known as the singing banker. Danner's films include the feature films *Meet the Parents*, *The Prince of Tides*, *Brighton Beach Memoirs*, *The Great Santini*, *The Love Letter*, *No Looking Back*, *Alice*, *The Myth of Fingerprints*, *The Farmhouse*, and *Homage*.

She has acted on stage and television. Her daughter and son are performers too, Gwyneth and Jake Paltrow.

Other actresses with Philadelphia connections include Katherine Hepburn (Swarthmore College), Candace Bergen (Penn), Lola Folana, Pearl Bailey, and Ethel Barrymore.[13]

James Michener (1907-1997)

The writer who has had the most success in the movies and the one whose movies most capture Penn's Quaker ideals was James Michener.

Michener grew up in Doylestown where he was raised a Quaker. He studied at a Quaker school, Swarthmore, and then began a literary career, which included numerous bestsellers and the award of the Pulitzer Prize.

His writings included travel to foreign places (foreign to Philadelphians) like *Hawaii*, *the South Pacific*, *Texas*, *Iberia*, *Alaska*, *Mexico*, and *Outer Space*. Filled with history, they captured the public's imagination. But what was at the core of his books, and later his movies, was his belief that neighborhoods/cultures should not result in divides. Contrasting cultures and beliefs should thrive together. His favorite song from *South Pacific* was "You've Got To Be Carefully Taught," sung by a white American who was in love with a Polynesian. The song title was a reference to the notion that prejudice had to be taught. Michener and his Quaker religion believed in the "Inner Light" which was predicated on the philosophy that humans were individually inherently good and an examination of this goodness was all one needed to get along in the world.

The movies from his books were many and included:

◊ *Bridges at Tokio Ri* with William Holden and Grace Kelly
◊ *Caravans* with Anthony Quinn and Joseph Cotton
◊ *Hawaii* with Julie Andrews, Max Von Sydow, Caroll O'Connor, and a young Gene Hackman
◊ *Return to Paradise* with Gary Cooper
◊ *Sayanora* with Marlon Brando and Red Buttons
◊ *South Pacific* with Rossino Brozzi and Mitzi Gaynor
◊ *Until They Sail* with Paul Newman and Joan Fontaine

Michener evidenced the Quaker ideal in other aspects. He participated in many organizations including serving on the Advisory Board of NASA and as a secretary to the Pennsylvania Constitutional Convention. He married Mari Sabusawa, a Japanese American, who was interred during WWII and helped in many of his projects. He gave to numerous charities from Swarthmore to Texas University to the Mercer Museum to the Museum that is named after him – the James Michener Museum in Doylestown. He purchased paintings only by people who were alive after he was born. Many of these paintings, worth tens of millions, were donated to The Honolulu Academy of Art and The University of Texas.

Brian De Palma

Brian De Palma grew up in Philadelphia where his father was an orthopedic surgeon. His credits include the Philadelphia film *Blow-Out*, which stars John Travolta as a sound producer who accidentally hears fatal gunfire.

De Palma began making films as a student, first at Columbia, later at Sarah Lawrence. He was born in New Jersey.

De Palma credits Alfred Hitchcock for his fascination with the graphic side of mystery. It is notably present in many of his films, which include Steven King's *Carrie* (1976), *Dressed to Kill* (1980), *Scarface* (1983), and *The Untouchables* (1987). Other films include one of his first successes, *Obsession* and one of his latest, *Mission to Mars*.

"Although De Palma works primarily in the genre of the psychological thriller, elements of romance, horror, and gangster melodramas are explored as well. De Palma's films are 'visually dynamic'. They include techniques such as the stalking, searching camera; the 'God's eye' point of view; and an expressively detailed *mise-en-scéne*. A master of rhythmic editing, he often opens his films with an extended, viscerally composed sequence. The now-classic prom sequence in Carrie, with its use of the split screen, slow-motion and cross cutting, typifies the rich versatility of De Palma's craft."[14]

David Lynch

David Lynch used his studies at the Pennsylvania Academy of Fine Arts in Philadelphia to help his film career ("Twin Peaks" on TV and movies such as *Mullholland Drive, Straight Story, Blue Velvet, and Elephant Man*).[15]

Mark Bowden

Mark Bowden, once a writer for the *Philadelphia Inquirer*, is author of *Black Hawk Down: A Story of Modern War*, recently released as a motion picture.

Bowden is also the author of the international bestseller *Killing Pablo: The Hunt for the World's Greatest Outlaw* (2001), which tells the story of the hunt for a Colombian cocaine billionaire. *Killing Pablo* was made into a film. Bowden is also the author of *Doctor Dealer* (1987), *Bringing the Heat* (1994), *Our Finest Day* (2002), and *Finders Keepers* (2002), and *Guests of the Ayatollah: The First Battle in America's War with Militant Islam (2006)* – among other books.

M. Night Shyamalan

Mr. Shyamalan is a writer, producer, and director whose films include at least two centered in Philadelphia – *Unbreakable, The Sixth Sense* (both starring Bruce Willis), and *Signs*. The latter was filmed in nearby Bucks County.

According to the *New York Post's* John Podhoretz, Shyamalan is likable because he understands the elements of great storytelling. Mood. Resonant characters whose journey viewers can identify with. Combining the familiar with the new.

Podhoretz points out that "Shyamalan doesn't exploit the pain of the characters he creates. He sets up believable situations for them and offers them a measure of resolution at the end."[18]

Roger Ebert confirms Shyamalan's storytelling prowess and his love of Bruce Willis's acting when he states in his review of *The Sixth Sense*. "I have to admit I was blind-sided by the ending. The solution to many of the film's puzzlements is right there in plain view, and the movie hasn't cheated, but the very boldness of the storytelling carried me right past the crucial hints and right through to the end of the film, where everything takes on an intriguing new dimension."[19]

Charles Fuller

Charles Fuller attended Villanova University and LaSalle University. He is the second African American playwright to win the Pulitzer Prize and is a co-founder of Afro-American Arts Theatre in Philadelphia, Pennsylvania. His plays include *Zooman, The Sign*, and *A Soldier's Story*.

A Soldier's Story is essentially about the roles of blacks in white society, particularly the military. The murder mystery/courtroom drama involves the search for the murderer of Sgt. Vernon Waters, played by Adolph Caesar on stage and in the film.

The story deals indirectly with the search for the meaning of Sgt. Waters' last words, "They still hate you!" Cpt. Davenport, played by Denzel Washington, is hired to find why Waters was killed. Davenport "discovers, in the face of white racist obstruction, not only the murderer of Sgt. Waters (by another black), but the painful reason for this fratricide."

According to Frank Rich's review of the play for the *New York Times* "[Fuller] has a compassion for blacks who might be driven to murder their brothers—because he sees them as victims of a world they haven't made. Mr. Fuller demands that his black characters find the courage to break their suicidal, fratricidal cycle—just as he demands that whites end the injustices that have locked his black characters into a nightmare."[20, 21]

Lee Daniels

Lee Daniels, from Philadelphia, produced *Monster's Ball*, a relationship movie, starring Halle Berry and Billy Bob Thornton, who fall for each other despite the differences in their races and their attitudes about race.

Daniel's movie *The Woodsman* stars Kevin Bacon as a pedophile returning home after a dozen years to try to start a new life. Much of *The Woodsman* was filmed in Philadelphia. Another Philadelphia-based movie by Daniels is *Shadowboxer*, which starred Cuba Gooding, Jr. and Helen Mirren. It is another relationship movie – this time between a mother and a stepson. The two are romantically linked, which isn't as odd as the fact that they're both contract assassins.

Other producers/directors with Philadelphia connections include:

Richard Lester (*A Funny Thing Happened on the Way to the Forum* and *The Three Musketeers*)

Arthur Penn (*Little Big Man* and *Bonnie and Clyde*)

Sidney Lumet (*12 Angry Men, Serpico, Dog Day Afternoon*, and *Network*)

Jon Shestack (*Bickford Schmeckler's Cool Ideas, Waiting, Firewall*, and *Dan in Real Life*)

It took theater (not film) a while to get going in Philadelphia because of Quaker restrictions. In the 1800s a number of theaters were built. Two of them, The Walnut Street Theater and the Academy of Music are still treasures. Many other theaters, built in the 1800s, burned or became burlesque houses.

The first movie motion picture shown in Philadelphia was at Keith's Bijou in 1895. In the 1900s, many theaters were built for a variety of purposes, including film. These theaters marked a trend in architecture. They were the "first time in architectural history that ornate and costly structures were commenced and executed primarily for the service of the common man." Some of the most extravagant theaters were built in the poorest neighborhoods. Demand for more theaters grew with more leisure time.

Many theaters had balconies, murals, and extravagant design in various styles including French Renaissance.

The Boyd was the only art-deco theater of its day. Opened in 1928, it had the following description:

"Art detailing, including polychrome mirrors cut in zigzag patterns, tiered chandeliers that resemble upside-down wedding cakes, a jagged stone facade, and the original, freestanding, pagoda-like ticket booth."[22]

Jerry Jonas of the *Bucks County Courier Times* wrote that the Sameric/Boyd (the Boyd was sold to the Sameric Corporation) was also known for the attention to detail of its uniformed ushers. Ushers were given classroom assignments on how to serve the movie patrons in a fashion that could have been suitable for a military drill team.[23]

The theaters had full stages with orchestra pits, in part, because the early movies were silent movies and an orchestra played the music. The Mastbaum was one of the most impressive with a seating capacity of 4,738. Other well-known theaters included: The Fox Theater, the Diamond, The Earle, the Uptown, the Circle, and the Midway.

The old theaters survived, in part, because they had a direct connection to the studios that released the films. In 1942, William Goldman sued Stanley Warner and a number of other companies. He won, on a conspiracy to monopolize theory, in the Supreme Court five years later. Goldman was awarded money and the right to run first run features but the other movie theaters couldn't depend on a steady release of films. This combined with the advent of television killed the big movie houses for the most part.[24] The Sameric/Boyd is one of the few movie-houses from the 1920s still standing. Efforts are being made to preserve it. By a unanimous 14 to 0 vote on August 8, 2008, the Philadelphia Historical Commission voted to add the Boyd Theatre to the Philadelphia Register of Historic Places.

The Irving R. Glazer collection at the Athenaeum includes "original photographs, dedication programs, playbills, news clippings, and correspondence relating to nearly 1,000 theater buildings, primarily of Philadelphia theater – including many photographs from the architectural firm of William H. Hoffman and Paul J. Henon, Jr., who designed thirty-two theater buildings in Philadelphia, including their masterpiece, the Mastbaum (1929)." The Glazer Collection is also supported by the photo and inventory files of the aforesaid Stanley-Warner Company, the leading motion-picture distributor in Philadelphia during the first half of the twentieth century.

RITZ Theaters and Ramon L. Posel

"Ramon L. Posel's father owned seven movie houses. Growing up the son preferred novels until he saw Vittorio De Sica's The Bicycle Thief, while attending Harvard Law School. He left his legal practice with the law form of Wolf Block LLP. In 1964, he built his first theater on Bustleton Avenue, the Leo, named for his father. In 1976 Ray Posel opened the Ritz Three in the Historic District of Philadelphia (Walnut Street, near Second Street), [in Society Hill] where he developed an "audience of independent and international cinema." The Ritz Three blossomed into the Ritz Five." Posel built additional theaters in Philadelphia and in New Jersey, which quickly turned a profit.

Posel's philosophy was the reverse of Robert Frost's. Frost thought that good fences make good neighbors; Ray Posel thought good theaters make good neighborhoods. His theaters, according to Swarthmore psychology professor Barry Schwartz, helped transform neighborhoods by making people want to go the neighborhoods to see great movies. After seeing the movie they'd want to see the neighborhood. And great movies were Posel's staple. The Ritz theaters show independent films for an audience that wants to see more than just the Oscar nominated films.

"One legend about Mr. Posel is that in the 1970s when a New Jersey mobster told him to use the mobster's vending machines or else, Mr. Posel looked him in the eye and shrugged, 'You'll just have to kill me.' The thug folded." Carrie Rickey wrote Mr. Posel's obituary for the Philadelphia Inquirer. Mr. Posel passed away in 2005.

David Grossman and Temple University Center City

For a long period in the later 1900s, David Grossman showed great movies at Temple's Center City Campus (TUCC). The setting was unremarkable, but Grossman's love of film was not. Grossman, a movie buff, writer, and teacher, introduced each film to the general audience by not only explaining the context but how the films were made. Mr. Grossman also ran the Philadelphia Film Forum, a successor to TUCC before he passed away.

Many movies that were filmed in Philadelphia include Philadelphia actors, directors, and producers. Other films are those with lots of recognizable scenes of Philadelphia. But the ones that leave a lasting impression are those that say something about the way Philadelphians live.

The most common characteristic played in the movie is the class one. Blue-collar workers compete with Rich Main Liners or those who don't belong to the proper clubs fight for the right to success and happiness.

PHILADELPHIA MOVIES

The Young Philadelphians (1959)

This film is discussed at the end of the legal section since the star, Paul Newman, portrayed an ambitious lawyer.

Fantasia (1940)[25]

While there are no Philadelphia scenes in this movie – after all it is a cartoon – there is one unmistakable film feature – the Philadelphia sound of the Philadelphia orchestra led by their conductor, Leopold Stokowski. The Walt Disney movie is known for its combination of wonderful colorful images and the "Philadelphia Sound." You might say there's no real clash of neighborhoods here and you'd be right. Yet you'd also be wrong. For this film was all about clash. The clash between the visual – the wildly colorful animations and the sound

of the best orchestra in the world – the Fabulous Philadelphians. In the most famous segment – "The Sorcerer's Apprentice" – the speed of the music drives the animation. Or is it vice-versa?

Music for *Fantasia*

Some of the musical compositions that Stokowski played are referenced in the following collection from the University of Pennsylvania Records.[26]

Leopold Stokowski: Making Music Matter *Curated by Marjorie Hassen Otto E. Albrecht Music Library University of Pennsylvania*

Oxford Theater by Rob Lawlor. Courtesy of Rob Lawlor

Fantasia **Contents:**

◊ "Toccata and Fugue in D minor:" director, Samuel Armstrong; music, Johann Sebastian Bach

◊ "The Nutcracker Suite:" director, Samuel Armstrong; music, Peter Ilich Tchaikovsky

◊ "The Sorcerer's Apprentice:" director, James Algar; music, Paul Dukas

◊ "Rite of Spring:" directors, Bill Roberts, Paul Satterfield; music, Igor Stravinsky

◊ "Pastoral Symphony:" directors, Hamilton Luske, Jim Handley, Ford Beebe; music, Ludwig van Beethoven

◊ "Dance of the Hours:" directors, T. Hee, Norm Ferguson; music, Amilcare Ponchielli

◊ "Night on Bald Mountain:" director, Wilfred Jackson; music, Modest Petrovich Mussorgsky

◊ "Ave Maria:" director, Wilfred Jackson; music, Franz Schubert.

Fantasia originally began as a short. Needing more money to recoup their investment in a Burbank studio, Disney decided to make it a feature film. The original orchestral recording was made by Stokowski and the Philadelphia Orchestra at the Philadelphia Academy of Music, said to be acoustically perfect.

Kitty Foyle (1940)

This film was based on the novel by Christopher Morley. It starred Ginger Rogers as a woman who marries into a Main Line family, though she is from the wrong side of the tracks. The marriage is annulled because the society family of the husband thinks she's below him.

The Rogers character becomes a success in New York, working as an executive in a Fashion House.

She then has to choose between her old Philadelphia husband who still wants to be with her and another suitor, a New York doctor.[27, 28]

The Philadelphia Story (1940)

Philadelphia Story, written by Philip Berg and starring Katherine Hepburn, was based on socialite Hope Montgomery Scott. It was a play before it became a movie. A musical version, *High Society*, with Grace Kelly was made about fifteen years later. In the movie version, Katherine Hepburn's first husband Cary Grant, a smooth socialite, seeks to remarry Hepburn who tests the waters with Jimmy Stewart before settling for Cary Grant. The dialogue is clever and very smart.

Trading Places (1983)

Eddie Murphy hilariously plays a con-man trying to survive on his wits. Jamie Lee Curtis plays a prostitute trying to make enough to get out of the profession.

The Philadelphia theme in this movie is the standard upper-class snobbishness of those who make their money in the city, join the Union League, but leave at the end of the day for the rich environs of the Main Line. The Main Line is the Western suburb where many of the richest Philadelphians live. In the movie and elsewhere (literature, the press), the Main Liners have been portrayed as being interested in money over people (namely their servants and people like the poor Mr. Murphy character). They're the type of people, as portrayed by Don Ameche and Ralph Bellamy (The Duke Brothers), who can make a one dollar bet without regard to how it might change the lives of two men (Murphy and Ackroyd).

Dan Ackroyd, who plays the Main Liner, learns the importance of people over money just in time for him to team with Murphy and the Jamie Lee Curtis character to send the rich Dukes crashing into bankruptcy.

Witness (**1984**)

Witness is another neighborhood meets neighborhood film. Harrison Ford plays a brash Philadelphia detective who is forced to hide out with Kelly McGillis in her Amish community when McGillis's son witnesses a crime at Amtrak's 30th Street Station. The community feelings of the Amish are best shown in the house-raising scene. Along the way each culture learns a little about the other. And though the romance between Ford and McGillis tempts Ford to stay – in the end he goes back to Philadelphia – albeit a little bit enriched for having experienced the Amish culture.

30th Street Station. Courtesy of Temple University. Urban Archives. Evening Bulletin Photo Collection.

Philadelphia (**1993**)

Philadelphia is essentially a story about the rights of an HIV positive lawyer to continue working while he has the disease. While it is set in Philadelphia, it could have been portrayed anywhere with the exception that the Philadelphia snobbery of the partners in the law firm where the Tom Hanks character works is another reminder that the elitism of Philadelphia extends not just to the Main Line but to the legal profession – a profession noted, in early Philadelphia, for its aristocracy at times.

Invincible (**2005**)

This inspirational film traced the successful efforts of a local South Philadelphia native, Vince Papale, to play for Dick Vermeil and the Philadelphia Eagles. Papale didn't play in college but still made the team.

The Philadelphia Experiment (**1984 and a sequel in 1993**)

A New Kensington resident by the name of Carlos Miguel Allende claimed to have seen an unusual experiment run by the U.S. Navy. He claimed that in October 1943, during the Second World War, that a DE-173 Destroyer, the USS Eldridge naval vessel, mysteriously became invisible and minutes later became visible.

Allende, who also went by the name of Carl Allen, claimed that the vessel had been transported to Virginia and back. Several books were written about the investigation to determine whether there was any truth to the Allende claim or whether Allende himself might have been an alien. Nothing ever concluded that such an experiment took place. Nevertheless, a fictional account of the Philadelphia Experiment was made into a movie in 1984.[29]

Rocky (1975-2006)
[For more see the Sylvester Stallone Section]

While there have been five sequels (the last and most recent, *Rocky Balboa*, getting great acclaim) so far, it is the first "Rocky" that is the best film and the most identifiable with Philadelphia. Rocky, as the story goes, is a South Philadelphia Italian barely making a living as a boxer when the opportunity of a lifetime, to fight the World Champion, gives him the opportunity to change his fortunes. Philadelphians identify with the down and out boxer because he doesn't dream too big. He just wants a better house, a girlfriend, and a chance to make a living where he doesn't have to hurt anybody. The neighborhood clash here is one of class. Rocky is Italian but more than that he's poor. The champion is out of his league. The film is notable for a variety of Philadelphia scenes from a small group of singers on the corner, to the famous run up the Art Museum Steps, with plenty of shots of the Parkway, Boathouse Row and South Philadelphia as well.

My Architect (2003)
Text reprinted with permission of the Philadelphia Inquirer and Carrie Rickey
Review By Carrie Rickey Philadelphia Inquirer Friday, November 14, 2003 [Excerpted]

Great men are not always great dads. Louis Kahn, the Philadelphia-bred architect, is a contender for most influential builder of the twentieth century. But no one would have nominated him for father of the year, least of all his son, Nathaniel, who was eleven when Lou died bankrupt. His three children – one each by a wife and two mistresses – met each other for the first time at his funeral.

My Architect, Nathaniel's rapturous and rigorous portrait, reconciles the great artist with the lousy paterfamilias.

Louis Kahn led a triple life and so does the movie about him. It's a mystery of pulse-pounding suspense, a melodrama of wrenching emotion, an epic of dramatic sweep. It takes the audience from the row house in Philadelphia where the new immigrant Kahn grew up to his dazzling National Assembly building in Dhaka, Bangladesh, where a new nation grew up.

When Nathaniel read his father's death notice he realized he did not officially exist. But instead of inviting us to his pity party, the bastard son – who proves himself a deft psychological architect – packs us along on his Odyssey to find his father and build a family structure that includes himself, his half-sisters, and their mothers. "Are we a family?" Nathaniel pointedly asks his siblings.

It's not blood that connects them; it's the buildings. The Salk Institute in La Jolla, the Kimbell Art Museum in Fort Worth, and the National Assembly in Dhaka are forms of Euclidean inscrutability that reveal themselves in the way they capture light, reflect water, and create community.

The film is enriched by the eloquence of silent buildings and by the insights of talking heads. Nathaniel consults a pantheon of architects (Philip Johnson, I.M. Pei, Robert A.M. Stern, Moshe Safdie, and Frank Gehry) who variously eulogize Kahn as a visionary, an inspiration, an artist among businessmen, a genius, a workaholic.

This is not the verdict of legendary Philadelphia city planner Ed Bacon. Standing in front of the brutalist Penn Center, built during his tenure, he declares Kahn a crackpot: "It would have been a tragedy if Lou had built anything in Center City."

It could be that the elder Kahn and Bacon were antagonists in a centuries-old war between architects and planners.

Or it could be, as Richard Saul Wurman suggests, that the Jewish architect and WASP planner were antagonists in a centuries-old Philadelphia skirmish between plebeian and patrician.

My Architect may begin with a father's obituary but it ends, transcendently and unexpectedly, with a son's rebirth as his father's legitimate artistic heir.

My Architect (Movie Poster).
Courtesy of Susan Behr

PHILADELPHIA LOCATIONS
IN THE MOVIES

One of the great reasons for filming in Philadelphia is the city's vast variety of architecture styles – interior and exterior. Every Saturday one can take a tour of many of the sites where Philadelphia films have been made while seeing clips of the relevant sites from those films. The Tour is sponsored by the Greater Philadelphia Film Office. Along with references to various locations the tour guide offers a variety of trivia such as that it is rare the interior and exterior of the same building are used. In National Treasure the good guys used the "Google" search engine while the bad guys uses "Yahoo." [This is not meant to be an editorial comment].

Rarely are films shot in sequence, from beginning to end. Two such Philadelphia films that were shot in sequence were *Philadelphia* and *The Sixth Sense*. Many films are shot in multiple locations. *Philadelphia* was shot entirely in Philadelphia. *Philadelphia* starred fifty-three gay men, forty-three of whom died shortly after filming from HIV-AIDS.

One of the attractions to filming in Philadelphia is that access to the government buildings is free. For many other locations, the producers often have to pay a fee, sometimes paying for a whole building or series of building for a night or more.

The bus tour began in 2006 and will add new films to the tour over time. Usually permission isn't granted to show the movie clips until the film has been released to DVD

The Corn Exchange Building was where the people in *Real World Philadelphia* were housed. *Shooter*, about a Presidential assignation attempt, being filmed in Philadelphia, used the PECO building to land helicopters.

South Philly

South Philly Two Bits was an Al Pacino depression era movie. The area around 7th and Wolf was used in the film. The power lines, public telephones, mailboxes, streetlights, TV antennas, and curb cuts were removed so the area would look like the Depression era. The film, penned by Philadelphia native Joseph Stephano (*Psycho*), also starred Mary Elizabeth Mastrantonio and Jerry Barone, and was directed by James Foley.

Fallen starred Denzel Washington, John Goodman, Embeth Davidtz, and Donald Sutherland. At 9th and Passyunk are Pat's Steaks and Geno's Steaks (arguably the two best places for Philadelphia cheesesteaks in the world). At the intersections the devil was passed from person to person in the movie.

The Italian Market on 9th Street was one of the places Sylvester Stallone jogged through in *Rocky* and where scenes from Johnathan Demme's *Philadelphia* were shot. More recently DiBruno Brothers and other Italian Market vendors could be seen in Jennifer Weiner's *In Her Shoes*, which starred Cameron Diaz and Toni Collette. Weiner, a Philadelphia native, can be seen in the film wearing a white scarf.

South Street

Jim's Steaks, at 4th & South, is at the center of a scene in *Mannequin Two On the Move*.

In Her Shoes used the back of the Jamaican Jerk Hut on South St. for the wedding reception.

Historic/Old Philadelphia

The Bell Tower of Independence Hall was used in *National Treasure*.

Washington Square Park was used to film *Beloved*, starring Oprah Winfrey, Danny Glover, and Thandie Newtown. It was directed by Jonathan Demme. Philadelphia was used for parts of the movie, even though it takes place in 1890s Cincinnati. An alleyway and the Sawyer Building are two of the locations in the movie.

The Curtis Center is at the intersection of 7th and Walnut. One of the most memorable shots in *Unbreakable* (2000), a scene featuring Bruce Willis and Robin Wright Penn sitting at a bar enjoying a cocktail, was shot here. The Curtis Center lobby area was transformed into a restaurant in the middle of the night for this short scene. The lobby is graced with the famous mural "The Dream Garden," by Louis Comfort Tiffany. This magnificent mural was comprised of thousands of glass mosaic pieces, and the design was taken from a Maxfield Parrish painting.

St. Augustine's Church: This historic church was a key location in *The Sixth Sense* (1998).

The Pennsylvania Convention Center at 11th and Arch Streets: Parts of the convention center were used in *Up Close and Personal* (1995), and the Great Train Hall was turned into an airport for *Twelve Monkeys*.

The Famous 4th Street Deli was where conversations took place in *Philadelphia*, *In Her Shoes*, and *Jersey Girl*, starring Jennifer Lopez and Ben Afleck.

Center City

At the intersection of Broad and Arch, look diagonally to the left at the Municipal Services Building. The top of the building can be seen in *Mannequin Two On the Move*. The production fashioned a large gondola basket attached to a balloon on the roof and floated it with cables across the city skyline. In *Up Close and Personal*, there was a lovely and romantic scene with Michelle Pfeiffer and Robert Redford, also shot on the rooftop. All of the equipment and actors had to be transported to the roof via a narrow ladder.

At 1735 Market St. is the Mellon Bank Center, called the Wheeler Building in the movie *Philadelphia*. It is where Tom Hanks' firm was housed in Philadelphia. Across the street is Pickwick Pharmacy where a fictional Penn law student tried to pick up Denzel Washington's character. Ironically, on the day of filming many law students were interviewing for jobs in law offices in the Mellon Bank Center, but the "Wheeler Building" sign threw them for a loop.

Reading Terminal Market was the venue for a chase scene in *National Treasure*. The movie was filmed on a Sunday, a day when the Reading Terminal Market was closed. [It has since opened for Sundays for the Winter Holiday season].

City Hall: This amazing example of French Second Empire architecture can be seen in a number of movies, including *Blow Out* (1980), when John Travolta drives a jeep through a narrow pedestrian passageway. The courtyard was featured in a scene where Denzel Washington and Embeth Davidtz had a secret rendezvous in *Fallen*. City Hall was also one of the important settings. The former famous John Wanamaker's is where *Mannequin* (1986) and *Mannequin Two On The Move* were shot. The Wanamaker Building has appeared in many other films. Kim Catrell, from "Sex and the City," played the "Mannequin." In *Blow Out*, John Travolta drove down Market St., through the City Hall courtyard, and crashed his jeep into Wanamaker's window. Bruce Willis and Madeleine Stowe shopped for new clothes to disguise themselves from the army of the *Twelve Monkeys* here.

The apron around City Hall was used as the site of an AIDS demonstration in *Philadelphia*, and Courtroom 243 was used as a key set piece in the movie.

21st Street and Fairmount Avenue: Eastern State Penitentiary was used as the insane asylum in *Twelve Monkeys*. In *Return to Paradise* (1997), starring Vince Vaughn and Anne Heche, it doubled as a Malaysian prison. In its day Eastern State Penitentiary was a model prison. Over 300 prisons were based on its design.

Elvis Costello sang a song in one of its restrooms in *Prison Song* (1999).

15th Street is home to the distinctive Clothespin sculpture, which Claes Oldenburg created in 1976. It can be seen in *Trading Places* (1982) in a scene with Jamie Lee Curtis and Dan Aykroyd.

On the corner of 15th and Chestnut is the Packard Building. The interior of this building was transformed into a train station for M. Night Shyamalan's *Unbreakable*.

At the corner of 15th and Walnut is (what used to be) Striped Bass restaurant where Bruce Willis went on his anniversary to find Olivia Williams finishing her dinner, paying her check, and ignoring him in *The Sixth Sense*.

St. Mark's Church is located on Locust Street between 16th and 17th. The interior was used in *Fallen* when Denzel Washington went inside to speak with Embeth Davidtz.

Cameron Diaz can be seen in *In Her Shoes* walking into and out of stores along Walnut Street.

On the corner of Broad and Locust is the Academy of Music. This authentic nineteenth century opera house was used for the opening scenes in *The Age of Innocence* (1992), the Martin Scorcese film starring Daniel Day-Lewis and Michelle Pfeiffer. Although it was shot over Memorial Day weekend, the winter scene called for 'movie magic' snow. In order to accomplish this, Broad Street was closed for three days. Dirt and snow were brought in, and hundreds of Philadelphians were adorned in period formal attire and hairdos.

At Broad and Sansom Streets is the Wachovia Bank (formerly Girard Bank). In *Trading Places*, directed by John Landis, the building was renamed Duke and Duke, the offices of the Duke brothers played by Don Ameche and Ralph Bellamy. Dan Aykroyd can be seen drunkenly stumbling out of the front doors dressed as Santa Claus and catching a SEPTA bus, and Eddie Murphy runs through the majestic lobby. Unfortunately, the interiors were shot in New York, which was so often the case in films shot in Philadelphia prior to 1992.

West Philadelphia

University of Pennsylvania's Frank Furness Library at 34th and Walnut can be seen as a law library in *Philadelphia*, starring Tom Hanks and Denzel Washington. It's where Denzel Washington, a cousin of Philadelphia journalist, Ukee Washington, first notices Hanks.

Across the street is the University Museum of Archaeology and Anthropology. The museum is featured in M. Night Shyalaman's *Wide Awake* (1995) when Joshua (Joseph Cross) and a classmate get stuck in a turnstile while on a field trip with teacher Rosie O'Donnell.

Follow Convention Avenue to South Street and turn right: Ahead is the South Street Bridge. In *Twelve Monkeys*, elephants can be seen crossing it. Real elephants were used as were other animals in *Twelve Monkeys*. The Greater Philadelphia Film Office had to acquire a state menagerie license to legally bring these 'animal actors' to town.

Near South Street Bridge – at 33rd and Spruce – is Franklin Field, the home stadium for the University of Pennsylvania. It was used to look like Veteran's Stadium in the inspirational story about Vince Papale, starring Mark Wahlberg – *Invincible*.

Papale made the Philadelphia Eagles roster and played for several years, despite making the team on a tryout. Papale was from South Philadelphia. (2005). Wigs were put on balloons to fill out the crowd scenes.

Art Museum Area

The Philadelphia Museum of Art: Rocky's famous run up the steps in front of the museum at the end of his workout in *Rocky*. The inside of the museum was also used in *Dressed to Kill* (1979), when Angie Dickinson was seductively pursued by a mysterious man.

30th Street Station can be recognized in a number of movies. In *Trading Places*, Eddie Murphy and Dan Ackroyd boarded a train from here to New York using the savings of Jamie Lee Curtis and Denholm Elliot who were at the station. In *Blow Out*, John Travolta, John Lithgow, and Nancy Allen used the station as a key meeting place. In *Witness* (1984), detective Harrison Ford quizzed a small boy about a murder that the boy had witnessed while hiding in a rest room stall at 30th Street Station. In *Fallen*, Denzel Washington chased a demon onto a train that stopped at this station.

Can You Hear the Music by Perry Milou.
Courtesy of Perry Milou

PHILADELPHIA SPORTS

Connie Mack by Dick Perez. Courtesy of Dick Perez

Picture – Connie Mack

Philadelphia Sports
"The tallest, steepest, swiftest, dizziest, dare-devil, death-defying dive ever undertaken by a baseball team came off with a rich and fruity climax yesterday when the Phillies toppled headlong into the World Series."

Red Smith, Sportswriter

PHILADELPHIA SPORTS

NOTABLE STYLES
Neighborhoods
Lunch Pail Players
Best Teams Ever. Worst Teams Ever.
Great Rivalries
A Taste for The Bizarre
Golden Throated Announcers

CONTENTS

PHILADELPHIA SPORTS

Volumes could be written about Philadelphia sports, including many books, most arranged by sport or chronologically.

This chapter tries to summarize, as best one can, the traits that are common to these teams, owners, players, and the media as well as the venues.

The early influences of Penn and Franklin apply, at both extremes. Some of the Philadelphia teams have been among the best … others, among the worst. Penn's influence is the coach to the system approach where each team has the style of its coach or owner. Villanova routinely plays a different style of basketball than Penn or St. Joseph's.

Franklin's practical view of the world helps explain why a multi-function Veterans stadium was built and why new stadiums in the twenty-first century are where the parking and other stadiums are. It also helps explain why some of the best coaches and best athletes have been teachers like John Chaney or craftsmen like Mike Schmidt. Many athletes would appreciate that Franklin was a self-taught swimmer. He learned to swim from reading books about swimming.[1] Franklin's style today would be more the coach to the talent approach, which appreciates the differences of all its players and tries to find the right chemistry.

Franklin also believed in the Andre Agassi line – "Image is everything."[2] He believed that if one is seen to be working hard that those who saw that would appreciate the effort. Perhaps this was the forerunner of the 'lunch pail' athlete – the fellow who, at least, is seen to be trying to win.

Bill Lyon, the celebrated writer for the *Philadelphia Inquirer*, noted that Dickens could have written about Philadelphia sports since the play has been the "best of times" and "the worst of times." When he first started covering sports for *The Philadelphia Inquirer*, the Eagles were 2-12,the Seventy-Sixers team set a record for futility, the Flyers missed the Stanley Cup playoffs, and Phillies pitcher, Steve Carlton, won almost half the team's games. In 1980, all four pro teams made the finals. Being a Philadelphia sports fan is a roller coaster ride, but as Lyon noted, "They're loyal and by far the most passionate."

Moe Berg, who was the first Jewish ballplayer to play for Princeton, referenced Franklin in a line that could apply to many Phillies team – "Good fielding and pitching, without hitting, or vice versa, is like Ben Franklin's half pair of scissors."[3]

In the best of Penn's and Franklin's world – neighborhoods voluntarily combine and share competition and even coaching strategies. Exhibit A: The Big Five teams of LaSalle, St. Joseph's, Temple, the University of Pennsylvania, and Villanova.

In the worst of Penn's and Franklin's world – the neighborhoods would be so caught up in competition and pragmatism that they would fail in their main objective – to be successful, to win. Philadelphia sports thrive on neighborhood rivalries at the high school and college level. Even professionally Philadelphia sports teams often have focused on winning the rivalries – New York, Dallas Cowboys, Boston Celtics, more than winning the championship. The rivalries, though, in pro basketball and football, between Army and Navy, St. Joseph's and Villanova, and Ali and Frazier have been some of the best.

This chapter tries to summarize the best and the worst of Philadelphia sports and some of the memories in-between.

The sayings: Dave Zinkoff's "Julius Errrrrrrving;" Harry Kalas's "Outta Here;" Bill Lyon's description of accuracy, "he could have threaded the football through a keyhole;" "The Hawk will never die;" "Gola goal;" "Yo! Adrain."

The clothes fit the body: John Chaney's ties; Chuck Bednarik's hands; Yo Yo's suit of clothes; Jack Ramsay's pants; Wilbur Montgomery's feet; Allen Iverson's tattoos; Andrew Toney's eye; Barbaro's ankle; William Penn's hat.

Monikers: Freddie "The Fog" Shero; "Chocolate Thunder;" "The Mound of Rebound;" The "Tall Tactician;" The "Kangaroo Kid."

The numbers tell it all: Fourth and 26; 1964; "fo', fo', fo;" "We owe you one;" 100; 90-47; Perfection.

CLUB SPORTS

Neighborhoods were influential in the rise of several sports: rowing, cricket, squash, and tennis.

Rowing clubs were organized along the Schuylkill River. Most were neighborhood clubs, except for a few college clubs. The best-known rowers were from the Vespers club, home to the Jack Kellys (father and son) who both won Olympic medals. It is the statue of Jack Kelly, rowing, that adorns the River Drive, which surmounts part of the Schuylkill River. Thomas Eakins painted rowers in a number of portraits.[4] [Several views of Boat House Row, the homes to many rowing clubs, can be seen at the end of the art section.]

In the mid-1800s cricket, imported from Rome, and in many ways a precursor of baseball's fame, arrived in Philadelphia. The three biggest clubs were The Germantown Cricket Club, Merion, and Philadelphia Cricket. Around the turn of the twentieth century there were fifty such cricket clubs in or about Philadelphia. The cricket teams from Philly fared well nationally.

Later, the cricket clubs would succumb to the popularity of tennis. Germantown produced one of the best tennis players ever, William H. Tilden.[5] Squash is still a popular sport in the cricket clubs.

A Struggle for Possession of the Puck, 1895.
Courtesy of Philadelphia Press – Public
Domain

PHILADELPHIA SCHOOL
OF GOLF ARCHITECTURE

The text is a rewrite of an article in Philadelphia Golf Magazine-04/2003 by Thomas E. Paul, a member of the Golf Association of Philadelphia and Pennsylvania Golf Association Executive Committees, who has been a member of Gulph Mills Golf Club for the past quarter century.

Many of the early golf courses in America were designed with the help of a local group of players: George Crump, George Thomas, Albert Tillinghast, Hugh Wilson, William Flynn, and William Fownes. Sharing their knowledge with each other, these golfers learned the ins and outs of planning golf courses and their style of design became known as the "Philadelphia School of Golf Architecture."

The first four were Philadelphia aristocrats. Fownes, an aristocrat from Pittsburgh was the son of H.C. Fownes, the creator of Oakmont. Four of the six did their designs for free.

The two premier courses designed by this group were Merion East and Pine Valley, in Clementon, New Jersey, which began in 1911 and 1912 respectively. Ninety years later they're still considered two of the best courses in the world. Wilson, who began the design of Merion East, and Crump, who began the design of Pine Valley, both took trips to Europe in 1910 to gain some expertise.

"A good case can be made that the idea of the uniquely American 'championship' style golf course originated from the Philadelphia School of Architecture, from the architectural collaboration at Merion and Pine Valley." The design of the courses, though begun by Wilson and Crump, was really a collaboration of ideas, primarily of the six mentioned, but also of other great golf architects of the day. Though Crump died in 1918 the course was finished with the help of Crump's friends in 1922.

Unlike other courses of their day, Pine Valley was designed to be "for the best, for a high caliber of player." [A debate raged over whether golf courses should be democratic (designed for all skill levels) or designed for players of skill.]

It was through mutual correspondence between Hugh Wilson, his brother Alan, C.V. Piper, and R.A. Oakley (the latter two of the U.S. Department of Agriculture) that the science and research of agronomy for golf course purposes took shape. They perfected the use and application of bent grasses as well as green construction methods and agronomic disease controls. Merion was a prime example of this collaboration.

"William Fownes won the 1910 U.S. Amateur, became President of the USGA in 1925-26, and spent the remainder of his life in architecture perfecting Oakmont.

William Flynn, primarily in partnership with engineer Howard Toomey, went on to produce forty to fifty original designs, including, among others, Shinnecock, Cherry Hills, Denver CC, CC of Cleveland, Indian Creek, Cascades, Lancaster, Kittansett, Philadelphia CC, Rolling Green, Huntingdon Valley, Lehigh, Manufacturers, and an additional nine at Brookline that became part of that course's U.S. Open Championship composite course."

Flynn's work can be seen to some degree in the greens and bunker style of Merion and the greens and sand designs of Pine Valley.

"Albert Tillinghast designed until the mid-1930s producing such notable courses as Baltusrol, Baltimore CC, Winged Foot, Bethpage, San Francisco CC, Ridgewood, Somerset Hills, Philadelphia Cricket (along with Flynn), and Sunnehanna, among others."

Merion hosted a number of golf championships, including the U.S. Open championships in 1934, 1950 (memorable for the play of Ben Hogan), 1971, 1981, and 1930 where Bobby Jones closed out his Grand Slam. The course is notable for its wicker flagsticks.

Other notable clubs in the Philadelphia region include the Whitemarsh Valley Country Club, and Arnonimink.

The Region's most successful golf player, as of this writing, is R. Jay Sigel.

ANNOUNCERS

Philadelphia has been lucky to have had some of the greatest voices in sports anywhere. The original voice that many fans know belonged to a television anchorman, John Facenda. Facenda was the voiceover for NFL Films, which showed a weekly telecast highlighting the past week in football. Facenda and his "golden throat" became a trademark for the NFL Films and a model for future Hall of Famers or soon to be Hall of Fame Sportscasters.

Bill Campbell

According to Angleo Catalidi, in his *Great Philadelphia Sports Debate* book with Glen Macnow, Bill Campbell, who was a broadcaster for fifty years covering mostly the Phillies, was the most knowledgeable and gifted announcer of all of Philadelphia's greats.

Dave Zinkoff (1910-1985)

Dave Zinkoff announced for the Philadelphia Athletics but made his fame with the Philadelphia '76ers. He was noted for his announcing of players such as Julius Errrrrrrrrrrrrrrrrving and Gola Goal. He often would remind (warn) the audience:

Attention: The owner of a gray Buick license number 12389. The key is in the ignition, the lights are on, and the engine is running. Later in the game the Zink would announce: "Attention. The owner of a gray Buick license number 12389. The key is in the ignition but the lights are no longer on and the engine is NOT running."

Merrill Reese for years has been the "golden voice" on the radio of Eagles football. Bob, "Buck the Bartender," Vetrone and Les Keiter were the voices of the Big Five.

Gene Hart (1931-1999)

Gene Hart was the voice of the Flyers during their championships of the 1970s, and the play in the '80s, and some of the '90s. What was remarkable was Hart's ability to describe the fast-paced motion of who was controlling the puck, who was receiving the puck and who was in position to get the next puck with a clarity that never mumbled words and never seemed to lose his train of thought.

Richie Ashburn (1927-1977) and Harry Kalas (1936-2009)

Hall of Famers Harry Kalas and Richie Ashburn were two of the best sports announcers Philadelphia ever had. Both Kalas and Ashburn passed away during the baseball season. Both announcers were mourned by players, the team, the city, and the country when they died.

Harry spoke with perfect diction. His voice was made for radio. He announced through the ups and mostly downs and, in 2008, the ups again of Phillies baseball, using his calm demeanor and sayings like "Outta Here, Michael Jack Schmidt" have been a treasure for Phillies Fans.

Richie Ashburn, the star player for the 1950 Phillies Whiz Kids, a great centerfielder, leadoff man and contact hitter made the Hall of Fame on his hitting skills but what made him another Philadelphia treasure was his homespun Nebraska way of telling stories and his honesty in critiquing managers for their decision making.

Ashburn loved a good tale. One of his classics was actually a true story about Honus Wagner (at least Mr. Wagner claimed it was true). The old baseball teams didn't have the best venues. Some of the teams played on nothing more than cow pastures. One day, as the batter, in one such field, hit the ball to Wagner a white rabbit sprung from a hole in the ground. Wagner, having to make a quick decision, fielded the rabbit and mistakenly threw the rabbit to first just beating out the runner. It was an historic first not just for Wagner, but also for all baseball. It was the first time, in recorded history that a runner was thrown out by a "hare."

Connie Mack and His Baseball Teams

Philadelphia's owners for the most part have been known for their unwillingness to spend money. The Phillies have lost more games, over 10,000, than any other sports franchise. In the 1920s, 1930s, and 1940s the Phillies best players were constantly sold to keep the team afloat.

A second negative characteristic over the years of all major franchises has been the poor evaluation of talent, especially in the free agent area, by the owners and their managers who were picked by the owners.

One owner who spent freely was Leonard Tose, whose 1980 Eagles team went to the Super Bowl. Tose would run into financial difficulty because of his spending habits, in and out of football, and eventually had to sell the team.

Connie Mack (1862-1956)

Mack, who owned and also managed the Phillies for a long time, was tight-fisted. Seeing baseball as a business, he once confided that it was more profitable to have a team get off to a hot start, then ultimately finish fourth. "A team like that will draw well enough during the first part of the season to show a profit for the year, and you don't have to give the players raises when they don't win," he said.

Connie Mack by Dick Perez. Courtesy of Dick Perez

He won nine pennants and five World Series with the Philadelphia Athletics. During that span his teams lost more than they won. He began with a quarter interest in 1901 and "eventually became sole owner." His partner, Ben Shibe, made baseballs and other sporting equipment. Shibe Park was named after Shibe. Unlike the teams of the twenty-first century concessions and ticket sales were his source of revenue. There was no corporate money, no city money, and no parking revenue to use.

In the early 1910s the Athletics won four pennants in five years from 1910 to 1914. Star players jumped to the newly formed Federal League or other teams. Mack sold off his other top players. The Athletics soon fell from first to last and stayed there for seven years.

Mack was legendary for being cheap. On July 10, 1932, the A's played a one-game series with the Cleveland Indians. To save train fare, Mack only brought two pitchers. When the starter was forced out in the first inning Mack had knuckleballer Eddie Rommel finish the game. Rommel pitched 17 innings and gave up 33 hits, but won the game, 18-17.

Mack was known as 'The Tall Tactician.' Though 6'1", he 'never raised his voice and seldom confronted a player in front of his teammates, but he could put a man in his place with a cutting sarcastic comment. He was called the tenth man on the field for his ability to move his fielders, using his scorecard, into the proper positions. He liked tall, strong pitchers and considered pitching eighty percent of the game. As a player, Mack played every position in the majors except third base and pitcher, but he was primarily a brainy, sometimes rule-bending catcher.

Unlike most other managers Mack wore a suit, not a uniform, when managing.

In the 1920s Mack built a new Athletics team that has been graded one of the best. From 1925 through 1933 the Athletics finished no lower than third, dethroning the Yankees in 1929-30-31. Again the salary demands of his players forced him to sell them and for the last seventeen years, until he retired at eighty-eight in 1950, the Athletics had only one first-division finish, fourth in 1948.

He won the World Series three of the first four times and in 1929 and 1930. His 1929 team is considered by many the best ever. These teams included numerous Hall of Famers.

Sadly, dynasty would never be a word that Philadelphia baseball or other professional teams would ever get to hear. Most owners have been concerned, like Mack, about the bottom line – making money on the team, though most, like Mack, like to win.

Four years after he retired, the Athletics were sold to Arnold Johnson and moved to Kansas City in 1955.[6]

Ed Snider

Text reprinted with permission of the Philadelphia Flyers (source: website www.flyers.nhl.com)

Ed Snider took a risk in 1966 that would come to characterize his career for the next five decades. He pledged his home as collateral for a loan to create the Philadelphia Flyers, and then used that foundation to build one of the preeminent sports and entertainment organizations in the world – Comcast-Spectacor. His role as Philadelphia's leading architect of the current sports scene was recognized by Philly's fans in 1999, when readers of the *Philadelphia Daily News* voted Snider as the City's greatest mover and shaker of the millennium.

When the National Hockey League decided to expand in 1966, Philadelphia was not on the radar of cities expected to receive an expansion team. Snider waged a one-man campaign to convince the League and succeeded. He had to promise the new team would have a home, and convinced City officials that, if they would provide him five acres of land on what was supposed to be part of the parking lot for the new Veterans Stadium, he would build an arena. Snider oversaw the construction of the Spectrum and eventually took control of it.

In 1974, Snider created Spectacor to oversee the Flyers and the Spectrum. This new company quickly became a major player in the national sports and entertainment scene. Nearly a dozen successful enterprises flourished under the Spectacor banner.

In 1996, Snider merged Spectacor with Comcast Corporation to form Comcast-Spectacor. That same year, he saw another dream come to fruition with the opening of the Wachovia Center, a $210 million state-of-the-art sports/entertainment complex. Today, the Wachovia Center and the Wachovia Spectrum comprise the most active sports and entertainment complex in the world.

While Comcast-Spectacor's success stands as testimony to Snider's vision and entrepreneurial skills, the creation of the Ed Snider Youth Hockey Foundation is Snider's true legacy. The Foundation was started by Snider in 2005 to provide a means to reach inner city children by giving them the chance to learn to play hockey. Hockey, however, is only the "hook" – the program will teach the children necessary life skills, and provide them with educational assistance to help them stay in school. The program has already touched the lives of over 1,000 children, and reflects Snider's strong commitment to give back to the community that has supported him.

Snider's achievements and his philanthropy have earned numerous awards and recognition. He was elected to the Hockey Hall of Fame in 1988 and serves on the NHL's Executive Committee. He is a recipient of the Lester Patrick Award for outstanding service to hockey in the United States and has been elected to the Pennsylvania Sports Hall of Fame, the Philadelphia Sports Hall of Fame, the Philadelphia Jewish Sports Hall of Fame, the Greater Washington DC Jewish Sports Hall of Fame, and the Flyers Hall of Fame. In 2005, Snider received the Greater Philadelphia Chamber of Commerce's William Penn Award, the most prestigious business honor in the region, and the Ellis Island Medal of Honor awarded to Americans of all ethnic backgrounds who have made significant contributions to our society.

In February of 2001, Snider received Temple University's First Annual Sports Leadership Award. In December 1999, he received the Anti-Defamation League's prestigious Americanism Award. In 1985, Snider received an honorary Doctor of Humane Letters degree from MCP Hahnemann University and in May of 1999, he received the same from Thomas Jefferson Hospital. He is also a Benefactor of the Sol C. Snider Entrepreneurial Center of the Wharton School of the University of Pennsylvania. Other Board memberships include the National Foundation for Celiac Awareness, The Atlas Society, the Simon Wiesenthal Center, and the Middle East Forum.

PROS

At the professional level Philadelphia coaches haven't compared to their college counterparts. A few who have compared include:

Fred Shero coached the Philadelphia Flyers hockey team in the early 1970s. He was known as "Freddy the Fog Shero," in part because of his glasses and in part because he was always "in a fog" – thinking up news strategies for the Flyers to win.

Dallas Green brought a lunch-pail view to coaching. His intensity along with that of Pete Rose's intensity changed the Phillies baseball teams of the late 1970s from a bunch of over-thinking players into a team that refused to lose.

Both Dick Vermeil and Buddy Ryan were "lunch pail" coaches of the Philadelphia Eagles football team. Vermeil displayed his intensity by working around the clock and sleeping at the stadium office. Ryan showed his intensity by supporting the players during the time they went out on strike. Andy Reid took the Philadelphia Eagles from futility to the NFC championship four times and the Super Bowl once [as of this writing].

COLLEGE

At the college level Philadelphia has had some of the best coaches in the country.

In football, Temple became prominent during the days of Glenn Pop Warner. Penn was successful in the 1940s and '50s under George Munger. Another Penn Coach, for only a brief period, was their ex-player John Heisman for whom the Heisman Trophy, college football's most prestigious award is named.

In track Jumbo Elliot led Villanova track teams to championships at the Penn Relays and always seemed to have the best milers, usually from Ireland, on his squads.

Glenn Warner (1871-1954)

Glenn S. Warner (Pop Warner) played football at Cornell, but he is best known for his coaching career. "Glenn S. Warner's (nicknamed Pop Warner) football career included playing at Cornell and coaching at a variety of schools including Carlisle where he taught Jim Thorpe. At Stamford University his star player was Ernie Evers. In 1932 he coached at Temple University.

Cradle of Coaches by Stan Kotzen. There have been coaching changes since this painting was drawn. Courtesy of Stan Kotzen

In 1929, Joe Tomlin thought football would be a good alternative to juvenile delinquency. Pop Warner lent his name to the project. The project, the Pop Warner Football League, still survives with an emphasis on academics as well as football.

Football historians credit Warner with being in the forefront of the movement which transformed the game from one of brawn to one of skill. Warner developed the "spiral punt, the screen play, single and double wing formations, the naked reverse, the three-point stance, numbering players' jerseys [thus the phrase 'you can't tell the players without a program'], and the use of shoulder and thigh pads."

[Biography from popwarner.com and Mountain Valley Conference Pop Warner Football and Cheerleading League]

Jumbo Elliot (1915-1981)

James 'Jumbo' Elliott ran track for Villanova, but it was as a coach, beginning in 1949, that he made his mark. His teams won numerous national indoor, outdoor, and cross-country championships, and his athletes excelled out all levels setting numerous world records – indoors and out.

Elliot's teams dominated the Penn Relays at nearby Franklin Field – at the University of Pennsylvania and at IC4A Championships.

Olympic competitors included Ron Delaney and Charles Jenkins in 1956, in the 1500m and 400 respectively, "Don Bragg in the 1960 pole vault, Paul Drayton in the 1964 4x100m relay, and Larry James in the 1968 4x400m relay."

He is best known for developing outstanding distance runners, including Delaney, Marty Liquori, Eamonn Coghlan, and Sydney Maree.

Basketball

In basketball, the Big Five has been a coaching cradle. A number of coaches have left for the professional NBA.

Penn was coached by Jack McClosky, the crew-cut sporting Dick Harter, "haberdashery" Chuck Daly, Bob Weinhaur, and Fran Dunphy (a former key player at LaSalle who left Penn for Temple).

Villanova by Al Severance, Jack Kraft, the cheery Italian Rollie Massimino (a former Penn assistant), Rollie's assistant Steve Lappas, and now Jay Wright.

Temple by the crafty caring Hal Litwack, Don Casey and John Chaney, and now Fran Dunphy.

St. Joseph's by Dr. Jack Ramsay, Jack McKinney, Jimmy Lynam, and now Phil Martelli.

LaSalle by the Shakespearean Professor Paul Westhead, Roman Catholic's Speedy Morris, the legendary Tom Gola's coach Ken Loeffler, Billy Hahn, and now Dr. John Giannini.

John Chaney and Sonny Hill

Two of the best coaches/teachers in the City have Temple roots and are known for their own value system.

John Chaney was hired by Temple President Peter Liacouras at the suggestion of Sonny Hill and with the help of Bill Cosby.

Chaney, a point guard in his high school days, wasn't able to play on a Big Five team during his college days. While the Big Five teams did have black players they didn't have too many.

Chaney went on to lead Philadelphia Textile to a national championship and with Temple continued the legacy of Temple coach Harry Litwack. He instilled in his players a work ethic that began with early morning practices and continued with a philosophy that said, "Be in

Sonny Hill by Sonny Hill.
Courtesy of Sonny Hill

control." His match-up-zone enabled his teams not only to compete but to reach the Elite Eight of the NCAA tournament multiple times. He is now a member of the National Basketball Hall of Fame. He retired in 2006.

Excerpted from Joe Clark, "The Sonny Never Sets." Philadelphia Daily News, 2/15/99.

Sonny Hill founded two basketball leagues. The first, league, the Baker League, was founded in 1960 to help professional players improve their games and to give college graduates a chance to prepare for the pros. His second league, the Sonny Hill league, begun in 1968 as a community involvement initiative. An alternative to juvenile delinquency and gang warfare, it now includes teams from six through college The programs don't begin and end with basketball. Their goal, Sonny's goal, is to use basketball as a teaching advice for life's lessons. Tutoring, mentoring, reading, and education are his main goals. Basketball is just the means.

Unlike most other sports, the appeal of basketball is to the poor. As Coach Chaney notes one basketball and basket can engage thousands.

Though they might have come from different lifestyles, Democratic presidential candidate and former U.S. Senator Bill Bradley credits Sonny Hill with helping him develop into a professional basketball star.

Hill has hosted a Sunday morning talk show, on WIP, longer than any other host on the popular sports talk station. He has also advised the Philadelphia Seventy-Sixers and served as a color commentator.

Harry Litwack (1907-1999)

Coach Litwack began as captain of Temple University's basketball team. He played seven years with the Philadelphia SPAHS (their uniforms were provided by the South Philadelphia Hebrew Association), helping them capture multiple championships. For twenty-two years he coached Temple's freshman basketball team (in the days where freshmen were not eligible to play for the varsity). Known as the "Chief," he became Temple's head coach in 1952. In twenty-one years his teams only had one losing season. They made the postseason thirteen times, including a remarkable run in 1969 when they won the NIT (National Invitation Tournament) when John Baum helped the Owls beat Boston College for the title. The Owls had third place NCAA finishes in 1946 and 1958. Guy Rodgers and Hal Lear were two of his best players.

"Basketball historians will say that Harry Litwack achieved more success with less talent than any coach in history. Litwack's flawless character, distinguished coaching ability, and outstanding sportsmanship made him a legendary figure in Philadelphia sporting annals." [Biography from Basketball Hall of Fame]

Jack Ramsay

"Perhaps more than any other individual, [Jack] Ramsay symbolizes Philadelphia basketball, home-grown and sown style. Smarts and guts. Inspiration and perspiration. Remarkable success and remarkable humility."

Ramsay's taught his St. Joseph's team the concept of pressure defense in which his players were in the face and on the ball at all times. Players dove for loose balls and got in the faces of opposing players so they couldn't think. His legend arguably began on February 26, 1958 when with six minutes left in a city-series game against LaSalle his team trailed by 16 points. Emphasizing "all-court traps" and his "pressure defense" the hawks rallied, tying the score and winning 82-77 in overtime.

Ramsay also coached the NBA Portland Trailblazers (with Bill Walton at center) to two championships, including one against the Philadelphia Seventy-Sixers. (B.G. Kelley. "Basketball is Art to Ramsay and He is One of its Greats." *Philadelphia Inquirer*, Editorial, September 23, 1995.)

Phil Martelli

Phil Martelli is the current coach of a St. Joseph's team that had a spectacular 2003-2004 season led by "the best backcourt in the nation," Jameer Nelson and David West. During his tenure at St. Joseph's, a small Jesuit School and a budget that is about ¼ the size of Duke's Martelli has managed to coach his team to two wins for every loss and several NCAA post-season tournaments. For Martelli it is his love of basketball and of the warm side of being a Philadelphian that has kept him from moving to bigger programs.

Martelli's love of basketball began on the Catholic playgrounds of his Southwest Philadelphia youth, expanded to the high school gyms, then the Palestra when the Big Five played all of its round-robin games there, and on to college basketball at local Widener. He then joined the local high school coaching ranks along with his longtime friend Geno Auriemma who went on to make Connecticut a powerhouse in women's basketball. After stints at Widener and Bishop Kenrick, Martelli became an assistant at St. Joe's. His hiring in 1995 was an exception for St. Joseph's, which likes to hire former graduates.

But Martelli excelled at St. Joe's and unlike many coaches who aspire to bigger offices, bigger gymnasiums, and bigger contracts, Martelli has made the frenetic pace of being a coach downright fun. He hosts a local talk-show called Hawk Talk, in which he wisecracks, imitates Johnny Carson's famous Carnac routine and has informal conversations with many of the locals. The St. Joe's field house barely holds 3000.

"Phil knows the janitor, the cleaning woman, everybody in his building," said Geno Auriemma, the ultra-successful Connecticut women's coach who is Martelli's closest friend. "I wish I could be like that."

There is, of course, nowhere in his office for Martelli to hide. Not that he'd want to. He relishes being the public face of St. Joe's basketball, chatting with the dry cleaner, the checkout clerk, the bank teller, all of whom know him or know somebody who knew him, or, at the very least, feel like they know him."[7]

PHILADELPHIA GUARDS

Philadelphia college basketball's table has long since been set by the play of its guards. Combining a mixture of smart athletic play with an ability to create one's own shot when the system the coach has ingrained in them doesn't let them get off a shot, the play of the guards is what often leads local college teams to upsets over the bigger known national teams.

Great guard play began with the tandem of Guy Rodgers and Hal Lear under the tutelage of Temple's Harry Litwack. The 1955 – 1958 Temple teams, led by Rodgers surprised many teams including a road victory against Kentucky in 1955.

Bill Conlin described the 1958 Final Four workout before the real game against Kentucky again, when Jay Norman had replaced Lear. In 1958 Litwack ran his 26-2 "juggernaut" through a dress rehearsal which was so finely run by Rodgers and Lear that when coach LItwack said "Good work, gang," the 500 writes applauded the workout. According to Conlin, Rodgers will be the lead guard in any celestial-all star game. Magic Johnson and Bob Cousy will have to find other roles. Temple lost to Kentucky 61-60. Their only other loss was to Cincinnati, who had a pretty good guard too – Oscar Robertson. (Bill Conlin. "Blackwell, Evans Keep A Tradition Alive At Temple." *Philadelphia Daily News*, 2/5/87).

All Big Five Schools each have had some of the best college backcourts, in basketball in the country. Each backcourt play has been representative of the jazz played in Philadelphia; Smooth and Easy.

All Big Five Schools each have had some of the best college backcourts, in basketball in the country. Each backcourt play has been representative of the Jazz played in Philadelphia, Smooth and Easy:

Villanova
Wali Jones and George Leftwich (1963-64).
Tom Ingelsby and Chris Ford (1970-72).
Penn
Jerome Allen and Matt Maloney (1994-95).
David Wohl and Steve Bilsky (1968-71).
LaSalle
Bernie Williams/Larry Cannon/Roland Taylor (1968-69).
Doug Overton and Randy Woods (1990-91)
St. Joseph's
Jim Lynam/Billy Hoy (1962-63)
Matt Guokas Jr./Billy Oakes (1964-66).
Jeffrey Clark/Bryan Warrick (1980-82).
Marvin O'Connor and Jameer Nelson (2001-02)
Nelson and Delonte West (2003-04)
Temple
Guy Rodgers and Hal Lear/Bill "Pickles" Kennedy(1955-58)
Nate Blackwell and Howard Evans(1986-87)
Nate Blackwell/Mark Macon(1987-88).[8]

In 2005-2006, Villanova did standard basketball teams two better when it played most of its games with a four guard offense of Randy Foye, Allan Ray, Mike Nardi, Kyle Lowry, and Nardi Lowry.

Guy Rodgers and Hal Lear. Courtesy of Temple University. Urban Archives. Evening Bulletin Photo Collection.

LUNCH PAIL PLAYERS

Philadelphia has always liked its athletes to be fighters. They like players who are willing to dive for loose balls, put winning above injury, are willing to lose teeth, and play above their potential. Mostly, they like players who refuse to lose. These players have come to be called "lunch pail" players because they represent Philly's working class. The rich can root for the cool players, but for most Philadelphians life is hard physical work. Shipyard workers, construction workers, people who work outdoors on rainy days, these are the people who live with team wins and die with team losses. They like seeing athletes who remind them of themselves.

Every Philadelphia team has had these players. Chuck Bednarik played offense and defense for the Eagles. He was the last of the 60-minute men (players who played offense and defense, full time). Bobby Clark lost his original teeth early. He wasn't the most skilled hockey player, no Wayne Gretzky, but he did the tough work, fought for the puck behind the goal, inspired his teammates by his grit and carried the early Flyers in 1974 and 1975 to two Stanley Cups with the aid of a tough coach, Fred Shero, and a tough goaltender, Bernie Parent.

Lenny "Nails" Dykstra was a remnant of the old days of baseball. He chewed tobacco, slid hard, and concentrated so hard he nearly hit .400 one year even though he didn't have a classic swing. He led a team of "lunch pail" players in 1993 to the brink of a World Series Championship. That team, the 1993 team, was probably more loved because of its players than the "cooler" 1980 team. Among Dykstra's teammates were John Kruk, Mitch Williams, and Darren Daulton.

Chuck Klein, the star player for the early Phillies teams, was a hard-nosed competitor. Charles Barkley (recently elected to the NBA Hall of Fame) was a 6-5 forward who played like he was 6-10. He out-rebounded most NBA forwards and many centers. He also was not afraid to speak his mind and was a beloved player even though he played a number of years for other teams.

Allen Iverson (until he wad traded to Denver) was the recent favorite lunch pail player. He shoots until he makes it. He has the quickest first step ever seen. Mostly though, he falls to the floor after being knocked down when trying to score among the taller NBA trees. What's remarkable and why the fans love him is he always gets back up. For many, he best represents life, if you get knocked down – and most of us do – get right back up and into the game.

Tommy McDonald was a lunchpail player for the Philadelphia Eagles.

Joe Frazier

If Muhammad Ali was the charismatic showman, Joe Frazier was the perfect foil – the steady tenacious boxer who just kept coming at his opponent without an ounce of quit. Ali's charisma overshadowed Joe Frazier and it was Ali who overcame the obstacles. He lost to Frazier once then beat him twice. Ali was stripped of his right to box after he was placed in jail for failing to fight in the Vietnam War. Ali challenged his conviction on the grounds of being a conscientious objector (because of his Islamic beliefs) and was later vindicated by the United States Supreme Court. Ali Silverman, no relation, summed up Frazier and Ali in a chapter of his sports book – *It's Not Over 'til It's Over*. Ali Silverman (Chapter 9 – Ali and Frazier) The Overlook Press 2002.

What made the Ali-Frazier fights extra- appealing was the differences in their styles and in their personalities.

Ali was a counter-puncher who used his feet and made quick jabs – he "floated like a butterfly and stung like a bee" Ali claimed. Frazier was the puncher who hit to the body while trying to knock his opponent out.

Text reprinted with permission of Overlook Press

Ali was more charismatic, more conscious of being a public figure. "For Joe Frazier, 'a blue collar worker' it was a chance to show that his value system of hard work mattered. For Frazier, nothing was easy. He was accused of being 'a Tom' by Ali and 'the Obedient Negro.' Frazier once said of himself, 'Joe Frazier is a natural person, like other people, a human being. Not a loudmouth. Not a machine you wind up to beat up. Not an animal.' He despised Ali for making him seem like an animal, always rapping that he was going to give Frazier a ghetto whipping. Frazier responded back, 'What he know about the ghetto'."

Frazier grew up "dirt-poor" in Beaufort, South Carolina. He moved to Philadelphia to support his young wife and their son. His first job was [a true Rocky job] working in a slaughterhouse. He became known as 'the slaughterhouse kid' in part because of his job and in part because of his quick rise to the top. In 1964 in Tokyo, Frazier, like Ali four years before him, won the Olympic gold medal. Both fighters were undefeated. Both were for their white and black investors corporations paid to turn a profit in the ring.

The first fight was fairly even throughout though Ali sensed that he needed a knockout to win in the 15th. Ali forgot a golden rule of boxing that said don't hook a hooker. When Ali led the round with a hook Frazier countered with a left hook that floored Ali. Frazier who always fought with another golden rule in mind, 'kill the body and the head will die' won the fight when the referee and two judges all ruled in his favor.

Ali would win the second 15 round fight in January of 1974 at Madison Square Garden and the 'Thrilla in Manilla', a 14 round victory, a year and 8 months later. "After the first fight and subsequent fights Frazier insisted that Ali apologize for all the 'rotten things' he said about Frazier. Ali decades later would apologize."

The fights and the careers of Frazier and Ali would be the stuff of numerous books. Two noted writers Mark Kram (father of Philadelphia sportswriter Mark Kram) and Gerald Early (from Penn) wrote books on Frazier and Ali respectively. Kram wrote the *Ghost of Manila* and Early the *Muhammad Ali Reader*.

Joe Frazier, it should be noted, was one of many famous Philadelphia boxers. Others included Tommy Loughran, Barney Lebrowitz ("Battling Levinsky"), Lew Tendler, Camden's Jersey Joe Walcott, Marvin Frazier, Joe's son, and Bernard Hopkins. One famous fight saw Philadelphia's Bob Montgomery lose to Trenton's Ike Williams.

Another famous Philadelphia boxing match at the Sesquicentennial Arena saw heavyweight champion Jack Dempsey ("the Manassa Mauler") lose his title, in a major upset, to Gene Tunney ("Gentlemen Gene"), a former Marine noted for quoting Shakespeare. 2,500 police were on duty at the fight, which included 300 writers and the largest crowd in boxing history to date. Tunney would also win the rematch in a famous "long count" which allowed Tunney time to get up before the 10 count.[9]

Len Dykstra by Dick Perez. Gouache on board. Courtesy of Dick Perez

A Lunch Pail Team

One team, the 1993 Phillies, captured the City's heart like no other. Virtually all of its player were like its centerfielder Lenny Dykstra and first baseman John Kruk. Just a bunch of 'dudes' who wanted to win and didn't care if they didn't look pretty doing it. They nearly won the World Series; however, both a 15-14 bizarre loss in the downpour of game 4 and a Mitch Williams homerun to Joe Carter, after the Phillies had rallied behind "Nails" Dykstra in game 6 were their downfall.[10] Three million fans saw the 1993 Phillies play that year. Their blue-collar style of play was the drawing card for Philadelphia's blue-collar fans.

AWARDS

Two of the most prestigious awards in football are the Heisman Trophy, named after a Penn coach and honoring the best college football player, and the Outland Trophy, named for Penn player John Outland and honoring the best interior lineman in college football.

Maxwell Award

Philadelphia's most prestigious football award is named after Robert W. (Tiny) Maxwell, who began playing college football at the University of Chicago in 1902 for Amos Alonzo Stagg. But it was the look on his face after playing for Swarthmore that changed the game. His nose was broken and eyes heavily swollen. His face had taken such a beating that the photo taken resulted in a demand to make the game more civil. The rules changes affected by the photo included increasing the first down yardage from five to ten, reducing the game time by fifteen minutes to sixty, legalizing the forward pass, allowing for a neutral zone on the line of scrimmage, and rules against rough play.

After his playing days, Maxwell became a referee, "helped create the first association of football officials, and later became a sports columnist and editor for the *Public Ledger*." A car accident ended his life, where even facing death he yelled to help the colliding truck, which was carrying Boy Scouts. "He was salt of the earth," wrote Damon Runyon of Maxwell.[11]

Bert Bell, the second Commissioner of the NFL, is honored when each year the Maxwell Club gives the NFL's best player the Bert Bell Award.

Heisman and Bell

"A Sculptor of the Gridiron." By Wincie King. 9/28/1922. *Philadelphia Public Ledger*. "Some men are satisfied with each day's work accomplished: others cannot find contentment until the results of today are forgotten in looking for a brighter tomorrow. Such a man is John W. Heisman, coach of the University of Pennsylvania football teams, who when dismal failure seemed to mark his efforts strove and modeled and tolled and forgot the day, looking forward always to the new method that would bring greater result and finer spirit in the way to win."

"On the Board of Strategy." Wyncie King. *Philadelphia Public Ledger*. 10/5/1922 "There are many men who can teach the fundamentals of the gridiron and who can even go beyond that and instruct in the advanced method and theory of the game; but those who are real strategists are rare. Such a one is Bert Bell, captain of that mighty 1919 team at Penn, and now assisting in the process of the Red and Blue by the lore and cunning in the fray that made him a great field general."

A Sculptor of the Gridiron by Wyncie King. Original Image from Philadelphia Public Ledger - Public Domain

Board of Strategy by Wyncie King. Original Image from Philadelphia Public Ledger - Public Domain

ALL-AROUND

Bill Tilden (1893-1953)

Of all the Philadelphia athletes, besides Wilt Chamberlain, the most complete athlete was Bill Tilden, a championship tennis player during the early part of the twentieth century.[12]

Tilden during his early life and career exemplified many lunch pail qualities. Tilden became an orphan at an early age. His father was active in the Union League. His tennis career floundered until he took a year off to develop his backhand. He was known to come back from defeat a number of times. In addition to being a champion player he was also a writer and a coach. He wrote several tennis books, including *Match Play – The Spin of the Ball*, a book that showed that Tilden was thinking several moves ahead of his rivals.

Tilden's play in the 1920s was summarized by the noted University of Pennsylvania Professor, E. Digby Baltzell, in his book *Sporting Gentlemen*.

Baltzell wrote that in 1927, "Tilden could have won the French championship against France's Henry Lacoste when Lacoste developed cramps. Tilden, in true sportsmanlike fashion, gave the younger Lacoste the time needed to recover. Tilden twice had match point at 9-8 when Tilden's apparent ace was called out. Lacoste went out to win 4-6, 6-4, 5-7, 6-3, 11-9."

"'There followed a tennis demonstration I have never seen repeated,' wrote Al Laney many years later. Here was a heroic defeat, which Tilden twice almost won. In accord with his rigid sportsman's code, he never, at the time or later, mentioned Cochet's close line call, even though it obviously upset him and contributed to his finally double-faulting on match point. 'I doubt that there ever has been a tennis battle,' wrote Al Laney, 'waged with more perfect sportsmanship under trying conditions, or with greater mutual admiration between adversaries'."

From 1920 to 1926 Tilden was the dominant player of his era. He won ten Grand-Slams in an age when players from America rarely played in the Australian tournament.

In the 1930s and 1940s he played the professional tour. His love of theater was his financial undoing as he sank money into financial ventures that failed.

Text sources: Tennis Hall of Fame website and Baltzell, E. Digby, *Sporting Gentlemen – Men's Tennis from the Age of the Human to the Cult of the Superstar* (The Free Press, Copyright © 1995)

Bill Tilden. Courtesy of Tennis Hall of Fame

Tom Gola

Tom Gola is one of only two players to lead his college team, LaSalle, to NCAA and NIT championships and to also lead his professional team, the Philadelphia Warriors, to the NBA championship. In 1969 he almost made it a quadruple by guiding his LaSalle team to a second place ranking in the polls. Unfortunately, LaSalle was on probation due to a prior coach's offenses so LaSalle didn't get its change to play UCLA for the championship. During his playing days he was college's leading rebounders. Gola was a three time All-American in college. He averaged 20 points a game and nearly 20 rebounds a game in college.[13, 14, 15]

Bob Vetrone, the voice of the Big Five, a sportswriter and a Sports Information Director for LaSalle, said in August of 2003 that "Gola was Magic before there was Magic" (referring to the Laker's Magic Johnson, another player who could dribble, rebound, pass, and score)

Wilt Chamberlain and Bill Russell. Courtesy of Temple University. Urban Archives. Evening Bulletin Photo Collection. The Philadelphia 76ers logo and Boston Celtics logos are used with permission from NBA Properties, Inc. ©2009. All rights reserved.

Wilt Chamberlain (1936-1999)

Wilt Chamberlain was the best athlete ever. With due respect to Michael Jordan, Chamberlain was so big and so strong that rules had to be written when he came into the game. He could score, rebound and create assists at will. No individual could stop him. Bill Russell tried but statistically Chamberlain was better. Russell unfortunately had the better teams and the best coach in professional basketball, Red Auerbach, and won most of his match-ups with Chamberlain.

Chamberlain began his basketball career in Philadelphia with Overbrook High and then for some reason he played his college ball at – of all places – Kansas. He returned to Philadelphia to play for the Warriors and then later for the 76ers. His 1967 '76er team is considered one of the best ever. His most famous day was scoring 100 points in an NBA game. [See more on Chamberlain in the review of his 100 point game.]

Dawn Staley
Text – Paraphrased from her website

Dawn Staley began her basketball career at Dobbins Tech High School (1986-1988) in Philadelphia where she led her high school to three straight Public League Championships. In college at the University of Virginia (1989-1992) she led her team to four NCAA tournament appearances and three Final Four appearances in all but her freshman year.

In 1994 she was chosen USA Basketball Female Athlete of the Year for 1994. In 1996, Staley led the USA Olympic Basketball team to the gold medal, in Atlanta, compiling a perfect record along the way. She captured her third women's basketball Gold Medal, in the 2004 Athens Games. She carried the flag for the United States in the 2004 opening ceremonies.

She recently coached the women's basketball team at Temple, where she guided the team to multiple conference championships and three postseason bids. She was also an All-Star player for the WNBA's Charlotte Sting.

Steve Carlton by Dick Perez. Courtesy of Dick Perez

GREAT CRAFTSMEN

A few Philadelphia athletes were notable for being seen as cerebral players who were always thinking about ways to improve.

Steve Carlton, refused to talk to the press after a losing season (which followed a tremendous season in which he won 15 games in a row and nearly half the team's games). Carlton spoke to the press a lot after the winning season, one of several Cy Young seasons but claimed all that talking distracted him the next year. Carlton claimed that not talking made the sportswriters use their imagination when writing a story, making their stories better.

Mike Schmidt should have been loved by the fans more. He was the best defensive third baseman of his day and hit over 500 homeruns. But Schmidt was always tinkering with his swing and never seemed to have the personality needed to carry the Phillies to victory. He had a love-hate relationship with the fans who loved him when he hit a homer and hated him when he struck out. Unlike Larry Bowa, Schmidt seemed to play without emotion.

Many credit Pete Rose with being the catalyst that carried the Phillies to victory in 1980 but it was Carlton who won the Cy Young and Schmidt the MVP.

Mike Schmidt by Dick Perez. Courtesy of Dick Perez

Robin Roberts by Dick Perez. Courtesy of Dick Perez

Philadelphia has been blessed with a number of wonderful sportswriters. Most of these writers have stayed local to Philadelphia for years. Television increased the difficulties of writing about sports. After all, if you saw the game, what is the writer to tell you that you don't already know? The answers range from putting the contest/players into some sort of context, using words to let you relive the images without replaying them on the VCR and still finding a way to tell you things you don't already know.

What follows are the writings of a few of Philadelphia writers or writers about Philadelphia sports and two full length articles by Bill Lyon, winner of numerous Pennsylvania and Philadelphia sports writer of the year awards.

The Philadelphia Daily News has one of the best sports writing sections in the nation, led by Bill Conlin, who has covered the Phillies for decades.

Red Smith who wrote for *The Philadelphia Record* for ten years (1936-1945) before moving to New York. A second Red Smith column highlights the Phillies' 1950 deciding game.

Red Smith (1905-1982)

One of Mr. Lyon's favorites was Red Smith, who wrote for *The Philadelphia Record* from 1936-1945. He later moved on to the New York newspapers. Perhaps it was the futility of the Phillies that spurred the movement.

Off the Highest Board
Reprinted from Red Smith on Baseball, copyright © 2000 by Phyllis W. Smith. By permission of Ivan R. Dee, Publisher.

The tallest, steepest, swiftest, dizziest, dare-devil, death-defying dive ever undertaken by a baseball team came off with a rich and fruity climax yesterday when the Phillies toppled headlong into the World Series.

For thirty-five years, the Phillies struggled to win a National League pennant. For the last twelve days they battled mightily to lose one Then in the tenth inning of the 155th game of their season, all snarled up in a strangling tie with the team that had closed eight laps on them in a fortnight, they were knocked kicking into the championship by the bat of Dick Sisler.

George Sisler, probably the greatest first baseman who ever lived, whose .400 average couldn't get him into a World Series, sat in Ebbets Field and saw his big son slice a three-run homer which shattered the pennant hopes of the Dodgers, whom George now serves.

Sisler's hit won the game, 4 to 1. Minutes earlier, lustrous pitching by Robin Roberts had saved it, after the Dodgers had come within a dozen feet of the victory which would have closed the season in a tie and brought Philadelphia and Brooklyn together for a playoff.'

"There hasn't been such a finish," said Mr. Warren Brown, the noted Chicago author, "since sporting British officials carried Durando over the line in the 1908 Olympic marathon."

On Sept. 19 the Phillies had the pennant won in every sense save the mathematical one. They were seven and a half games ahead of the Boston Braves, and Brooklyn was third, nine games

off the pace. The Dodgers won fourteen of their next seventeen games, the Phillies three of their twelve.

[The game was tied going into the ninth.]

To say tension was growing is to abuse the mother tongue. Things reached such a pass that when a bug flew into the eye of Mike Goliat, the Phillies second baseman, Mr. Babe Alexander, of Philadelphia, cursed. "Those Dodgers," he said, "have adopted germ warfare."

But shucks, things were practically lethargic when compared to the Brooklyn ninth, when the Dodgers put their first two batsmen on base and Duke Snider lashed what had to be the deciding hit into center field. Richie Ashburn fielded the ball on one hop, threw swiftly and superbly to the plate, and Cal Abrams, coming home with the winning run, was out by twelve fat feet.

Nobody ever saw better pitching than Roberts showed then. With runners on second, third and one out, he walked Jackie Robinson purposely to fill the bases, then reared back and just threw that thing through them. Carl Furillo popped up. Gil Hodges flied out.

Ken Heintzelman and Ken Johnson ran all the way from the bullpen to shake Roberts's hand. Eddie Sawyer patted Robert's stomach. Those were gentle hands. Sisler and Roberts felt others later…

Begging Mr. Sullivan's Pardon [Frank Sullivan was known as the "cliché" expert. In this piece Red Smith upped the ante.]
Reprinted from Red Smith on Baseball, copyright © 2000 by Phyllis W. Smith. By permission of Ivan R. Dee, Publisher 4/15/52

Question (by sports editor): What is baseball?
Answer: The national pastime.
Q. Good, very good. Now, what is the game played with?
A: The horsehide and ash.
Q: Excellent. And what else?
A. The sphere, hassocks.
Q: Yes, yes. I see you have the idea. And what is the game played on?
A: It is played on the velvety sward.
Q: Identify the home team?
A: Our heroes.
Q: And they oppose?
A: The hated visitors.
Q: Now, where do both teams go in the spring?
A: They head for sunny climes.
Q: Where do they go on road trips?
A: The hinterlands.
Q: Fine, Fine. What is another name for umpires?
A: The arbiters, the men in blue, or, collectively, the Three Blind Mice.
Q: What is a rookie?
A: A rookie is the New Dazzy Vance. The new Babe Ruth. The New Ty Cobb, in special circumstances. The Left-Handed Dizzy Dean.

Q: What does the rookie who is The New Ty Cobb run like?

A: A deer.

Q: What has he for an arm?

A: A rifle.

Q: On days when he doesn't run like a deer, what does he run like?

A: The wind.

Q: Anything else?

A: A gazelle.

Q: Corking, corking! What is the manager?

A: The Gallant Skipper, the Silent Strategist, The Tall Tactician, The Brain…

Q: Fine, that's enough. What is the president of the club?

A: The prez.

Q: And as a group?

A: Magnates.

Q: What is a pitching arm?

A: A soupbone.

Q: What sometimes happens to old soupbones?

A: They get chips.

Q: Where do the chips go?

A: To John Hopkins.

Q: What happens after they are removed?

A: GIANT HOPES SOAR AS JANSEN PREDICTS 20 WINS.

Q: What is the name of that type of headline?

A: Set and hold for spring…

Q: Good, good, you're doing splendidly. Now, let me ask you this: What do you call it when two men are retired on one play?

A: A double play.

Q: A double play! A double play! Anything else?

A: Well, a—er, rippling double play.

Q: Think, boy, think! Isn't there—uh—say, a twin answer to the question?

A: A twin answer?

Q: Yes, twin, twin, t-w-i-n.

A: I'm sorry, sir, it's just a double play to me. I can't think of anything else to call it.

Q: Well, son, maybe I'm being a bit hasty about this. Maybe I don't need a new baseball writer. Tell you what I'll do. I'm going to put your name on the list. Leave your address here and I'll drop you a line if anything turns up.

Bill Lyon

Bill Lyon is a veteran writer for the *Philadelphia Inquirer*. His columns (he's now retired and writes on special occasions) have been the first read in the morning for many years.

One of his best bits of writings was not a column, however. It was a write-up of the legendary Charles Bednarik in a book called *When the Clock Runs Out* – a book about what happens to old time football players when their playing days are over.

Bill Lyon on Chuck Bednarik

Text reprinted with permission of Bill Lyon, Bill Lyon, Christine Zordich, When the Clock Runs Out (Triumph Books, 2001).

Those hands. You cannot help but stare at them. They are hypnotic. Mesmerizing.

It is thought that the oldest living thing on the planet is a tree that dwells on a bleak, hardscrabble, windswept spit of desolation, and it is so cantankerously hardy, so unyieldingly stubborn that it seems to take root in rock. You can't kill it, and it won't die on its own.

Those hands, they belong on that tree.

As a player, Mack played every position in the majors except third base and pitcher, but he was primarily a brainy, wily, sometimes rule-bending catcher. He was a popular player for his smarts. He distracted batters with his chatter, was not above tipping a hitter's bat just before a swing, and learned to make a slapping sound as a batter swung and missed that made it sound like a foul tip.

The fingers are bent at grotesque angles, the knuckles hideously swollen. The pinky on the right hand wanders out at a ninety-degree angle, almost as though it belongs to another hand.

Those fingers have been stepped on. Chewed on. Twisted. Bent. Yanked. Cleated. Caught in the ear holes of helmets. Caught in face masks and violently shaken about. All that, plus whatever other atrocities football players commit on each other when they are hidden from the view of the whistle-blowers and the yellow flag-throwers, down there at the bottom of the pile, when the rule is to grab hold of the handiest extremity and practice extreme sadism.

Those hands…imagine the stories they could tell.

Well, those hands are the property of Chuck Bednarik. He is beamingly proud of them, and he will gladly recount for you each dislocation, each firecracker pop that meant yet another fracture, each ligament torn, each muscle shredded, each bit of cartilage ripped loose from its moorings. He can give you down and distance and gruesome detail.

Chuck Bednarik. Last of the Sixty-Minute Men. Iron Man. Concrete Charlie.

When the Eagles won the pro football championship in 1960, Concrete Charlie played all but ninety seconds of the game. He had retired two years prior, but had come back. He was thirty-seven years old. And on the last play of the game, the Green Bay Packers' brutish fullback Jim Taylor caught a pass and was heading to the end zone for what would have been the winning touchdown.

Except Concrete Charlie got him, wrestled him to the cold, hard ground like a rodeo cowboy bulldogs a steer and then sat on the squirming, seething Taylor until the clock blinked down to all zeros.

"You can get up now, Jim," Concrete Charlie told Taylor. "The game's over."

It became a line for the ages.

Also for the ages was Concrete Charlie's hit on Frank Gifford. It remains even now the definitive tackle in the sport of football. Coaches still scrounge around for the grainy black and white shot from November 20, 1960, to show their charges how to legally decapitate another human being.

It was in Yankee Stadium, the Eagles were winning 17-10 inside the last two minutes, and Gifford was running a pass route directly into the Bermuda Triangle, over the middle, into the Dead Zone, reaching back for the pass that was thrown behind him, snaring it with an elegant ease, the graceful nonchalance that was his signature, turning to head upfield and …

Wham!

If he'd been hit full with a baseball bat, he wouldn't have flown backward with such velocity. The ball flew forward. Gifford lay like a corpse.

"Chuck knocked him right out of his shoes," insists Tom Brookshier, who was Concrete Charlie's teammate.

Gifford sustained the king of concussions, and he was knocked out of not only the game, but the rest of the season … and the season after that!

And this is what Gifford has said: "'It was perfectly legal. If I'd had the chance, I'd have done the same thing Chuck did."

At the card shows he does, Concrete Charlie has two stacks of 8x10 photographs ready for autograph seekers. They can select one that shows him crouched, poised to pounce on an unseen opponent. Or they can opt for the other one, that famous shot, Bednarik looking down at the unconscious Gifford.

"Nine out of ten choose this one," says Concrete Charlie, holding up the most famous picture in the history of professional football.

Bill Lyon on Julius Erving. *Sports Humanitarian*, October 14, 2002 <sportshumanitarian.com/induction/jerving>.
Text reprinted with permission of Bill Lyon.

He saved one league…He kept another one afloat…He popularized the single most entertaining shot in the sport…He made a fast game even faster…He defined free-form basketball, injecting into a game that already throbbed with its special rhythms a choreography of aerial improvisation that took our breath away… He spawned a whole generation of cloud-hopping, wing walking imitators and, in the process, changed forever the way the game was played…And beyond all of this – and vastly more important, he came to represent the essence of citizenship and sportsmanship. He came to be the conscience of sport, the forceful, ever present reminder that there is room up there on the marquee for comparison and humanitarianism. He came to be, in short, what, rightly or wrongly, we have always wanted the athlete to be – a role model…And that of course, is his most meaningful legacy… Other than that, Julius Winfield Erving II didn't have much of an impact on professional basketball.

*From Top:
Charles Bednarik
(University of
Pennsylvania). Courtesy
of Temple University.
Urban Archives. Evening
Bulletin Photo Collection.*

*Julius Erving by Larry
Berman. Courtesy of Larry
Berman. The Philadelphia
76ers logo is used with
permission from NBA
Properties, Inc. ©2009.
All rights reserved.*

VENUES

Many of the venues for sports in Philadelphia are noteworthy more for the competition of the teams and players rather than the stadiums. Like the Spectrum, Veterans Stadium, and the Villanova Ski Lodge, they are clean and airy and nobody goes there just because of the arena. These arenas lack the character and ghosts and charisma of the older sports locations.

Others are noted for their failure. The Flyers are the only team in the country that can fairly claim to have had a stadium that conformed to the elements. Their old venue, the Spectrum, had to be closed for repairs when the roof blew off. Another, JFK Stadium, gained notoriety when a fence couldn't hold a number of men in uniform at the annual Army-Navy Game.

The main exceptions are the old baseball parks where the Athletics and Phillies used to play and two venues at the University of Pennsylvania – Franklin Field and The Palestra. One other early venue of note is the Merion Cricket Club, which has hosted several prestigious tournaments in golf and in tennis.

Dick Perez

Text reprinted with permission of Dick Perez
Dick Perez – The Dream, Too.
www.dickperz.com

The Dream, Too by Dick Perez. Courtesy of Dick Perez

Dick Perez, born in 1940 in San Lorenzo, Puerto Rico, lived from the age of six in New York City's Harlem. His family moved to Philadelphia in 1958. After completing high school Perez attended the Philadelphia College of Art and the University of Pennsylvania and served briefly as illustrator for the United States Air Force. He apprenticed in both a graphic design studio and a printing company. His work experience included a position as assistant art director with an advertising agency and a position as art director for a publishing company. He was co-owner of a design and printing consulting firm and a partner in an ad agency before striking out on his own in 1976. The culmination of these experiences resulted in a strong sense of design, command of composition, and an evident artistic maturity. Fortuity brought him design and illustration work from the Philadelphia Eagles and the Philadelphia Phillies in the 1970s, thus beginning his involvement in sports art. He has been the winner of numerous design awards including the winning entry for the national contest held in 1976 to create the official centennial logo of baseball's National League. He also designed and illustrated the 1983 World Series program cover.

Currently, Perez is a partner in Perez-Steele Galleries, a well-known publisher of sport art. Perez is official artist for the Baseball Hall of Fame and Museum.

Dick Perez works primarily in oils, watercolors, acrylics and gouache. His subjects show his wide range of interests but predominantly Perez enjoys portraiture. His portraiture shows the influences of such masters as John Singer Sargent, Anders Zorn, Joaquin Sorolla, and Diego Velazquez. He derives his inspiration for his landscapes from the American Impressionists.

Baseball Parks

The Philadelphia Professional baseball teams have played at a number of parks like Forepaugh Park at Broad and Dauphin Streets, Philadelphia Park at Broad and Jefferson and Jefferson Park at 25th and Jefferson. The best known parks were Recreation Park, Columbia Park, the Baker Bowl and Shibe Park. Veterans Stadium opened in 1970 as a multipurpose park where baseball and football were played.

Separate stadiums for the Phillies and Eagles have recently opened.

Recreation Park and Columbia Park

The Phillies played their first game at Recreation Park, on April 2, 1883, against a semipro team from Manayunk. The park was on an odd shape of land so that centerfield was 369 feet from home plate while right field a mere 247. The cost of a game was 50 cents, which the owner, Alfred J. Reach, tried to offset by offering two free horse-trolley tickets worth 12 cents. The offset was to entice fans who were going to Columbia Park to see the Athletics.

Columbia Park was located at 29th and Columbia and was home to the Athletics for eight seasons starting with 1901. The first manager of the Athletics was Cornelius McGuillicuddy, a.k.a. Connie Mack. The cost of building the stadium was $35,000. The stadium had a seating capacity of 9,500. Athletic games were only a quarter and included some great players like Napolean Lajolie, Chick Fraser, and Bill Bernhard, who had been lured away from the Phillies. The A's won the pennant in 1902 (the National League refused to play the American League, thus there was no World Series) and in 1905 the A's lost to John McGraw's New York Giants, 4-1, all five games being shutouts.

A memorable game was the September 30, 1907, match-up with Ty Cobb's Tigers. The first game of the scheduled doubleheader was 9-9 in the fourteenth when the A's Davis hit a ball that should have been a ground-rule double. Detroit centerfielder Sam Crawford claimed that a policeman interfered with him. While the umpire, Silk O'Loughlin deliberated, a melee broke out which even included the street clothed Connie Mack. O'Loughlin ruled for Detroit so the single that followed did not produce what would have been the winning run. The game was called after 17 innings at 4-4 and the second game of the doubleheader was not played. The result was that Detroit won the Pennant and the A's, who would have won the pennant, if only O'Loughlin had ruled differently, came in second.

The other games of note at Columbia Park were the City Series preseason games between the Phils and A's. They evenly split the 26 games played at Columbia Park.[16]

One of the most famous paintings of the early baseball era was Thomas Eakins "Baseball Players Practicing" (1874). Frank Fitzpatrick wrote of the painting for the *Philadelphia Inquirer* on 7/23/07.

Eakins painting depicts an afternoon practice at North Philadelphia's Jefferson Street Grounds in the 1874 season. The team is the Philadelphia Athletics (not the antecedent of Connie Mack's Athletics). By 1874 baseball's popularity had exceeded cricket's and Eakins was capturing the new modern sport.

The batter, Weston Dickson Fisler, of Camden, would on April 22, 1876, score the first run in major league baseball history when the National League A's lost 6-5 to the National League Boston team. The

A's folded a year later. In 1883 the Phillies became the local National league entry. The shoes, caps, and stockings (teams were often named for the color of their stockings) were popular in their day.

The Baker Bowl and Shibe Park (a.k.a. Connie Mack Stadium)

The Phillies played in the Baker Bowl from 1887-1939. The most notable feature of the Baker Bowl was the short right field wall, an ugly long wall originally 300 feet from home plate, later reduced to 280 and ½ feet. It was a pitcher's nightmare and a hitter's delight.[17] The clubhouse was in centerfield. The Phillies during their tenure lost more than they won. Their only World Series appearance was in 1915. They lost. The most notable impression of the Baker Bowl was Edgar William's newspaper line – "It was a lovely place. It was beautifully decrepit. They don't make ballparks like that anymore."[18] During its day the park was used for bike racing, around the perimeter, football, boxing, wrestling, and other events.[19] Eventually, the ballpark, like the occupant, the Phillies, began to deteriorate and the team moved to a better stadium, Shibe Park, at 21st and Lehigh in 1938, where the A's had been playing since 1909. At the time it was built, Shibe Park was in the wilderness of Philadelphia. The park was known as being more for the poor man than the rich man.[20]

The park was hailed a marvel when built. Years later, a mezzanine was built and so were upper decks. In the 1930s the outfield wall was raised 22 feet so fans who were viewing the game from neighborhood rooftops couldn't see. The wall became known as the "spite wall." In 1939 neighborhood fans again became upset when lights were installed. In 1953, the last major change took place. The park was renamed Connie Mack Stadium. In 1954 the A's moved to Kansas City and the stadium was purchased by the Phillies owner Bob Carpenter whose son, Ruly, would also own the Phillies.[21]

The park was also known for its obstructed views, boobirds, curfews, and great hotdogs. Dave Zinkoff of 76er fame announced many A's games there.[22] In its day, the playing conditions were considered superb. The A's played in the Series eight times there (05, 10, 11, 13, 14, 29, 30, and 31) winning five times. Alas, only the 1950 Whiz Kids made it for the Phillies. The best game was when the A's roared to a 10-8 victory after being down 8-0 in a Series game against the Chicago Cubs. While many memorable games were played there, the most lasting memories in the 1960s, its last decade, were the '64 collapse and Richie "don't call me Dick" Allen writing words in the dirt, asking to be traded.

Veterans Stadium

The Phillies most successful years were at Veterans Stadium, an all purpose park where the Eagles also played. The Phillies won the World Series in 1980, two pennants in 1983 and 1993, and made the playoffs numerous times.

Citizens Bank Ball Park

In 2004 the Phillies moved around the corner to their new baseball only stadium, Citizen's Bank Ballpark. The field is natural grass and dirt, there's a view of the Philadelphia skyline, and many enticing features like Ashburn Alley for remembrances of teams past. The Phillies made the playoffs in 2007 and won the World Series in 2008.

Connie Mack, Night 10" x 16", oil on board by Max Mason. Courtesy of Gross McCleaf Gallery

500 Level at the Vet, Original Oil, 36" x 108", installed mural, 120" x 360" Citizens Bank Mural #3 by Max Mason. Courtesy of Gross McCleaf Gallery

*Citizens Bank Park in the Sun 24" x 30", pastel by Max Mason. Courtesy of Gross McCleaf
Gallery*

*Rounding First at Citizens Bank Park by Max
Mason. Courtesy of Gross McCleaf Gallery*

NEW STADIUMS

Lincoln Financial Field is the new home of the Philadelphia Eagles. An effort was made to follow the trend of other cities and place the stadiums, especially the Phillies stadium, in downtown Philadelphia. But Franklin's practical side won out. To avoid litigation over the location of the stadiums and to capitalize on Penn's view of the world – sports venues should be in one neighborhood, movies in another (old city), museums in another, the parks remained in South Philadelphia along with the Wachovia Center (host to the hockey team, the Philadelphia Flyers, and the basketball team, the Philadelphia Seventy-Sixers).

CLASSICS
Franklin Field[23]

Franklin Field, the best named Philadelphia venue after the Palestra, was built in the early 1920s when football, not basketball, was king at the University of Pennsylvania. It is a classic horseshoe stadium where the clock doesn't have numerals, just the twelve letters of Pennsylvania starting with the P at noon.

For years the Eagles played at Franklin Field. Penn played national powers, including Notre Dame.

Mostly though it was and is still the site of the Penn Relays, a wonderful tradition of sprint relays and other track and field events held each year for college and high-school athletes and other amateurs. The relays began in 1895. The relays are the longest uninterrupted collegiate track meet in the country. During the era of Jim "Jumbo" Elliot at Villanova, the Villanova track team won at least one championship, often the combined distance medley, for years against the best competition in the World.

Recently, it has been kept afloat by people like Bill Cosby, who occasionally runs in an old-timers distance medley.

The finish of a Penn Relay Race is shown.

Penn Relays. Courtesy of University of Pennsylvania – Athletics

Franklin Field. Courtesy of University of Pennsylvania – Athletics

COLLEGE BASKETBALL

Over the years there have been hundreds of great games played by Big Five Teams. The best, the city series games, are almost sure locks to be down-to-the-wire barnburners. LaSalle won a championship in 1959 against Bradley with Gola, Charley Singley and Frank O'Malley leading the way, while Villanova won a championship against Georgetown in 1985 [see the best games section].

Notable games begin with the "Holy War" between St. Joseph's and Villanova, the most intense rivalry, pitting the Augustinian Wildcats against the Jesuit St. Joe's Hawks. The most memorable game in the series was in 1966, when the heavily favored Hawks beat the upstart Villanova Wildcats on a last second 29 foot shot by defensive player, Steve Donches.

In 1971, the Penn Quakers beat the favored Villanova Wildcats in a great stall game won by the score of 32-30. The next year Penn would go through the regular season undefeated only to be demolished in the NCAA tournament by Villanova by the score of ..., well I went to Penn, so you can look it up.

Upsets

Each of the Big Five teams has had notable upsets. Temple beat Boston College in 1969 for the NIT championship, Villanova beat Georgetown for the NCAA title, Penn Basketball. LaSalle beat Jim McDaniel's Western Kentucky team in 1971. Two absolute stunners were captured in the press the next day as the highlights which follow show.

Penn/North Carolina

Tom Cushman. "Penn Puts Torch to Carolina," Philadelphia Daily News, 3/12/1979

In 1979 Penn beat North Carolina 72-71. They had just squeaked by Iona just to earn the right to play the Tar-Heels. They went on to beat Syracuse and St. John's to win probably the last truly Eastern-Eastern regional to reach the Final Four – a remarkable achievement for an Ivy League school.

St. Joseph's/Depaul

Phil Jasner. "Hawk's Dream Alive," Philadelphia Daily News, 3/16/81

In 1981 St. Joseph's played DePaul, the No. 1 team and one of the favorites to win the NCAA March-Madness tourney, in a first-round game. Phil Jasner, a sportswriter for the Philadelphia Daily News captured the ending moments. "The five St. Joe's players on the floor at the end of the game are John Smith, Tony Costner, Lonnie McFarlan, and Bryan Warrick. Warrick, with 11 seconds left, flashes the ball through his legs, behind his back, leaving the two defenders flailing after him. He spots McFarlan along the right baseline and sends the freshman a swift, accurate pass. McFarlan, in turn, squares his shoulders to face the basket and goes up for glory. Halfway through the motion, he realizes the only people in front of him are Smith and 6-10 Tony Costner. Lonnie drops the ball inside to Smith, who lays in the points heard 'round the basketball world."

(Phil Jasner. "Hawk's Dream Alive." *Philadelphia Daily News*, 3/16/81)

The Big Five

While Philadelphia cherishes its neighborhoods, the Big Five, along with the Mummers, are two prime examples of where neighborhoods come together for a better good.

The Big Five is a league based on geographical and historical connections to a city: Washington, D.C., New York, Boston, Chicago. None of these cities has their own college basketball league. But Philadelphia does.

Before it's creation in 1955 some of the teams didn't play each other. Villanova and Penn played doubleheaders at the Penn Palestra. The other three schools played at the home of the Philadelphia Warriors. They played at nearby Convention Hall. In 1955, Jerry Ford (not the U.S. President, but Penn's athletic director) discussed with the other athletic directors the formation of the Big Five. Putting aside their differences, in 1955, a round robin among the five schools began. All five schools would play at the Palestra (Penn's home gymnasium). Since 1955, the Palestra has hosted more regular season and post-season games than any other gym. Hundreds of schools have played there, often as part of a doubleheader. The Big Five has given pleasure to many and has often been a unifying activity for the diverse Philadelphia community. It has exposed many of these communities not only to the teams but to the spirit of each other.[24]

The Palestra

"The Palestra was built in 1927, adjacent to Franklin Field and next to Penn's math and science facilities. The 'ancient Greeks had gymnasia, in which athletes trained, and attached to them palaistra, rectangular courtyards where those skills, once perfected, were publicly displayed. The Palestra, where some Big Five games and Penn games are played, fits the Greek mold since the Palestra is next to the school's gym – Hutchinson gymnasium. The Palestra is braced by 10 arched steel trusses'."[25]

What makes the Palestra college basketball's best arena is not just the layout of the building. It is one of those few arenas that says – only basketball should be played here.

Unlike most arenas Penn from 1955 through 1989 was host to the other Big Five Schools. For many years the tradition was that the Palestra would host doubleheaders. The first game would usually pit a Big Five team against some of the best teams in the country. The second would be a contest between two locals where the stands would be half filled with cheerers for one local and the other half supporters for the rival local.

Traditionally, the Big Five local would pull a major upset against the higher ranked team. LaSalle, in 1971, upset Western Kentucky with Jim McDaniels. St. Joe's beat Wichita State, in 1964, when Wichita had Nate Bowman and Dave Stallworth, two future NBA stars and Bowling Green in 1962 when Bowling Green starred Nate Thurmond and Howard Komives.

Streamers (Palestra).
Courtesy of Drew Hallowell.

The second game always began and ended with the warning, 'You can throw their records out the window." The local games consisted of players who knew each other's moves from previous games and often from Summer League play. The number of Big Five games that have gone down to the wire is countless.

Text reprinted with permission of Alexander Wolff. (Big Game, Small World (Warner Books, 2002)).

"The Palestra had other traditions. Streamers were thrown after a team scored its first basket. Rollouts would be the first sign that the fans were ready for the game. Rollouts were paper messages that schools unrolled to support their team and ride their rival. Some of the popular rollouts were 'HAWKS BANK ON MCFARLAND TO CHASE MAHAT-TAN' and 'PENN HAS HOT DOG STARTERS AND BEANS AND FRANKS ON THE BENCH,' 'HAWKS ARE SO VAIN THEY PROBABLY THINK THIS ROLLOUT IS ABOUT THEM.' The real fun was the counter rollout. When Villanova would rollout – 'THE HAWK IS DEAD,' St. Joseph's would respond with a dozen banners that said, 'THE HAWK WILL NEVER DIE.' Unfortunately, the rollouts became crude and were ended when rollouts like 'WHAT'S THE DIFFERENCE BETWEEN CHRIS FORD AND A DEAD BABY? A DEAD BABY DOESN'T SUCK' began to appear.

The favorite attendee at many Big Five games was Bernie Schiffran, whose moniker was YoYo. YoYo sadly spent his nights 'amid the newsprint rolls by the loading dock behind the *Bulletin* building at 30th and Walnut.' 'But ushers never asked to ask to see his ticket, and fans always shared a piece of their pretzels, and coaches made sure to let him follow them to Cavanaugh's Restaurant, where he'd deliver malaprop-laced monologues about...' Frank Scenario of Hobobroken. Jack Ramsay gave him his shirt, Litwack his pants, and McCloskey of Penn his suit coat."

When Princeton beat Penn in their miracle comeback game, a game in which Penn led 40-13 with 15 minutes to play, Neil Hartman remarked the next day – 'Just think, in the old days, last night's game would have been only half of a double-header'."[26]

Alas, in the late 1980s the Big Five schools started to go their own way when television became more of an influence and the locals joined their own leagues. More money could be made if games were played at the Spectrum or First Union Center or newly built gyms like Temple's Apollo and Villanova's Pavilion. The Big Five for a decade played only a half of a Big Five.

Fortunately, in the late 1990s, the full round robin schedule of the Big Five was reinstated. Penn and St. Joseph's play their Big Five games at the Palestra. And in 2001 a new concourse around the Palestra was built highlighting the teams, the games, the writers, and the traditions at the Palestra.

By Joe Rhoads

"This [The Palestra] is a place with magic in the air... The Palestra has the acoustics of a big bass drum. It's a basketball echo chamber where every sound is amplified, where 100 people sound like a thousand, where a thousand sound like 10,000 and where 10,000 sound like nothing you've ever heard before. When the bleachers are full and the games are good, this is the best place to watch a college basketball game in America. There are other great gyms, other great crowds. But they are not the Palestra. It is the best basketball gymnasium in the country—by far."[26]

Immaculata College: Immaculata College, in Chester County on the Main Line, was a national powerhouse in women's college basketball, winning their national tournament the first three years the tournament was held and losing the next two in the finals. Their firsts included the first women's collegiate basketball championship, the first-ever regular season nationally televised women's college basketball game, and the first women's college game played in Madison Square Garden.

RIVALRY

If Philadelphia Sports has excelled in one area it has been that they've had some of the best rivalries in sports. What makes these rivalries special is that the opponents usually have just as many similarities as differences. For example, the Dallas Cowboys and Washington Redskins have had great football contests but the cities themselves couldn't be more different.

The '76ers/Celtics rivalry is based on two cities, Philadelphia and Boston, that are both old northern cities, both are NOT New York, both were established on religious foundations (Penn's Holy Experiment and Boston's Puritanism). The first level of rivalry was between two centers – Wilt Chamberlain and Bill Russell. The second level was between two forwards – Julius Erving and Larry Bird. The most recent rivalry was focused between two guards – Allen Iverson and Paul Pierce.

The Celtics won most of the playoff match-ups, though the 1967 Seventy-Sixer team with Wali Jones, Hal Greer, Chet Walker, Lucius Jackson, Chamberlain, and 6th Man – Billy Cunningham – is considered one of the best NBA teams ever.

Ditto the rivalry between the Julius Erving led teams against the Larry Bird teams in the 1970s and early '80s. While the Sixers lost the match-up more often than not, the 1983 championship team with Maurice Cheeks, Andrew Toney, Erving, Moses Malone, Bobby Jones, and 6th Man Clint Richardson is also considered one of the best NBA teams ever with the arguable exception of the '67 team. [Maybe it takes overly-talented individuals to beat a team that plays true team ball?]

Penn and Princeton have competed for over a century in a variety of sports. Both are near each other, both since 1955 are members of the Ivy League. Both claim to be the better school. The rivalry really began when Princeton, with Bill Bradley, became a national power. Penn, which had been quiet in Ivy League sports (they disbanded their national football program to join the Ivy League) wanted to keep pace with Princeton and ever since the Penn/Princeton games have almost always determined who wins the Ivy League basketball title.

Army/Navy is the premier college football rivalry in the country between two branches of the national services. While neither team is located in Philadelphia, Philadelphia, for most years of the rivalry, has been the natural host to the teams because of its central location.

Frazier/Ali: As the article on Joe Frazier summarizes, the three fights between these two greats was one of boxing's best rivalries. It was between two African-Americans who both won Olympic Gold.

Holy War: Of all the rivalries in the Big Five, the most intense has been the one between two Catholic Schools, one Augustinian and one Jesuit; between two suburban schools; between two academically similar schools, St. Joseph's and Villanova.

Tilden/The Four Musketeers: The Digby Baltzell piece explains why this rivalry may have been the best. After all, it took four Frenchmen to beat one American and after the French won in America they built one of the best arenas in the world, the clay of Roland Garros, to make sure they could beat "Big Beel" in France.

Giants/Eagles: Begin with Chuck Bednarik's hit on Frank Gifford, run through the fumble in the Meadowlands, and end with a few nail biting seasons in which the Eagles and the Giants games determined the division winner. Add in that Philadelphians love to beat New York and New York expects to beat Philadelphia and you have a prescription for a great Northeastern rivalry. Eagles fans love to beat the Dallas Cowboys. They consider them –well, pretentious – America's team and all that. But the Cowboys consider the Redskins their rival, so the Giants and Eagles gets the nod for best pro-football rivalry.

In other sports, the rivalries aren't as intense. Philadelphia is more like St. Louis, Chicago, and Pittsburgh than the baseball cities of Atlanta and Montreal and Miami Gardens. The Mets and Phillies have rarely been good at the same time until recently. In hockey the rivalries with New York and Pittsburgh and New Jersey have rarely been competitive. The Flyers and the New Jersey Devils often compete for the division lead, though the rivalry in the past decade has been rather one-sided with the Devils bedeviling the Flyers and winning a number of Stanley Cups. The Flyers did win their division in 2004.

PHILADELPHIA
SPORTS FAN

Philadelphia fans. Long suffering. Boo-Birds. Knowledgeable. Passionate. Rowdy. Unlike any other city the adjectives about Philadelphia fans roll off the tongue. Sports books have even been written about the famous/even notorious Philadelphia fan. Glen Macnow and Anthony L. Gargano, in *The Great Philadelphia Fan Book*, explain the phenomenon.

Any mention of the "Philadelphia fan" seems to begin with an episode in 1968 where the fans booed Santa Claus at an Eagles game. Setting the stage, they explain how the 1960 Championship Eagles team had been dismantled. Sonny Jurgenson was traded to the Redskins for Norm Snead by "Joe must go" coach Kuharich. By 1968 they were a woeful 2-12. When a Christmas halftime pageant had to be cancelled because of snow a nineteen-year-old recruit was found in the stands. When he jogged onto the field between two columns of cheerleaders the fans took out their frustrations on the team, the coach, and the owner, Jerry Wolman. A few fans did boo. Other episodes have worked in their favor. The most notable was the hooting of Dodger Burt Hooton in a crucial playoff moment against the Phillies. Hooton succumbed to the hooting and walked his batter.

Joe Queenan's *True Believers, The Tragic Lives of Sports Fans* is another look at Philadelphia's heartache over its failure to win its proper share of championships. Angelo Cataldi and Mr. Macnow teamed up to write *The Great Philadelphia Sports Debate* – the pro and con sides of fifty great Philadelphia sports questions.

The passion of the Philadelphia fan is the reason behind the success of WIP's sports radio show (see the humor section) and Comcast's live television sports talk show in which Michael Barkann brings newspaper columnists and sports figures into the fan's home for a daily roundtable. The Eagles' Post Game Live, for football, includes Philadelphia's number one sports fan – the Governor and former Mayor – Ed Rendell, whose commentary is on a par with long time NFL and Eagles sportswriter Ray Didinger and former Eagle player Vaughn Hebron.

BEST TEAMS

Like the players, there are just too many great teams to review in a short chapter on sports. What does make Philadelphia unique is that among the teams that have won championships are some of the very best in all of their respective sport.

NBA Teams

The 1967 Seventy-Sixers included Wilt Chamberlain, Luke Jackson, Hal Greer, and sixth-man Billy Cunningham. The '83 Sixers had Julius Erving, Moses Malone, Bobby Jones, Andrew Toney, and Maurice Cheeks and were coached by Billy Cunningham. The 1967 team finally beat the Boston Celtics to win the East and ultimately the NBA Championship. The 1983 team nearly swept the playoffs as Moses Malone's prediction of a fo', fo' fo', sweep nearly came true. The 76ers swept the Lakers in the finals and only lost one game to the Milwaukee Bucks.

Philadelphia SPHAS

Of all the Philadelphia Pro Teams, the one that had the most success was the early basketball team called the SPHAS, which stood for South Philadelphia Hebrew Association. The SPHAS played in local leagues, the Eastern Basketball League and later the early American Basketball League. Their team was formed by Eddie Gottlieb, Harry Passon, and Hugie Black. The team was composed of primarily Jewish ballplayers and won the ABL 7 times between 1933 and 1946. It defeated the Original Celtics and the New York Rens for the first basketball world championship.

Gottlieb, by the late 1940s, was involved in the formation of the first NBA franchise in Philadelphia – the Philadelphia Warriors. Before the age of computers, Gottlieb was the sole schedule-maker of the NBA for thirty years.

The SPHAS were sold to Red Klotz in 1950. Klotz changed the name of the team to the Washington Generals. The Generals became the favorite foil for the Harlem Globetrotters.[28] One of their players for a short time was Wilt Chamberlain.

1974-1975 Philadelphia Flyers

After decades of losses, after the 1964 collapse, after the Eagles trading Sonny Jurgenson to the Redskins, and losing so much that chants of "Joe must go" led to the firing of their coach, Joe Kuharich, and seeing the 76ers unable to score – the unexpected wins by the Philadelphia Flyers in 1974 and '75 lifted the city. For the record, the Flyers beat both the Boston Bruins and then the Buffalo Sabers. The Flyers squads included Hall of Famers, Bobby Clarke, Bill Barber, and Bernie Parent. Even those who never played hockey, never watched hockey, and didn't even know how to skate were warmed by the Flyers win. It gave Philadelphians hope and led to the success of all the other teams so that in 1980 all four professional teams played for the Championship.[29]

1980

In 1980 all four professional teams made the Championship Finals. It was the first time in the history of sports that four finalists came from one city. The Philadelphia Seventy-Sixers were led by Julius Erving and George McGinnis. They lost to Jack Ramsay's Portland Trailblazers led by Bill Walton. The Philadelphia Eagles probably were flat after beaching their arch-enemy the Dallas Cowboys. They were led by Ron Jaworski and coached by Dick Vermeil and won the NFC Championship. They lost the Super Bowl to Oakland. The Philadelphia Flyers lost to the New York Islanders 4-2.

1980 Phillies

After years of coming close in the mid-1970s, the Phillies pulled it all together for their first and only World Series win to that point in 1980. Mike Schmidt's home run helped defeat the Montreal Expos to clinch a regular season win. The team was helped by the verbal leadership of their skipper Dallas Green. In the playoffs the five games against the House Astros were some of the most amazing ever. Game four saw a triple play that was a double play then a single out and finally a double play. Runners were caught going to home too soon. The fifth game saw the Phillies rally against Nolan Ryan who almost never gave up a lead in the late innings.

Sparked by the solid play of veterans like Manny Trillo, Bake McBride, Bob Boone, and Gary Maddox along with the play of their stars, Mike Schmidt, Steve Carlton, and Tug McGraw, the 1980 Phillies won the first two games against George Brett's Kansas City Royals, lost the next two, and rallied in the fifth leading to the clincher in the sixth. Every player seemed to play at or above his potential. Along with the play by play of Legends, Harry Kalas and ex-Phillies legend Richie Ashburn, the season has been etched into the memories of Phillies fans for years. Perhaps the icing on the cake was when ex-New York Met Tug McGraw said in his speech at the parade that New York could stick it (a reference to the New York Media which somehow couldn't believe that the Yankees or Mets weren't in the Series) because the Phillies were Number One.

2008 Phillies

After twenty-five years without a professional championship in Philadelphia in the four major professional sports, the 2008 Philadelphia Phillies put together a championship season.

In June the team swooned against the American League Competition. But with Ryan Howard getting hot in September, with reliever Brad Lidge being perfect in save chances (as he would be in the postseason), with steady pitching by their Ace, Cole Hamels, and with the return of Brett Myers from a minor league stint the Phillies surged in September and continued that surge through October. They beat the Milwaukee Brewers, Los Angeles Dodgers, and Tampa Ray Devil Rays in succession – losing only one game in each series to take the World Series home to Philadelphia – in a heart-warming parade.

Perfection St. Joe's 2003-2004

St. Joseph's finished the regular season with a record of 27-0, the only time a Big Five team has gone undefeated in the regular season except for the 1970-'71 Penn squad led by Bilsky and Wohl. St. Joseph's finished the regular season ranked number one in the country, the only time a Big Five team has done that since the Temple 1988 team led by Mark Macon

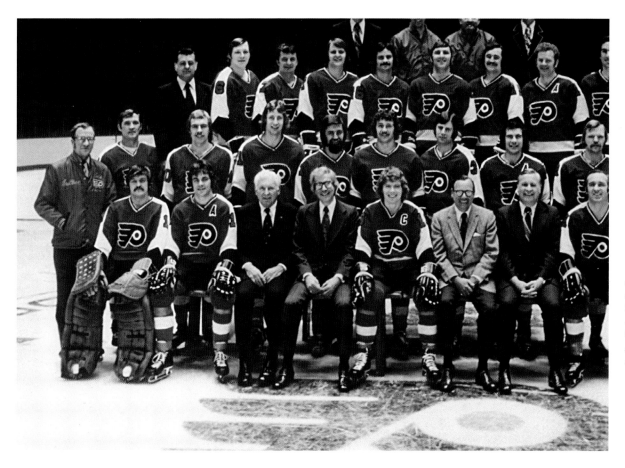

Philadelphia Flyers – Stanley Cup Winners 1973-1974. Courtesy of Philadelphia Flyers

St. Joseph's did it with the best backcourt (Jameer Nelson – the National Player of the Year and Delonte West) in the nation in years. They did it with five players who could shoot 3 pointers. Pat Caroll, Tyrone Barley, and Chet Stachitas and the two guards. They did it with pressure defense and speed and making the extra pass. They did it even though they rarely passed the ball into the post/middle to their big men John Bryant and Dwayne Jones who specialized on defense. They did it with the best mascot in sports – The St. Joe Hawk – who never stops flapping his/her wings. They did it with the beautiful coaching of Phil Martelli, the Coach of the Year.

Even though St. Joe's is one of the smaller schools in the country, they were the talk of the nation. When they lost their first game to Conference rival Xavier, the basketball elites turned on them. When broadcaster Billy Packer said they weren't really good enough to play with the big football-oriented schools or with the storied Atlantic Coast Conference, Coach Martelli and his team took offense. In three great games, two wins against Bobby Knight's team and Wake Forest and a down to the wire loss to Oklahoma State, the Hawks proved not only that they could play with anyone in the country, but that they were the most fun team to watch. Why even Temple's Bill Cosby was seen wearing a St. Joe's hat and Penn alumni Governor Ed Rendell was seen standing next to the president of St. Joseph's University cheering every Hawk shot made. The Final Four, for 2004, was anticlimactic. Some team won. It really didn't matter. The most exciting team to watch, the team of the year had already played.

1929 Athletics

"The 1929 Philadelphia A's, not the '27 Yankees, may have been the greatest baseball club ever." The above statement is no mirage. The A's, under Connie Mack, won the Series in 1929 and '30. They lost the Series in '31 and still won 91 games in '32 when Mack started to dismantle the team. The '29 A's included four Hall of Famers, first basemen Jimmie Foxx, center fielder Al Simmons, catcher Mickey Cochrane, and starting pitcher Lefty Grove. Connie Mack is also in the Hall of Fame.[30]

The 1929 A's team went 100-50 in the regular season. Their ace was Lefty Grove, who led the league in strikeouts. Two other star pitchers were Rube Walberg and George Earnshaw. Earnshaw won the most games – 24. "Despite these three great pitchers, Connie Mack started Howard Ehmke in game one against the Cubs. Ehmke was thirty-five years old and hadn't pitched in weeks, but Ehmke struck out 13 and won the opener 3-1. In game four the A's were losing 8-0, in the bottom of the seventh. But the A's came back with ten runs in the bottom of the seventh and Lefty Grove came in – in relief, and tossed two shutout innings to seal the win. In game five they were losing 2-0 in the bottom of the ninth with one out but Max Bishop hit a single, Mule Haas a two run homer, Cochrane grounded out, Simmons doubled, Foxx was intentionally walked, and Bing Miller hit a double off the scoreboard to seal the win and the Championship."[31]

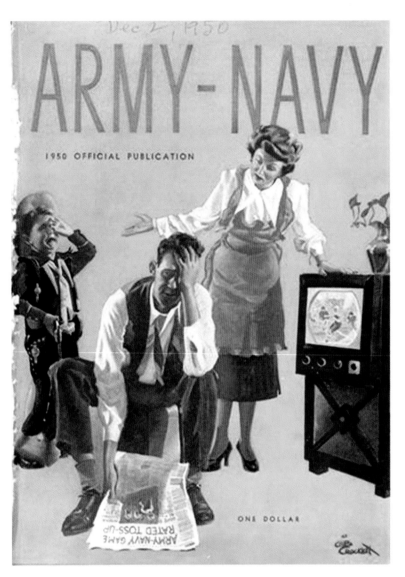

Army Navy Cover (1950). Courtesy of United States Naval Academy

BEST GAMES

Trying to pick the best games often depends on one's favorite sport. For those who claim to like all sports the following games are ranked by the author in order of their claim to Philadelphia fame, keeping in mind the level of competition of the game, the upset value, the intensity, and all the things that make sport interesting.

1. Georgetown – Villanova: The 1985 Championship game, won by Villanova 66-64, was the culmination of a magnificent run by Coach Rollie Massimino's Wildcats. During the year the team had a number of losses and barely was selected to make it to the NCAA tournament. They were underdogs in virtually every playoff game they played but managed to upset Dayton, Maryland, Michigan, and Memphis State in succession. The Georgetown team they faced in the finals was a prohibitive favorite, having beaten Villanova twice earlier in the season, having won the title the year before, and having one of the best players in the game in center Patrick Ewing. Villanova played the game of its basketball life, shooting 90% in the second half. With the inspired play of Ed Pinckney, the shooting of Dwayne McLain and Harold Jensen, the rebounding of Harold Pressley, and the passing of Gary McLain, Villanova pulled off one of the biggest upsets in sports history to give Philadelphia it's first NCAA men's basketball championship since Tom Gola led the LaSalle Explorers in 1954 past Bradley.

Villanova shot close to 80% for the game, 9-10 in the second half, against a Georgetown team that prided itself on defense. In an up and back game Harold Jensen hit a two pointer (there were no three point shots back then) to put Villanova ahead for good. Ewing was bested by Ed Pinckney and Dwayne McClain hit jumpers from every angle possible.

2. The 2008 World Series clincher that spread over three days: It has a been a fundamental tenet of Philadelphia sports that it is tinged with the bizarre. The World Series clincher was remarkable in that the bizarre (calling the game after Tampa Bay scored the tying run in an inning that should have been called off) did happen – but with the "Rich and Fruity climax" of which Red Smith wrote about in 1950. The second half of the game was played in sunshine with the remarkable play of Chase Utley's deking a Tampa Ray runner into going for home and then throwing him out at home. The win occurred in a warm sunshine that continued through the home team parade. While it is easy for people to forget individual plays no Phillies fan will forget that the game stretched over three days making the 2008 championship unforgettable.

3. Any 1980 Philles/Astros playoff game: If Pete Rose's miracle catch was the highlight of the 1980 World Series, the prelude was certainly the best divisional playoff series ever. Each game was a nail biter. Each game came down to the last at bat. Games 2-5 went extra innings. Games 4 and 5 had some of the most bewildering, "I can't watch anymore" plays ever. Game 4 had the single that was a double play that was a triple play that was then a double play and several runners being called for leaving the base before the fielder caught the ball. Game 5 had a comeback against Nolan Ryan, the most feared pitcher of his day, in the top of the eighth inning, which was started by a bunt and then followed by a couple of seeing-eye hits, followed by an Astros rally in the bottom of the ninth followed by another rally by the Phillies in extra innings only to end when a starting pitcher, Dick Ruthven, in relief, got the last out.

4. Any Joe Frazier/Muhammad Ali Fight: Pick your fight. The first fight was Ali's first test for the championship after he had been suspended (the suspension was overturned by the U.S. Supreme Court). Frazier floored Ali, something unheard of prior to then. Ali would go on to win the next two fights, which went the limit, winning the rubber game in the famous "Thrilla in Manilla"

5. Flyers vs. Russia: Though they won two championships in 1974 and 1975, the Flyers biggest victory may have occurred on January 11, 1976, when the Flyers bested one of two Russian teams barnstorming the country. Undefeated going into the game, the Red Army team lost 4-1, pulling its team from the ice when the going got a little too rough for them. The inspiration for the game was a Flyer standard-bearer during their glory years – Kate Smith's rendition of "God Bless America."

6. Chicago Cardinals Championship game: Won by the Eagles 7-0 in a game that was played in a blizzard.

7. The 1950 Army/Navy Game: Considered one of the greatest upsets ever, Navy beat Army 14-2. Army hadn't lost in 28 straight games and was ranked No. 2 in the nation.... Navy, meanwhile, had won only two of eight games and hadn't beaten Army since 1943. In the previous year, Navy suffered a 38-0 shellacking from Army, its worst in the fifty-one-year history of the series. With Army a solid three touchdown favorite, Navy's rookie coach, Eddie Erdelatz, was pitted against Army's legendary Earl "Red" Blaik, who publicly proclaimed that his team should be ranked number one. From the opening kickoff, Navy stunned Army, Army fumbled five times, and was intercepted five times. The dominant performer in the game was Bob "Zug" Zastrow, Navy's quarterback, who was in on all 16 points scored. (See the Grif Teller write-up in the Business section for a wonderful painting of the trains for passengers for the Army - Navy game at Municipal Stadium).

8. 1929 A's/Cubs World Series: Game 4 or 5. For the reasons stated in the "team" section.

9. 1950 Phillies/Brooklyn Game: Dick Sisler hit a late inning home run to win the game to secure the pennant in the last game for the Phillies. [See the Red Smith write-up.]

10. 1982 Boston/76ers game 7: Philly wins unexpectedly. Philadelphia went ahead in the series 3-1 only to see Boston rally in Boston and then Philadelphia. The Sixers went to Philadelphia and everyone expected them to lose because of their long tradition of losing series with the Celtics in Sports "Greatest Rivalry." The Sixers unexpectedly won and even Celtic fans were heard to cheer "Beat L.A." at the end of the game. The Sixers didn't win the Championship until the next year.

11. (Tie) Penn/Princeton 1999: Princeton comeback. This game is summarized in the selection on the Palestra.

St. Joe's/Nova 1966 Donchez game winner: By 1966, the Villanova /St. Joe's games had been renamed "the Holy War" because of its fierce intensity and the desire of these nearby schools to prove which one was superior. The St. Joseph's team was ranked and expected to win easily. Villanova, however, played a terrific game, and was ahead most of the game. St. Joseph's won only when Steve Donches, a little used player, put up a miracle shot to win the game in the last seconds.

LaSalle-Bradley: Tom Gola led the Explorers to Philadelphia's lone collegiate championship until the Villanova Wildcats in 1985.

TRIPLE CROWN

Smarty Jones, the "St. Joseph's" of Philadelphia horse racing, outran a horse named Lion Heart to win the Kentucky Derby in 2004. Smarty Jones, from Philadelphia Park, won the next leg of the triple crown, but came in second in the last leg to a horse that won only because he was fresher. The jockey was Stewart Elliott, who won many a race at Philadelphia Park but who had never raced at Churchill Downs before. The trainer, John Servis, also trained horses, including Smarty Jones, at Philadelphia Park. The owners were Roy and Patricia Chapman from Bucks County, Pennsylvania. The horse was bred in Chester County, Pennsylvania.

Afleet Alex, also locally trained, won the Preakness and the Belmont the following year, coming in second in the Kentucky Derby.

Barbaro, owned by nearby Chester County's Roy and Gretchen Johnson, won the 2006 Kentucky Derby. Sadly, his ankle shattered in the next race and he was forced to be euthanized, months later, after a gallant effort to save him.

BEST MOMENTS

1. World Championship Memories

Tug McGraw struck out Willie Wilson with the bases loaded in the bottom of the ninth to give the Phillies their first World Championship in 1980. The vision of McGraw, who sadly passed away from cancer too early, will always be engrained in Phillie fans' minds.

Game 3 of the 2008 World Series started after a rain delay. The game went back and forth. It ended on a dribbler at one-thirty in the morning when Carlos Ruiz, with the bases loaded and one out, made contact – a dribbler down the third base line that allowed Eric Bruntlett to score the winning run.

2. Other Championship Memories

Baseball: Pete Rose's 1980 Series Catch. Prior to 1980, the Phillies history was bleak. They had only managed to reach the World Series twice, in 1915 and 1950. They lost quickly both times. In 1964 they collapsed by losing ten games straight. In the 1970s, they had marvelous talent but lost to the Cincinnati Reds once and the Los Angeles Dodgers twice. By 1980, fans had given up hope. But one player was added to the team of great talent, Schmidt, Carlton, Boone, McGraw, Maddox, Trillo, Bowa, and other. That was Pete Rose, "Charlie Hustle," who had previously led the Reds teams to several World Series Championships. Rose came to the Phillies for one purpose. The thought was that the Phillies thought too much and they needed someone, with talent, who played on emotion to let them win. They needed someone like Pete Rose, who wouldn't let them lose.

But failure has a way of making a team and its city of supporters fatalistic. Even though the Phillies beat the Astros in five marvelous games and even though they had a 3-2 lead (thanks, in part, to another moment, the near beaning of Kansas City's George Brett in game five), game six saw the Phillies collapsing again. Their 4-0 lead was cut to 4-1 and the Royals had the bases loaded in the bottom of the ninth. When Bob Boone dropped a one-out foul ball the heart of every Philadelphian ached "there they go again." But before the ache could have time to settle, there was Pete Rose catching Boone's bobble before it hit the ground. Rose had, by that one catch, refused to let the Phillies lose. Tug McGraw would make the last out, striking out Willie Wilson, but every Philadelphian who has watched the Phillies knows that Rose, despite his subsequent failures, had saved the day, the year, the century, and the lifeblood of the Phillies with that one remarkable, "how did he know to be there" catch.

As described in the Team section, Bing Miller hit a double off the scoreboard to win the 1929 Series for Connie Mack's Athletics.

Basketball: The Seventy-Sixers came close numerous times between 1967 and 1983, always losing out, mostly to Boston and Los Angeles. The smile on guard Maurice Cheeks (who would later coach the Seventy-Sixers) as his team sealed a 'fo, five', 'fo sweep of the NBA erased all the pain of the previous years.

Football: Bednarik sits on Taylor to preserve the Championship. An alternative number two would be Bednarik's hit on Frank Gifford to preserve an upset win in a key game over the Giants. See Bill Lyon's writing on Chuck Bednarik above for both plays.

Hockey: Rick MacLeish scored the most important goal in Flyers history, a game-winning goal in Game 6 of the 1974 Stanley Cup Finals against the Boston Bruins. It gave the Flyers a 1-0 win and their first championship.

3. Playoff Memories

Baseball: "Whoomp! There it is." It was the catch-phrase that ignited the 1993 Phillies to a game 6 against the defending World Champion Toronto Blue Jays. In 2008, Brett Meyers coaxed a walk out of C.C. Sabathia (the Milwaukee Brewers and maybe the league's number one pitcher) from an 0-2 count after fouling off numerous pitches. It set the tone for the playoffs.

Basketball: Julius Ervings' Dunk around the World – In an NBA final against the Los Angeles Lakers, Julius Erving couldn't dunk over one of the NBA players, so he did the next best thing. The move was described by Gary Smith in his column, "Doc Leaves 'Em Dumbstruck:" "Erving faced four obstacles to the basket – 3 Lakers, Landsberger, Jabaar, and Chones, and the end line. Erving went up, around the three men, around the backboard, 'Reached from behind the backboard, reached from out of bounds, reached around the flailing snake arms of Abdul-Jabbar and Chones and flicked it up with impossible perfect English off the glass,…, and in…' Julius, with typical modesty, called it a nice reverse lay-up. Smith said that's like calling 'Kilimanjaro' a goose bump."

Football: Four Philadelphia teams made it to the World Championship. The one that was perhaps the biggest surprise was the football Eagles. The Eagles were good but Tom Landry's Dallas Cowboys always seemed to win the big game. But in 1980 with Ron Jaworksi at quarterback and Harold Carmichael out-leaping all defenders the Eagles made it to the championship game at home. Wilburt Montgomery, running with a bad knee, broke the game open with his cut-back against the grain running totaling close to 200 yards, His runs included a 42 yard scamper on the Eagles first possession to set the tone for the day.

"First down Freddy" Mitchell snared a Donovan McNabb 4th and 26 pass for a crucial catch leading to a field goal by the Eagles to tie the 2003 divisional playoff game against the Green Bay Packers. The Eagles won the game in overtime. Chad Lewis' great "Catch" in the End Zone helped Philadelphia beat Atlanta and launch the Eagles into the 2005 Super Bowl against New England. It was the first championship win for Coach Andy Reid, whose three prior teams had lost in the NFC championship.[32]

Hockey: Flyers beat Pittsburgh in five overtimes. This "longest game in NHL history" with the Penguins helped send the Flyers into the Eastern conference championship against the New Jersey Devils. John LeClair and Mark Recchi scored goals in the 2-1 victory.[33]

4. Regular Season Moments

Baseball: Jim Bunning's Perfect Game. Jim Bunning pitched his first no-hitter for the Detroit Tigers in 1958. His second no-hitter was even better. It was a perfect game on June 21, 1964, against the New York Mets on Father's Day. It was the first perfect game in the National League for 84 years. Bunning and the country knew it was really big when he was invited to appear on New York's Ed Sullivan show.

Basketball: Wilt's 100. On March 2, 1962, in Hershey, Pennsylvania, the Philadelphia Warriors beat the New York Knicks 169-147. The story, though, was how Wilt Chamberlain shattered the previous one-game scoring record by scoring 100 points in a game. A notoriously poor free three shooter – Chamberlain made 28 of 32 free throw attempts to match his 36 field goals (when field goals were only 2 points). He set or tied nine records in the game. Chamberlain played on the 1966-67 Seventy-Sixers teams which is considered perhaps the best ever. His epic battles with Boston Celtic Bill Russell were legendary. But he will always be remembered for doing what no other NBA player could do – score 100 points.

A Football Miracle: The Miracle of the Meadowlands. All Joe Piscarcik of the Giants had to do was hold on to the ball and kneel to the ground. Instead, he tried a handoff that Herman Edwards of the Eagles recovered when the Giant's running back couldn't hold on to the handoff. Edwards recovered in the End Zone and the Eagles won a game everyone thought they had lost. The call by Eagles announcer Merrill Reese repeatedly exclaimed "I don't believe it, I don't believe it!"

Jack Kelly wins the Olympics: See the section on Grace Kelly in the film chapter.

Hockey: December 22, 1985, the Flyers, under the leadership of goalie Pelle Lindbergh, extend their record breaking unbeaten streak to 35 games. Lindbergh would lead the Flyers to the Stanley Cup Flyers against the Edmonton Oilers. Tragically, Lindbergh would die in a car accident before the next season.

Other sports: According to the artist and architect Alfred Bendiner (see the art section), Philadelphia was famous for its fights at the "Arena." One noted boxing enthusiast was Dr. J. William White, a noted society surgeon who was always eager to "put up his dukes." "Legend has it that he was once seated in the audience in a New York arena when the announcer announced with a sneer that the next bout was forfeited because the fighter from Philadelphia hadn't shown up. Dr. White arose and climbed into the ring, took off his Prince Albert coat but not his white vest, took off his starched cuffs and adjusted the boxing gloves, walked to the center of the ring and with a single blow knocked cold the New Yorker, thereby upholding the honor and name of Philadelphia."[34]

Phillies 2008 Celebration by Derek Johnson. (baseballderekthirteen@yahoo.com) Courtesy of Derek Johnson

PHILADELPHIA FOOD

Book cover from
the *Frög Commissary
Cookbook by Steven Poser,
Anne Clark, and Becky
Ruller. (Philadelphia
Camino Books, Inc.,
2002). Courtesy of
Camino Books*

Commissary Cookbook Cover

The Philadelphia Food Renaissance

*"The experiment of mixing heretofore
unmixed flavors that [Steve] Poses began
at Frög [his storefront restaurant where
Maxine Keyser states the Philadelphia
Food Renaissance began], captured the
attention of Philadelphians and let loose
a chain reaction of innovative eating
establishments that cropped up all over
the city."*

Maxine Keyser
Food Critic

PHILADELPHIA FOOD

PHILADELPHIA FOOD

NOTABLE STYLES
Something for Everyone
Mixing Up all the Styles
Neighborhood Restaurants

CONTENTS

PHILADELPHIA FOOD

Ben Franklin arrived in Philadelphia with three cents to his name. Legend has it, believed now to be true, that he spent the money on three loaves of bread (the original finger food). He would never run out of money or food thereafter.

Legend has it, now believed to be false, that George Washington, who made part of his living selling shad, survived at Valley Forge in the winter of 1778 when shad swam up the Schuylkill during a warm spell, saving the soldiers from famine.

Philadelphia, like many eastern seaport cities, has been and still is noted for its seafood. Boston may have their chowder, Baltimore their terrapins, but Philadelphia seafood and Philadelphia pepper pot are best served in Philadelphia. For decades everyone, in and out of town, ate at John Taxin's Bookbinders, where lobsters and shad and scallops and other fish adorned the plate and satisfied the palate.

Apples and Roses, Oil, 24 x 32 inches, by Frank Trefny. Courtesy of Gross McCleaf Gallery

According to John Lukacs, Philadelphia families used to dine at four. Many of the men cooked. Standard items on some of the more patrician tables and the working families were "chicken salad and fried oysters, oyster croquettes, fresh shad and shad roe, soft-shell crabs, Philadelphia ice cream, cream cheese, cinnamon buns, terrapin, snapper soup and scrapple." It was considered vulgar to entertain in a hotel, and you gave a ball at your own house.[1]

The famous caterer in the 1900s (early) was Augustine, a black man, with an impressive establishment on Fifteenth Street.

Philadelphia has a variety of foods named after it: Philadelphia soft pretzels, Philadelphia cheesesteaks and pizza-steaks, and Philadelphia TastyKakes. The list goes on and on even if Philadelphia can't legitimately claim Philadelphia Cream Cheese (made by Kraft foods out of New York).

Philadelphia is also known for its neighborhood food—South Philly Italian, Chinese from Chinatown, the Club House Diner, "Everyone eats at Melrose."

Two Markets—the Italian Market, in South Philadelphia, and Reading Terminal Market, in Center City—combine the fun of shopping for the ingredients with really good eating.

If you can't find your food in the markets, there's a chance that some of the dishes on your table include food from local manufacturers such as Campbell's Soups, Kennett Square mushrooms, and Whitman chocolates.

The Philadelphia Food Renaissance, a new seasoning mix of neighborhood cuisines that put Philadelphia on the national food map, took advantage of its willingness to share to experiment across different cultures—different types of foods. A second Food Renaissance added more attention to the décor and surroundings as well as the food.

George Perrier's Le Bec Fin was one of a dozen five star restaurants. There are plenty of four star places and many places with upscale and international tastes.

If expensive French desserts from Perrier's places aren't your fare – then Philadelphia dessert is often either water ice or some old fashioned Philadelphia ice cream.

Philadelphia food: Whether you're from the local neighborhood or out of state, there's plenty to make one's dining experience savory, yet satisfying. Whether it's eating at home or dining out – there's nothing like Philadelphia cooking.

Oranges and April Tulips, Gaouche, 25 x 19 inches, by Frank Trefny. Courtesy of Gross McCleaf Gallery

COOKBOOKS AND RECIPES

"Recipe" is a perfect choice of word to describe the unique marriage of the two ingredients for preparing food:

The scientific formula of cooking, the nouns boullebaise, jambalaya, say which ingredients to have, how many, and what order to prepare them. The verbs: sauté, flambé, remouillee, etc. and the adjectives: a touch, a pinch, a smattering, etc. are the "art" of cooking. The combination of the three provides the verbal lesson of how to prepare a dish.

Philadelphia cooking as Mary Anne Hines, Gordon Marshall, and William Woys Weaver wrote in *The Larder Invaded, Three Centuries of Philadelphia Food & Drink*, has cultivated a unique combination of recipes.[2]

Decaf, Oil on Board, 27 x 31 inches, by Bertha Leonard. Courtesy of Gross McCleaf Gallery

I'll Get the Tip, Oil on Board, 28 x 24 inches, by Bertha Leonard. Courtesy of Gross McCleaf Gallery

Old Time Recipes

Thirty-five receipts from the "Larder Invaded" includes some of Philadelphia's best known dishes, including fried oysters[3] and such greatly named dishes as:

◊ Gooseberry Marmalade
◊ Fricasse of Pigeon, the Italian Way
◊ Whipped Syllabub – the precursor to the ice cream soda
◊ Dredging Mixture of Roast Mutton
◊ Bobotje – African "cured minced meat"
◊ Rosucrucian Chili

Others recipes like Philadelphia pepper pot, Philadelphia snapper, and Philadelphia scrapple are discussed throughout this chapter.

Some well known Philadelphia cookbooks include the recipes of Sarah Tyson Rorer, who was a leader in explaining cooking. Her *Philadelphia Cook Book* was a classic of her day.

Sarah Hale wrote numerous cookbooks and was one of the advocates for making Thanksgiving a national holiday. Elze Leshie and Elizabeth Pennell also wrote and collected cookbooks. James W. Parkinson's *Confectionaire's Journal* was the first American culinary journal.

One of the most popular cookbooks was the *Frog's Commissary Cookbook* mentioned above. Other notable cookbooks include the *White Dog Café Cookbook* by Judy Wicks and the *Rittenhouse Cookbook*, which includes recipes from the Rittenhouse Hotel.

The Original Philadelphia Neighborhood Cookbook by Irina Smith and Ann Hazan presents the many tastes of over fifty Philadelphia neighborhoods. Other compilations include recipes from the Main Line, and from The Italian Market. They also compiled a *Reading Terminal Cookbook*.

The Book and the Cook is a recent Philadelphia tradition where local restaurants come together once a year for about ten days to serve food, display there cookbooks, and to serve the community by providing master classes, cooking demonstrations, culinary festivals, and health classes.

In the spirit of Penn and Franklin, the variety of restaurants in Philadelphia now come together, not only for the Book and the Cook, but for several new ventures.

Philly Cooks!™ is a competition where the local chefs compete for the best appetizer, the best entrée, and the best desert at a site open to the public in January. Later in January many of the city's restaurants have a weekend where their food can be tried for a flat rate ($30 in 2005).

Reviews

There are almost as many reviews of Philadelphia restaurants as there are Philadelphia cookbooks.

Each year, for the past few decades, *Philadelphia Magazine* has profiled the best places to eat in and around the city (as well as the best in a whole host of other categories). Other issues of the magazine review current trends, review restaurants old and new, show who's involved in the restaurant scene, and even discuss the latest in kitchen tools. Many newspapers have their own food critics. Maxine Keyser writes for the *City Paper* and Craig LaBan is the current ace reviewer for *The Philadelphia Inquirer*. His latest book is *Savoring Philadelphia*.

Shopping at Giordanis, oil on canvas, 36" x 48", © 2002 (private collection) by Elaine Moynihan Lisle. Courtesy of Elaine Moynihan Lisle

MARKETS

Italian Market 9th Street

In the 1800s many immigrants, Italians, Jews, blacks, and others, began to settle in South Philadelphia between Fourth and Eleventh Streets. They all lived side by side.

Many of the Italians were attracted to the neighborhood Parishes. Early on the Italians, like their Jewish neighbors, tried to serve meals that reminded them of their home-countries. Jews served Bett Zigerman Zolfstein's cabbage soup, borscht, and brisket. Italians looked to C. Antonio Marano who imported food from Italy and other sites. Marano purchased the old piano factory of John Wanamaker's at Eleventh and Christian Streets and began The Philadelphia Macaroni Company. In addition to serving the locals, Marano's Macaroni products were used for the alphabet soup in the nearby Campbell's factory as well as in Franco-American Spaghetti-O's.

The Italian cuisine in South Philadelphia has roots in Naples and Salerno, which liked "lots of tomato sauce with the consistency of a gravy." Marono was from Naples. Frank Palumbo ran a catering business for special parties, including the likes of Frank Sinatra.

From 1900 through 1930, the Italian Market's main address was the 800 block of Christian Street. During this time the importing of Italian products to South Philly became routine. Locally, oils, spices, herbs, and vegetables were home-grown.

Around 1920, maybe earlier, the Italian Market gravitated to South Ninth Street. One of the early notables was Pasquale "Pat" Oliveri who is credited by most with creating the "pizza steak." Other local sandwiches included pepper and eggs, baloney and eggs, any meat with cheese, tomato and lettuce that was "hoagie-like" and roasted pork and beef sandwiches. Some of the local traditions include fire barrels for heat and using the awnings for hanging peppers to dry out.

The Italian market became, and still is, known as a "Mecca for Bargains." It includes today, not only a vast variety of Italian flavors, but the flavors of East European Jews, Latin locals, Caribbean and Continental African Cuisine, Asian, and Lebanese.[3,4]

Reading Terminal Market

12th and Arch Streets

Text reprinted with permission of Reading Terminal Market (source: www.readingterminalmarket. org)

Markets have been a part of Philadelphia's history since the city's development by William Penn in the late seventeenth century. When William Penn's managers established the town of Philadelphia, one of their first actions was to herd the ragtag crowd of farmers, fisherman, and huntsman, who were hawking their goods all over the bustling settlement, into an open area at the foot of what was known as High Street, along the Delaware River. Soon the so-called 'Jersey Market' (because most of the hucksters were from the neighboring state) began to expand westward in the middle of the thoroughfare that had been appropriately named Market Street. With the growth of Philadelphia came the expansion of public markets. By the middle of the nineteenth century, the string of market sheds had become six blocks long, making the easternmost mile of the city's main street a veritable babble of farmers and food purveyors on most days.

Markets Move Indoors

Not long after, open air markets fell out of favor with the general public. They were considered health hazards and nuisances. They also created obstacles for the ever-increasing streetcar traffic. Bowing to complaints of nearby residents, city fathers decreed that the street markets would have to go, and in 1859 summarily dismantled them. It was then that two main markets sprang up at 12th and Market Streets. They were known as the Farmers' Market and the Franklin Market. It would be these two markets that would become the forerunners of what is now Reading Terminal Market.

The Reading Terminal Market is Born

In the 1880s and 1890s great train terminals sprung up in many of the nation's large cities as the Industrial Revolution chugged on and corporate competition grew. One manifestation of this corporate rivalry was architectural braggadocio, a phenomenon in which giant railroads were building magnificent palaces for their passenger trains, their riders, and, most of all, their own corporate images.

In 1889 the Reading Railroad announced it would build a state-of-the-art train shed in Philadelphia at 12th and Market Streets. The new train shed promised to be the biggest of them all, fronted by a splendid pink and white eight story office building. Fortunately, after much debate, it was decided that the markets currently occupying the same location on which the railroad proposed to build its new terminal would be purchased for one million dollars. The markets would be relocated within the new train shed beneath the elevated rail tracks. Reading's new train shed would be different from all others in that it had a gastronomic bazaar tucked away in its cellar. Reading Terminal Market was born.

Reading Terminal Market – The Early Years

Reading Terminal Market opened its doors in 1892. The new Market was approximately 78,000 square feet and held nearly 800 spaces for merchants, each positioned in six foot stalls. The Market was laid out in a grid system similar to the streets of Philadelphia. There were twelve aisles and four avenues. It was the perfect location for easily receiving and shipping goods.

Soon after opening, the new state-of-the-art Reading Terminal Market would boast that its refrigeration facility was by far the biggest in Philadelphia with its half-million cubic feet of space and 52 separate rooms, each cooled to individual temperatures, 15 - 25 degrees for meat and poultry, 34 degrees for fruits and vegetables. The refrigeration system included an array of special pumps, compressors, and other equipment to handle the brine and ammonia used in its operation. When the cold-storage facility reached full stride a few years later, a visitor to its chilly climes would regularly find stored there 200,000 pounds of meat, 50,000 crates of eggs, thousands of cans of cream, 10,000 - 20,000 boxes of poultry, 10,000 barrels of berries and cherries, 25,000 barrels of apples, and 10,000 tons of ice....

As horse-drawn wagons gave way to refrigerated trucks in the years after World War I, the Market was able to improve its earlier attempts at home delivery. The trucks provided service every hour to some 60 suburban towns and resorts along the New Jersey shore.

In November 1931, the Reading Terminal Market and the Merchants' Association jointly celebrated the Market's 40th anniversary with a week-long 'Food and Home Progress Exposition,' which drew tens of thousands of people from all over the region. A proud Reading president, Agnew T. Dice, bragged that the railroad's unique food emporium had won nationwide fame, touting that it was the biggest market in Pennsylvania, and the largest under one roof in the country.

Reading Terminal Market – The Middle Years

The Depression years of the 1930s were difficult for the railroad and the Market alike, but both institutions managed to struggle through the hard times. By the end of the decade, in fact, 10 of the 64 merchants in the Market were among the original stand holders from 1892. During World War II, the Market became a Mecca for Philadelphians seeking relief from the rigors of rationing. Even with the war on, the vendors managed to provide a surprising variety of scarce victuals. Despite labor shortages and other problems brought on by the war, 97 percent of the stalls were occupied even in 1944, the penultimate year of the conflict.... A severe cash shortage and declining freight and passenger traffic finally forced the railroad company into bankruptcy in 1971, after which the Market suffered from almost total inattention from upstairs. In 1976, the Reading ceased to exist as a railroad corporation. But a new Reading Company continued functioning, essentially as a real estate business, with Reading Terminal and the Market as one of its prime assets. Various ideas were discussed by the bankrupt company to dispose of the Market so that it would be easier to sell the Terminal building....

Finally, in the 1980s, the Reading Company appointed a general manager of the Market and slowly but steadily the dismal slide ended and, in fact, the Market began a dramatic turnaround.

Reading Terminal Market Revitalized

In 1985, the train shed above the Market fell silent when the city's commuter-rail system was rerouted to bypass the terminal. After several years of negotiations and false starts, the Pennsylvania Convention Center Authority was created to convert the Reading Terminal into a spectacular entranceway to the new convention center under construction. Philadelphians, with fire in their eyes, immediately demanded assurances that the venerable gustatory jewel under the silent tracks would be part of the rehabilitation plan for the building. It was agreed and construction to revitalize the Market began in the early 1990s.

Reading Terminal Market. Courtesy of Reading Terminal Market Corporation

Reading Terminal Market Today

Today, Reading Terminal Market is once again the gastronomic bazaar that its original planners had envisioned. Many of the historic Market stands survived the reconstruction and are once again filled with local produce, fresh eggs, milk, meats, poultry, seafood, handmade crafts, jewelry, and clothing. The Market is home to 75 merchants, two of whom are descendants of the original stand holders from a century before. On any given day, one can find an eclectic array of fresh baked Amish goods, produce direct from the field, unusual spices, free range meats and poultry, flowers, ethnic foods, and much more. More than one hundred thousand Philadelphians and tourists pass through the Reading Terminal Market every week enjoying its exceptional products, history, and people.

A mix of fruit and vegetables and food items shares space with fashion and plants and everything to make a kitchen fashionable at the Reading Terminal Market.

FINGER FOOD/FUN FOOD
The Philly Cheesesteak

Arguments abound as to which is the best finger food – soft pretzels, TastyKakes, or what many claim to be the original Philadelphia food – cheesesteaks. Of course, originally, they were called pizza steaks because they were topped by a pizza sauce, but the classic Philadelphia version is the cheesesteak. The debate rages over which is the best place to get a cheesesteak. Some say Pat's in South Philadelphia. Others say Geno's, also located in South Philadelphia. Both on Passyunk Avenue. Both stay open all night. Jim's Steaks on South Street claims it has the best. Others say Dallessandro's in Roxborough. To settle this argument for yourself, you will just have to try cheesesteaks from each of these establishments … repeatedly.

South Philadelphians claim to be the original inventors, back in the 1930s.

Most will agree though on the requirements:

"Real cheesesteaks are cooked fresh, covered with American cheese, provolone or Cheese-Whiz and rest in a roll dripping with grease. A proper Philly cheesesteak is made with real beef – fresh, not frozen. It is cooked on a grill using grease. As it is cooked, it should be chopped to bits. You then choose which cheese you prefer and whether you want onions, peppers or other toppings.

When the sandwich is served the juices should drip from your cheesesteak. In order to avoid ruining their clothes, Philadelphians have learned, what is referred to as, the 'Philadelphia Lean', bending forward to eat the cheesesteak, instead of bringing it to your mouth."[5]

A 2002 survey done by Craig Leban and four high school seniors rated the following places tops:

1. John's Roast Pork of Snyder Avenue and Weccacoe St.
2. Tony Luke's Old Philly Style Sandwiches, 39 E Oregon Avenue
3. Chink's Steaks, 6030 Torresdale Ave
4. McNally's H&J Tavern, 8634 Germantown Avenue.[6]

Breafast at Pats, Oil on Canvas, 40" x 40", © 2000 (private collection) by Elaine Moynihan Lisle. Courtesy of Elaine Moynihan Lisle

Pretzel Museum

Soft Pretzels are sold everywhere in Philadelphia – at intersections where lazy drivers can have their pretzels delivered, ball games, train stations, and by street vendors.

"The pretzel is believed to have been invented by an Italian Monk in the sixth century who rewarded church-going youngsters with this doughy bribe. The word pretzel probably descends from the Latin word 'Pretzola', or 'little reward', and evolved into the Italian word 'brachiola' which means 'little arms'. Legend has it that the pretzel represents arms crossed in prayer, and that the three holes represent the Trinity. The pretzel probably traveled to America with the Palantine Germans who were later known as the Pennsylvania Dutch. Not too surprisingly, the German word for pretzel is 'bretzel'.

"A few interesting twists according to the Pretzel Museum:

"Helen Hoff holds the record, twisting 57 pretzels in one minute.
"Pretzels without salt are called baldies.
"An 1859 parade in New Orleans featured a float carrying a pretzel-baking machine.
"An average pretzel has 3.5 grams of fat and 260 calories.
"German kids wear pretzels around their neck for good luck on New Year's. Pretzels top some Christmas trees in Austria."[7]

Philadelphia Scrapple

Scrapple, for the uninitiated, is a fried slice of pork-mush. It was created by the Pennsylvania Dutch (transplanted German frugal farmers who learned to use every part of a hog). The Pennsylvania Dutch reside outside of Philadelphia but Philadelphia has made it home. The term scrapple means just what it sounds like. Made from leftover pig scraps with cornmeal and spices. After the ham, bacon, and chops are cut out, what's left of the pig goes into the making of scrapple.

Hoagie

Text reprinted with permission of Linda Stradley and What's Cooking America at http://whatscookingamerica.net.

Hoagies are built-to-order sandwiches filled with meat and cheese, as well as lettuce, tomatoes, and onions, topped off with a dash of oregano-vinegar dressing on an Italian roll. A true Italian Hoagie is made with Italian ham, prosciutto, salami, and provolone cheese, along with all the works. It was declared the "Official Sandwich of Philadelphia" in 1992.

The Hoagie was originally created in Philadelphia. There are a number of different versions to how the Hoagie got its name, but no matter what version is right (historians cannot seem to agree on the correct version), all agree that it started in Philadelphia or the town's suburbs.

Subcontractors by Bruce Johnson. Courtesy of Bruce Johnson

(1) The most widely accepted story centers on an area of Philadelphia known as Hog Island, which was home to a shipyard during World War I (1914-1918). The Italian immigrants working there would bring giant sandwiches made with cold cuts, spices, oil, lettuce, tomatoes, onions, and peppers for their lunches. These workers were nicknamed "hoggies." Over the years, the name was attached to the sandwiches, but under a different spelling.

(2) Another version on this story says that workers at Hog Island did bring this type of sandwich for lunch, but it was never called a hoagie. The story goes, that one day an Irish worker, who every day carried an American cheese sandwich, looked enviously at

his co-workers' lunches and said; "**If your wife will make me one of those things, I'll buy it from you.**" The man went home and said to his wife "Tomorrow, make two sandwiches, one for me and one for Hogan," his co-worker's name. So everyone started calling the sandwich "hogans," which eventually was shortened to hoagie.

(3) Another version says that hoagies got started in A. DiCostanza's grocery store, when a late-night gambler in an after-hours card game got hungry.

(4) The last story says that during the Depression (1929-1939), out-of-work Philadelphian Al DePalma went to Hog Island near the naval shipyards to find work. When he saw the workers on lunch break eating their giant sandwiches, his first thought was, "**Those fellas look like a bunch of hogs.**" Instead of applying for a job at the shipyard, he opened a luncheonette that served these big sandwiches. He listed them on the menu as "hoggies" named for the hogs he saw during that lunch hour.

During the late 1930s, DePalma joined forces with Buccelli's Bakery and developed the perfect hoagie roll (an eight-inch roll that became the standard for the modern-day hoagie). By World War II, during the 1940s, he turned the back room of his restaurant into a hoagie factory to supply sandwiches to workers at the shipyard. DePalma became know as "The King of Hoggies." At some point after World War II, the "hoggie" became the "hoagie." It is said that because his customers kept calling them hoagies, he changed the name.

SEAFOOD

Philadelphia has for over a century been home to a number of good seafood houses.

Shad

Early in the city's history shad ran along the Schuylkill River. George Washington sold thousands of shad fish commercially.

During his stay at Valley Forge during the winter of 1777-1778, Washington and his men found their supplies in all areas to be running vastly short and they struggled to stay alive.[8] John McPhee in his book, *The Founding Fish*, examined whether the legend of the shad's early run enabling the soldiers to break the famine was true. McPhee's research showed that shad in the spring and salt shad the rest of the year were food staples in the early 1700s. Feuds would arise between various groups trying to catch the fish. One such feud involved Daniel Boone's family. Large fees were paid for good shad fisheries. William Penn, in his negotiations with the Lenape, bargained for the rights to fish on the Schuylkill. Penn's special interests were in the "whales, sturgeon, and shad."

According to McPhee's research, several sources mentioned the early shad run at Valley Forge, including Harry Emerson Wilde's "Valley Forge."

Other investigations by McPhee included checking the weather to see if there were enough warm days for the shad to make their run. McPhee's research makes for a good read. As McPhee points out, there is a "Philadelphia" style to cooking shad that makes the shad to Philadelphia what cod is to Boston."[9-11]

Thomas Eakins noted watercolors include Shad Fishing at Gloucester on the Delaware River.[12]

Today, in the twenty-first century, Lambertville, New Jersey, about twenty-five miles north of Philadelphia along the Delaware, is home to an annual shad festival. Mr. McPhee lives nearby and fishes for shad there often and his written about his efforts for the *New Yorker Magazine*.

Biscuits were a common compliment to seafood.

Bookbinders
125 Walnut Street

Bookbinders claims to have been founded in 1865 by Samuel Bookbinder at 2nd. Street. A relative founded another Bookbinders on 15th Street. Its known for its seafood, including five-pound lobsters and great cuts of meat. The Taxin family took over Bookbinders in 1941. The Taxins encouraged celebrities to eat there. The list of people who have dined at Bookbinders is a who's who. It includes military personnel who ate there during visits for the Army Navy game, U.S. presidents, athletes and famous entertainers. Notables include Joe Dimaggio, Liillian Russell, Richard Nixon Bob Hope and Frank Sinatra, Elizabeth Taylor and Julius Erving. Bookbinders survived the ups and downs of the neighborhood including the building of Society Hill Towers and the Food Distribution Center. It was renovated in 2005. Beth Gillin, Beth, "The World Was Their Oyster," The Philadelphia Inquirer (The (PA) February 24, 2002) Section: Inquirer Magazine Page: 08 and Old Original Bookbinders website (www.bookbinders.biz)

The Sansom Street Oyster House

Begun by the Kellys on Mole Street, the Sansom Street Oyster House was run by the Mink family at 1516 Sansom Street. After the renovation, the Sansom Street Oyster House reopened in the Sprint of 2009.

Shad Fisherman (1890s). Courtesy of Philadelphia Press – Public Domain

Philadelphia Pepper Pot

Supposedly this soup began during the winter of 1777-1778 when Washington's army had to make the best with what was around. More likely, it was originally from West Africa and brought over with the slave trade. It is a direct descendant of "Caribbean callaloo."[13] The main ingredients are honeycomb tripe, onions, potatoes, bay leafs and peppercorns, and a veal or beef bone.

Philadelphia Snapper Soup

This soup was and is a staple of Philadelphia's Bookbinder's Restaurant. Its main ingredients are turtle beef, onions, carrots, celery, beef stock, tomato puree, flour, garlic, corn starch, paprika, flour, and parsley. When hot, the soup is best topped off with a little sherry.

Oyster Eaters.

L. Boilly, Oyster Eaters, Litho, Paris (?), ca. 1825. Courtesy of Historical Society of Pennsylvania

DRINK

KARL LAMPE,
Karl Lampe & Co., Bottlers.

Ale Cartoon. Original from Philadelphians in Cartoons – Public Domain

Of course, what is good food without some delicious drink with which to wash it down? Peter Thompson in his *Rum Punch and the Revolution* book discusses the various types of taverns and their influence on the politics of the city and the nation.[14]

Thompson illustrates that taverns and alehouses were a very democratic institution in early Philadelphia. In the early 1700s, the city had more taverns per capita than even France. Taverns were not only places for drink, but also for food and lodging.

Penn and the Quakers discouraged drunkenness but they were not averse to drink. Franklin, as his *Drunkard's Dictionary* (See the Humor Section) shows, knew all too well the pros and cons of imbibing.

The early taverns were places where all classes of citizen could get together and discuss local news from the *Pennsylvania Gazette* and elsewhere. More importantly, since there was no cable or Internet or TV or radio, the tavern was a place to express and exchange opinions.[15]

It was a place where behavior and the character of individuals could be examined by all the patrons. Toasts were a popular way of making everyone feel equal. But drink also led to telling tall tales, something that was frowned upon.[16]

As time went on in the 1700s, some proprietors tried to target their places to certain classes. One that had some success was William Bradford's Old London Coffeehouse, which served coffee. Bradford's Coffeehouse had a bar on the first floor and a merchant's exchange on the second. The existence of the exchange encouraged people with a few dollars to visit the bar.

As the Revolutionary War approached there was a concern, somewhat like today, that the opinions in the taverns were "planted artfully by incendiaries" and by those in favor of a certain view.

By the time of the Continental Congress, The City Tavern, like Bradford's Coffeehouse, attracted similar people – namely delegates like John Adams. The City Tavern became their tavern for reviewing the workings of the Congress in a more informal setting.

After the war, the times changed. Essays and pamphlets replaced the oratory of the tavern-speakers. Reasoned argument replaced the passionate outburst. Voting was the preferred way to contact leaders, rather than drinking together.[17]

While taverns still exist in Philadelphia, there have been plenty of changes. Oelle's Hotel led the way to other hotels, though many hotels today have their own bars. Diners ate at restaurants that didn't serve alcohol. Leagues like the Union League screened their applicants. Sports bars opened up. True Coffeehouses now exist. As for the level of exchange – well there's always some but it's more targeted to people with the same interests or people who can afford the same tastes. It may be more democratic, but it's less republican than the colony days.

Since the early days, Philadelphia has been best known for its breweries. These included, in the late 1800s, John F. Betz and Son, F. A. Poth Brewing Com., White, Hertz and Co., Alexander Young Company, Moore and Sinnott.[17] In the twentieth century, one of the best known local beers was Ortliebs. But prohibition, then labor wars, then beer wars where national beer-companies out-commercialized local breweries, led to its closure as well as that of many other breweries. "Henry A. Ortlieb, who owns and operates Poor Henry's brewery and restaurant, located at 829 N. American Street, is proud to be a fourth-generation brewmaster and to continue his great-grandfather's legacy. At Poor Henry's, Ortlieb [who reacquired the trademark after the brewery his great-grandfather started closed] operates a seven-barrel pilot brewery for test beers and a 60-barrel brewery for beers to be sold wholesale.[18]

Another popular drink that had roots in Philadelphia was Coca Cola.

The Lenni Lenape Indians named Manayunk. It means "the Drinking place." Anyone who has climbed the hills and ridden them in the annual bike race knows why it was so named.

Two other popular Philadelphia drinks included [Charles E.] Hires Root Beer and "Fish House Punch." The punch drink has been described as a relatively sweet, citrusy concoction that shakes down the throat, then, according to one veteran "can strike as suddenly as lightning and kick like a mule."[19]

Afternoon Tea (2/19/1893).
Original from Philadelphia Press
– Public Domain

EARLY DAYS

Text reprinted with permission of Philadelphia Inquirer
"MEMORIES TO SAVOR PHILADELPHIA'S RESTAURANT RENAISSANCE WAS JUST THAT – A REBIRTH OF THE FINE DINING THE CITY WAS LONG KNOWN FOR." By Craig LaBan, Inquirer Restaurant Critic – Philadelphia Inquirer, The (PA) January 9, 2000.

A mischievous spark lights Sam Bushman's eyes. With slicked-back silver hair and pendulous jowls, the ageless publicity man settles into his chair and smiles. So you want to know the history of restaurants in Philadelphia? How much time do you have? The question unlocks a flood of memory, a river of names forgotten twice over by most but still remembered by a precious few of Bushman's dwindling generation. Benny the Bum's. Shoyer's. Kugler's. Boothby's. Jack Lynch's Walton Roof. The boxers Frankie Bradley and Lew Tendler. All three Kelly's. And Ralph's, which turns a century old this year.

The memories scan wide. There were German restaurants in Olney and Center City – the Schwarzwald Inn, Hoffman House, and Ostendorff's. The Italians were below South. The great oyster houses were near Dock Street. The speakeasies of Prohibition. The grand hotels. The exclusive clubs. And the lesser-known neighborhood restaurants. In West Philadelphia it was Oscar's at 52d and Market Streets and Joe Littleton's at 40th and Lancaster Avenue. Bushman's father, Max, worked as a chef there from 1915 to 1925. And there was Fritz Pflug's Arcadia International Restaurant, a post-repeal nightspot frequented by such performers as Rudy Vallee, Guy Lombardo, and Gene Krupa. In 1936, the Arcadia became Bushman's first restaurant publicity job, and so, even 64 years later, the 85-year-old can't resist a plug: 'It was the city's first big restaurant nightclub with good food'. ..."

A typical first class lunch counter (1893). Original from Philadelphia Press – Public Domain

First Golden Age Of Philadelphia Food

By 1900, the first Golden Age of Philadelphia food had already ended. As food historian William Woys Weaver writes in *The Larder Invaded: Reflections on Three Centuries of Philadelphia Food and Drink*, the period began in the 1790s with the city's tenure as the cosmopolitan capital of a new country. Cut off from the British (no culinary loss there), the city gained a talented new pool of cooks and confectioners, thanks to the French Revolution and the Haitian slave rebellion.

This golden era came to an end in 1895 with the death of James W. Parkinson, "perhaps the greatest American cook," according to Woys Weaver.

The dawn of the new century revealed a city in flux, and its eateries reflected the chasm between very different worlds. Members of the privileged old society were feted at their annual banquets with clear green turtle soup, maraschino punch, and planked shad at exclusive clubs and hotels. At a nine-course Founder's Day meal held at the Union League in 1900, they dined on terrapin, venison, and canvasback duck.

Society catering was still dominated by some of the nineteenth century black catering families such as the Dutrieuilles. But the ubiquitous women who stood on market street corners in the late nineteenth century selling spicy Creole soup with the hawker's cry, "Perpper-ee pot! All hot!" had been replaced by the "hokey-pokey" man, the Italian selling ices and antipasto salads stuffed into torpedo-shaped "Pinafore" rolls, the sandwiches that came to be known as "hoagies."

Immigrant laborers gathered at restaurants for sustenance and the familiar comforts of their homeland. Many arrived at the Washington Avenue docks with the word Palumbo pinned to their coats, speeding their journey to the famed South Philadelphia restaurant of the same name that doubled as a boarding house and entertainment hall.

Ralph's Italian Restaurant began the same way in 1900 on Montrose Street, moving to an old boarding house on South Ninth Street in 1915. The pasta and red gravy menu hasn't changed at all, says fourth-generation family operator James Rubino, and the tile-work floor, rediscovered during renovations in 1993, is preserved as it was when Ralph Dispigno's father, Francesco, moved the family business in.

Down by the Dock Street markets, another immigrant family called Bookbinder – this one Dutch Jewish – had already moved its oyster saloon and restaurant to Walnut Street in 1898. The Bookbinders joined a vibrant oyster trade already thriving at Kugler's (34 S. Broad), Boothby's (13th and Chestnut) and Shoyer's (412 Arch), which was also known for its German pot roast and sweet-and-sour tongue. They were soon to be followed by Snockey's and Kelly's on Mole Street.

The once-great oyster house tradition has nearly withered away. The Bookbinders split into two restaurants in 1935, when founder Samuel Bookbinder's grandson, Sam, married a waitress who wasn't Jewish.

The Mink family bought Kelly's on Mole Street in 1947, and their business has survived in the form of the Sansom Street Oyster House. But like an old-world refugee from the city's redevelopment, Kelly's was pushed aside twice to make way for Center Square and then Liberty Place. As the Sansom Street Oyster House, it still serves the unique Philadelphia combination of chicken salad and fried oysters.

Philadelphia, the city where cast-iron stoves, Mason jars, and ice-cream makers were patented, was on the verge of another industrial innovation: fast food.

The Automat

On June 12, 1902, Joseph Horn and Frank Hardart opened the country's first Automat at 818 Chestnut, where hot coffee (the first drip-filtered brew in town) poured from silvery wall-mounted dolphin heads, and nickels opened glass doors onto beef pot pies, Harvard beets, and tapioca pudding.

The H&H chain reached 80-strong around Philadelphia and New York at its peak. It spawned an all-night rival in Linton's, whose apple brown betty, fish-fry platters, and the "Biggest Breakfast in North America" (including a dozen eggs and a pound of bacon) rattled out of the kitchen on conveyor belts. Horn & Hardart's also left its wholesome mark on a generation of future gourmets, including Deux Cheminees' Fritz Blank.

"The coconut custard pies were magnificent," said Blank longingly. "The creamed spinach was to die for."

The Speakeasy and Hotels

John Wanamaker opened the country's first department store restaurant here with the Crystal Tearoom. When it opened on April 5, 1911, the menu offered caviar with potato puffs, Sole Marguery, sweetbreads, and, of course, Philadelphia cream cheese.

While public dining thrived in Philadelphia for society events and basic sustenance, the city's conservative Quaker roots did not foster dining as nightlife. It was not until Prohibition that restaurant speakeasies, or "speaks," as they were called, drew crowds to dinner venues for nighttime entertainment. Many of them blossomed into legitimate restaurants after repeal in 1933.

There was the Embassy, where lobster thermidor and chicken a la king ruled. There were the Saxony and the 21 Club, which was sued by the New York institution for using the same name.

There was the Three Threes, at 333 Smedley St., which was opened in 1928 by Gene Fornarol, who narrowly missed going down on the Titanic with Philadelphia millionaire George Widener, who had hired him to be chef at the Ritz-Carlton. The restaurant survived under the same family management until 1989.

Most famous of the speakeasy converts was Benny Fogelman, a k a "Benny the Bum," who made enough money on gambling at the ritzy Quaker Outing Club on Pine Street to open his namesake restaurant on Broad Street in 1938.

"He was a rough-spoken guy," said Bushman of the former cab driver and train "candy butcher." "But Benny the Bum catered to upscale stockbrokers and high society."

Another well-known figure was Jack Lynch, who operated the Prohibition-era Friar's Club in Delaware County. He also ran the famed roof garden club at the Walton Hotel, where Scott's uncle bragged of having seduced actress Lillian Russell with ruddy duck.

The Walton, at Locust and Broad, was one of many hotels that boasted roof-garden nightspots. The old Continental had bark-covered columns for a Tarzan jungle theme. The Adelphia had its "wind-swept" Hawaiian roof. The Ben Franklin had "El Patio Grill." The original Ritz-Carlton had a roof garden before it closed in 1954. And the Bellevue-Stratford had its own elegant style of roof garden, which Mary Wickham Bond remembered from pre-World War II days in a 1979 *Inquirer* article, "with white fences, straw-strewn paddocks ... and waiters in 'pink' coats, black riding caps, and boots. ... We all kicked off our satin slippers and danced in stocking feet ... filling the room with a secret sort of sound like rustling silk."

These and others stamped a long Philadelphia tradition of hotel fine dining that continued after the war with the Barclay and the Warwick, where chef George LaMaize popularized his signature shrimp cocktail with zipped-up Russian dressing. Eventually, the Rittenhouse and Four Seasons would carry the hotel flame until the end of the century.

One of the more interesting hotels of the first half of the century was the Majestic at Broad and Girard. Torn down in 1966, it was eulogized as the "hotel of the stars."

Baseball legends such as Babe Ruth and Casey Stengel stayed there when playing at the nearby Baker Bowl and Shibe Park. Operatic stars such as Enrico Caruso and Geraldine Farrar stayed at the Majestic during their engagements at the Metropolitan Opera House close by on North Broad. The dapper Polish gangster of the 1920s, Mickey Duffy, also made the Majestic his home, and reportedly held a summit there with Al Capone…

And before the arrival of steak-house chains like Morton's, the Palm, and Ruth's Chris, local chop houses thrived: the manly Arthur's Steak House, which moved to Walnut Street from Society Hill before it died in the 1980s after 54 years; Mitchell's on Juniper near Locust; and two restaurants named for old-time boxers, Lew Tendler's Tavern and Frankie Bradley's, which closed after 49 years at Juniper and Chancellor Streets.

Bradley was a Jewish prizefighter in the 1920s whose actual surname, Bloch, was turned Irish for the appearance of toughness in the ring. In the kitchen, though, it was the Jewish recipes for matzo ball and kreplach soups and rib steak with garlic that were coveted by his guests.

In the 1940s and 1950s, Chinatown was starting to flourish as the chop-suey and chow-mein houses that fed sojourning bachelors over laundries in the 1940s came into their own as bona fide restaurants.

The Clubs

But for society's elite, Philadelphia 's exclusive private club dining rooms were still the mainstay. The staid Union League, the Vesper Club, the Racquet Club, and the Locust Club – which catered to a Jewish membership that was excluded elsewhere – were among many of the clubs that fed the city's movers and shakers. Though not a private club, the Stouffer's at 16th and Market was a power breakfast destination for the same clubby set, said City Councilman Thacher Longstreth, who recalls having as many as five important meetings there during one meal.

"We were a little in-grown," concedes Longstreth, 80, who ate a club sandwich and iced tea at the Princeton Club (now Deux Cheminees) every day for 20 years. "The clubs gave us a chance to see the people we liked to see."

"We were lazy," said Scott. "It was easy to go to the clubs. ... But in those days, there really were not that many other places to eat."

All that was soon to change.

By the mid- to late-1960s, Philadelphians were ready.

Society Hill's redevelopment in the 1950s had infused new affluence into Center City. Changes in immigration laws depleted old money households of the servants that once kept them coddled in a world of home-cooked meals. Some of the city's restrictive blue laws were repealed in 1971, when restaurants could finally serve alcohol on Sunday. And a generation of young baby boomers – educated, world-traveled, and searching for identity – turned to the restaurant industry as a logical medium to express its creative and entrepreneurial spirit. ...

In 1974, Jay Guben founded the Restaurant School. What began as a venue for a handful of motivated career-changers to hone their skills and launch Renaissance-era restaurants such as Under the Blue Moon in Chestnut Hill has evolved into a serious professional program. Now, under president Daniel Liberatoscioli, the school educates more than 500 students in each class, offering a continuous supply of fuel for a restaurant scene that never seems to stop growing, transforming neighborhood by neighborhood as it expands, from funky South Street to Walnut Street to trendy Manayunk, quaint Chestnut Hill, Old City, and the Main Line.

NEIGHBORHOOD FARE

In between the seafood houses and the junk food and the high cuisine, Philadelphia has traditionally been home to a number of neighborhood diners and local fare. Some of the more famous diners include the Melrose Diner and the Country Club Diner. Famous Deli at Fourth and Bainbridge, Hymies and Murray's have been serving good Jewish food for decades.

Soul Food

Ms. Tootsie's Soul Food Café is owned by Keven Parker who includes many of his mom's recipes in the menu including lots of fried foods, fresh catfish "inside a greaseless buttermilk crust, the juices perfumed with a lime based marinade." Much of the food includes recipes from Virginia with Louisiana spices. The yams move "from boiling pot to cast-iron pan to griddle and then steamer. They are the epitome of yummy yamdom." [And they're not just for yuppies!][20]

Delilah Winders runs several restaurants with a Soul Food theme including Bluezette on 2nd and Market Street and two counters at the Reading Terminal and the 30th Street Station.

More South Philadelphian

Another eating established known for its waiters who sang Italian arias is Victors' Restaurant, also in South Philadelphia. Frank Sinatra was also known to frequent Ralph's Restaurant (as well as Palumbo's which burned down in the 1990s), which is over 100 years old. James Darren, another famous singer and movie star grew up nearby and makes it a point to eat at Ralph's when he's in town. Other customers have included Dom DeLuise, Cardinal Bevilauqua, the leader of Philadelphia's Roman Catholic Church, and Connie Mack.[21]

Dom DeLuise, a gourmet cook in his own right, had heard about Ralph's Calamari and wanted to find out if it was as good as it was reputed to be. He sat alone in the restaurant, ate the Calamari, escarole, and a loaf of Italian bread and then got up and left. "He had walked down here from Center City," Rubino said, "and when he was done he raved about the meal, thanked us, and then walked through the Italian Market and disappeared."

Chinatown
Arch to Vine and 8th to 11th

Some of the favorites of *Philadelphia Inquirer* food critic Craig Laban include:[22]

Shiao lan King salt-baked seafood and steamed dumplings with ginger sauce.
Sang Kee Peking duck rolls, E-fu "long life" noodles, and wonton soup.
Penang Roticanai pancakes and coconut prawns.
Cherry Street Chinese Vegetarian Mack chicken imperial and salt-baked oyster mushrooms.
Rangoon spicy crisped lentil cakes and flaky thousand-layer bread.

THE FOOD RENAISSANCE

Text reprinted with permission of Maxine Keyser (City Paper) and Penn Arts and Sciences (Spring 2001)

Just to the right as you go through the door of an old brick-and-mortar warehouse in the Northern Liberties section of Philadelphia—a little north and east of the action in Center City—a thick, rough-hewn sign that says "The Commissary" is bolted to the wall. A quiet hum, like electric snoring, issues from the walk-in refrigerators in the nearby industrial kitchen, now suspended in stainless-steel sleep. The sign was carved by Steve Poses, College '69, and hung above the sidewalk outside the innovative and upscale cafeteria he started downtown in the mid-'70s. With the Commissary and some half dozen other eating enterprises, he is credited with launching Philadelphia's restaurant renaissance, which lifted the city out of what one food critic named the "dark ages of dining."

Guided by Ignorance

The renaissance germinated at Penn, when Poses, a sociology major living off campus, was deprived of his mother's cooking and had to fend for himself. "I was this sheltered kid with no strong ethnic roots," he explains, "just this homogenized, suburbanized, white-bread product of the 1950s." That indifferent culinary upbringing, with its lack of allegiance to how food should taste, was reflected in Philadelphia's uninspired meat-and-potato restaurant scene.

Unencumbered by ethnic predilections, Poses was free to experiment with whatever flavor combinations seemed to taste good. "I could take this from here and that from there and come up with something that's 'fusion'," he says. "That's what they call it now." A summer in Spain, France, and Italy awakened his palate to cuisines with more spark than American bland. Returning home, he subscribed to the Time-Life international cookbook series to inform his culinary experiments.

"I was really guided by ignorance and a certain sense of adventure and a reasonable palate to come up with flavors." ...After a brief Peace Corps stint, he took the first step toward becoming a restaurateur by accepting a position as busboy, parsley chopper, and pheasant plucker at La Panetiere, then Philadelphia's premier French restaurant. He kept Julia Child's *Mastering the Art of French Cooking* beside his bed like a Bible and eventually found a place sautéing vegetables on the cooking line.

Working in the kitchen were a number of young men from Thailand who had fled the wars igniting across Southeast Asia. The exotic tastes of the staff dinners they prepared delighted Poses—the pickled vegetables, the lemon grass and fish sauce, the many-colored sweet and fiery curries. "Only in America and only at that time," he writes in his best selling *Frog/Commissary Cookbook*, "could a Jewish kid from Yonkers, having graduated from the University of Pennsylvania, be working and learning how to cook in a French restaurant alongside a substantial contingent of Thais."

Adding an Asian culinary tradition to his Western repertoire supplied the critical mass for an unheard-of fusion of multicultural ingredients, tastes, textures, and cooking methods. At the age of twenty-six, he opened Frög—with an umlaut and an investment of $35,000. The storefront restaurant was hobbled together with mismatched chairs and church pews, green marble slabs

Philadelphia Chinatown by Howard N. Watson. Courtesy of Howard N. Watson

from a soda fountain top he was paid to remove from a defunct drugstore, and a card-table salad station whose leg had to be tied to a sturdier piece of scavenged furniture. The umlaut was dropped eventually but Frog would become his flagship, and by 1984 Poses had a string of wildly popular eateries that served about 5,000 customers daily and did about $11.5 million a year in business.[23]

The experiment of mixing heretofore unmixed flavors that Poses began at Frog, captured the attention of Philadelphians and let loose a chain reaction of innovative eating establishments that cropped up all over the city. Many aspiring chefs who became part of the restaurant renaissance learned the trade by working for the man who fathered it. Paul Roller, C'74, who has set up three restaurants in Chestnut Hill, started out at the Commissary. Frog and the Commissary, he has commented, were "seminal to the food movement overall. It was a wonderful, experimental time."[24]

… "Our cuisine, Philadelphia cuisine, was heavily influenced by the Thais," he says, although the "sociological phenomenon" of Asian refugees who came and mixed new ways of cooking into the melting pot "changed how Americans thought about food and flavor. Now you didn't have to go to Chinatown to taste ginger. You could taste it at this little storefront restaurant named Frog."

Philadelphia's restaurant resurgence has continued to cook but has left Poses behind. His dining empire eventually fell apart, and he now oversees Frog/Commissary Catering, which is housed in the Northern Liberties warehouse. The business serves 700 to 800 events a year, and employees number about 50 in the off-season, ballooning to nearly 300 at the peak.[25]

A STANDARD-BEARER

One of the many famous Philadelphia restaurant owners is Georges Perrier. *"Bellwethers still – Three of the city's finest flourish despite changes in the kitchen." Philadelphia Inquirer, The (PA) February 17, 2002. Author: Craig LaBan.*

Georges Perrier – Le Bec-Fin
[Le Bec-Fin] – an idiom for "The Good Taste"

Georges Perrier, originally from Lyon, France, began his culinary career at age fourteen. He trained at some of France's best restaurants with some of the top chefs. Work was from 5:30 am till midnight.[29]

Peter von Starck, who ran Philadelphia's La Panetière brought Chef Perrier over to Philadelphia in 1967 as Head Chef. In 1970, Perrier opened his first and world-acclaimed restaurant, **"Le Bec-Fin,"** a French idiom for "the good taste." Le Bec-Fin soon became a required stop for anyone traveling between New York and Washington, D.C.

"In 1976, Chef Perrier was inducted into the Maîtres Cuisiniers de France, the premier international society of French chefs. Its 200 members include the finest French chefs in the world. In 1989, those members voted Perrier "Chef of the Year" and awarded him with the Silver Toque, the most coveted trophy in the world of haute cuisine."

Georges Perrier, Le Bec-fin Recipes (Image for Cover). Courtesy of Perseus Books

NEWER CUISINES and the SECOND RENAISSANCE

1980s

In the early 1980s the restaurant scene was beginning to blossom thanks to Steve Poses and Kamol Phultek whose "Thai seasonings on French cuisine" had started a new sensation at Alouette's on Fifth Street.

French food could be found at Peter von Starck's La Panetière and Déjà Vu, La Camargue a La Terrasses, in addition to Georges Perrier's Le Bec-Fin. [Some credit Von Starck with being a major influence on the Food Renaissance.]

South Street had restaurants (fortunately some have still survived) including Lickety Split, Wildflowers, Bridget Foy's, Montserrat and Knave of Hearts were steaming along, and some still are. "Old City had yet to be discovered, and Manayunk was still a dream in Dan Neducsin's head."

Bookbinders had two dining establishments for Seafood. As did the Sansom Street Oyster House. Seafood? Neil Stein worked at the Fish Market.

Le Bec-Fin moved to 1523 Walnut Street, in 1987, when Perreir purchased an historic art deco building which added the elegance he desired to his elegant cuisine. He added a private banquet room, a separate smoking room, downstairs bar, and bistro, **Le Bar Lyonnas**, finishing touch to his restaurant was added in 1990. It's an intimate downstairs bar and bistro.

Along with continuing personal honors (in 1998 Chef Perrier was honored by America's leading culinary organization when he was awarded Best Mid-Atlantic Chef by the James Beard Foundation). Le Bec-Fin has received numerous accolades. Le Bec-Fin is the only dining establishment in Pennsylvania to receive the five-star rating from the Mobil Travel Guide and has been for twenty-four years standing. In 1994, readers of Condé Nast Traveler magazine chose Le Bec-Fin as the #1 restaurant in the country. It still continues to acclaim in the country's leading food and travel magazines such as *Gourmet, Food & Wine, Esquire,* and *Wine Spectator*.

Philadelphia is glad to have Perrier and Perrier has returned the favor by refusing invitations to relocate to the nation's other major cities. In addition to his restaurants Perrier has received awards from numerous charities that he helps including SCAN (Stop Child Abuse Now), Amyotrophic Lateral Sclerosis (ALS) Association, the Breast Health Institute and the Arthur Ashe Tennis Foundation. In addition to being a business magnate, Perrier owns his own restaurants, he also has charity dinners, gives cooking classes in person and occasionally on television.[30] "The Perrier personality is as important a commodity as the food."[31]

The jacket for his book, Georges Perrier *Le Bec-Fin Recipes*, is shown. The book includes more than 100 recipes from Le Bec-Fin and Le Bar Lyonnas.

Perrier opened several more restaurants:

Brasserie Perrier. Opened January 1997. 1619 Walnut Street, just a block away from Le Bec-Fin. "A more relaxed, less expensive alternative to Le Bec-Fin, the first-rate Brasserie offers modern French cuisine with Italian and Asian influences."

georges' Opened in December 2000. 503 West Lancaster Avenue on Philadelphia's prestigious Main Line. "The restaurant serves an eclectic and affordable menu in a relaxed setting, reminiscent of a country inn. When it opened, Esquire Magazine named it one of the country's "Best New Restaurants in 2001."

Brasserie Perrier Café at Boyd's. Opened in the Spring of 2005

Mia. Opened in 2008. A Mediterranean bistro in Caesars Atlantic City

Perrier was knighted into the French National Order of Merit, the second-highest distinction accorded by France to civilians.

"'I plan to be the best for at least thirty more years,' says Perrier, which is good news to his fans, the patrons of his restaurants, and the culinary world." (main source- www.signaturerg.com)

Quietly, Two Quails opened in the space on Spruce Street (now the home of Vetri) that was vacated by Le Bec-Fin. The owners were Jon and Lori Weinrott, who have become the area's premier caterers with Peachtree & Ward. Vin Hoa and Saigon were early Vietnamese restaurants, and are still benchmarks for the proliferation of this wonderful cuisine.

For Italian there was Villa Di Roma on Ninth Street, Cous' Little Italy, and other center Italian restaurants (not forgetting, of course, all the Italian places in South Philadelphia). There was the Garden, which is alas no more.[32]

Neil Stein opened other seafood places – Rock Lobster and later the Striped Bass, Rouge and Bleu, and Avenue B. The successful restaurants made it because of the quality of the fresh fish, the great locations, and the entertainment value Stein provided such as open places where customers could see the chefs. Striped Bass was named by *Esquire Magazine* as the best new restaurant in the country. Reservations for it were backed up six months. Striped Bass grossed seven million in the first year. But future choices (Blue and especially Avenue B) showed the pitfalls of the restaurant business. These choices but personal problems led Stein's fortunes south. Striped Bass was recently brought out by the current restaurant mogul – Stephen Starr.[33, 34]

1990s and Twenty-first Century

Starting in the mid-90s, Poses noted, big chains, such as the Four Seasons hotel, sparked a second renaissance, with investors spending lavishly to finance splendid decors, fabulous linens, gorgeous silverware, professionally trained chefs, and staff skilled in the intricate theater of presentation that now accompanies fine dining in the city. "I think the food is probably superior to anything we served in the first wave, and on top of that, they added a layer of sizzle. I think both the steak has changed and the sizzle has gotten a lot brighter."[35]

There's Café Habana and Cuba Libre, Nuevo Latino at ¡Pasión!, Cibucán, Azafran, Las Cazuelas, Zocalo, Tequila's.

In short, there isn't any cuisine that is unavailable to diners in Philadelphia now — Vietnamese, Cambodian, Afghani, more sushi bars than I can count, Indian at so many places, the best being Cafe Spice, and plenty of soul food at spots like Bluezette.

Not only has the food diversified, it's gotten much more sophisticated and true to its origins. There's authentic Italian in many places, from smaller spots like Tre Scalini and L'Angolo to big guns like Il Portico and the incomparable Vetri. Wander into Brasserie Perrier or Bistro St. Tropez and you will find France well represented. Everyone knows about seared tuna and pea shoots and fava beans and steak frites, and the proper wines to accompany them....

Striped Bass by Perry Milou. Courtesy of Perry Milou

STEPHEN STARR

Unlike many other restaurateurs who grew up with food, Stephen Starr began as a club owner, a concert promoter, and even a radio talk-show host. He put the promotional knowledge to use with an ever-expanding array of restaurants that, as Steven Poses noted, emphasize the sizzle and the atmosphere in places where the setting is almost as important as the food. Tangerine gives the customer an Arabian-nights feel. Buddakan has a 10-foot-tall Buddha. According to Starr, "I'm selling the experience."[36]

The Philadelphia restaurant scene is always changing. According to *Philadelphia Magazine's* 50 Best Restaurant Issue (May 2009), Zahav Israeli cuisine restaurant is the best restaurant in the city and Jose Garces is the new "hot" restaurateur.

Pare Bistro, Rittenhouse Squre, by Charles Cushing. This was one of Georges Perrier's restaurants. Courtesy of Charles Cushing

MANUFACTURERS

Philadelphia and the neighboring counties were and are home to many farms producing a variety of foods for local and national consumption.

Some of the city's contributions included Lemon Meringue Pie, Pigeon, Seckel Pears, Trenton Crackers, Whitman's Chocolates, Nabisco Cookies, and Campbell's Beefsteak Tomatoes. Two of the best-known providers are Campbell's Soups in nearby Camden, New Jersey, across the river from Philadelphia and mushrooms, which are grown in KennettSquare.

Campbell's Soup
(Text, paraphrased from the website of Campbell's Soup Company.)

Campbell's Soup Company was formed in 1869 when Joseph Campbell, a fruit merchant, and Abraham Anderson, an icebox manufacturer, joined together. The business produced canned tomatoes, vegetables, jellies, soups, condiments, and minced meats. In 1897, Dr. John T. Dorrance, a chemist, introduced the idea of condensed soup, which meant soup could be packaged without water, thus reducing the cost.

Campbell's used innovative advertising including "cherubic Campbell Kids" and the slogan 'M'm! M'm! Good!' Through the use of the condensed soup in recipes and through business transactions, which have allowed Campbell's to grow, the soup company prospered. Brand names and products now include "Pepperidge Farm" breads, cookies, and crackers, "Franco-American" gravies and pastas, "V8" vegetable juices, "Swanson" broths, and Godiva Chocolates.

Additional slogans are "Wow! I could've had a V8!," "Uh-oh Spaghetti Os," and "Pepperidge Farm Remembers."

Mushrooms and Kennett Square

"Mushroom cultivation in the United States first began in Kennett Square in 1896 when two local florists wanted to make more efficient use of their greenhouses by utilizing the area underneath the shelves used to grow ornamental plants. This set-up was less than ideal, however, with improvements in technology over many years, and many generations later, the cultivation of mushrooms in the United States is greater than ever.

"Every year Kennett Square holds a major mushroom festival where portabella, white, shiitake, criminal, oyster, and enoki mushrooms can be fared, often in the best mushroom soups around."

[http://www.mushroomfestival.org/mushrooms.htm]

Tastykake

Text reprinted with permission of Tastykake
[Tastykake Web Site – www.tastykake.com]

"A Pittsburgh baker and a Boston seller of eggs teamed up in 1914 to make small pre-packaged desserts. Their treats include Juniors, Krimpets, KandyKakes, Creamies, Cupcakes, various fruit pies, and more. From a local bakery, Tastykake has expanded country-wide."

Back in 1914, a Pittsburgh baker, Philip J. Baur and a Boston egg salesman, Herbert T. Morris, went into business in Philadelphia to produce goods using only the finest ingredients, delivered fresh daily to the bakery. The products were so good that Morris' wife, after trying some of the samples, said they were "tasty," so they eventually named the business Tasty Baking Company and came up with the catchy name, Tastykake.

Tastykake. Courtesy of Tastykake

Chocolate Juniors were the first new product developed, then they put in electric ovens for cupcakes. By 1918, sales reached $1 million. By 1930, with the introduction of Butterscotch Krimpets and the expansion to five buildings, Tastykake was selling $6 million of these new snack cakes. In the '30s, as Americans looked toward economy, Tasty Baking Company came up with a revolution – individually packaged lunchbox-sized pies, at a nickel apiece they became immediate hits. The apple led to peach and lemon and blueberry, and the rest as they say is history.

Other Philadelphia food traditions include funnel cakes with lots of sugar and the various brands of ice cream discussed in the science section. Philadelphia Cream Cheese is actually made by Kraft, and named after that well-known oxymoron – Philadelphia, New York.

DESSERT

"**Water Ice, a.k.a. Italian Water Ice or Italian Ice,** is a legendary summertime treat in Philadelphia.

"It is a water-based product made with real fruit blended in fine ice to form a soft, velvety smooth texture. It contains no fat, no cholesterol, and is the ideal ice cream alternative for those who are lactose intolerant. Water Ice is a very labor-intensive product. Preparation of water ice begins with real fruit or fruit puree mixed with water, sugar, and other ingredients which undergoes a 'quick-freezing' process that generations of Philadelphians have come to expect."

[http://www.jimjims.com/pages/What_is_Water-ice.htm]

ICE CREAM

(c) 2006. History of Philadelphia Ice Cream. Coleman Poses and Chilly Philly Ice Cream
Text reprinted with permission of Coleman Poses (source: www.chillyphilly.com)

The early history of ice cream in Philadelphia owes much to the contribution of the French. The French involvement starts with one Emanuel Segur, believed to be the person who taught Philadelphians how to make ice cream after the Revolutionary War.

There is good reason to believe that African Americans played the dominant role in Philadelphia's ice cream business throughout the middle of the nineteenth century. Possibly the most influential of these tradesmen was Augustus Jackson, an African American, who worked as a cook in the White House. Legend has it that he may have been the head chef at the White House. Legend also has it that he is the inventor of ice cream, an absurdity that ultimately belittles his real accomplishments. Jackson moved to Philadelphia in the late 1820s and started his own catering business. He made ice cream for his own customers as well as two other African American owned ice cream parlors on South Street. He ran a successful business for at least the next thirty years and became one of Philadelphia's wealthiest African American citizens. One source claims that African Americans had a monopoly on the ice cream trade in the mid-nineteenth century.

The revolution in ice cream production occurred on September 9, 1843, when a Philadelphia woman: Nancy Johnson, received a patent for an "artificial freezer." This new invention had only three main parts: a tall tub, a slender cylinder with a close fitting lid, and a dasher with a removable crank. By placing the dasher in the cylinder, and by attaching the dasher to the crank through a hole in the cylinder lid, a person could turn the crank with less work than rotating the lid of a pot freezer.

The ice cream sold on Philadelphia's streets was generally superior to the substandard "hokey-pokey" hawked in other cities, where peddlers routinely sold an inferior product under rather unsanitary conditions. Much of the credit for the superiority of Philadelphia's ice cream should go to Mary Engle Pennington, who, though originally denied her chemistry baccalaureate from the University of Pennsylvania because of gender, subsequently completed her doctorate and became head of Philadelphia's municipal bacterial lab. She first built a reputation for creating a system to inspect cattle and dairies in the city (remember that much of Philadelphia was still rural in the late 1800s) thereby ensuring that the city's milk supply was safe. She subsequently targeted the city's ice cream peddlers, and persuaded them to employ sanitary methods such as cleaning their utensils in boiling water.

Philadelphia ice cream has always connoted an ice cream made with pure, natural ingredients. By strict definition, however, Philadelphia ice cream is simply ice cream made without eggs. Philadelphia ice creams have other connotations as well: they are cooked before freezing, and there are vanilla bean specks in the vanilla ice cream. Chilly Philly is made with all of the above characteristics.

The year was 1861... It was during this period that a Quaker farmer and schoolteacher from Salem, New Jersey – Louis Dubois Bassett – had a better idea: to develop one of the world's truly great ice creams – Bassetts of Philadelphia. Eventually, he moved into the city and set up shop in the Reading Terminal Market in 1893. The original store continues to be operational. The founder's grandson, Louis Lafayette, LL, inherited the business, and experimented with flavors such as kiwi, papaya, and yellow tomato. Louis Lafayette's genius was responsible for many of the flavors that are available today. However, if it were not for the business acumen of LL's daughter, Ann, the business might have floundered. She restored order to the business and successfully expanded it beyond the Philadelphia region.

Perhaps nobody epitomized the superiority of street sold ice cream in Philadelphia more than William Breyer. In 1854, all of Philadelphia County became incorporated into Philadelphia city, including the Frankford and Kensington neighborhoods where, a dozen years later, Breyer would run his business. He hand-cranked his ice cream in his kitchen and traveled through Frankford and Kensington in a horse drawn wagon. Before his death in 1882, he had opened six retail stores. His sons, Henry and Fred, incorporated the business, expanded it into Philadelphia's suburbs and beyond. Both William and Henry Breyers insisted on using pure, natural ingredients, limiting themselves to milk, cream, sugar, and flavorings. Such ice cream is known today as Philadelphia ice cream.

The most successful Philadelphia ice cream company of modern times is Jack & Jill, founded by Max Schwartz in the early part of this century, who peddled his ice cream in a box that he carried on his shoulder as he walked through the streets of Philadelphia.

PHILADELPHIA HUMOR

*Bill Cosby.
Courtesy of
Kennedy Center
Honors*

Picture – Bill Cosby

"On the whole, I'd rather be living in Philadelphia."

W.C. Fields
Comedian
What he wanted on his gravestone

PHILADELPHIA HUMOR

PHILADELPHIA HUMOR

NOTABLE STYLES

Stories. Not Jokes

  Clean

    Reflective of their neighborhoods

CONTENTS

PHIA HUMOR

PHILADELPHIA HUMOR

Benjamin Franklin can properly be considered one of Philadelphia's first humorists. His *Poor Richard's Almanac* was a primary source for his famous witticisms. In other arenas, from politics (where he is credited for creating the first political cartoon) to the neighborhood meetings of his Junto group, humor was a constant staple.

Before photography, many newspapers employed artists such as Joseph Pennell and Alfred Bendiner to create scenes of the city. Along with these creations, these artists and others added their own humorous take on the scenes they had sketched. Occasionally the newspapers had columnists with a humorous biting edge to them such as the *Philadelphia Inquirer's* Steve Lopez. Sadly, that tradition has vanished with most of the daily newspapers. Humor seems confined to the funny pages and to the cartoonists, an area where Philadelphia has shined.

Wyncie King came to the Philadelphia *Public Ledger* by way of Georgia and Louisville, Kentucky. While with the *Public Ledger* he did a series of Philadelphia caricatures that have been described as some of the best of its kind. Tony Auth has been the political cartoonist for *The Philadelphia Inquirer* for decades. Auth is one of the best and his cartoons are picked up by many newspapers nationwide. Signe Wilkinson is a Pulitzer Prize winning cartoonist for the *Philadelphia Daily News* and other publications. Several other local newspapers have their own cartoonists also. The *Philadelphia Tribune's* Sam Joyner and *The Northeast Time's* Tom Stiglich are two of the best.

In other mediums, television and film, Philadelphia comedians from W.C. Fields to Larry Fine to Will Smith have made their mark. Joey Bishop grew up in Philadelphia and then made his fame with Frank Sinatra and the "Rat Pack." The comedians who grew up in Philadelphia but who became famous elsewhere include South Philadelphia's Jack Klugman, Strawberry Mansion's Carl Reiner, and Upper Darby's Tina Fey whose television hits include *Saturday Night Live's* and *30 Rock*.

Where Philadelphia has shined most, though, is in a specific invention of the twentieth century – the comedy routine. Bill Cosby is the one Philadelphian who made the comedy routine the most famous. His style is rare among comedians in that he tells stories instead of jokes. His routines are notable because of the lack of punch lines. His facial expressions are his trademark and no story is complete without them. His range expanded from the comedy sketch to television, movie, stage performances, records, books, and more. He became one of the nation's premier comedians.

Other Philadelphia comedians who have made their reputation have employed local humor to make their mark. David Brenner's humor is constantly flavored with references to growing up in Philadelphia and is drawn from life's experiences. Like many other humorists, his career began elsewhere, as a writer/producer/director of documentaries.

Joe Conklin does impressions of most of the city's famous politicians and sports figures. For radio station WIP, Conklin often employs Ben Franklin's old trick of pretending to be other people – when the show's master of ceremonies, Angelo Cataldi, wants that "extra special" caller.

And speaking of sports, Philadelphia's penchant for losing more often than what seems like all the other teams combined has led to another humor staple – self deprecation. After all, if one can't laugh at oneself like Cataldi and Morganti and Rhea Hughes do on The WIP Morning Show, well – one might be inclined to move to some "serious" city, like Boston. Their most celebrated act is the staging for the past two decades of "Wing Bowl," where husky gentleman assume monikers like "El Wingador" and gorge themselves on eating more food in a half an hour than normal people eat in three days.

There's also the essayist: A Philadelphia favorite is a St. Joseph's graduate – Joe Queenan. Even the Main Line has a humorist – David Brooks, though his departure to the *New York Times* makes Philadelphians wonder.

CARTOONISTS

Political Cartoon

Benjamin Franklin is credited with creating the first political cartoon. By combining both his wit and political convictions, he portrayed his own reflections on issues affecting society. Since then, the political cartoon has become a staple of modern culture and thought. The picture, titled "Join or Die," is the first political cartoon ever. Appearing in Franklin's *Pennsylvania Gazette*, it concerns the Albany Plan of Union and the author's stance on the matter.

One notable cartoonist story involved Pennsylvania's Governor Pennypacker (1903). When cartoonists portrayed him unkindly he got upset. When one cartoonist showed him as a parrot, Pennypacker had a law passed holding that humans could not, in Pennsylvania, be portrayed as birds or animals. Well, when one door shuts, a window opens. Cartoonists then portrayed him as a fish and the Philadelphia *North American* devoted a page of Walt MacDougall caricatures to portraying Pennypacker and those who supported him as vegetables. The law was never enforced and when the next administration repealed the law politicians were "fair game" again.[1]

In the 1890s newspapers didn't have editorial pages. The editorial cartoon in the *Philadelphia Press* appeared on the front page. A sample cartoon from the *Press* is shown. In the 1890s cars hadn't been invented yet, so the first day of May, the first reliably warm day of the year, everybody would march off to Washington.

Wyncie King (1984-1961)

Wynice King worked in Louisville, from 1910 to 1921. He came to the Philadelphia *Public Ledger* in 1921. According to the *Saturday Evening Post* (where King was also a major contributor), critics hailed one particular series of caricatures King sketched for the *Public Ledger* as "the finest work in caricature ever done in this country." This series profiled mostly Philadelphians in a variety of professions. Two others are shown in the legal and sports chapters. He was married to a Bryn Mawr professor and poet. Bryn Mawr holds some of his paintings. Other paintings can be seen at the Franklin Inn Club, a club devoted to great writers, including its founder, Silas Weir Mitchell. Mitchell, who was also a physician, was considered one of the leading writers of the nineteenth century. His historical novels, *Hugh Wynne, Free Quaker* (1897), *The Adventures of François* (1898), and *The Red City* (1909), take high rank in this branch of fiction.

Live Free or Die by Benjamin Franklin. Courtesy of Public Domain

First of May. Courtesy of Philadelphia Press – Public Domain

Nothing but Work and Worry, 1921, by Wyncie King. Original from Philadelphia Public Ledger – Public Domain

Classicists of the Comic Strip, 1922, by Wyncie King. Original from Philadelphia Public Ledger – Public Domain

An Artist in Dialectics by Wyncie King. Original from Philadelphia Public Ledger – Public Domain

Three Thrifty Political Housekeepers, 1921, by Wyncie King. Original from Philadelphia Public Ledger – Public Domain

Alfred Bendiner

A wonderful drawer of Philadelphia was the noted architect Alfred Bendiner, who drew and wrote for the *Evening Bulletin*. His drawings included wry observations of many of the most famous locations in the city. Drawings included landscapes, museums, government offices, buildings and all parts of the city.

He wrote the following about the madness of trying to drive the Schuylkill Expressway:
"I try and remember everything which I have read and heard from the adjoining seat in forty-five years of fairly safe driving. Keep in your lane and don't straddle the white line. Stay seventy-five feet behind the maniac in front. Turn off the radio. Watch the blond in the midget cutting into your fender. Push off the left turn signal. Oops, watch the truck birdie, duck your head and be ready to ditch as the trailer tilts over the guardrail. Hold your hats as she levels off. Now head into the left lane and speed her up. No! The cop in the Red Car is looking into your rear mirror."

Now you're past the mob and can breathe until they start mowing you down on all sides. Make up your mind—will you turn off toward North Philly, or cut into the slot and go down the East River Drive. It's clogged.

Maybe the entrance to West River is clear.

Comedians by Alfred Bendiner. Courtesy of University of Pennsylvania Architectural Archives

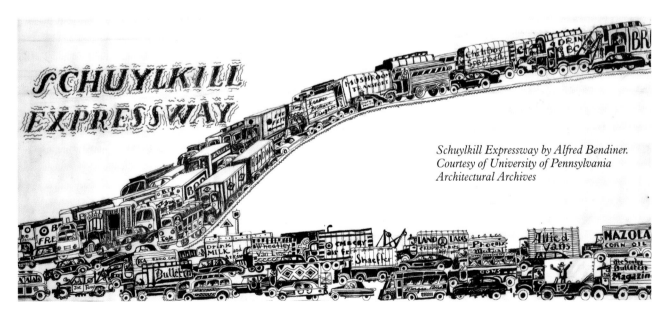

Schuylkill Expressway by Alfred Bendiner. Courtesy of University of Pennsylvania Architectural Archives

But that guy sitting on your rear fender will kill you. So it's straight through. You should make a right at 30th Street, but you're boxed by trucks and trailers –so now for Center City. There goes 15th, 12th, Holy Market! Next chance off is the Bridge and Camden. Maybe it would be better to stay off the Expressway or let your wife drive."[2]

Drawings shown include: The Schuylkill Expressway and The Athenaeum.

The Athenaeum, according to the artist, is "about the last private library in Philadelphia... To become a member you have to wait for another old Philadelphian to die and his family to relinquish the share. The Library is on Washington Square, and the building was designed by Charles Noram, and is still the best architectural thing around. The most awe-inspiring room is the Main Library on the second floor."

*Atheneum by Alfred Bendiner. Courtesy of
Atheneum of Philadelphia.*

Wall Street – Week of 1/21/2008 by Signe Wilkinson. Courtesy of Signe Wilkinson

Signe Wilkinson

Text reprinted with permission of Signe Wilkinson

Signe Wilkinson is one of contemporary America's few women cartoonists, an area in which Philadelphia has shone. A native Philadelphian, Wilkinson began her career as a journalist for the *Daily Local News* in suburban West Chester, Pennsylvania. She soon realized her interest in cartooning as she began drawing the subjects she was supposed to be covering. After attending the Pennsylvania Academy of the Fine Arts and freelancing, Wilkinson joined the staff of the *San Jose Mercury News*. In 1985 she returned to Philadelphia as the editorial cartoonist for the *Philadelphia Daily News*.

In addition to her political cartoons, she draws a daily comic strip called "Family Tree," which is also syndicated nationally. The first woman to receive a Pulitzer Prize for cartooning, Wilkinson has won three Nast Awards from the Overseas Press Club and two RFK, Jr. awards for her cartoons about issues of poverty and the dispossessed. Her most coveted accolade was being named "Pennsylvania's Official Vegetable Substitute."[3]

Tony Auth

Text reprinted with permission of Tony Auth

"Tony Auth was raised in California and worked as a medical illustrator for a large teaching hospital before doing political cartoons. He began doing the cartoons for the UCLA *Daily Bruin*, but since 1971 has been an editorial cartoonist for *The Philadelphia Inquirer*. He is currently a member of its editorial board.

"Auth has won several awards, including the Pulitzer Prize for editorial cartooning and the Sigma Delta Chi Award for distinguished service in journalism."

Tony Auth personal selection.
Courtesy of Tony Auth

Sam Joyner

Text reprinted with permission of Sam Joyner

Sam Joyner started out delivering *The Philadelphia Tribune* as a young boy. Today, he is their resident cartoonist. "Samuel Joyner is a great classic style cartoonist with a voice for hard working people."[4]

Mr. Joyner was forced for a long time to hide his race, to work anonymously. Fortunately his talent was too good and he works for a variety of publications among other graphic arts ventures.

Mr. Joyner taught advertising art, silkscreen printing, poster design, and graphic communication courses as an art teacher for nineteen years for the Philadelphia Board of Education for the Edward Bok Vocational/Technical High School in South Philadelphia. Mr. Joyner credits his one black teacher, Samuel Brown, from his own public schooling, for encouraging his art.

Sam Joyner. Courtesy of Sam Joyner

Sam Joyner Selection. Courtesy of Sam Joyner

Our Schools will continue to stay in trouble as long as we pay the best teachers *less* than we pay the worst football player.

Tom Stiglich

www.tomstiglich.com

Text reprinted with permission of Tom Stiglich

Cartooning is Tom's life. He started as a child and hasn't stopped. Born and raised in Philadelphia, drawing has been a great way to support a serious cheese steak addiction.

While in high school, his first cartoon was published by the *Philadelphia Daily News*.

Tom attended the Art Institute of Philadelphia in June 1988.

His cartoons have appeared in *USA Today*, *The New York Times*, *Newsweek*, *Newsweek Japan*, *TIME Magazine*, King Features Syndicate's *The New Breed*, *The Philadelphia Inquirer*, *The Philadelphia Daily News*, *The Chicago Sun-Times*, *Mad Kids* magazine, and in the annual book series *Best Editorial Cartoons of the Year*.

Recently, he received a Citation of Excellence 2007 Ranan Lurie award from the United Nations and currently has two cartoons on exhibit at the Charles M. Schulz museum in Santa Rosa, California.

Tom's editorial cartoons appear in many newspapers throughout Pennsylvania and New Jersey. He is a member of the National Cartoonists Society and the Association of American Editorial Cartoonists.

Biography Reprinted with permission of Tom Stiglich

Disconnected by Tom Stiglich

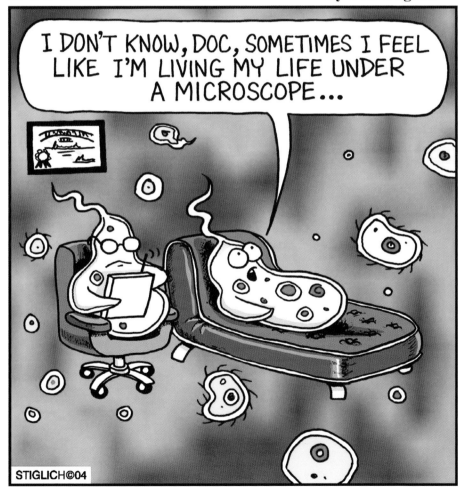

Disconnected © 2004 by Tom Stiglich. Courtesy of Tom Stiglich

William Keane

William Keane began drawing at Northeast Catholic High School. He draws a comic strip that is family friendly. He has his own comic strip – Family Circus. Keane also worked for *The Philadelphia Bulletin*.

Other Newspaper Cartoonists[5]

The Philadelphia Cartoonist Community runs the gambit from Wally Neibart (who taught at the University of the Arts) to a loose confederacy of comic book/strip cartoonists. The Philadelphia Cartoonist Society has a wide variety of cartoonists.

Among many other Philadelphia cartoonists, Charles Burns does comic-books, Renee French is an illustrator, Pauline Comanor draws the "Chunky Monkey" cartoons and teaches cartoon drawing, among other endeavors.

Wally Neibart

www.wallyneibart.net

Text reprinted with permission of Wally Neibart

Wally Neibart, a graduate of the Philadelphia College of Art, now the University of the Arts, is an internationally known humorous illustrator. His work appears in advertising campaigns, national magazines, text books, etc Clients include Rohm & Haas, United Phosphorus, Inc., *Penn Medicine Magazine*, *Highlights for Children*, to name a few.

A Professor of art and guest lecturer in many colleges and universities, Wally Neibart is also involved in programs at libraries and public schools, bringing his whimsical creativity to adults and children of all ages.

Biologics. Hal Lewis Design Group *by Wally Neibart. Courtesy of Wally Neibart*

HUMORISTS

NORTH PHILLY
BILL COSBY

www.billcosby.com
Text reprinted with permission of Bill Cosby

Bill Cosby is, by any standards, one of the most influential stars in America today. Whether it be through concert appearances or recordings, television or films, commercials or education, Bill Cosby has the ability to touch people's lives. His humor often centers on the basic cornerstones of our existence, seeking to provide an insight into our roles as parents, children, family members, and men and women. Without resorting to gimmickry or low-brow humor, Bill Cosby's comedy has a point of reference and respect for the trappings and traditions of the great American humorists such as Charlie Chaplin, Will Rogers, W.C. Fields, and Groucho Marx.

The 1984-92 run of *The Cosby Show* and his books *Fatherhood* and *Time Flies* established new benchmarks on how success is measured. His status at the top of the TVQ survey year after year continues to confirm his appeal as one of the most popular personalities in America. His lifelong contributions to American culture were recognized with a Kennedy Center Honor in 1998 and the Presidential Medal of Freedom in July 2002, America's highest civilian honor.

The Cosby Show – The 25ᵗʰ Anniversary Commemorative Edition, released by First Look Studios and Carsey-Werner, is available in stores and online at www.billcosby.com. The DVD box set of the NBC television hit series is the complete collection of one of the most popular programs in the history of television, garnering twenty-nine Emmy® nominations with six wins, six Golden Globe® nominations with three wins, and ten People's Choice Awards.

"*The Cosby Show* is a message for all time: the family and raising your children matters most," said Bill Cosby. "Many people approach me and say that the show made them aware that there could be a better life out there for them. At the same time they say that the show still makes them laugh."

Come On, People! On the Path from Victims to Victors, written by Bill Cosby and Alvin F. Poussaint, M.D., professor of psychiatry at Harvard Medical School and civil rights veteran, lay out their message of hope and empowerment in this *New York Times* bestseller. *Come On, People*, published by Thomas Nelson, provides real-life examples of the problems plaguing communities throughout America and the time-tested solutions that can help turn things around. The audiobook is available online at www.billcosby.com and read by accomplished actress CCH Pounder, currently in the critically acclaimed FX series, "The Shield."

Bill Cosby Presents The Cosnarati: State of Emergency, this rap album was made as a companion to *Come On, People!* All song story concepts are by Cosby and was assembled by his longtime musical collaborator Bill "Spaceman" Patterson with guest rappers providing the rhymes about the value of an education, respecting one's self and ... giving (listeners) a chance to raise their self-esteem and confidence. Sold exclusively online at www.billcosby.com.

Cosby has touched the hearts of a new generation of young children with his Emmy Award winning *Little Bill* animated series, which aired daily on Nickelodeon and Saturday mornings on CBS. The show was based on Cosby's popular children's books. His interest in young people also spawned his best-selling book, *Congratulations! Now What?*, published by Hyperion. The book contains his amusing yet wise take on college life and what lies ahead for the new graduate in the real world.

Friends of a Feather: One of Life's Little Fables, a HarperEntertainment book released in 2003, is a collaboration with his daughter, Erika, who did the illustrations. It is a beautiful story that explores the theme of being true to yourself.

I Am What I Ate ... and I'm frightened!!!, published by HarperCollins, was released on September 21, 2004, was also on the *New York Times* Best Seller List. It offers a hip, humorous, hard-earned wisdom on the healthy lifestyle and the behavior behind it.

"Fatherhood" was launched appropriately enough on Father's Day as an animated series on *Nick at Nite*.

Bill and Camille Cosby produced a live action/animated Fat Albert motion picture in 2004. A box office success, the movie introduced a new generation to the loveable character and his friends initially famous through the unforgettable Cosby comedy routines about them. The Fat Albert television show and feature are now available on DVD.

He often neglected his studies for athletics and, after repeating the tenth grade, he left school to join the Navy. He finished high school via a correspondence course while still in the service. When he was discharged, he enrolled at Temple University with an athletic scholarship and earned academic honors. His goal was to become a physical education teacher. He probably could have made it as a professional football player, but the world is richer in laughter because he decided on show business.

As busy as he is with his many ventures, Cosby has been a crusader throughout his career for a better world and for better understanding between people. Besides his involvement with a host of charity organizations, Cosby is also an active trustee of his alma mater, Temple University of Philadelphia. As philanthropists, Bill and Camille Cosby have made substantial gifts in support of education (most notably to predominantly African American colleges) and to various social service and civil rights organizations.

In addition, Cosby earned a Masters Degree in Education (M. Ed.) in 1972 and his Doctorate in Education (Ed. D.) in 1977 from the University of Massachusetts. His doctoral thesis was titled "The Integration of Visual Media Via Fat Albert and the Cosby Kids Into the Elementary Schools Culminating as a Teacher Aid to Achieve Increased Learning."

Cosby's been busy raising a family, too. He married the former Camille Hanks on January 25, 1964, while she was still a student at the University of Maryland. They raised four daughters (Erika, Erinn, Ensa, and Evin) and one son (Ennis Cosby) and now have three grandchildren. The family resides in New England.

When speaking of Camille, Cosby has urged an amendment to the saying, "*Behind* every good man there's a good woman." He suggests that "behind" should be substituted by "Three miles ahead." Camille has not only raised five children, but has also been totally involved in her husband's career. She produced his last album and has taped several concerts over the years. She has received her doctorate in education and plays an active role in a number of important national organizations.

Camille enjoyed great success adapting the best-selling book *Having Our Say: The Delany Sisters' First 100 Years*. First she produced the property as a Broadway play and then as a television movie. The play was nominated for three Tony Awards and the television film won a Peabody Award. Camille also produced a one-hour sociological documentary film *No Dreams Deferred*, which aired on over 150 public television stations. When Oprah Winfrey debuted her new magazine in April 2000, she chose Camille Cosby as her very first interview.

For more than five decades, Bill Cosby has graced us through virtually every entertainment outlet.

Joe Conklin

Conklin, a product of Temple University and North Philadelphia, made the rounds at open mike shows and comedy clubs until landing a gig with the WIP morning show. His routines are distinguished by his uncanny impressions of local sports figures and commentators, Philadelphia celebrities, and politicians. Impressions of national figures are also part of his repertoire.

One celebrated routine during the Eagles drive towards the Super Bowl (it failed in a loss to Tampa Bay) was his takeoff on the Jimmy Stewart character in the film, *It's a Wonderful Life*. Seems the Eagles star quarterback injured his ankle in midseason and he watched on the sidelines while such name products as Koy Detmer and A. J. Feeley led the Eagles into the playoffs. Through a variety of impersonations from Donovan McNabb through Coach Andy Reid, Conklin parodies the Eagles fortunes and misfortunes.

While he could have left for New York, Conklin has chosen to stay in Philly. Some of the coaches like Dick Vermeil and Ray Rhodes couldn't stand him while others like Andy Reid figure that Conklin singing the "Refrigerator Dash" to the tune of "Monster Mash" is better than Cataldi blaming him for another rare loss. At least that's nicer than his spins on Flyer's coach Bobby Clarke.

Conklin's routines can be heard on sportsjoker.com

SOUTH PHILLY
Joey Bishop (1918-2007)
Though born in Brooklyn, Joey Bishop rose to fame while growing up and living in South Philadelphia. His comedy routine essentially consisted of a doom and gloom countenance, deadpan humor, a healthy cynicism, and the catchphrase "Son of a gun!" Bishop began with three friends in a singing nightclub group called the Bishop Brothers.[6] He also had a career in Burlesque.

He made a friendship with Frank Sinatra that he used to become Masters of Ceremonies of the Famous "Rat Pack," which also included Dean Martin and Sammy Davis Jr. as well as Peter Lawford. From there he went on to numerous television appearances, including two of his own shows of the same name – "The Joey Bishop Show." The first was a sitcom where he played a talk show host. In the second show he was an actual talk show host, with Regis Philbin as the second banana.

Bishop was also a semi-regular host of the "Jack Paar Show" and "The Tonight Show" with Johnny Carson.

WEST PHILLY
(via South Philly on the Way to Center City and Beyond)
Will Smith [See the film section]

David Brenner
Text reprinted with permission of David Brenner (email communication)
As a kid in the poor sections of South and West Philadelphia, Brenner was a gang leader who used humor as a powerful weapon. From fourth grade through high school, Brenner was elected class president, as well as "the class comedian." He then went to Temple University where, in spite of being funny, he graduated with honors, majoring in mass communications.

Before stepping on stage, Brenner enjoyed a successful career behind the camera as the writer/producer/director of 115 television documentaries and headed the distinguished documentary departments of both Westinghouse Broadcasting and Metromedia Broadcasting. Brenner's documentary work earned him a total of nearly thirty awards and citations including an Emmy Award.

Brenner added another dimension to his career by writing a best-selling autobiography entitled *Soft Pretzels with Mustard*. The success of the autobiography resulted in a multiple book deal for Brenner. Other books by Brenner include *There's a Terrorist in my Soup, How to Survive Personal* and *World Problems with Laughter, Seriously*. He has had numerous HBO specials and is often a guest on comedy and political talk shows.[7]

Many of Brenner's bits included growing up in Philadelphia. A classic was a practical joke he used to pull. He and some friends would wait at a bus stop. Brenner would board the bus with a whisk broom. He would stand on the bus and whisk the other passengers. Finally, he would get off to the applause of the passengers. But Brenner would then get in the car that his friends had brought to an agreed spot, drive ahead – and you guessed it – board the exact same bus again. Broom in hand.

A second notable was – Mr. Brenner, once while a guest on Johnny Carson (he appeared on Carson 158 times, the most of any guest), said in response to a discussion on leadership:

"I don't think anyone in the political arena today is capable of leading this great nation of ours, so what we've got to do is reincarnate the bravest man who ever lived and let him lead our country." Carson asked "Well, David, who is the bravest man who ever lived?" Brenner's reply, "Johnny, I think the bravest man who ever lived in the history of mankind was the first man who drank milk." Off camera Brenner said, "Wait a minute Johnny, I'm wrong. The bravest man who ever lived was the first man who ate an egg." / *David Brenner Soft Pretzels with Mustard* (Arbour House, 1983), David Brenner, *Revenge is the Best Exercise* (Arbour House, 1984 55-59).

One of Mr. Brenner's books, *Revenge is the Best Exercise*, shows Brenner at his crazy best. Its premise is that he's tired of the exercise craze so he constructs a number of better ways to work out. One, called "Conversation," shows the proper way:

"When emphasizing a point, poke the person in the chest or shoulder. Use a different finger and your thumb with each poke. Then use your other hand. Now bend the fingers and poke with your knuckles. Then take off your shoes and poke with your toes."

"When being introduced to someone, make at least six aborted attempts to shake his or her hand. When in conversation, interrupt the speaker with the statement, 'Wait a minute; let's see what the person over there thinks about this.' Then walk across the street or across the room or halfway down the block and make believe you are talking to someone. Return and say, 'He didn't know' or 'He had no opinion.' Let the other person continue talking."

"If you hear your name spoken, no matter how softly, spin around as if you were frightened. Respond to someone's conversation by saying, 'I love it' and then do a little dance."

Calorie-Burning Activities/Activity

Activity		
Staring straight ahead	....	*50*
Staring upward	....	*55*
Staring downward	....	*55*
Blinking one eye at a time	....	*60*
Blinking both eyes *at the same time*	....	*75*
Smacking lips after a meal	....	*30*
Smacking lips for *no reason*	....	*40*

Several comedians have made their fame in television and radio. Larry Fine, Ed Wynn, and Will Smith are covered in the Film Section.

ESSAYISTS

Benjamin Franklin

If Bill Cosby is Philadelphia's best known comedian, Benjamin Franklin was the first. His humor covered wonderings about daily life that he wrote about in his *Poor Richard's Almanac*, and other publications. Some of the best ones follow:

Stories

While conversing with some friends at a local Philadelphia tavern, Franklin was accosted by a drunken man who had overheard him discussing the Declaration of Independence. Slandering the document, the young fellow shouted at Franklin: "Aw, them words don't mean nothing at all. Where's all the happiness the document says it guarantees us." The quick-witted statesman sympathetically replied, "My friend, the Declaration of Independence only guarantees the American people the right to pursue happiness. You have to catch it yourself!"

While serving as an American representative in France during the American Revolution, Franklin was told that General Howe, the British commanding officer, had captured Philadelphia. However, Franklin, aware that maintaining control of the city would be a great burden, replied, "I beg your pardon, Sir, Philadelphia has taken Howe."[8]

Sayings from *Poor Richard's Almanac*:
Diligence is the mother of good luck.
Fear to do evil and you need fear nothing else.
Fish and visitors stink in three days.
Fools make feasts and wise men eat them.
Having been poor is no shame, but being ashamed of it is.
He that hath a Trade, hath an Estate.
He that lies down with dogs shall rise up with fleas.
Hear no ill of a friend, nor speak any of an enemy.
Ill Customs & bad Advice are seldom forgotten.
Little rogues easily become great ones.
Love your enemies for they tell you your faults.
Must not speak all he knows nor judge all he sees.
One today is worth two tomorrows.
Pride dines on Vanity, sups on Contempt.
Success has ruined many a man.
There are no gains without pains.
There are three faithful friends—An old wife, an old dog, and ready money.
They who have nothing to trouble them, will be troubled at nothing.
To err is human, to repent divine, to persist devilish.

The Drinkers Dictionary
...Tho' every one may possibly recollect a Dozen at least of the Expressions us'd on this Occasion, yet I think no one who has not much frequented Taverns would imagine the number of them so great as it really is. It may therefore surprize as well as divert the sober Reader, to have the Sight of a new Piece, lately communicated to me, entitled *The Drinker's Dictionary*.

A
He is Addled,
He's casting up his Accounts,
He's Afflicted,
He's in his Airs.

B
He's Biggy,
Bewitch'd,
Block and Block,
Boozy,
Bowz'd,
Been at Barbadoes,
Piss'd in the Brook,
Drunk as a Wheel-Barrow,
Burdock'd,
Buskey,
Buzzey,
Has Stole a Manchet out of the Brewer's Basket,
His Head is full of Bees,
Has been in the Bibbing Plot,
Has drank more than he has bled,
He's Bungey,

As Drunk as a Beggar,
He sees the Bears,
He's kiss'd black Betty,
He's Bridgey.

C
He's Cat,
Cagrin'd,
Cherubimical,
Cherry Merry,
Wamble Crop'd,
Crack'd,
Concern'd,
Half Way to Concord,
Has taken a Chirriping-Glass,
Got Corns in his Head,
A Cup to much,
Coguy,
Copey,
He's heat his Copper,
He's Crocus,
Catch'd,
He cuts his Capers,
He's been in the Cellar,
He's in his Cups,
Non Compos,
Cock'd,
Curv'd,
Cut,
Chipper,
Chickery,
Loaded his Cart,
He's been too free with the Creature,
Curv'd,
Cramp'd,
Sir Richard has taken off his Considering Cap,
Capable,

D
He's Disguiz'd,
He's got a Dish,
Kill'd his Dog,
Took his Drops,
It is a Dark Day with him,
He's a Dead Man,
Has Dipp'd his Bill,
He's Dagg'd,
He's seen the Devil,

E
He's Prince Eugene,
Enter'd,
Wet both Eyes,
Cock Ey'd,
Got the Pole Evil,
Got a brass Eye,
Made an Example,
He's Eat a Toad & half for Breakfast,
In his Eleement,

F
He's Fishey,
Fox'd,
Fuddled,
Sore Footed,
Frozen,

Well in for't,
Owes no Man a Farthing,
Fears no Man,
Crump Footed,
Been to France,
Flush'd,
Froze his Mouth,
Fetter'd,
Been to a Funeral,
His Flag is out,
Been at an Indian Feast.

G
He's Glad,
Groatable,
Gold-headed,
Glaiz'd,
Generous,
Booz'd the Gage,
As Dizzy as a Goose,
Been before George,
Got the Gout,
Had a Kick in the Guts,
Been with Sir John Goa,
Been at Geneva,
Globular,
Got the Glanders.

H
Half and Half,
Hardy,
Top Heavy,
Got by the Head,
Hiddey,
Got on his little Hat,
Hammerish,
Loose in the Hilts,
Knows not the way Home,
Got the Hornson,
Haunted with Evil Spirits,
Has Taken Hippocrates grand Elixir,

I and J
He's Intoxicated,
Jolly,
Jagg'd,
Jambled,
Going to Jerusalem,
Jocular,
Juicy

K
He's a King,
Clips the King's English,
Seen the French King,
The King is his Cousin,
Got Kib'd Heels,
Knapt,
Het his Kettle.

L
He's in Liquor,
Lordly,
He makes Indentures with his Leggs,
Well to Live,
Light,
Lappy,
Limber.

M
He sees two Moons,
Merry,
Middling,
Moon-Ey'd,
Muddled,
Seen a Flock of Moons,
Maudlin.

N
He's eat the Cocoa Nut,
Got the Night Mare,
Nimptopsical.

O
He's Oil'd,
Eat Opium,
Smelt of an Onion,
Oxycrocium,
Overset.

P
He drank till he gave up his Half-Penny,
Pidgeon Ey'd,
Pungey,
Priddy,
As good conditioned as a Puppy,
Has scalt his Head Pan,
Been among the Philistines,
In his Prosperity,
He's been among the Philippians,
Wasted his Paunch,
He's Polite,
Eat a Pudding Bagg.

Q
He's Quarrelsome.

R
He's Rocky,
Raddled,
Rich,
Religious,
Lost his Rudder,
Ragged,
Rais'd,
Been too free with Sir Richard,
Like a Rat in Trouble.

S
He's Stitch'd,
Seafaring,
In the Sudds,
Strong,
Been in the Sun,
As Drunk as David's Sow,
Swampt,
His Skin is full,
He's Steady,
He's Stiff,
Seen the yellow Star,
As Stiff as a Ring-bolt,
Half Seas over,
His Shoe pinches him,
Staggerish,
It is Star-light with him,

He carries too much Sail,
Stew'd
Stubb'd,
Soak'd,
Soft,
Been too free with Sir John Strawberry,
He's right before the Wind with all his Studding Sails out,
Has Sold his Senses.

T
He's Top'd,
Tongue-ty'd,
Tann'd,
Tipium Grove,
Double Tongu'd,
Topsy Turvey,
Tipsey,
Has Swallow'd a Tavern Token,
He's Thaw'd,
He's in a Trance,
He's Trammel'd.

V
He makes Virginia Fence,
Valiant,
Got the Indian Vapours.

W
The Malt is above the Water,
He's Wise,
He's Wet,
He's been to the Salt Water,
He's Water-soaken,
He's very Weary,
Out of the Way.

The Phrases in this Dictionary are not (like most of our Terms of Art) borrow'd from Foreign Languages, neither are they collected from the Writings of the Learned in our own, but gather'd wholly from the modern Tavern-Conversation of Tiplers. I do not doubt but that there are many more in use; and I was even tempted to add a new one myself under the Letter B, to wit, Brutify'd: But upon Consideration, I fear'd being guilty of Injustice to the Brute Creation, if I represented Drunkenness as a beastly Vice, since, 'tis well-known, that the Brutes are in general a very sober sort of People. – by Ben Franklin.

TRANSPLANTED PHILADELPHIANS

Steve Lopez

Philadelphia humor is not confined to Philadelphians. Steve Lopez, a transplanted Californian, wrote for the *Philadelphia Inquirer* for over a decade before transplanting himself back to California.

While in town, Lopez's daily column for the *Inquirer* focused on an outsider's views of the highs and lows of Philadelphia politics and Philadelphia life. A reading of his columns shows a fascination with the variety of neighborhoods from Mt. Airy and Center City to North and West and South Philadelphia. Lopez's columns were written with a humorous but sharp edge.

In one column Lopez came to Philadelphia's defense.

"WHADDYA MEAN WE'RE HOSTILE"

Lopez, Steve. "Whaddya Mean, We're Hostile." *Philadelphia Inquirer* 5/14/94. It begins:

"You saw the story. You saw it. You heard about it, whatever.

"Some guy from Duke University, calling himself a doctor, says Philadelphia is the most hostile city in the United States. Which would be fine, of course. Except when you learn more about it, you realize it was not meant as a compliment."[9]

Fields, W.C. (1880-1946)

Born Claude William Dukenfield in Philadelphia, W.C. Fields used his vaudeville and ad-lib skills to launch a famous movie career. His comic movies included *The Bank Dick* and *My Little Chickadee* (both 1940) and *Never Give a Sucker an Even Break* (1941).

Fields character was pompous and celf centered. He was known for his "nasal drawl and wooden expression." "He often played a heavy drinker who detested all children and dogs, wore a top hat and frayed gloves, and carried a walking stick."[10]

His most famous quote comes from a *Vanity Fair* article in 1925 – "Here lies W.C. Fields. I would rather be living in Philadelphia."[11]

Many of his famous quotes were made famous by his movie characters.

OTHERS – A SAMPLING

Bob Saget, a graduate of Temple University, starred in "Full House" and "America's Funniest Home Videos." He works as a stand-up comedian and also as a producer.

Tina Fey, from a predominantly Greek neighborhood in Upper Darby, became the first female head writer for "Saturday Night Live." Ms. Fey also wrote the script for the movie *Mean Girls*. In 2008, she was one of the most successful comedians in America – producing and starring in "30 Rock" and portraying Vice Presidential candidate Sarah Palin.

Imogene Coca, born in Philadelphia, went on to become a comedic actress best known for her sketch comedy on Sid Caesar's "Your Show of Shows."

Other humorists of Philadelphia and related areas of note are S. J. Pearlman, Dorothy Parker, and George S. Kaufman, and even that is a stretch. They were part of the "genius belt" that lived in neighboring Bucks County along with other famous writers like Pearl Buck and James Michener.

BIBLIOGRAPHY

Sextuplet. Original from Philadelphia Press – Public Domain

Skaters. Original from Philadelphia Press – Public Domain

BIBLIOGRAPHY

Anderson, John. *Art Held Hostage. The Battle over the Barnes Foundation*. New York, New York: W.W. Norton & Co., 2003.

Archer, Dennis, Mayor. "Speech at the Detroit Athletic Club." *Michigan Supreme Court Historical Society* (4/13/2000).

Baltzell E. Digby. *Philadelphia Gentlemen*. Philadelphia, Pennsylvania: University of Pennsylvania Press, 1979.

_____. *Sporting Gentlemen – Men's Tennis form the Age of the Human to the Cult of the Superstar*. New York, New York: The Free Press, 1995.

Bell, Robert R. *Philadelphia Lawyer – A History 1735-1945*. Columbia, Pennsylvania: Susquehanna Press, 1992.

Bendiner, Alfred. *Bendiner's Philadelphia*. New York, New York: Franklin Publishing Co. (A.S. Barnes and Company) and Betty Bendiner, 1976.

Benjamin, Michael D. *The African-American Bar*. Philadelphia, Pennsylvania: Philadelphia Lawyer Anniversary Issue, 2002.

Binzen, Peter and Joseph R. Daughen. *The Wreck of the Penn Central*. Location Unknown: Beard Books, 1999.

Bissinger, Buzz. *A Prayer for the City*. New York, New York: Vintage Books, 1999.

Bok, Curtis. "Ulen – the Flowers – Tra-la." *The Shingle* (January 1941).

Brands, H.W. *The First American*. First Anchor Books, 2000.

Brenner, David. *Revenge is the Best Exercise*. New York, New York: Arbour House, 1984.

_____. *Soft Pretzels with Mustard*, New York, New York: Arbour House, 1983.

Burt, Nathaniel. *The Perennial Philadelphians: The Anatomy of an American Aristocracy. The Leisure Class in America*. Philadelphia, Pa: University of Pennsylvania Press, 2007.

Capuzzi Giresi, Joan. "The Good Citizen." *Pennsylvania Gazette* (3/4/2003).

Clark, Joe. "The Sonny Never Sets." *Philadelphia Daily News* (2/25/1999).

Collins, Herman LeRoy, A.M.Litt.D. *Philadelphia A Story of Progress, Volume IV*. New York, New York: Lewis Historical Publishing, 1941.

Conlin, Bill. "Blackwell, Evans Keep a Tradition Alive at Temple." *Philadelphia Daily News* (2/5/1987).

Conlin, Bill. "Tug Never Wasted a Second." *Philadelphia Daily News* (1/5/2004).

Conn, Steven. *Metropolitan Philadelphia*. Philadelphia, Pennsylvania: University of Pennsylvania Press, 2006.

Cushman, Tom. "Penn Puts Torch to Carolina." *Philadelphia Daily News* (3/12/1979).

David Hildebrand. "True Confessions." *Philadelphia Inquirer* (1/19/2003).

DeCurtis, Anthony and James Henke with Holly George Warren. *The Rolling Stone. Illustrated History of Rock and Roll*. New York, New York: Random House, 1992.

Dell, John Edward and Walt Reed. *Visions of Adventure. N.C. Wyeth and the Brandywine Artists*. New York, New York: Watson-Guptil

Publications, 2000.

DeLombard, Jeannine. "Renaissance Women." *City Paper* (2/19-26/1998).

Didinger, Ray. "The Final Four and the Big Five Philly Teams have had their Shares of Triumphs and Tainted Moments." *Philadelphia Daily News* (3/31/1988).

Dobrin, Peter. "The Kimmel Center." *Philadelphia Inquirer* (12/9/2004).

Dorwart, Jeffrey M. with Jean K Wolf. *The Philadelphia Navy Yard from the Birth of the U.S. Navy to the Nuclear Age*. Philadelphia, Pennsylvania: University of Pennsylvania Press, 2000.

Eckhard, Joseph. *The King of the Movies*. Madison, New Jersey: Farleigh Dickinson Press, 1997.

Eckhard, Joseph and Linda Kowall. *Peddler of Dreams: Siegmund Lubin and the Creation of the Motion Picture Industry*. Philadelphia, Pennsylvania: National Museum of American Jewish History, 1984.

Ershkowitz, Herbert. *John Wanamaker Philadelphia Merchant*. Champaign, Illinois: Combined Publishing, 1999.

Firth, Susan. "Now Playing on the Big Screen." *Pennsylvania Gazette* (1/2/2005).

_____. "The Global Garden." *Pennsylvania Gazette* (7/8/2004).

Fitzpatrick, Frank. "In Hoops Heaven." *Philadelphia Inquirer* (2/29/2004).

Fleishmans, Bill. *Philadelphia's Greatest Sports Moments*. Sports Publishing Inc., 2000.

Franklin, Benjamin. *Benjamin Franklin's Autobiography*. Philadelphia, Pennsylvania: Barnes and Noble, 1994.

Gillin, Beth. "The World was their Oyster." *Philadelphia Inquirer* (2/24/2002).

Glover, Chad G. *The Barnes Foundation – In the Press*. Philadelphia, Pennsylvania: *Tribune* Staff, 1999.

Greenlee, Edwin J. "Comments." *U. Penn Law Review – Sesquicentennial Issue* 150 (6/2002), 6.

Heller, Karen. "Join the Club." *Philadelphia Inquirer* (6/7/2003).

Home, William I. *Robert Henri and His Circle*, Ithaca, New York: , Cornell University Press, 1969.

Goldhaber, Emil, Hon. "In the Matter of Joseph S. Lord III." *The Shingle* (April 1972).

Hughes, Samuel. "The Most Beautiful Front Lawn in America." *Philadelphia Magazine* (November 1984).

Hunt, Donald. *The Phladelphia Big Five*. Champaign, Illinois: Sagamore Press, 1996.

Hunt, Ray Parillo. "Big Time Big Five Backcourts." *Philadelphia Inquirer* (3/7/2004).

Hunter, Al. "Blues for Philly Jazz, City's Swing Thing Ain't What it Used to Be." *Philadelphia Inquirer* (2/6/1998).

Isaacson, Walter. *Benjamin Franklin An American Life*. New York, New York: Simon and Schuster, 2003.

Jasner, Phil. "Hawk's Dream Alive." *Philadelphia Daily News* (3/16/1981).

Jonas, Jerry. "Boyd Theater, Last Survivor of a Fabulous Era." *Levittown, Bucks County Courier Times* (5/5/2002).

Keating, Douglas J. "Princely Debut the City's Latest Theatrical Venue." *Philadelphia Inquirer* (3/16/1999).

Kelley, B.G. "Basketball is Art to Ramsay and He is One of its Greats." *Philadelphia Inquirer* (9/23/1995).

Knott, A Smith, Philip Chadwick, and Foster Smith. *Philadelphia On the River, Philadelphia Maritime Museum*. Philadelphia, Pennsylvania: University of Pennsylvania Press, 1986.

LaBan, Craig. "Bellwethers Still Three of the City's Finest Flourish Despite Changes in the Kitchen." *Philadelphia Inquirer Magazine* (12/17/2002).

_____. "The Cheese-steak Project." *Philadelphia Inquirer* (8/11/02).

Labovitz, Sherman. *Being Red in Philadelphia*, Philadelphia, Pennsylvania: Camino Books, 2002.

Lacey, Robert. *Grace*, New York, New York: G. Putnam's Sons, 1992.

Lapsosky, Emma Jones and Anne A. Verplanck. *Quaker Aesthetics*. Philadelphia, Pennsylvania: University of Pennsylvania Press, 2003.

Levy, Maury Z. "Movies." *Philadelphia Magazine* (April 1976).

Longman, Jere. "Football's Looniest Stadium has its Last Hurrah." *New York Times* (1/15/2003).

Lopez, Katherine Jean. "NRO talks to Black Hawk Down author Mark Bowden." *National Review Online* (1/7/2003).

Lopez, Steve. "Senator Leftovers, Food for Thought." *Philadelphia Inquirer* (11/1/1992).

_____. "Thelma's Luncheonette." *Philadelphia Inquirer* (4/6/1987).

_____. "Whaddya Mean We're Hostile." *Philadelphia Inquirer* (5/14/1994).

Lounsberry, Emile. "The Judge Who Will Sentence Beloff et al." *Philadelphia Inquirer* (8/2/1987).

_____. "Legacy of a Judicial Scandal." *Philadelphia Inquirer* (9/16/1990).

Lukcas, John. *Philadelphia Patricians and Philistines. 1900-1950*. New York, New York: Farar Straus and Giroux, 1980.

Lyon, Bill. "Erving." *Sports Humanitarian* (10/14/2002).

Lyon, Bill and Christine Zordich. *When the Clock Runs Out*, Chicago, Illinois: Triumph Books, 1999.

Marimo, William and Christopher Hepp. "Writers Probe Links Union Gifts to 10 Judges." *Philadelphia Inquirer* (2/14/1986).

McGrath, Tom. "The 20 Greatest Philadelphia Movies." *Philadelphia Magazine* (October 2005).

McPhee, John. *A Sense of Where You Are*. New York, New York: Farrar Strauss and Giroux, 1978.

_____. *The Founding Fish*. New York, New York: Farrar Straus and Giroux, 2002.

Miers, Charlene. *Independence Hall*. Philadelphia, Pennsylvania: University of Pennsylvania Press, 2002.

Morell, Celeste. *A Philadelphia Italian Market Cookbook. The Tastes of South 9th Street*. Philadelphia, Pennsylvania: Jeffries and Manz, Inc., 1999.

Morris, Charles, Ed. *Makers of Philadelphia*. Location Unknown: L.R. Hamersly & Co., 1894.

Morris, Robert. *Audacious. Portrait by Frederick Wagner*. New York: Dodd Mead & Company, 1976.

Murrell, William. *History of American Graphic Humor*. New York, New York: Whitney Museum, 1933-38.

Muschamp, Herbert. "Slinky Winter Garden Opens in Philadelphia." *New York Times* (12/13/2001).

Paulos, John. *Mathematics and Humor*. Chicago, Illinois: University of Chicago Press, 1980.

Paxson, Ellis Oberholtzer. *Philadelphia – A History of the City and It's People A Record of 225 Years*. Location Unknown: S. J. Clarke Publishing Company, 1912.

Pennell, Joseph and Elizabeth Pennell. *Our Philadelphia*. Philadelphia, Pennsylvania: J. B. Lipincott Press, 1914.

Peterson, Brian H. *Pennsylvania Impressionism*. Philadelphia, Pennsylvania: University of Pennsylvania Press, 2002.

Philadelphia Inquirer. "Millennium Philadelphia, The Last 100 Years." *Philadelphia Inquirer* (2000).

Platt, Larry. "The Reincarnation of Stephen Starr." *Philadelphia Magazine* (September 2000).

Podhoretz, John. "Review." *National Review Organization* (8/6/2002).

Pose, Steve and Anne Clark. *Frog Commissary Cookbook*, Philadelphia, Pennsylvania: Camino Books, 2002.

Rickey, Carrie. "A Hundred Toasts to Phila's Queen of the Silver Screen." *Philadelphia Inquirer* (6/15/2003).

_____. "Film at the Prince: Place for all kinds of Audiences." *Philadelphia Inquirer* (3/16/1999).

_____. "Review of My Architect." *Philadelphia Inquirer* (11/14/2003).

_____. "Ritz Cinema Founder Ramon L. Posel Dies." *Philadelphia Inquirer* (6/24/2005).

Rodrick, Stephen. "The Last Neil Stein Story." *Philadelphia Magazine* (September 2000).

Rottenberg, Dan. *The Man who Made Wall Street, Anthony J. Drexel and the Rise of Modern Finance*. Philadelphia, Pennsylvania: University of Pennsylvania Press, 2000.

Saffron, Inga. "Film Fans Vow to Save City's Last Grand Movie House." *Philadelphia Inquirer* (6/19/2002).

Schiff, Stacey. *A Great Improvisation: Franklin, France, and the Birth of America*. Philadelphia, Pennsylvania: Owl Books, 2003.

Sellers, Nicholas. "Portrait Collection of the Bar Association." *The Shingle* (October 1965).

Shapiro, Howard. "Growth Factor." *Philadelphia Inquirer Magazine* (2/23/2003).

Silverman, Al. *Ali and Frazier*, New York, New York: The Overlook Press, 2002.

Slobodzian, Joseph A. "Church-State Precedent has Roots in Philadelphia." *Philadelphia Inquirer* (6/29/2003).

Sozanski, Edward. "Nothing is Quite Something." *Philadelphia Inquirer* (4/28/2004).

St. John, Gerard J. "Ben and I." *Philadelphia Lawyer* (Summer 1993).

_____. "This is Our Bar." *Philadelphia Lawyer Anniversary* (Winter 2002).

_____. "When You Call Me That, Smile." *Philadelphia Lawyer* (Spring 2003).

_____. "Workshop of the World." *Philadelphia Lawyer Anniversary Issue* (April 1976).

Stark, Jayson. "Schmitty Made it Look So Easy." *Philadelphia Inquirer* (5/30/1989).

Stearns, David P. "Kimmel's Reviews Mixed Among Out of Towners." *Philadelphia Inquirer* (12/18/2001).

Strange, Harry. *Philadelphia Stories from the City of Brotherly Love*. Philadelphia, Pennsylvania: Temple University Press, 1955.

Talbott, Page and Patricia Tganis Sydney. *The Philadelphia Ten*. Philadelphia, Pennsylvania: Galleries at Moore, 1998.

Talley, Audrey C. "Walking with Destiny. Women Lawyers in Philadelphia." *Philadelphia Lawyer* (Winter 2002).

Taylor, Alan. *American Colonies*. New York, New York: Penguin, 2001.

Thomas, George E. and Donald R. Broukee. *Building America's First University*. Philadelphia, Pennsylvania: University of Pennsylvania Press, 2000.

Thompson, Peter. *Rum Punch and Revolution, Tavern Going and Public Life in Eighteenth Century Philadelphia*. Philadelphia, Pennsylvania: University of Pennsylvania Press, 1999.

Van Horne, John. *Traveling the Pennsylvania Railroad, Photographs of William H. Rau*. Philadelphia, Pennsylvania: University of Pennsylvania Press, 2002.

Vrato, Elizabeth. *The Counselors: Conversations with 18 Courageous Women Who Have Changed the World*. Philadelphia, Pennsylvania: Running Press, 2002.

Wallace, Benjamin. "Georges Perrier." *Philadelphia Magazine* (January 2001).

Watt, George. *Experiences of a Philadelphia Lawyer*. Self Published, 1948.

Westcott, Rich. *Philadelphia's Old Ball Parks*. Philadelphia, Pennsylvania: Temple University Press, 1996.

Westcott, Richard. *A Century of Philadelphia Sports*. Philadelphia, Pennsylvania: Temple University Press, 2001.

Wiegley, Russell F. *Philadelphia. 300 Years of History*. New York, New York: W.W. Morton and Company, 1982.

Willis, Arthur C. *Cecil's City: A History of Blacks in Philadelphia 1638-1979*. New York, New York: Carlton Press, 1989.

Wolf, Edwin, 2nd. *Portrait of an American City*. Mechanicsburg, Pennsylvania: Stackpole Books, 1975.

Wolff, Alexander. *Big Game, Small World*. New York, New York: Warner Books, 2002.

ENDNOTES

Montgomery Avenue Bridge by Rob Lawlor. Courtesy of Rob Lawlor

ENDNOTES

Preface

1. Buzz Bissinger. *A Prayer for the City* (Vintage Books, 1999), 5-11.

2. Russell F. Wiegley. *Philadelphia, 300 Years of History* (W.W. Morton and Company, 1982), 218.

3. John Lukcas. *Philadelphia. Patricians and Philistines. 1900-1950.* (Farar, Straus and Giroux, 1980).

4. Peter Thompson. *Rum Punch and Revolution* (University of Pennsylvania Press, 1999), 9.

5. Jim Powell. "Quakers. Ideas on Liberty. William Penn, America's First Great Champion for Liberty and Peace." (January 16, 2003). <quaker.org/wmpenn>

6. Ibid.

7. Powell.

8. Alan Taylor. *American Colonies.* (Penguin, 2001) 264-265.

9. Ibid.

10. September 14, 2005 <williampenn.org>

11. September 14, 2005 <williampenn.org>

12. Ibid.

13. Ibid.

14. Encyclopedia Britannica. Volume 17 (William Benton Publisher, 1961), pp.473-474. (The article on Penn also supports the other historical text on Penn).

15. January 16, 2003 Technical University Eindhoven <win.tue.nl/~engels/discovery/penn.>

16. Taylor, 265.

17. Technical University Eindhoven.

18. Ibid.

19. Taylor, 266.

20. Ibid.

21. Technical University Eindhoven.

22. Taylor, 268-270.

23. Ibid.

24. Luckas, 17-18.

25, Weigley, 3-5.

26. Weigley, 17.

27. Weigley, 5.

28. Weigley, 29.

29. Weigley, 29-30.

30. Pennell, Joseph and Elizabeth. *Our Philadelphia* (J. B. Lipincott Press. 1914).

31. David McCollough. *John Adams.* (Simon and Schuster 2000).

32. Weigley, 9.

33. Charles Adams, III. *Philadelphia Ghost Stories* (Exeter House Books, 1998).

34. Samuel.Hughes. "The Most Beautiful Front Lawn in America." *Philadelphia Magazine* (1984), 130 et seq.

35. Hughes.

36. January 16, 2003, Navpoint/Internet <navpoint.com/~arpit/benjamin.>

37. "Philadelphia." Encyclopedia Britannica, 708 (Both quotes).

38. American Studies William Penn Plans the City. *University of Virginian* January 19, 2003 <xroads.virginia.edu/~CAP/PENN/pnplan.>

39. Benjamin Franklin. *Benjamin Franklin's Autobiography* (Barnes and Noble, 1994), 104-11.

40. Walter Isaacson. *Banjamin Franklin: An American Life* (Simon and Schuster 2003).

41. Stacey Schiff. *A Great Improvisation: Franklin, France, and the Birth of America.*

42. "Philadelphia." Encyclopedia Britannica (1961 edition), 707.

43. Weigley, 229.

Law

1. Edward Rendell. *Penn Arts and Sciences* (Spring 2001).

2. Gerard St. John. "This is Our Bar." *Philadelphia Bar Association Anniversary Issue* (Winter 2002).

3. Dan Rottenberg. "One Shining Moment. Why Philadelphia Lawyes are Different." *Philadelphia Bar Association Anniversary Issue* (Winter 2002), 118, 121.

4. Lukacs, 36-27.

5. Rottenberg, 121.

6. "The Trial of John Peter Zenger: An Account By Doug Linder." (2001) University of Missouri-Kansas City School of Law (from an article posted on the school website).

7. Robert R. Bell. *Philadelphia Lawyer – a History – 1735-1945* (Susquehanna Press 1992), 33-35.

8. Bell.

9. Rottenberg, 121.

10. Lindner.

11. *Philadelphia Bar Association News Release, January 8, 2002.*

12. *Charlene Miers. Independence Hall (University of Pennsylvania Press, 2002), 3-8.*

13. *A complete list can be viewed in the Winter 2002 issue of The Philadelphia Lawyer.*

14. *Gerard St. John. "This is Our Bar." The Philadelphia Lawyer (Winter 2002), 54.*

15. *University of Pennsylvania Law School Website.*

16. *Burt. The Perennial Philadelphians: The Anatomy of an American Aristocracy. The Leisure Class in America (Little Brown and Co., 1975), 132-133.*

17. *Late 1800s - early 1900s in the Bar Association's Legends.*

18. *Burt, 131.*

19. *Gerard St. John. "Workshop of the World." The Philadelphia Lawyer (Winter 2002), 69.*

20. *Bell, 177-184.*

21. *Nathaniel Burt. Perennial Philadelphians (Little Brown, 1963).*

22. *Burt, 134.*

23. *Morgan Lewis LLP Website (January 16, 2003) <morganlewis.com>*

24. *Information on City provided by Reprinted with permission of Eric. S's website – http://www.ajaxelectric.com/cityhall/noframemenu.htm His site notes Special Thanks to the Philadelphia Historical Commission for invaluable assistance and photos and to Greta Greenberger for her support & love of City Hall.*

25. *Liberty Bell Museum, libertybellmemorial.com*

26. *Philadelphia Yearly Meeting Website.*

27. *Jerome J. Shestack, Esq. Email note (10/30/02).*

28. *Studs Terkel Interviews (1970_. Four part interview http://www.studsterkel.org/radio.php?gallery=sub--Teens*

29. *St. John, Gerard. "When You Call Me That, Smile." Philadelphia Lawyer (Spring 2003).*

30. *J. Greenlee Edwin. "Comments." University of Pennsylvania Law Review.Sequcentennial Issue 150(66), 2002.*

31. *Michael A. Mugman. "Broadsheet Bullies Designated Pubic Forum and Established Newspapers Effects to Rid Philadelphia Public Transit System of a Government-Sponsored Competition." University of Pennsylvania Law Review (6/2002).*

32. *Gerard St. John. "Workshop of the World." The Philadelphia Lawyer (Winter 2002), 108-9.*

33. *Michael D. Benjamin. The African-American Bar Philadelphia Bar Association 200th Anniversary Issue (Winter 2002).*

34. *Arthur C. Willis. Cecil's City. History Of Blacks In Philadelphia (Carlton Press 1990).*

35. *Burt, 229.*

36. *Philadelphia Bar Association 1802-1952. Comments of George Wharton Pepper, 60.*

37. *Ibid., 229.*

38. *Gerard St. John. "Workshop of the World." The Philadelphia Lawyer (Winter 2002), 69.*

39. *Burt, 228.*

40. *Vidal et al. v. Girard's Executors, 43 U.S. (2 Howard) 126, 188 (1844).*

41. *Ibid., 229.*

42. *Terry v. Adams. 345 US. 461, 373 (1953).*

43. *Willis, 146-154; Girard Will Case. 386 Pa. 548; 127 A.2d 287; (1956) Pennsylvania Et Al. V. Board Of Directors Of City Trusts Of The City Of Philadelphia 353 U.S. 230, *;77 S. Ct. 806;1957. Brown v. Board of Education, 347 U.S. 483. 230-231.*

44. *Pennsylvania Public Accommodation Act of May 19, 1887. L. Sec 1, as amended, 18 S. Sec4654. Civil Rights Act of 1870, Sec 16, 42 U.S.C. Sec 1981 and Civil Rights Act of 1871, 42 U.S.C. 1903 and 28 U.S.C. Sec 1343. Commonwealth of Pennsylvania vs. Brown [one of the Trustees]. 260 F. Su 323(1966), 260 F.Su 358 (1966), 270, F.Su 782 (1967). 373 F2d. 771. (1967). 292 F.2s. 120 (1968). Evans v. Newton. 382. U.S. 296 (1966).*

45. *Elizabeth Vrato. "Norma Shapiro." The Counselors: Conversations With 18 Courageous Women Who Have Changed the World (Running Press, 2002).*

46. *Audrey C. Talley. "Walking with Destiny. Women Lawyers in Philadelphia." The Philadelphia Lawyer (Winter.2002), 72-78*

47. *Vorchheimer v. School Dist., 430 U.S. 703. (1977). Ruth Badee Ginsburg filed a brief on behalf of Petition. Solicitor General Robert Bork filed an amicus brief on behalf of the United States in court of the School District.*

48. *Elizabeth NEWBERG, a Minor, by Herbert NEWBERG and Babbette Josephs, her Parents and Guardians, Pauline H. King, a Minor, by Hugh King, her Parent and Guardian, Jessica S. Bonn, a Minor, by Anne Bonn and Jerrold Bonn, her Parents and Guardians v. BOARD OF PUBLIC EDUCATION, School District of Philadelphia, Dr. Constance E. Clayton, Superintendent of Schools, and Dr. Richard D. Haunsey, Assistant Superintendent for Field Operations. Aeal of STUDENTS CURRENTLY ATTENDING PHILADEL-*

*PHIA HIGH SCHOOL FOR GIRLS et al. 330 Pa. Super. 65, *. 478 A. 2d 1352. (1984).*

49. *The Japanese American Citizens League Website.*

50. *Gerard St. John, 109.*

51. *Pepper Hamilton website.*

52. *Trenton State, May 5, 2003. <tnstate.edu/library/digital/hastie>*

53. *May 4, 2003. <icasinc.org/bios/shestack.>*

54. *Rottenberg, 125.*

55. *St. John, 92.*

56. *Websites of Morgan Lewis and Dechert LLP as of 4/8/06.*

57. *Nicholas Sellers. "Portrait Collection of the Bar Association." The Shingle (October 1965), 167-170.*

58. *Regina Smith, Jenkins Law Library Director. Conversation 8/30/2005.*

59. *Sherman Labovitz. Being Red in Philadelphia. (Camino Books. 2002).*

60. *[The will can be viewed at .fi.edu/franklin/family/lastwill.]]*

61. *George Wharton Pepper (Lippincott 1941), 350-352.*

62. *Gerard J. St. John. "Ben and I." Philadelphia Lawyer (Summer, 1993), 42, 58-59.*

63. *Johnson Trust 9 Fiduciary Reporter 57, 1959.*

64. *Chad G. Glover. "In the Press: The Barnes Foundation – In the Press 1999 and Staff of The Barnes Foundation." Tribune. Staff.*

65. *Pennsylvania law 24 Pa. Stat. S 15-1516, as amended, Pub. Law 1928 (Su 1960) Dec. 17, 1959.*

66. *Joseph A. Slobodzian. "Church-State Precedent Has Roots in Phila." The Philadelphia Inquirer (6/29/03).*

67. *Freethought Society v. Chester County Commissioners, 334 F.3d 247 (3d Cir. 2003).*

68. *William K. Marimow and Christopher He, Inquirer Staff. "Writers Probe Links Union Gifts To 10 Judges." Philadelphia Inquirer, The (PA) (February 14, 1986).*

69. *Emil Lounsberry. "Legacy Of A Judicial Scandal." Philadelphia Inquirer, The (Pa) (September 16, 1990).*

Business

1. *Steven Conn. Metropolitan Philadelphia – Living with the Presence of the Past (University of Pennsylvania Press, 2006), 14.*

2. *Edwin Wolf 2nd. Philadelphia. Portrait of an American City. (Stackpole Books. The William Penn Foundation, 1975).*

3. *Dorwart, Jeffrey M. with Jean K. Wolf. The Philadelphia Navy Yard From the Birth of the U.S. Navy to the Nuclear Age (University of Pennsylvania Press, 19xx), book jacket and first chapter.*

4. *January 6, 2003. Federation of American Scientists. Military Analysis Network. <fas.org/man/company/shipyard/Philadelphia>*

5. *Baltzel, Philadelphia Gentlemen, 124*

6.*Globusz Publishing January 27, 2003 <globusz.com/ebooks/BigBusi/00000015>*

7. *Elaine Rothschild. A History of Cheltenham (College 1976).*

8. *August 14, 2004 www.scriptophilly.com*

9. *June 26, 2007. www.membrane.com/philanet/railroads*

10. *John Van Horne. Traveling the Pennsylvania Railroad. Photographs of William H. Rau. (University of Pennsylvania Press, 2002).*

11. *April 9, 2006. www.philanet.com*

12. *June 26, 2007. www.membrane.com/philanet/railroads*

13. *Peter Binzen and Joseph R. Daughen. The Wreck of the Penn Central. (Beard Books. 1999).*

14. *Philip Chadwick Foster Smith. Philadelphia on the River. (Philadelphia Maritime Museum (1986), jacket.*

15. *Wiegly, 482.*

16. *Cheltenham Township January 16, 2003 <cheltenhamtownshiorg/wallhouse/stetson.>*

17. *Benjamin Wallace, editor along with other contributors. "The 40 Richest Philadelphians." Philadelphia Magazine (November 2002), 108, et seq.*

18. *Herman LeRoy Collins, A.M., Litt D. Philadelphia A Story of Progress, Volume IV (Lewis Historical Publishing Company, 1941), 541-543.*

19. *Herbert Ershkowitz. John Wanamaker Philadelphia Merchant (Combined Publishing, 1999).*

20. *Wolf, The William Penn Foundation, 1975.*

21. *Ibid.*

22. *January 16, 2003 <freepages.genealogy.rootsweb.com/~apassageintime/johnwanamakermerchant.>*

23. *Baltzell, Philadelphia Gentlemen, 123-124.*

24. *Lukcas.*

24a. *Robert Morris. Audacious. Portrait by Frederick Wagner (New York: Dodd Mead & Company, 1976).*

25. Raken, January 16, 2003 <raken.com/american_wealth/bankers/girard_private_banker3.asp>

26. http://www.newsmakingnews.com/lm7%2C1%2C02%2Charvardtoenronpt5.htm> July 16, 2004 Linda Minor © 2002.

27. Burt Struthers. The Holy Experiment (DoubleDay, and Co. Inc. 1945), 329-333.

28. Note: Girard bank is known now only by its name. "Girard Bank" was revived by Benjamin Wood Richards, when he founded in 1835 the Girard Life Insurance Annuity and Trust Co. of Philadelphia and named it in honor of the great philanthropist. Later renamed Girard Trust, the company merged with Corn Exchange Bank in 1951, and was acquired in 1983 by Mellon Bank under the name Girard Bank. This Girard Bank is not the successor of Stephen Girard's financial institution, which was liquidated by his executors in the year following his death.

29. Weigley, 303-304.

30. Baltzell, Philadelphia Gentlemen, 89-90.

31. Dan Rottenberg. The Man who Made Wall Street, Anthony J. Drexel and the Rise of Modern Finance (University of Pennsylvania Press, 2000), 9, 21-25.

32. Rottenberg, 27-29, 44-47.

33. Rottenberg, 65-70.

34. Rottenberg, 73-81.

35. Rottenberg Jacket.

36. Rottenberg, 172.

37. Rotteberg, 174-181.

38a. Wikipedia.

38. Lukcas.

39. Independence Hall Association, January 16, 2003 <ushistory.org/betsy/flagtale.>

30. Stringband.com January 16, 2003 <stringband.com/mummer.>

41. Greetz.com August 16, 2003 <greetz.com/mummers/view.?ms3.gif>

42. Lukacs 27.

43. Charles Maris. Makers of Philadelphia (L.R. Hamersly & CO. 1894) and (Oberholtzer), 235

44. Karen Heller. "Join the Club." Philadelphia Inquirer (June 7, 2003).

45. Heller.

46. <philaathenaeum.org/tuw/index.html> April 23, 2004.

47. Lower Merion Services. Historic Preservation Lecture Series (February 3, 2003) <vws0100.safepackets.com/hpls.>

48. Architects section and 75th Anniversary Sections. Free Library of Philadelphia (February 3, 2003) <Free Library Website>

49. African American Registry (April 23, 2004) <http://www.aaregistry.com/african_american_history/1525/Julian_Abele_an_architectural_pioneer>

50. National Park Service (February 3, 2003) <10/9=10/03 cr.nps.gov/history/online_books/allaback/vc2a.>

51. David B. Brownlee. "The Philadelphia School of Architecture 'Philadelphia Schooldays'." The Philadelphia Architect (September 2003).

Science

1. Independence Hall Association. <www.ushistory.org > 4/14/06.

2. Philadelphia Zoo (July 8, 1993). <phillyzoo.org> 3/26/03.

3. National Aeronautics and Space Administration Lyndon B. Johnson Space Center. July 30, 2003. Houston, Texas <77058./jsc.nasa.gov/Bios/bios/bagian.>

4. Bartram's Garden <bartramsgarden.org/franklinia/index.>

5. Bill LeFevre John Bartram Association.

6. Bartram's Garden <bartramsgarden.org/franklinia/index.>

7. Wikipedia. 4/14/06.

8. Philadelphia Flower Show September 16, 2003 <philaflowershow.com/pr_history>

9. Howard Shapiro. "Growth Factor." Philadelphia Inquirer Magazine (2/23/03), 11-16.

10. Susan Firth "The Global Garden." Pennsylvania Gazette (7/8/2004), 28-33.

11. Carl Van Doren. Benjamin Franklin. (Penguin Books, 1938, 1966), 157-167.

12. LibraryThinquest.org

13. Benjamin Rush Society (September 5, 2003) The Benjamin Rush Society Website.

14. Penn in the 18th Century. University of Pennsylvania Archives

15. Franklin Institute January 17, 2003 <sln.fi.edu/index>.

16. H. W. Brands. The First American (First Anchor Books, 2000), 114-117.

17.Brands, 117.

18.Brands, 122-125.

19. Brand, 128-129.

20. Winslow, ?

21. Baltzell, 49.

22. Ellis Oberholtzer Paxson, PHD. Philadelphia – A History Of The City And Its People – A Record Of 225 Years. (S. J. Clarke Publishing Company).

23. Wiegley, 300.

24. Wiegley, 454.

25. Wiegley, 628-9.

26. Wiegley, 630, 691.

27. Joan Capuzzi Giresi. "The Good Citizen." Pennsylvania Gazette (Mar/April 2003), 32.

28. Giresi, 32.

29. Weigley, 630, 691.

30. Wallace, 108, et seq.

31. Wiegley, 514.

32. Saturday Evening Post Spartacus International (January 28, 2003) <spartacus.schoolnet.co.uk/USAsaturday>.

33. Broadcast Pioneers (July 22, 2003). <broadcastpioneers.50megs.com/Farnsworth>.

34. Broadcast Pioneers (July 22, 2003). <broadcastpioneers.50megs.com/Farnsworth>.

35-36. [Deleted]

37. The Atwater Kent Museum – History (September 8, 2004) http://www.philadelphiahistory.org/akm/history/#company

38. "Philadelphia radio." Members.aol (July 20, 2003). <members.aol.com/philaradio/curr1210>.

39. Collphyphil.org (July 23, 2003). <collphyphil.org/gnifhist>.

40. Wistar Institute. University of Pennsylvania (July 25, 2003). <wistar.upenn.edu/about_wistar/history>

41. Free Library of Philadelphia (July 12, 2003) lib.library.phila.gov/CenCol/exhibition-fax.

42. Dupont (June 12, 2003) <Dupont.com>

43. Franklin Institute (July 25, 2003) <sln.fi.edu/tfi/exhibits/bower/>

44. Dena Sher. "Fairmount Water Works: Past & Future." From the Friends of the Wissahickon Website with thanks to the following two publications for permitting the use of their material: The Pennsylvania Gazette, "Rebirth on the River" by Susan Lonkevich (Jan/Feb 2000), and The Chestnut Hill Local and http://www.fairmountwaterworks.com/about.php?sec=3&subsec=0 and Wolf, pp. (fillin – 290s)

45. Free Library of Philadelphia (July 12, 2003) lib.library.phila.gov/CenCol/exhibition-fax.

46. Free Library of Philadelphia (July 12, 2003) lib.library.phila.gov/CenCol/exhibition-fax.

47. http://etext.lib.virginia.edu/railton/yankee/cymach1.html

48. Free Library of Philadelphia (July 12, 2003) lib.library.phila.gov/CenCol/exhibition-fax.

49. Free Library of Philadelphia (July 12, 2003) lib.library.phila.gov/CenCol/exhibition-fax.

50. Rohm and Haas (June 12, 2003) <RohmHaas.com>

51. Franklin Institute (July 12, 2003) <sln.fi.edu/tfi/info/history>

52. Jim McWilliams. "The Heart" Franklin Institute.

53. Acnatsci.org (July 12, 2003) <acnatsci.org/learn/index>.

Art

1. Independence Hall Association (ushistory.org/birch).

2. Smithsonian Institute (March 23, 2003) <npg.si.edu/exh/peale/index-papers>

3. The Getty Museum (*/27/04) <getty.edu>

4. State Museum of Pennsylvania (March 23, 2003) <statemuseumpa.org/Potamkin/creating/>

5. Emma Jones Lapsosky, and Anne A. Verplanck. Quaker Aesthetics. (University of Pennsylvania Press 2003), Chapter 8.

6. Registrar's Department Worcester Art Museum 55 Salisbury Street Worcester, MA 01609-3123

7. James Michener Museum Website. www.michenermuseum.org 4/19/06. Edward Hicks.

8. Independence Hall Association (ushistory.org/birch).

9. Philadelphia Museum of Art (February 4, 2003) <philademuseum.org>

10. Philadelphia Museum of Art (February 4, 2003) philamuseum.org/exhibitions/webprojects.s

11. Thomas Eakins (February 4, 2003) <sunsite.dk/cgfa/eakins/eakins_bio>.

12. Moore College of Art Website.

13. Springfield Museum of Art Biography of Henry Ossawa Tanner (June 24, 2007) <springfieldart.museum/content/view/127/164/>

14. Laurence S. Cutler, Coauthor with Judy Goffman of Maxfield Parrish. Maxfield Parrish. National Museum of American Illustrators. (Crescent Books, Random House 1993).

15. Independence Hall Association (February 4, 2003) <ushistory.org/districts/parkway/swann>.

16. Calder Foundation.

17. *Calder Foundation.*

18. *Catalogue of the Etchings of Joseph Pennell. Compiled by Louis A. Wreath? (Little, Brown and Co, 1928).*

19. *Nicholas B. Wainwright. Pennsylvania Magazine of History and Biography. Volume 84 (July, 1960), 325-340.*

20. *<Philadelphia Sketch Club - _sketchclub.org>*

21. *Franklin Institute. Print Collection.*

22. *Franklin Institute. Print Collection.*

23. *Illustration House (February 12, 2003) <illustration-house.com/bios/pyle_bio>*

24. *Howard Pyle Nation Makers Brandywine Museum.*

25. *John Edward Dell. Visions of Adventure, N.C. Wyeth and the Brandywine Artists. (Watson Guptill Publications © 2000), 22-23, 112-115 (Walt Reed) 252, 255.*

26. *Wyeth Hurd Gallery (February 4, 2003) <wyethhurd.com/familytree>.*

27. *Brandywine Museum (February 4, 2003) <brandywinemuseum.org/ncstudio>.*

28. *NC Wyeth Gallery (February 4, 2003) <ncwyeth.com/links>*

29. *John Edward Dell. Visions of Adventure, N.C. Wyeth and the Brandywine Artists. (Watson Guptill Publications © 2000), 22-23, 112-115 (Walt Reed) 256, 258.*

30. *Philadelphia Museum of Art. Biography for his 2006 Exhibit.*

30a. *Jamie Wyeth Website (February) <jamiewyeth.com/biography>*

31. *N.C Wyeth Biography Website.*

32. *New Britain Museum of American Art.*

33. *Andrew Wyeth Gallery (February) <awyethgallery.com/andrew/chris>*

34. *Andrew Wyeth Gallery (February) <awyethgallery.com/andrew/chris>*

35. *N.C Wyeth Biography Website (February) <ncwyeth.com/wyethsworld>*

36. *New Britain Museum of American Art (February) <nbmaa.org/Gallery_s/Wyeth>*

37. *William Innes Homer. Robert Henri and His Circle (Ithaca, NY and London: Cornell University Press, 1969), 80, sheldon.unl.edu//ARTIST/Henri_R/PortWGlackens_RH.*

38. *Butler Institute of American Art (April 29, 2003) <butlerart.com/pc_book/pages/john_sloan_1871>.*

39. *Brian H. Peterson is Senior Curator at the James A. Michener Art Museum and has more than twenty years of experience as a curator, critic, artist, and arts administrator in the Philadelphia area. He is the author of a new book called Pennsylvania Impressionism published by the University of Press Website. The quotes are excerpted from the Penn Press website. upenn.edu/pennpress/img/covers/13857.l.jpg*

40. *Penny Balkin Bach Public Art in Philadelphia. Website Notes.*

41. *Independence Hall Association (April 14, 2003) <ushistory.org>*

42. *Virginia Western Distance Learning (April 14, 2003) <webed.vw.cc.va.us/vwbaile/Media/clothspn.jpg>*

43. *Rodin Museum (June 25, 2007) <rodinmuseum.org>*

44. *Pennsylvania Academy of Fine Arts (March 5, 2003) <pafa.org/info/history/3.s>*

45. *The material in [] is from John Anderson's Art Held Hostage. The Battle over the Barnes Foundation. (W.W. Norton & Co., 2003), 7-45.*

46. *Weigley, 514.*

47. *http://www.liunet.edu/cwis/cwp/library/aavaahp.htm#pippin*

48. *http://www.thegalleriesatmoore.org/publications/howardbct.shtml*

49. *Plasticlibertynet.org (February 12, 2003) <plasticc.libertynet.org/history>.*

50. *Page Talbott and Patricia Tanis Sydney. The Philadelphia Ten (Philadelphia: Galleries at Moore : Kansas City, MO : American Art Review Press, [1998]).*

51. *PortraitArtist.com (February 12, 2003) <portraitartist.com/bookstore/arthistory>*

52. *Philadelphia Art Alliance (April 16, 2003) <philaartalliance.org>*

53. *Through the Heart of the City. An Exhibition where the Schuylkill River is the Source of Inspiration. Philadelphia Art Alliance. Philadelphia Free Library*

Music

1. *Philadelphia Music Alliance (January 3, 2003) <phillymusic.org/stars/>*

2. *Wiegley, 473-4.*

3. *Anthony DeCurtis and James Henke, with Holly George Warren. The Rolling Stone. Illustrated History of Rock and Roll (Random House, 1992). Quotes by Phil Spector.*

4. *Cash Box (March 9, 1963) and Philadelphia Music Alliance Biographies.*

5. *February 5, 2003 < yesterdayland.com/popopedia/shows/saturday/sa1373.php*

6. *The popular style and Sweet 16 come from the Philadelphia Music Exhibit at the Philadelphia Free Library.*

7. *Philadelphia Music Alliance.*

8. *Al Hunter. "Al Blues for Philly Jazz, City's Swing Thing Ain't What it Used To Be." Philadelphia Daily News (2/6/98) and (www.explorephiladelphiahistory.com).*

9. *explorePhiladelphihistory.com*

10. *Dizzy Gillespie Cosmopolis (April 18, 2003) <cosmopolis.ch/english/cosmo2/dizzy>*

11. *Wikipedia.*

12. *The John Coltrane Foundation. Website. Biography.*

13. *John Coltraine ATT April 18, 2003 home.att.net/~dawild/john_coltrane*

14. *NPR Radio. "John Coltrane's A Love Supreme." (11/25/2002) <npr.org/display_pages/features/feature_855350.html>*

15. *David Whited (January 21, 2003) <Peacock Gospel Classics. Ink19.com>*

16. *Gospel Highway (February 24, 2003) <gospelhighway.50megs.com/DIXIE/hummingbirdsindex>*

17. *Copyright © 2000 Smith/McIver.com. Afgen.com*

18. *Copyright © 2000 Smith/McIver.com. Afgen.com*

19. *Tom Moon. The Philadelphia Inquirer.*

20. *Savedow. Letter. 2/3/03.*

21. *Charles L. Blockson. Philadelphia 1639-2000 (Arcadia Press, 2000), 43, 63, 75.*

22. *Tom Moon The Philadelphia Inquirer.*

23. *Bessie Smith PBS <pbs.org/jazz/biography/artist_id_smith_bessie.>*

24. *"Lady Day at the Emerson," Bristol Riverside Theater. 2/1/03.*

25. *Bessie Smith PBS <pbs.org/jazz/biography/artist_id_smith_bessie.>*

26. *Ask Men (July 16, 2004) <askmen.com/women/singer_100/146_jill_scott.html>*

27. *Curtis Music (June 4, 2003) <curtis.edu//50000.s>*

28. *Peter Dobrin. "The Kimmel Center." Philadelphia Inquirer, The (PA) (December 9, 2001) S04.*

29. *Girard Avenue News, Inc. August 18, 1983.*

30. *Rodgers and Hammerstein Organization (January 8, 2004) http://www.rnh.com/bios/index.html*

31. *Douglas J. Keating. "Princely Debut The City's Latest Theatrical Venue, The $10 Million Prince Music \ Theater, Opens Tomorrow On The Avenue Of The Arts. It Will Strive To Match The Innovation Of Its Namesake, Broadway Director Harold Prince." The Philadelphia Inquirer (March 16, 1999).*

32. *Carrie Rickey. "Film At The Prince: 'Place For All Kinds Of Audiences'." The Philadelphia Inquirer (March 16, 1999).*

33. *Kennedy Center Honors.*

34. *Philadelphia Radio (June 4, 2003) <members.aol.com/philaradio/curr1210>*

35. *WMMR (June 4, 2003) < wmmr.com>*

36. *Charles L. Blockson. Philadelphia 1639-2000 (Arcadia Press, 200_), 120.*

Film

1. *Thomas Eakins: American Realist (10/4/01-1/6/02), Philadelphia Art Museum.*

2. *Joseph Eckhard and Linda Kowall. Peddler of Dreams: Siegmund Lubin and the Creation of the Motion Picture Industry (National Museum of American Jewish History, 1984).*

3. *Joseph Eckhard. The King of the Movies (Farleigh Dickinson Press, 1997). Selected excerpts and photos from his websites. The photos are alss as per the Philadelphia Free Library – Rare Book Department.*

4. *3-Stooges (February 3, 2003) <3-stooges.com/text/larry>*

5. *James Darren (February 3, 2003) <jamesdarren.com/>*

6. *Robert Lacey. Grace (G. Putnam's Sons, 1994), 135.*

7. *Lacey, 133.*

8. *Lacey, 17-20.*

9. *The Flattering Word and Farewell to the Theater CurtainUp.com (February 3, 2003) <curtainup.com/georgekelly-book.>*

10. *Lacey. (G, Putnam's Sons, 1994).*

11. *Geocites Janet Gaynor geocities.com/classicmoviestar/janet.*

12. *Carrie Rickey. "A hundred toasts to Phila.'s queen of the silver screen." Philadelphia Inquirer (6/15/03). Philadelphia music alliance website.*

13. *Levy. "Movies." Philadelphia Magazine (April 1976). (Other women and men actors and other producers/directors.)*

14. *Brian DePalma (February 3, 2003) <nextdch.mty.itesm.mx/~plopezg/Kaplan/people/depalma>*

15. *Geocites February 3, 2003 <geocities.com/Hollywood/2093/lynch.>*

16. *Kathryn Jean Lopez. "NRO talks to Black Hawk Down author Mark Bowden about Somalia,terrorism, movie making, and much more." NRO Executive Editor (January 7, 2002).*

17, *February 5, 2003 National Review <nationalreview.com/interrogatory/interrogatory010702.s>*

18. *John Podhoretz. "Mr. Podhoretz is a columnist for the New York Post." Review for National Review Online (8/6/02).*

19. *Roger Ebert. Chicago Sun Times (08/06/1999).*

20. *bridgesweb.com/fuller. Baraka, Amiri. "The Descent of Charlie Fuller into Pulitzerland and the Need for African American Institutions." Black American Literature Forum (Summer, 1983), 51-54. Fuller, Charles and Esther Harriott. American Voices: Five Contemporary Playwrights in Essays and Interviews. (McFarland and Company, Inc., Publishers, 1988), 112-125. Kerr, Walter. "A Fine Work from Forceful Playwright." The New York Times (December*

6, 1981), 3. Linda Metzger. *Black Writers* (Detroit: Gale Research, Inc. 1989). Frank Rich. "Negro Ensemble Presents 'Soldier's Play'." *The New York Times* (November 27, 1981), 3. _____. *Contemporary Literary Criticism* (25), 181-182.

21. February 5, 2003 <artlex.com/ArtLex/a/ashcan.>

22. Inga Saffron. "Film Fans Vow To Save City's Last Grand Movie House." *Philadelphia Inquirer* (6/19/02), E01.

23. Jerry Jonas. "Boyd Theater, Last Survivor Of A Fabulous Era." *Bucks County Courier Times* (5/5/2002).

24. Levy.

25. *Just Disney* (February 5, 2003) <justdisney.com/Features/Fantasia/>

26. Library University of Pennsylvania (April 7, 2003) <library.upenn/edu/speical/gallery/stokowski/fantasia.html>

27. February 7, 2003 <2.cs.cmu.edu/afs/cs.cmu.edu/user/mleone/pub/movies/fantasia-soundtrack.txt>

28. "Rotten Tomatoes" (February 5, 2003) <rottentomatoes.com/m/KittyFoyle-1011684/about.php>

29. Philadelphia Experiment – http://www.history.navy.mil and //www.crystalinks.com/phila.html

Sports

1. "Benjamin Franklin." PBS. WHYY. November 19 and 20, 2002, Broadcast.

2. Franklin – PBS show.

3. Rank Russo. "The Dead Ball Era." (August 2003). <thedeadballera.crosswinds.net/QuotableQuotes>.

4. Nathaniel Burt. *The Perennial Philadelphians: The Anatomy of an American Aristocracy The Leisure Class, in America.* (Little Brown and Company, 1975), 297, 298.

5. Ibid., 303-307.

6. Baseball Library (November 4, 2002) pubdim.net/baseballlibrary/ballplayers/M/Mack_Connie.stm

7. Frank Fitzpactrick. "In Hoops Heaven" *Philadelphia Inquirer, Image Section* (February 29, 2004).

8. Hunt, p 131. Ray Parillo. "Big-Time Big Five Backcourts." *Philadelphia Inquirer* D12 (3/7/04).

9. Richard Westcott. *A Century of Philadelphia Sports* (Temple University Press, 2001), 70-71.

10. <bigfool.com/kruk/> 12/29/03. Check kruk vs. Phillies photo.

11. Robert Maxwell. "Profile Ralph Keyes, Sports Illustrated" (November 12, 1984, January 5, 2003) Maxwell Football Club <http://www.maxwellfootballclub.org>, Condensed version of an article by Ralph Keyes reprinted with permission of Sports Illustrated from the November 12, 1984 issue...Copyright 1984, Time, Inc.

12. Westcott, 43-450.

13. LaSalle University (June 27, 2007) www.lasalle.edu

14. La Salle University webiste.

15. NBA Hall of Fame.

16. Rich Westcott. *Philadelphia's Old Ball Parks* (Temple University Press, 1996), 1-27.

17. Westcott, 32.

18. Westcott, 83.

19. Westcott, 87, 99.

20. Westcott, 107.

21. Westcott, 99-116.

22. Westcott, 121-122.

23. University of Pennsylvania (November 12, 2003). pennathletics.com and Penn archives website – football and Franklin Field.

24. Alexander Wolff. *Big Game, Small World* (Warner Books, 2002), 254.

25. Wolf, 266.

26. Dallas Based Writer – Joe Rhoads University of Pennsylvania (upenn.edu).

27. Donald Hunt. *The Big Five* (Sagamore Press, 1996), 11-13.

28. Jewish Sports Hall of Fame (January 14, 2003) <jewishsports.org > 8/16/03.

29. October 18, 2002

30. Neyer. *Baseball Dynasties.* (W.W. Norton and Company, 2000).

31. Neyer, 112-117.

32. Bill Fleishman. "Philadelphia's Greatest Sports Moments." – Staff *Philadelphia Daily News* (Sports Publishing, Inc, 2000), 63.

33. Canoe and QuebecCor Media (January 16, 2003) <canoe.ca/2000NHLPlayoffsPhiPit/may9_phi_pit. >

34. Alfred Bendiner. *Bendiner's Philadelphia.* (Franklin Publishing Company, © 1976 Betty Bendiner), 15.

Food

1. Lukacs, 17.

2. William Woys Weaver and Mary Anne Hines, Gordon Marshall. *The Larder Invaded, Three Centuries of Philadelphia Food and Drink.* (Philadelphia Library Company and Historical Society of Philadelphia 1987).

3. Morello, A. Celeste. *Philadelphia Italian Market Cookbook – The Tastes of South 9th Street.* (Jeffries and Manz, Inc. 1999), 17-19, 20-28, 30-51, 59-68, 270.

4. Ibid., 120.

5. "Philadelphia." About.com (May 7, 2003) <philadelphia.about.com/library/weekly/aa041700c>

6. Craig Laban. "The Cheesesteak Project." *Philadelphia Inquirer* (8/11/02).

7. Independence Hall Association.

8. John McPhee. "The Founding Fish" (Farrar, Straus, and Giroux, 2002).

9. McPhee, 150-153, Harry Emerson Widles. Valley Forge. (Macmillan, 1938).

10. McPhee, 190-191.

11. McPhee, 249-250.

12. McPhee, 254.

13. The Kitchen Project. <Kitchen Project.com>

14. Peter Thompson. *Rum Punch and Revolution. Tavern Going and Public Life in Eighteenth Century Philadelphia* (University of Pennsylvania Press, 1999).

15. Thompson, 113.

16. Thompson, 112, 143-147.

17. Thompson, 179-180.

18. Anonymous. *Philadelphia and Popular Philadelphians* (North American, 1891).

19. Shazia Iftakhar. "The Ortlieb Legacy Lives on at Poor Henry's." *Philadelphia Magazine* (3/16/2001). Temple University. March 12, 2003 <philly!/brewery.html>

20. LeBan, "Savoring Philadelphia." *Philadelphia Inquirer* (2002).

21. Ralph's (March 12, 2003) <ralphsrestaurant.com/celebrit>

22. Craig LaBan, "Savoring Philadelphia." *Philadelphia Inquirer* (2002).

23. Steve Poses and Anne Clark. *Frog Commissary Cookbook.* (Camino Books, 2002 – Reprint). With Pictures by Becky Roller.

24. Poses.

25. Penn Arts and Sciences – Spring 2001 (University of Pennsylvania).

26. Georges Perrier Restaurant Port.com March 14, 2003 http://www.restaurantreport.com/features/ft_perrier.html

27. Wallace, 153.

28. Wallace, 180.

29. Benjamin Wallace, "Georges Perrier," *Philadelphia Magazine* (2001 January 8).

30. Wallace, 82.

31. Wallace, 152.

32. Traditions and New Styles [small parts quoted] from the City Paper by Maxine Keyser © 2003

33.Stephen Rodrick, "The Last Neil Stein Story." *Philadelphia Magazine* (September 2000).

34. Traditions and New Styles [small parts quoted] from the City Paper by Maxine Keyser © 2003 March 15.

35. Penn Arts and Sciences – Spring 2001 (University of Pennsylvania).

36. Larry Platt, "The Reincarnation of Stephen Starr." *Philadelphia Magazine* (September 2000).

Humor

1. William Murrell. *History of American Graphic Humor. Volume 2.* (Whitney Museum 1933-1938), 173-174.

2. Alfred Bendiner. *Bendiner's Philadelphia* (B.A. Bergman 1964).

3. Moore College Online Site.

4. Creative License Studio Cartoonists _ award Cartoon - .clstoons.com/paoc/sjoyner.

5. AngelFire (January 5, 2003) <angelfire.com/art/pcs/awards.>

6. Blockbuster (September 5, 2003) <blockbuster.com/bb/movie/details/0,7286,VID-V++++97236,00.?>

7. David Brenner (September 5, 2003 and August 7, 2004) <davidbrenner.net/bio.>

8. Source: Compton's Interactive Encyclopedia. Copyright © 1994, 1995 Compton's NewMedia, Inc.

9. Lopez, Steve. "Whaddya Mean, We're Hostile." *Philadelphia Inquirer* (5/14/94).

10. January 5, 2003 <edr.uct.ac.za/~mj/W.C.Fields/wcfields>

11. June 4, 2003 <historycarper.com/resources/twobf2/pg> 36-37.

INDEX

Boathouse Row by Charles Cushing. Courtesy of Charles Cushing.

INDEX

SUBJECTS

PLACES

Vincent Does the Museum by Perry Milou. Courtesy of Perry Milou

Philly Flash #1 by Perry Milou. Courtesy of Perry Milou